LORETTE WILMOT LIBRARY
Nazareth College of Rochester

Thomas Folan

SONGS FROM THE HILL

SONGS FROM THE HILL~

A HISTORY OF THE

Cornell University Glee Club

MICHAEL SLON

Cornell University Glee Club

ITHACA, NEW YORK

First published 1998.

Printed in the United States of America

The paper in this book meets the minimum requirements
of the American National Standard for Information Sciences—
Permanence of Paper for Printed Library Materials, ANSI Z39.48-1984.

Library of Congress Cataloging-in-Publication Data

Slon, Michael, 1970–
Songs from the Hill : a history of the
Cornell University Glee Club / by Michael Slon.
        p.   cm.
Includes index.
ISBN 0-9620103-1-6
1. Cornell University. Glee Club–History.   I. Title.
ML421.C66S5   1998
782.5'06'074771–dc21   98-35215

Excerpt from "Ithaca" in *The Complete Poems of Cavafy* translated by Rae Dalvan,
copyright © 1961 and renewed 1989 by Rae Dalvan, reprinted by permission of
Harcourt Brace & Company.

*To all who have been, are, and
will be a part of the Club*

Contents

Foreword

A history of the Cornell University Glee Club embraces not only singing and the study of music but a wide variety of subjects including student life, education, artistic endeavors, performing ensembles, entertainment, finances, and people and ideas—all in an historical context. Singing was inexorably woven into scholastic life even before the first universities evolved from medieval monastic and cathedral schools. Over twelve hundred years ago, in 789, Emperor Charles the Great ordered all his monasteries and bishoprics to teach schoolboys psalms, notes, and chants—along with grammar. Later, during the Renaissance, choristers and occasionally trumpeters or pipers performed music for academic and religious ceremonies, while in the classroom music was studied as a science in the quadrivium. In the centuries between the Renaissance and the mid-1800s, university music reflected and absorbed some of the practices of world music by gradually incorporating its technical and aesthetic changes. These changes affected the mixture of secular with sacred, folk with national, and eventually popular with classical.

The beginning of musical activity at Cornell was mentioned in anecdotal form by Morris Bishop in *A History of Cornell* (1962), and its development was chronicled more extensively in Harold Samuel's article "The First Hundred Years of Music at Cornell" (1965). In the late 1960s, while plans were underway for the Glee Club's 100th anniversary celebration, the Club's executive committee proposed compiling a "history of the Cornell Glee Club." For the next two decades student historians and managerial staff collected pertinent information and began archival research.

In the early 1990s Glee Club officers formalized the project by commissioning Michael Slon to write the history. A former Glee Club singer, accompanist, assistant conductor, and executive committee member, Michael received his

Bachelor of Arts degree *magna cum laude* in English and Music in 1992. He was elected to Phi Beta Kappa, awarded the Barnes Shakespeare Prize by the English department and the Falconer Prize by the music department, and in 1993 began the grand task of researching and writing *Songs from the Hill*.

The Cornell Class of 1957 Fund has generously underwritten the costs of preparation of this book as it did for *Songs of Cornell* (1988) "for the enrichment and preservation of music at Cornell."

THOMAS A. SOKOL

Ithaca, New York

Preface

In his book *Stories of God,* Rainer Maria Rilke tells of old Timofei, a Russian peasant who spends the last days of his life singing songs to his son. Each song carries in its words and melody some place or legend from their people's heritage, and for weeks the two remain together—one singing, the other listening—until the son is himself ready to sing their story. As he tells this tale, Rilke laments other songs no longer part of an oral history—songs that once lived carelessly on many lips, but at some point had no further heirs, and were eventually "buried with all honors in a book."

As a preface let it be said there are several things this book cannot replace; one of them is the oral tradition that has kept stories of the Cornell University Glee Club alive in a vital and colorful way. Every decade has brought alumni and veteran singers, Timofeis, who pass on CUGC lore to the younger members, and this tradition presumably will continue as long as there is a Cornell Glee Club and tales worth telling.

Nor can this book (or Glee Club oral history for that matter) replace or even capture save in its highest moments the music making itself. Some will notice the center around which this book revolves—those moments when the Glee Club is engrossed in song—in many places is conspicuously absent, or at best, only intimated. In truth there is little one can say, as Leonard Bernstein points out in *The Joy of Music:* "Can anyone explain in mere prose the wonder of one note following or coinciding with another?"[1] In the same way, the music at the center of this book is largely untranslatable, and therefore absent by necessity. There is no replacement for actually going and hearing (or singing with) the Glee Club in concert or informal singing—much will make far more sense then. In lieu of that, the musical presence in this book might be imagined as the music many people claim is always playing in their heads, the song beneath the story, recognized in the morning or in the evening as having been there, underneath everything, all along.

In the story of Timofei, Rilke also laments the disinherited person "who could not sing, or at least knew only a small part of the songs of his father and grandfather, and lost with the other songs that great piece of experience which all these [songs] represent."[2] In that light, this book serves a greater purpose. Few things in life demonstrate short-term memory better than a student body, which turns over completely every few years. Even with the aid of faculty and alumni, history is eventually forgotten, and personalities and moments evaporate. This book recalls some earlier moments and older stories (either completely forgotten or hazily known), and preserves some of the more contemporary history—for those who have been a part of it and the generations to come. Then, at least, Cornell and its Glee Club will not lose a piece of experience well worth remembering. Moreover, oral tradition does not generally concern itself with painting the whole picture, restoring it to its original context, or analyzing larger trends. In that sense this book offers a distinctive biography of one ensemble, and insofar as it recounts artistic trends, landmark influences, and significant achievements, it should shed insight on Cornell's cultural history, the lives of other musical ensembles, and choral music in America.

This book was commissioned in conjunction with the 125th anniversary of the Glee Club, and consummates several other projects, either envisioned or attempted, to chronicle the organization's history. On an objective scale, the history of a collegiate glee club is a subject relatively small in scope when compared with other topics a historian might conceivably tackle. Indeed, during this project I have gained great respect for historians who organize voluminous amounts of history into accounts at once honest, compelling, and insightful. Nevertheless, much has happened in this ensemble's life (one could write an entire book on CUGC tours), and putting the puzzle together involved study of a wealth of material on the subject. The *Cornell Era,* a student weekly dating from the university's beginnings, was invaluable (not to mention seductively entertaining to read) in constructing the earliest years. Yearbooks, scrapbooks, songbooks, a biography of the group's first long-term director, the *Cornell Daily Sun,* and a host of other sources likewise contributed information and, at various junctures, some essential clues. As the group grew from an informal handful of singers to an ensemble with an international reputation, the paper trail widened. Glee Club managers have left a fairly complete record from the late 1920s on—thousands of pages of correspondence, newspaper clippings, and reports for the diligent historian; there are volumes of correspondence concerning tours never even taken. Correspondence in the university archives, interviews, recordings, histories of Ithaca, Cornell, and music at Cornell, and photographs also served as significant sources, together with tales from the oral tradition and firsthand experience.

If someone from the 1900 Glee Club were still around to read their section, I'd be curious to see how they might find it. With firsthand documentation of the early years harder to come by, interpretation was a longer stretch for the imagination. Clearly, it takes good scholarship to be able to tell you correctly what any janitor could have told you at the time. Nevertheless, there is safety in the distance of the earlier years. At a remove, retrospect more clearly resembles destiny and the historian is not tempted to be influenced by knowing anyone personally, whereas in more recent years assessing the import of something is handicapped by proximity, and by not knowing how things turn out. As he enters the final decade in *A History of Cornell*, Morris Bishop readily admits his historical confidence is fading, and shifts to a "just the facts, ma'am" approach. The book reveals that—he spends more than half the book (350 pages) on the first three and a half decades of the university, and only seven pages on the last (1951–1962). I too felt myself shy from the last decade, but in contrast to Bishop's book, and despite the historical pitfalls, this book gives more space to the last five decades or so, for two reasons: a far greater amount of information is available for those years and, perhaps more simply, more happened. In this period the group began to appear in the concert halls of Moscow and the papers of Malaysia, rubbed shoulders with such musicians as Eugene Ormandy and Sir Keith Falkner, and developed an ever stronger sense of its own history and traditions.

A few thoughts on writing history. The eminent author and Cornell professor Vladimir Nabokov once said, "I know more than I can express in words, and the little I can express would not have been expressed, had I not known more."[3] In a sense, another way of indicating the song beneath a story. But the historian can, for his own purposes, misrepresent the sentiment slightly to convey the nature of writing history. Having spent several years researching and writing this book in between responsibilities as an assistant conductor with the Cornell choral groups and more recently as a graduate student, I now probably know more than anyone cares to know about the Cornell Glee Club—what color the programs were in 1895, what the prefect of Harrow School in London said after a Club visit, what kind of grades the directors got in college. Most of the thousands of pages of material sorted through did not make it here, and rightly so. But if an extra thousand pages of research yielded ten items of real interest to this history, and seven of the ten made the cut into the book, better to have viewed them. And so, the historian can justly say, "I knew more than I could fit in this book, but . . ." One only wonders how much Edward Gibbon or Winston Churchill actually knew.

On the other hand, there are those who would argue the historian never knows enough, and to this I must also confess. In his essay "The Hedgehog and the Fox," Isaiah Berlin offers some thoughts on Tolstoy's view of history, along with a generous share of other insights. At one point he recounts a Tolstoyan attack on historians who peg the outcome of Borodino on Napoleon's having had a cold. To Tolstoy's mind, Napoleon knew "as little of what actually went on during the battle of Borodino as the lowliest of his soldiers; and that therefore his cold on the eve of it, of which so much was made by the historians, could have made no appreciable difference." More certainly, the complex web of actual decisions, orders, actions, and conditions on the field conspired to create the outcome, and "because the number of causes upon which events turn is too great for human knowledge or calculation," historians were deluding themselves with such "heroic" or "liberal" views of history.[4] Now, writing a history of a glee club is relatively simple by comparison, and there are enough knowns to merit historical account and interpretation. But I'm sure there are a few colds littered throughout the book. Moreover, the necessity of narrative coherence (which may be the stumbling block of many histories) undoubtedly led to unintended emphases on certain points, emphases picked up only because this or that point followed logically in the narrative, or came in numbers, offering a pattern by which to structure the book. So be it—the reader can enjoy the Napoleonic colds, and then weigh them with a little Tolstoyan wariness.

During this process there were the moments of genuine excitement—the exhilaration of discovery or of turning a good phrase, the pleasure of recalling friends, songs, and scenes from Glee Club life. Then too, there were the moments of despair—when facing a tedious mountain of material in the archives, wondering who would ever read the book, or encountering yet another published and misinformed account of the Glee Club. In those moments writing history can be humbling, as it can be when paging back through generations of students who tread the same slope and have all but passed from memory. An awe and sense of history came in still other forms, as when the university archives managed to find and hook up a 78 rpm record player so I could listen to a c. 1909 recording of the Glee Club singing the Alma Mater, or when writing Chapter 7, I realized I was telling the story of the Glee Club's 1895 tour to England essentially one hundred years to the day. And there were the moments of humor, often arising from the Glee Club's sense of humor, or the vagaries of writing history. A line from one interview—"And he did a lot in early radio with WGBH," said about G. Wallace Woodworth, one-time director of the Harvard Glee Club—was transcribed from the garbled audio tape as: "And he did a lot in early reggae with Billy Jean Lynch."

Despite the inscribed and ineffable difficulties, time and again as I made my way through decades of directors, managers, presidents, and singers who had given so much of themselves to this one ensemble, I concluded the honor was mine to be a part of this group, and to have the opportunity to write the story. Whatever else it may be, the Cornell University Glee Club is an organization that has meant a tremendous amount to a tremendous number of people, particularly the thousands of students who have found in it a home and a pinnacle experience during a significant time of youth. I hope that those who are a part of the Club will find the height of that experience somewhere in these pages, and those who do not know the Glee Club firsthand will feel, upon reading the history, that should they ever happen to meet the group some day they would be meeting a familiar and good friend.

MICHAEL SLON

Ithaca, New York, and Bloomington, Indiana

Acknowledgments

There are numerous people to thank for their contributions to this book. First, my gratitude to Professor Tom Sokol, without whom much of the history contained herein would not have happened. He was supportive and wise at every step of the project, and graciously spent long hours in our taped interview sessions offering his recollections and thoughts on the Glee Club's history. Recognition for initiating the project goes to former associate director of the Club Ron Schiller, who when I first expressed interest in the book over dinner one evening had the ball rolling before the food was cold. Charlie Stanton provided financial backing to the project (by way of the Class of 1957 Memorial Fund), and his friendly but persistent phone calls kept the book on track if not on time. He also prepared the index. Cornell's former university archivist Gould Colman and current archivist Elaine Engst were always interested and helpful, and great thanks are owed to the staff of the archives—Lucy Burgess, Joanne Busse, Nancy Dean, Mark Dimunation, Herb Finch, Eileen Keating, Laura Linke, Phil McCray, Margaret Nichols, Cheryl Rowland, Jim Tyler—who became familiar friends through the months of research. I am grateful to Jane Dieckmann, who edited the manuscript and whose knowledge of local history proved an added benefit, and to Dick Rosenbaum, who designed the book and managed its production.

Further thanks go to the publishers, institutions, and individuals who generously granted permission to reprint material. Assistance in pursuing those permissions was provided by Sandy Litweiler, Kathleen Parkhurst, and John Hedlund. This book also benefits from letters, photos, journals, and other information pertaining to the ensemble's history sent by alumni members and friends of the Glee Club. Audio tapes from the interviews with Professor Sokol were transcribed by Coraleen Rooney. I am also very grateful to Mary Lou

Tracy and the late Deane Malott (who was 95 at the time) for the interviews they granted. My appreciation goes to the managers and presidents of the Glee Club on whose watch this project took flight. And a word of thanks to Jane Belonsoff in the music department office for her remarkable efficiency in keeping track not only of the business of this project but of music at Cornell.

Finally, my special thanks go to those friends who read excerpts from the manuscript or shared in the experience of writing the book, and to my family, who (in the case of one or two benevolent skeptics) refused to believe this book existed until it appeared in print, and whose love and support are as constant as the stars. As Cornell's "Evening Song" says, "Joy to all we love the best."

Permission has been granted by the Division of Rare and Manuscript Collections, Cornell University Library, for use of material from the *Cornell Alumni News, Cornell Daily Sun, Cornell Era,* Cornell University Glee Club Records, *Cornellian,* Deane Waldo Malott papers, Edmund Ezra Day papers, Roger Henry Williams Scrapbooks.

Permission to use quoted material, granted by the following, is gratefully acknowledged: from Romeyn Berry, *Behind the Ivy,* © 1950 by Cornell University, used by permission of the publisher, Cornell University Press; from Morris Bishop, *A History of Cornell,* © 1962 by Cornell University, used by permission of the publisher, Cornell University Press; the Estate of Wilfred Owen, for lines from "Bugles Sang," "The Next War," and "Strange Meeting," from *The Collected Poetry of Wilfred Owen,* ed. C. Day Lewis (London, 1961), published by Chatto and Windus, quoted in Chapter 4; Harvard University Press, publisher of Elliot Forbes, *A History of Music at Harvard to 1972* (Cambridge, Mass., 1988).

Credits for photographs are as follows: figs. 1, 2, 3, 4, 5, 6, 7, 9, 22, 27, 28, 40, 43, 44, 45, Division of Rare and Manuscript Collections, Cornell University Library; figs. 10, 11, 12, 13, 14, 15, 16, 17, 18, 19, 20, 21, 23, 24, 25, 26, 29, 30, 36, 37, 42, 46, 47, Cornell University Glee Club Archives, Sage Chapel; figs. 31, 32, 33, 34, 35, from *Cornell Alumni News;* figs. 8, 38, 39, 41, used courtesy of the DeWitt Historical Society of Tompkins County; fig. 48, Media Services, Cornell University.

In addition to the support of the
Class of 1957 Glee Club Memorial Fund,
the generous financial assistance of the following in making
this book a reality is gratefully acknowledged:

Philip E. Batson and Deirdre Courtney-Batson

Richard C. Dehmel

Richard and Gail Erali

George Gull and Nancy Potter

Scott and Sherry Haber

Richard and Carole Howard

Barry (B. J.) Jacobson and Linda Case

H. Michael Newman

John C. Nicolls

Donald and Laurie Peck

Charles P. Stanton

William and Frances Welker

Anonymous

Office of the Provost, Cornell University

SONGS FROM THE HILL

1 The Origins,
1868–1889

"Quant' è bella giovinezza . . ., Di doman non c'è certezza"

("How beautiful is youth . . ., of tomorrow there is no certainty")
—Lorenzo de' Medici (used in Walter Piston's "Carnival Song")

When the first stones of Cornell were set, the new institution already stood on a firm foundation. Founder Ezra Cornell and first president Andrew Dickson White had realized their dream in this university, a dream brought to life by their generous vision and ample pocketbooks. But while this backing proved the force that held the stones together, in the early days little else did. Cornell University was a new place, not yet defined by the mythologies, folklore, and traditions that gave roots to older institutions. On Inaugural Day, October 7, 1868, the sun was shining, but the institution awaited the growth that only generations of faculty, leaders, and students could bring. The stones had yet to take on the hue of legend, and the air hung silent, not yet home to the reverberation of familiar songs and hallowed stories. Slowly, during the first months and years, the institution grew, tradition began to develop, and history began to take hold.

On November 28, 1868, a little over a month and a half after the university's opening, the first issue of the student weekly *Cornell Era* raised a question: "Several attempts have been made to organize a Glee Club in the University. Will some one give us the result?"

The answer was not long in coming. A week later the *Era's* second issue carried the following announcement:

A vocal quartette and orchestra has been formed in the University, under the name of "The Orpheus." The following are the officers: President, Harry H. Seymour; Vice-President, Thomas Castle; Secretary and Treasurer, E. L. Parker; Leader of Quartette, Harry G. Wells; Leader of Orchestra, D. S. Dickinson; Poet, George K. Birge.[1]

Membership in this first ensemble in part was the result of familiarity—Castle, Parker, Birge, and several other members all hailed from Buffalo, where a few had attended the Buffalo Academy together before matriculating at Cornell. Dickinson came from a musical family in Binghamton, bringing his violin together with talent well suited to leading the orchestra. The singers of this newborn crew were led by H. G. Wells (not the science fiction author, who across the ocean was just then learning how to walk), and as the listing shows, some doubled as instrumentalists. Most of the singing ensembles at the university in the early years took a similar form, quartettes or quintettes (to use their spelling) with singers arranged one to a part and at times enjoying the accompaniment of a small band. As to the club's poet laureate George K. Birge 1872, though he was omitted from the group's listing in the first *Cornelian* yearbook,[2] we shall hear more from him later.

On the very same page that announced the Glee Club's existence the editors of the December 5 *Era* included their own commentary:

> GENIUS cannot be kept in obscurity. Sooner or later it must come out. We learn that the Orpheus Glee Club have already made themselves known, and "won golden opinions from all sorts of men," (young ladies included.) We also hear that they have been invited to take part in a grand concert soon to be given in Ithaca.

Welcome praise for a young ensemble, but not entirely trustworthy. On the whole the *Cornell Era* was a professional and outspoken weekly, acting as a general gadfly to the university community and publishing student poetry alongside interesting articles on coeducation, Latin verse translating, and anatomical evolution. Nevertheless it tended to mix news with not-so-newsworthy gossip, hyperbole, and opinion. Just a year later the same paper would brazenly protest, "OUR Glee Clubs are becoming a decided nuisance." But before investigating the grounds for this complaint or the success of the grand concert in Ithaca, let's sketch a backdrop for the ensemble's early years.

Ithaca in the 1860s was already established on the map, in part owing to its position in a major network of waterways. Surrounded by farmland, the village numbered 6,000 inhabitants, largely merchants, farmers, artisans, and manual laborers who might be found in the Fall Creek mills where Ezra Cornell had worked as a young man. These were serious people, as Morris Bishop describes in his prelude to *A History of Cornell*:

> Life in Ithaca was, on the whole, grim. . . . Diversion was frowned upon, as a needless distraction from man's duty, which was to labor in this world and to strive for the privilege of resting in the next. This rule of life, this ethic was a product of mid-century needs and environment. There was so much work to

Orpheus.

OFFICERS.

HENRY H. SEYMOUR, . . PRESIDENT.
THOMAS CASTLE, . . VICE-PRESIDENT.
E. L. PARKER, . SECRETARY AND TREASURER.
H. G. WELLS, . . LEADER OF QUARTETTE.
D. S. DICKINSON, . " ORCHESTRA.

QUARTETTE.

| H. G. WELLS, . | . Bass. | H. M. BRIGGS, . | Tenor. |
| E. L. PARKER, . | Air. | THOMAS CASTLE, . | Alto. |

ORCHESTRA.

D. S. DICKINSON,	THOMAS CASTLE,
B. V. B. DIXON,	D. A. OGDEN, JR.,
H. G. WELLS,	E. L. PARKER.

Collegensia Quintett.

CHAS. W. RAYMOND, . . DIRECTOR.
CHAS H. RAMSEY, ... Soprano.
CLARENCE BEEBE, . . . Tenor.
C. W. RAYMOND, ... Alto.
H. W. VAN WAGENEN, . . . Bass.
D. B. WILMOT, . . . Baritone.

1. Listing for the Orpheus Glee Club in the first *Cornelian,* which came out in 1869.

be done, in the transformation of wilderness into civilization! All honor was paid to the pioneer virtues of strength, endurance, frugality, and to the builder, the maker, the doer.[3]

On the southeast corner of Seneca and Tioga Streets stood the Cornell Public Library, a gift of Ezra Cornell and the village's first public library when it opened late in 1866. A few blocks away, the impressive Clinton House rose as a proud landmark. The canopy of trees shading the community led some to call Ithaca the "Forest City."

Moving outward, the dirt-ridden, often mud-drenched roads gave way to the beauty of the surrounding hills. The sun set in splendor over the western shore of Cayuga Lake, as fields of wheat waved, orchards blossomed, and pasture lands rippled on the opposite hill. Up between Cascadilla and Fall Creek gorges, Ezra Cornell owned what had formerly been the DeWitt family farm. In 1857, at the age of fifty, he wrote his wife about the land he had just acquired. "Here I can transplant my affections and cultivate a garden of Eden for my bird of Paradise."[4] For several years he devoted the land to farming with skill and vision, but the soil was soon to harbor a far greater seed.

In 1862 the U.S. Congress passed the Morrill Land Grant Act. Under its provisions land would be given to each state to support colleges providing education in agriculture and the mechanic arts. For New York, which received the largest share, the land provided by the grant was to be sold, the generated income then going to support an agricultural college. In Albany, state senators Ezra Cornell and Andrew Dickson White (who later became Cornell University's first president) bonded together to secure New York's share of the Congressional land grant for a university to be constructed on property donated and endowed by Cornell. Elected to the senate in 1864, the two men had first crossed paths when White, as chairman of the Committee on Literature, received a bill proposing Cornell's library for Ithaca. White was struck by the generosity of the gift, and realized the munificent Cornell was already contemplating a wider field in which to sow his philanthropy. White had long harbored the dream of a great university and, recognizing the opportunity before him, waged a small political war against adversaries who wished to see the grant go to other colleges. He and Cornell prevailed, and on April 27, 1865, the bill constituting the charter of "the Cornell University" was signed.

Three years later the university on a hill opened its doors and set out, soon to become a flagship among American universities. White's dream as a young man "during my working hours, in the class-rooms, in rambles along the lake shore, in the evenings, when I paced up and down the walks in front of the [Geneva] college buildings, and saw rising . . . the worthy home of a great university,"[5] and what Ezra Cornell envisioned as "a university of the first magnitude—such as we have to go to Europe to find"[6] had taken its first step. At the new institution's opening a single building stood with wide open doors to wel-

2. The early Cornell campus, c. 1875 (Sage Chapel in foreground).

come people to the main campus—Building No. 1, or South University Building (Morrill Hall today). As Morris Bishop points out, the open doors were as
necessary as they were symbolic—the hinges had yet to arrive. Nearby a half-
completed North University Building (now White Hall) completed the quad,
while the nine bells given by Jennie McGraw were housed in a make-shift
wooden structure near the site of the present-day chimes tower. Across the
gorge Cascadilla stood as the only other building, ready to provide living quarters for faculty, students, and president alike. Some found these first buildings
attractive, others such as Professor Goldwin Smith disagreed. "Nothing can re-
deem them but dynamite," he later commented.[7]

Entrance examinations were administered at the Cornell Library downtown,
and a class of 412 (including 80 upperclassmen) was accepted to begin studies.
Tuition was set at $10 a trimester, and students had a choice of three courses of
study: Science, Philosophy, or Arts. Ranging in age from fifteen to thirty, class
members hailed from all corners of the country and could boast fellow students
from Canada, England, Brazil, and Russia. Some had served in the Civil War,
some were headed to the U.S. Senate; most were poor, but almost all had a rugged
spirit befitting a pioneer institution.

From this class emerged the first members of a glee club at Cornell. The new
students instinctively gravitated toward organizing themselves in clubs and societies, but in the context of the gray sobriety of the original buildings and the
predominantly conservative population of Ithaca, the appearance of a musical
group was notable. Even the founder of the university was reported to have only
an elementary taste in music. After one concert Cornell wrote that a rendition
of "Home, Sweet Home" was "so distorted by artistic skill that it made me nervous."[8] President White was more cultured, having spent time in the artistic centers of Europe, and he counted music among his diversions. Nevertheless the
local residents were just beginning to admit amusement into their lives, still
cautious lest it amount to an insidious snare of the devil. After a dance at Cascadilla hosted by Ezra Cornell, local clergy complained that the university
should not tolerate such activity; one wonders if a skeptical view of singing was
not far off.

While a glee club even in name was a novelty in Ithaca, the group had precedents at other institutions. A group of Harvard students had organized a glee club in 1858, generally acknowledged to be the first such organization in America. Other schools, including Michigan and Yale, soon followed suit, and a host of such clubs appeared on campuses during the decades that followed. Drawing on minstrel shows, the vaudeville stage, and an American brand of college songs for the style and substance of their performances, these groups developed a distinctly American character. The original ancestors of Cornell's Glee Club and other such groups, however, can be traced back across the ocean.

What, after all, is a glee club? The word "glee" is Anglo-Saxon, coming from "gliw" or "gléo," which meant entertainment, musical entertainment, or music itself. Used in this last sense, the word appears in the oldest of English epic poems, *Beowulf*. In the mid-seventeenth century, glee was first used to indicate a distinct musical form, referring to a simply harmonized, English composition for three or more unaccompanied male voices. "Con., Tenor, Base" was a popular designation for the voices, with a male alto or countertenor taking the top line. The glees often sang of eating and drinking, or other themes including love, patriotism, and the hunt. Some maintain that glees, frequently distinguished from catches and canons, developed in part as a reaction to the vulgarity of catches; as proof, one late-eighteenth-century book of glees announced "Words consistent with Female Delicacy." By this time glees written for mixed voices had appeared, ranging from three to eight voices. The late eighteenth century also brought the first accompanied glees. The term thereafter was liberally applied to everything from traditional glees to arrangements of solo songs, accompanied glees, and ensembles extracted from opera. Traditional glees disappeared as an active form by the end of the nineteenth century but were survived by the part song, which drew on the glee's gradual shift toward increasingly homophonic texture and sentimental melody.[9]

As early as the late 1500s, catch singing was recognized in England as a popular social pastime among men. Initially enjoyed by artisans and other men of the working class, the art soon caught on in all classes, leaving many a gentleman singing Restoration catches that juxtaposed words to great and bawdy effect. During the eighteenth century social clubs organized around this pastime, most notably the Noblemen and Gentlemen's Catch Club founded in 1761 "to meet for dinner and music-making." The club met every Tuesday from February to June in London's Thatched House Tavern and, despite its name, sang glees and canons as well as catches. Glee singing reached its peak in the late 1700s, and in 1783 the Glee Club was founded in London by a group who met to dine and sing at the house of Robert Smith in St. Paul's Churchyard. The original members included musicians Samuel Arnold, Thomas Linley, Samuel Webbe and his son Samuel, and John Callcott, along with a number of amateurs, for whom such clubs were principally intended. After all, a glee was supposed to be simple enough to provide "something grateful to listen to and not too demanding for the singers."[10] After dinner the Glee Club traditionally opened the singing with a three-voice canon by Byrd: "Non nobis, Domine! non nobis, sed nomini tuo da gloriam" ("Not unto us, O Lord! not unto us, but unto thy name be the praise"), drawn from Psalm 115. In 1790 the senior Samuel Webbe composed a three-voice glee, "Glorious Apollo," which thereafter opened the meetings of the Glee Club, the Byrd piece serving as a grace. This first of glee clubs was disbanded in 1857, about the time similar groups started appearing in America, and its library was sold. The Noblemen and Gentlemen's Catch Club, and another London organization known as the City Glee Club (tracing roots back to the Civil Club founded in the 1670s) both survived into the twentieth century.[11]

While these groups were the principal forefathers of American glee clubs, several other musical lineages are worth noting. The German *Männerchor,* for which Schubert, Brahms, Schumann, and Mendelssohn wrote, was particularly prominent during the nineteenth century, and crossed the Atlantic as an imported cultural heritage. Moreover, Scandinavia's rich male chorus tradition also bore fruit in the States, particularly among immigrants who settled in the Midwest. And most simply, perhaps, until the eighteenth century European choruses were male choruses (with boys, and later castrati, taking the treble parts); women were not allowed to sing except in the convent.

At Cornell the Orpheus Glee Club and Orchestra, as designated in the first *Cornelian,* made its way, rehearsing every Tuesday night according to the first Cornell Register (a listing of faculty and classes). Although the grand concert in Ithaca never materialized, the group did make at least one formal appearance. On the evening of Thursday, January 21, 1869, at a belated celebration of the second anniversary of the Cornell Library Association, the Orpheus Glee Club was invited to enliven the exercises with a song.[12] Standing before a capacity crowd in downtown Library Hall, they opened the concert history of Cornell ensembles with the first Cornell song, "The Chimes." Another college song came later in the program, and with these two small selections the first Cornell glee club met with thundering success. "The singers were loudly cheered, and called on to repeat,"[13] and though fairly reticent about the group's performance, the January 26 *Ithaca Journal* called the evening "one of the pleasantest entertainments ever given in Ithaca." Thus, after an acclaimed premiere that would also prove its pyre, the Orpheus Glee Club eventually bowed out of existence with only one official appearance to its name.

Such a fate was not unusual for the university's first music groups—in the early years formal concerts were rare. Impromptu music making was the order of the day, taking the form of spontaneous serenading (often accorded to endeared professors and finding further use once the women arrived permanently in 1871),[14] midnight notes wandering from a troubadour's violin, or the rowdy singing of an entire class as they paraded through the streets, celebrating the election of their new officers. Groups sprang up with varying degrees of formality. In October 1869 the Collegensia Quintette was founded (see fig. 1), a group that would outlive the Orpheus ensemble and eventually supply several members for the first "Cornell Glee Club."[15] Likewise, several fraternities had their own glee clubs and/or orchestras, including the Alpha Delta Phi Philharmonic, the Chi Phi Quartette, and the Kappa Alpha Harmonia.

With the first musicians came the first critics, and the impromptu manner of performance lent itself all too easily to detractors. On December 15, 1869, the *Cornell Era* burst forth:

> OUR Glee Clubs are becoming a decided nuisance. The numerous groups that, having learned the words and part of the air to three or four worn out songs, go prowling around the streets nearly every night racking the nervous system of all who have to listen by their "melodious discords," would do well to show a little more taste in the selection of parts, singers, and pieces to be sung. In short, our *best* advice to some of these clubs is for them never to attempt singing at all where any one can hear them; but if they persist in so doing, we suggest that not more than four or five take the parts of soprano and base, especially when there is tenor or alto. . . . We have had several quartette clubs in organization since opening of the University that often produced fine music, bnt [sic] we have heard nothing of them for some time. Have they dissipated their talent by merging it into such institutions as we have been speaking of, or has the superabundance of spurious "Music (floating) in the air" so disgusted them as to kill the enterprise?
>
> Far from any desire to cool the ardor of those musically inclined do we write these lines. No! we cry, give us *music,* soul stirring, heart swelling, tree heaving, stone moving music! all you can, even till Hades resounds in the charming noise, or till
>
> > Ixion, too, the magic shall feel,
> > And for a moment stop his wheel,—
>
> but save us from any further imitations of those nocturnal howlings on Mount Cythera.[16]

Supposedly still in existence at this time, the Orpheus Glee Club apparently did little to advance musicianship at Cornell. The group disappeared entirely by 1870–1871, most likely because several founding members were no longer in town. Over the next few years the absence of good singing would become a familiar complaint, particularly on the pages of the *Cornell Era*. With regularity almost equal to the seasons, the editors would air their semiannual grievances about music on campus. In October 1870 "there should be a dozen quartette clubs among so great a body of students as ours, to say nothing of a good University choir"; in February 1872 "Cornell is not guilty of the title of a 'Singing College,'" and in fall 1873 "other colleges with a much smaller number of students are able to form Glee Clubs, excellent enough even to give entertainments abroad, and yet Cornell has not even its quartette."[17]

Admittedly this last remark was an exaggeration, for the Collegensia Quintette was still around, as were several fraternity ensembles, and other flash-in-the-pan groups such as the "Qui Vive" serenaders and the University Quartette had also put in appearances. Moreover, unlike today whole classes would get involved in singing; though often led by a quartette the senior class sang en masse at both Class Day and Commencement exercises. Song was a vehicle for the camaraderie of shared identity, and more than once the pages of the *Era* mention the class of so-and-so should establish a rousing class song. Even so the natural impulse (and the *Era's* hope) was to establish a formal organization for the making of music, and after several false starts a meeting was called for Thursday, October 29, 1874, to organize a musical society. The result of this and a subsequent meeting was the formation of the Cornell University Musical Association, out of which emerged a glee club and orchestra. The latter provided music at association meetings from time to time, and a quartette was soon out serenading. The policy for admission to the group required a vote of the whole association on prospective members. However a further restriction governed membership, which raised some eyebrows and created a heated controversy—no women were allowed.

A proponent of coeducation before the first female students ever set foot on the campus, the *Cornell Era* sounded the alarm:

It is with some surprise that we heard of the action of the Musical Association in excluding from its membership the lady students. . . .

It was said that if ladies were admitted to the association the gentlemen would pay more attention to them than the singing, or, to state the matter plainly, the singing-school would virtually become a courting school. Poor susceptible mortals, we pity you from the bottom of our heart! . . . We have yet to be convinced that men and women, having a common, definite object in view cannot refrain from such boy and girl foolishness. . . .

[A student] should endeavor to crush all ideas which militate against that system [coeducation], whatever may be his own opinion of its merits. Of such ideas, the one embodied in the argument for the exclusion of ladies from the Musical Association seems to be the most dangerous, and we trust that it will not again find expression in the constitution of any student organization.[18]

Most of the university's early extracurricular organizations, including the fledgling athletic teams, excluded women, suggesting the need for an activity in which they were welcome. But in an age when coeducation itself was still an isolated experiment in American colleges, the Musical Association felt itself on defensible ground, and aired a rebuttal in the *Era* the following week, which read in part:

> Now we are willing always to take the back seat in favor of the ladies; will at all times give them full sweep of sidewalks; in fact are willing to do almost anything "to keep peace in the family," but cannot the gentlemen have *something* to themselves besides military drill, if they choose? . . .
>
> The whole upshot of the matter is this: A number of students met and organized themselves into a body for the purpose of improvement and culture in music. Instead of admitting ladies, and thereby creating a certain reserve and straight-backed decorum, which would have repelled very many who can learn enough of parlor aesthetics elsewhere, it was concluded best not to admit ladies as members. If the Association choose to do this, it is the business of nobody but themselves.[19]

In the end the 1875 *Cornelian* listed C. Harris, Instructor of Orchestra, E. H. Bartley, Instructor of Vocal Music, and a 57-member ensemble, all male.

Plans were made for a spring concert, but a conflict arose with another benefit slated for the Navy (that is, the crew). The Musical Association's performance was also intended as part of an evening of entertainment "for the benefit of the University Six," who would compete in a regatta in Saratoga. In the early years of organized musical and athletic activity on university campuses, the musical groups often plied their trade for the good of the "University Six" or the "College Nine." Not wishing to overtax the Cornell crew's supporters, the Musical Association's concert was moved to May 1, and the Wilgus Opera House downtown secured for the occasion. That evening's program proves to be one of the most eclectic in the history of the Glee Club: "1. Gymnastics . . . 2. Music: vocal by the University Glee Club, the Collegensia Quintette and the Engineer Quartette; instrumental by the University Orchestra. 3. A Heart-Rending Tragedy, presented by the University Amateur Dramatic Association."[20]

The concert was deemed a success, and marked the first time the "University Glee Club" appeared in name. The *Cornelian* of the next year (1876) listed a group of twenty as the Cornell Glee Club; having become an official representative of the university in name, the group began to entertain requests to participate in official university activities.

After the first half of 1875–1876 passed in quiet inactivity the Musical Association regrouped in the spring to offer another successful concert, this time sans tumblers and tragedians. Confidence was running high, and the organization decided to try their luck out of town. A train was booked, and on May 5, 1876, the CUMA gave a concert in Cortland, the first "concert tour" of a Cornell ensemble. For some members of the ensemble the train ride proved an unexpected sacrifice. Forced to switch cars en route, the unlucky ones ended up in a cattle car where they found themselves serenading "a few aborigines of both sexes." Moreover, once in Cortland the group met with wary local citizens, who like some of their apprehensive Ithaca brethren regarded the group as a possible compromise of puritanical principles. Though a financial failure, as most of the Glee Club's early trips would prove to be, the concert was success-ful musically, and "the singing was continued all the way home."[21]

At this time the musical activity of the campus and community was largely indebted to the efforts of two men: Estévan Antonio Fuertes and Max Piutti. Fuertes was head of the College of Civil Engineering (then housed in Lincoln Hall), and fondly referred to as "the Mogue" (in part because he smoked Mogul cigarettes). A native of Puerto Rico, where he was once imprisoned for politi-cal subversion, he worked with both the Glee Club and orchestra. Piutti was educated in Leipzig and elsewhere in his native Germany before emigrating to the States and becoming a professor of music at Wells College in fall 1874. With uncommon generosity he made the trip to Ithaca weekly, asking no payment other than his expenses. In addition to leading several musical ensembles he offered the first music classes at the university, which were directed toward the improvement of singing. He also brought his abilities as a pianist, playing Liszt's "Second Hungarian Rhapsody" in the Glee Club's spring 1876 concerts. (Fuertes contributed a flute solo.) Piutti is listed as leading the Glee Club in their 1877 spring concert, while Fuertes was at the helm of the orchestra, and the in-fluence of these two men is evident in the *Era's* review: "The concert . . . was one of the most enjoyable amateur performances ever given in Ithaca."[22] The article acknowledges their gifted assistance, as well as that of Charles Schaeffer, a professor of chemistry and mineralogy.

That the two Cornell professors guiding student music making were profes-sors of science should not come as a complete surprise—the first appointment of a professor in music was still more than twenty-five years off.[23] In the mean-time the dedicated Piutti and Fuertes took matters into their own hands. Late in 1875 they founded the Mozart Club of Ithaca, pledged by its constitution to perform "the great Classical composers," and to advance the musical culture of both town and university. The *Era* believed such performances would im-prove the outside world's estimation of Cornell—"It would be highly instruc-tive to watch the expression upon the faces of these auditors [Cornell critics] as they listened to the masterpieces of Haydn, Mozart, Mendelssohn, and Wagner interpreted by the 'young hayseeds' assisted by the talent of the 'Forest City'"[24]—and expressed the hope that the club might become a forerunner to a profes-sorship of music at the university. Gathering in the Sage parlors or Library Hall, the group held a handful of "rehearsals" a year, which in every regard other than name far more resembled concerts. Members were expected to arrive able to perform their parts (which had been previously distributed), programs were printed, and season ticket subscriptions made available to the public. Students, including some from the Glee Club, took part in the Mozart Club Chorus, and the performances were of such high quality that audience numbers began to exceed the seating capacity of the club's private settings.

With this healthy state of affairs 1877–1878 promised to be a strong musical year. Early in the term the Musical Association announced the "third of its successful concerts" would take place middle of the term, the earliest any concert had been scheduled. But the announcement proved presumptuous—the concert never took place. Instead, mention of Mozart Club rehearsals replaced mention of the Cornell University Musical Association, and the association fell out of existence the same year. The Mozart Club kept musical culture viable, offering a formal concert that year, and Piutti became further involved, having begun to deliver the university's first lectures in music. A series on Haydn, Mozart, and Beethoven was followed in the spring of 1878 with a set on Schubert, Schumann, and Chopin. The usual complaints about singing were aired—including comments that "Chapel singing has not been remarkable . . . for a rigorous adherence to the notes of the organ," and a choir might be formed that "others may sing at least with some sort of approximation to time and tune"—but with no glee club they were directed at the singing in Sage Chapel.[25]

Even with the efforts of the Mozart Club, a glee club was missed, and in the winter of 1878–1879 the *Era* took up the lament: "Cornell University formerly had a glee club. It might have been long ago, somewhere in the dark age of fable, but it is certain that we *once* had a glee club, and now are pursuing the even tenor (no pun intended) of our way without one. . . . Nothing has taken the place of our glee club, and it is for this that we mourn and refuse to be comforted."[26]

The dark days were at hand. The brass band started in the early 1870s, with instruments purchased by the generous donations of students and citizens alike, had long disappeared (apparently with the instruments, though some were destroyed in a fire). The orchestra formed from the Musical Association led a precarious and periodic existence. The quartettes and quintettes that had attained some success, like the Collegensia, had long since vanished. That group's demise in the mid-1870s may have been hastened by the last recorded report of their singing—"The song, 'Parting Day' . . . was not a decided success; a discord at the beginning threw the boys into confusion from which they recovered with difficulty."[27] And the departure of Piutti at the end of the decade sounded the requiem for the Mozart Club. The early 1880s in particular suggested what Harold Samuel, author of "The First Hundred Years of Music at Cornell," attributes to the whole decade: "resignation to the idea of an unmusical Cornell." But before giving in to this fate, the Glee Club made another go of it. As Samuel says, "The Glee Club was the only organization to attain some success [in the 1880s], and its ups and downs were determined by the availability of adequate leaders."[28]

In March 1880 a glee club was organized and with only two months rehearsal took the stage downtown at the Wilgus Opera House. "The first concert of the

University Glee Club took the audience by storm. Perhaps no entertainment ever given by any student organization has been better received. . . . The manner in which the various selections were rendered quite surprised the audience. . . . Every piece was encored, and some of them twice, and as the encores were generally college songs, they were enthusiastically received."[29]

The review mentions the distinct diction of the group, which became a trademark of Cornell choral ensembles. As for the manifest ability of the Club to pull together in a short period of time and rise to the occasion, it has become a habit.

Having impressed the townspeople of Ithaca, the Glee Club decided to take the entertainment abroad, perhaps encouraged by reports that other college glee clubs had earned reputations by touring around the country. In the space of a week (May 24–29) the group visited Trumansburg, Auburn, and Syracuse. The reviews were again laudatory, the financial outcome again lamentable. Still, on the steamboat trip down the lake, the "old hills echoed back the melodious harmonies of good old college songs,"[30] and by a late train, the group returned buoyed by the sound of double encores ringing in their ears.

In the fall of 1880 the Glee Club organized under Ludwig Thomas, who was not on the faculty at Cornell, and began rehearsing in the parlors of Cascadilla Place.[31] A concert was intimated for as early as Thanksgiving, but never given, and the Club had to completely reorganize the following January, with a small outstanding debt from past tours still lingering. For those familiar with the continuity of present-day ensembles, it is hard to imagine the uncertain and informal (not to mention impecunious) existence of the Glee Club. Clearly the problem in the first twenty years of the ensemble's history was that, even after a successful concert or particularly active year, of tomorrow there was no certainty. Leaders came and went, singers wandered in and out, plans were made and dropped, and only a few months after an acclaimed concert everything had to be restarted from scratch. The early history might well be interpreted as a search for continuity. In this struggle for survival one source of support became particularly helpful to the Glee Club in the 1880–1881 year—the *Cornell Era*. One of the Club's soloists, F. R. Luckey, also happened to be an editor for the *Era*, and so we find the weekly pledges "to persist until a Cornell Glee Club is an established fact," for otherwise the group "will have to be relegated to the catalogue of things that have died young."[32]

Similar to the Noblemen and Gentlemen's Catch Club, which offered prizes for new compositions, the *Era* offered to publish songs "dedicated to the Glee Club of Cornell," and with the incitement "there is nothing like making an honest effort to attain excellence in singing,"[33] the publication attempted in spring 1881 to recruit singers after only ten men attended a rehearsal led by Thomas. Ironically, the same *Era* issue also announced the group's concert in three weeks. The concert did take place, in Library Hall, but received only moderate kudos; as was often the case the instrumental selections on the program were considered more artistic. The group traveled to Elmira, and a joint trip to Geneva with the baseball team was planned. Only the Glee Club kept the engagement. Another proposed trip to Buffalo was abandoned, but the group gave its first Commencement concert, and the *Era* closed the year with the proclamation that in all probability "there is to-day no college in New York State that could boast a glee club the equal of ours."[34]

Morris Bishop writes, "With the formation of the Glee Club of 1880 Cornell musical history really began." Not quite.[35] The very next semester the Glee Club was reported abandoned by its members, and silence reigned for the next two years. The 1881–1882 *Cornelian* took advantage of the absence to publish a fictional and burlesque roster of the Glee Club (see fig. 3). The following year the yearbook did not mention a single student musical organization. An attempt to form a Glee Club was made in the winter of 1882–1883, but in addition to lack of interest the effort was hampered by a problem that has plagued most choral groups at one time or another—a lack of tenors. In reference to "the Glee Club Question" an 1885 *Era* would quote the proverb "the darkest hour is just before dawning." Nowhere was it more true than here—the Glee Club, and music at Cornell, were in the dark before dawn.

In these earliest years the face of life at Cornell, like the face of any child in youth, had changed rapidly and remarkably. By the mid 1880s, A. D. White's dream of "sermons in stone" had come true with the addition of such buildings as the president's house, Franklin (today Tjaden) Hall, and Sage Chapel. The student body had grown to more than 600 in 1885–1886, and was past 800 by the following year. The *Cornell Daily Sun* had come out for the first time in 1880, and literary, religious, departmental, and secret fraternal societies flourished. Athletics, off to a slow start in the first years, had gained momentum and popular support, and several teams excelled in competition. In addition to crew Cornell had its own brand of football (something of a combination of soccer, rugby, and football); it was not too popular with the faculty, and A. D. White once denied the team a trip saying, "I refuse to let forty of our boys travel four hundred miles merely to agitate a bag of wind."[36] Baseball was the first sport to catch on in a lasting way, and final scores, which might run as high as 42–26 in the early days, began to drop through the 1880s as the rules of the game changed. So much was flourishing on the campus, and yet the Cornell climate was proving hostile to formal music making.

Several factors accounted for this state of affairs. With the exception of Sage College for Women there was no campus dormitory, which meant most of the men lived downtown and had to trudge up the hill for rehearsals. Musical meetings were consequently held in the late afternoons to avoid an extra trip, but attendance still suffered. The musical organizations had to compete with the downtown attractions, including the almost nightly offerings at the Wilgus Opera House; Ithaca had sloughed off some inhibitions and now sought

CORNELL GLEE CLUB

O. B. SQUINT.   -   -   -   -   -   -   -   -   -   -   *Manager.*

First Tenors.	*Second Tenors.*
F. S. CIPHER,	J. L. MINUS,
G. W. MYTH,	R. S. AETHER,
J. T. IDEAL,	JAS. E. ZERO,
GEO. SPRITE.	H. S. WANTING.
First Basses.	*Second Basses.*
C. W. NAUGHT,	H. W. ABSENT,
M. S. GONE,	T. K. VIRTUAL,
F. J. FICTION,	P. S. NONE,
B. N. NONEST.	E. H. MISSING

A. D. ABSCOND,   -   -   -   -   -   -   -   *Treasurer.*
L. G. R. BEER,   -   -   -   -   -   -   -   *Starter.*
DAN. NELLIGAN,   -   -   -   -   -   -   -   *Stopper.*

3. Spoof Glee Club roster from the 1882 *Cornelian.*

entertainment in the regular run of plays, variety shows, and operettas. By contrast there was no concert series or schedule of visiting artists on campus, and the administration remained indifferent to both student musical efforts and general pleas for a professorship in music. In his last two reports to the Board of Trustees A. D. White recommended the establishment of a college in music and the fine arts, but the first professor in music was still a distant dream. And finally, if apparent to no one else, the *Era* perceived an antagonism between sports and music. On one occasion early in the decade the paper suggested the advantage of organizing a glee club in the winter months, when there would be no draw for athletic contests and the university audience could turn its attention to the vocal talent of the school. And in 1886, the *Era* observed that apparently the university could excel in athletics or music, but not both, seeing as the "blue waters of Cayuga [i.e., attention to crew] . . . seem to dampen the wings of song."[37]

Against these odds students labored in the fall of 1883 to resurrect the Glee Club. In a way, their situation resembled the earliest days of the university, which David Starr Jordan 1872 (who went on to become the first president of Stanford), described as being "without experience or tradition to guide or hinder."[38] Under the leadership of George B. Penny 1885 the group was reorganized on October 11, 1883, at a meeting that was "largely attended" (thirteen were present). The *Era* wrote, "Last evening the University Glee Club was made a permanent organization." While the club had by no means escaped its precarious situation, there is some truth to the claim. Every year since, with the exception of hiatuses caused by the two World Wars, there has been a Cornell Glee Club. Penny, who had originally served as an accompanist and piano soloist, moved up to musical director, apparently rounded up enough tenors, and focused enough enthusiasm to rally the troops to committed rehearsals and a first-term concert. The *Era* reported the ensemble "showed from the first a determination to have a concert this term," and after the December 6 appearance at the Wilgus Opera House, "a marked success in more ways than one," remarked that the Glee Club was "capable of making 'goodly melodie with much harmonie.'"[39] Not only the first concert of the Cornell Glee Club before the winter break, the entire program was given by performers drawn from within the group. Instrumental solos were still included (Penny performed brilliantly on a "miserable apology" for a piano), but never before had the group been entirely responsible for its own program.

With this ensemble and the following group of 1884–1885 (a good number of the members carried over and Penny remained as musical director) the Glee Club began to show a clearer sense of purpose. In 1880 the *Era* had suggested in addition to being enjoyable in itself the Club brought fame to its alma mater, and proved useful in teaching students the songs and how to sing them. The paper restated this idea in the spring of 1884, commenting that the group's duty was to perpetuate new college songs and revive old ones. In May 1885, however, an editorial for the first time revealed—at least on the part of the *Era's* editors—

a long-term vision for the group. Stating that "the object of the Glee Club has been pleasure rather than profit, to give concerts rather than to gain a knowledge of music," and criticizing that "the standard for admission to the glee club has not been sufficiently high to make membership any special honor . . . [or to foster any] musical *esprit du corps* in the organization," the article argued that improvement in these areas would ensure the success and perpetuity of the Club.[40] A qualified teacher should be found to train voices and lead the organization, whereby it would earn a high reputation and begin to attract musically inclined students who would in turn have the incentive to work for a position in the ensemble. And the article suggested the Club be reorganized immediately (the end of the spring term was approaching), not to give a concert but to lay a foundation for improvement in the following year. As a whole, the editorial demonstrated a new commitment to an enduring rather than expedient glee club, and can be taken as a significant statement about the group's purpose and philosophy. For whether Penny and company read their *Era,* these very ideas began to change the shape of the Glee Club.

Already in the fall of 1884, before the editorial even appeared, the group had begun to hold auditions to weed out poor singers. Unfortunately this did not secure the well-being of the group, and that ensemble did not survive the year. The next fall, campus singers regrouped and undaunted by the previous failure, again held auditions, with the intention of limiting the group to sixteen. Considering twenty or so singers formed the current ensemble, it was mentioned some would have to yield their places to better singers, and the possibility of two glee clubs was put forth. F. W. Hebard 1887 was elected director and ordered each man to report to rehearsal with a copy of "Cornell Songs." The group sputtered and halted, however, and for the second year in a row the Glee Club did not take part in the Commencement concert. A visit of the relatively healthy Amherst Glee Club prompted the *Era* to shake its head: "There must be some other reason for this neglect of the muses." But the last word on the Glee Club that year was a portent: "The good time is not far hence."[41] The next year, in November 1886, A. H. McKenney was secured as vocal instructor; when a sufficient number of interested singers submitted their names, it was announced, a meeting would be held and he would choose the voices "on merit alone." The new Glee Club (which began to resemble the vision of the *Era* article) held together but proceeded quietly, prompting the *Era* to say as late as April, "Are we to know nothing of this organization except that it exists? . . . It is not too late for the Glee Club to make its *debut* and show that it is possible for Cornell to support such an organization."[42] The somewhat humorous reality was that almost every other year the inchoate Glee Club could make a legitimate debut, having been completely reorganized as an ensemble. This time, after a trip to Owego and Trumansburg with the newly formed Banjo Club, the group gave a well-received Commencement concert at the Wilgus, launching a series of successful performances over the next few years.

Between 1887 and 1889 the Glee Club went on to make more formal appearances than it had during the rest of the decade combined, but an informality of approach typical of the 1880s lingered. In 1881 a call had gone out to round up additional singers just three weeks before a concert. This same casual attitude toward performance was evident in 1885 when the Glee Club sang for the inauguration of Cornell's second president, Charles Kendall Adams. That appearance had been the result of a last-minute request (the group had not been notified till the evening before that they were singing) and members could scarcely have had a chance to *see* the music they were to perform, let alone rehearse it. In spring 1884 a tour was announced to Syracuse, Auburn, Lockport, and Buffalo with concerts beginning in ten to fourteen days time. The Glee Club manager was to inform the alumni in those cities, and that was the last word on the subject.[43] Another trip (this one actually taken) to Owego in 1888 proved a high-spirited fiasco for those involved; that story is told in Chapter 7. Even as late as the 1888–1889 year, the beginning of the first semester found the officers and others trying to revive the organization, each year seemingly bringing a new cast of enthusiasts rushing to save the sinking ship. This perennial matter of reorganizing the ensemble and the Glee Club's informal ways could only perpetuate each other so long as both remained a way of life for the group.

Toward the end of the decade, however, better organization began to pay off. After the Commencement concert of 1887, which included a collaboration with the soprano Henrietta Beebe-Lawton, the group got off to a quick start the following term, with a certain continuity evident in the request that all old members attend the first meeting. Though the usual problem of finding first tenors prevailed, the Club made steady progress during its Wednesday evening rehearsals and in January announced a performance in Ithaca the night before the Junior Ball. It was a musical success, with the audience calling for encores for more than half of a program that included Cornell songs, a virtuoso whistler, a string quartette, and a bit of comic relief resembling the more contemporary "tour burn." (Omitting the last word of a song, seven singers turned around with the word Cornell spelled on placards across their backs.) A concert was given the Saturday before the 1888 graduation; though not considered as successful as the winter appearance, it was an undeniable improvement over the previous year's Commencement performance. Trips were taken over two April weekends to Cortland, Cazenovia, Binghamton, and Elmira. Even the relationship between sports and music was looking up—with the baseball team in Elmira the same day as the concert, everyone was encouraged to cheer the team in the afternoon and the Glee Club in the evening.

After some early obstacles in 1888–1889, the group took shape under McKenney as an ensemble of sixteen, four to a part. They concertized in Cortland before the Junior Ball, and then took the stage at the Wilgus Opera House in early February. The concert was "a revelation and a surprise to the friends of the organization. The club sang with a precision and harmony never evinced in a glee club here previously."[44] Next came a joint performance with the Amherst Glee and Banjo Clubs, the first collaboration with another ensemble. Here, the group's blend was criticized; the Cornell singers were good—they simply sounded as though every man wanted to be a soloist. The happy news, however, was that the "Amherst Warbler . . . was wholly eclipsed by our whistler, Mr. Kolb."[45] An April trip to Elmira was highly acclaimed by the local press, and in June the Glee Club made its third appearance of the season at the opera house. Not only was it the third Ithaca appearance of the year, it was the first time a Cornell Glee Club had put together three consecutive Commencement concert appearances.

This growing continuity and reliability were not merely demonstrations of the ability to survive. The Glee Club from 1886 to 1889 was making steady progress toward a new standard of music making, and their commitment did not go unnoticed. After the 1889 Commencement concert, the *Era* summed it up: "On the whole, there can be no doubt but that the Cornell Glee and Banjo Clubs have made wonderful improvement since their first appearance this season. They have labored hard and faithfully."[46] The darkness of the group's early years with its hopeful but inconstant flashes of light had given way to the steady light of dawn. A sense of purpose had begun to take root, traditions were gradually amassing, and an increasingly musical song filled the air. The group was now ready to engage a new director—Hollis Dann.

2 Hollis Dann,
1889–1921

Song is at once the alpha and omega of music.

—Hollis Dann

In the small village of Canton, Pennsylvania, not far from a creek fed by the Susquehanna River, the seasons turned over the land with comforting regularity. After the turbulence of the Civil War, new fields had begun to grow over the scarred earth near the state's southern border. Life went on rather quietly on the small farms, in town trades, and in the schoolhouses.

In 1869, 8-year-old Hollis Dann had no idea a group of men were struggling to launch a university and a group of still younger men to found a glee club some miles to the north. But with his early steps he unknowingly set out in a direction that would one day lead him from Canton to Cornell.

Born Hollis Ellsworth Dann on May 1, 1861, to parents who had a sense for the simple and the aesthetic in life, he later recalled: "As a child my home life was strongly influenced by music. Prior to my school days and throughout the years in elementary school I listened and later, with my mother and sister, joined in the singing of hymns almost every night after dinner." On Sunday the hymns were led by Dann's grandfather, described thus: "Although over seventy years old (he sang after he was eighty), grandfather would turn to father and sound the key, singing 'm-faddle-la' (do-so-do or la-mi-la) and then start the hymns, singing the melody and father singing the bass. I was particularly interested and often very much excited by the 'fugue tunes' such as 'Lenox' and greatly impressed by the hymns set to minor tunes such as 'Broad is the Road that Leads to Death.'"[1]

Growing up the youngest in a household of five, the boy began at 10 to study the piano with his sister Celia and at nearly the same time began to sing alto at the singing schools conducted by his father each winter. "These singing schools were organized in our home village and in communities within a radius of twenty miles," Dann later remembered. "Each term of singing school, consist-

4. Hollis Dann, 1908. From *Cornell Era,*
1907–1908.

ing of twenty lessons, was followed by a 'Musical Convention' held in a local
church, the singing school class augmented by the church choir and other experienced singers of the village. Sessions were held morning, afternoon and
evening, beginning Monday morning and closing with a 'grand concert' on Saturday night."[2] Within five years he was competent enough to accompany his
father at these conventions, playing a cabinet organ, and during his teens he took
part in other musical conventions led by nationally known conductors.

Very early in his career Dann began to follow his educational instincts. After graduating from Canton's high school in spring 1879 he took an opening to
teach a summer term in the country and continued for two years to teach in
the grammar grades of Canton's schools. At the same time he sang in a church
choir and served as the "chorister," a respected position of leadership, as his sister noted in admiration, usually reserved for older men. Somewhere in those
two years Dann decided music was his calling and in 1881 chose to go to Rochester, New York, to further his formal training. Singing in a church choir to support himself, he studied piano and organ for a year, after which he headed for
Boston, America's capital of music education at the time. For two years he dili-
gently studied voice and piano while sampling the city's cultural fare. The Boston
Symphony exposed him to symphonic repertoire, he heard oratorios performed by the Handel and Haydn Society and the Cecilia Society, and he took
in an occasional opera troupe at the Music Hall.

Dann returned from Boston to Canton, where he taught privately, headed a
church choir, and organized his first community chorus. In 1886 he took a job

as principal of the Montour Falls Academy near Watkins Glen. But as he wrote in a 1932 letter, his days as a music student in Boston had awakened an interest in music education. So when the chance came in 1887 to teach in the Ithaca public schools, he packed his bags and made his way northeast. He was engaged primarily to teach penmanship and commercial subjects but had been promised part-time work in music. Arriving in Ithaca a young man of 26, he soon found (as was the case across the country) that there was no organized study of music in the schools. Superintendent Luther Clark Foster became an immediate ally, and working against the skeptical school board the two men scored a triumph when the high school chorus made its first appearance at Commencement the following spring. Parents and other townspeople were struck with surprise, and Dann was soon made supervisor of music. It was just the beginning. Driven by seemingly boundless energy, Dann took on voice students, directed the Presbyterian Church Choir, and joined the only community musical organization around, the Ithaca Choral Club, all in addition to responsibilities in teaching nonmusical subjects.

The Choral Club, composed of Cornell faculty, students, and townspeople, annually staged light opera at the Wilgus Opera House, and for three years Dann sang a variety of roles, after which he became the group's conductor. His most memorable role probably was as Frederic in Gilbert and Sullivan's *Pirates of Penzance* and mainly for his offstage performance. Backstage one evening in the winter of late 1889, cast members realized "Mabel" had an engagement ring on her finger and discovered "Frederic" was the intended. The curtain went up late that night, and Dann married Lois Hanford the next summer.

For Dann 1889–1890 proved to be a big year for other reasons as well. That fall, having impressed the community with his musicianship, he was engaged to conduct the Cornell University Glee Club. According to Harold Samuel in "The First Hundred Years of Music at Cornell," the invitation came from the Choral Union (the Choral Club), who supposedly administered the Glee Club. Given that A. H. McKenney had ties to the Choral Club and that local businessmen Charles Treman 1889 and Charles Blood 1888 (both involved in Glee Club affairs) took part in its productions, the connection is entirely plausible. Why McKenney himself did not stay on as Glee Club director remains a mystery.

The Glee Club organized on November 29 that year, somewhat later than usual, and sang several selections for Founder's Day, January 11 (Ezra Cornell's birthday). The first real test for the group and its new director came at the second annual Junior Week concert in early February. The *Cornell Daily Sun* reported, "The choruses and solos with humming accompaniment to be sung at the Glee Club concert, next Wednesday, have been carefully rehearsed during the past season under Professor Dann, a well known local musician."[3] Following the concert, the *Era* raved, "It was by all means the best concert ever given at Cornell."[4] The season however went downhill from there—a spring trip to Utica, Albany, and Troy proved a financial failure, a manager resigned throwing further tour plans up in the air, and the *Era's* loquacious parting comment was, "It is hoped that next year the Glee Club will not be so unfortunate as to be unable to maintain an existence up to Commencement week."[5] The next fall Dann returned a year wiser, and the Glee Club soon began to show clearer signs of his presence. The Junior Week concert of 1891 went off very well, and the *Era* wrote, "It is safe to say that never before in the history of Cornell clubs has there been such a success." As if there were no ceiling, the hyperbolic (and somewhat amnesiac) *Era* claimed the next year the Glee Club had "made great progress," calling the entertainment "perhaps the best of the kind given at Cornell for several years."[6]

The press was not always so positive—one might hear on occasion the Glee Club was out "looking for the half tone they had dropped in the previous evening's concert." But with Dann's guidance the group became consistently more organized, more polished, and more ambitious. Indeed the 1890s proved to be a decade of great growth for the Glee Club—not only in reputation, but in size, sound, and scope of endeavor.

In the early years Dann made it a practice to hold auditions in his home at 12 North Aurora Street. In his first five years he kept membership at about twenty singers; with the growing Banjo and Mandolin Clubs the Musical Clubs totaled about forty. The competition for spots was keen—in fall 1893 it was reported fifty had tried out for the Glee Club and twenty were chosen for further competition. From these auditions Dann culled and carefully trained the "twelve-story tenors and sub-cellar bassos" whom the *Era* felt were "so joined that the voices blend like the colors of the solar spectrum."[7] The group's improving intonation apparently gave local critics the impression the sound had a greater strength and volume, even though there was no increase in group size until the latter half of the decade.

Together with their sound, the Glee Club's schedule was growing. The first Junior Week concert had been given in 1888, and in 1891 (the same year the spring tour expanded) the group restarted their traditional Commencement concert appearances. A typical year included several short trips to nearby towns, including Syracuse, Auburn, Elmira, Binghamton, and Cortland, and in spring 1893 the Glee Club made its first appearance in New York City (much to the delight of the pining Manhattan alumni), appearing with the Columbia Musical Clubs at the Madison Square Garden Concert Hall. Between January and June of 1894 alone the Glee Club had nineteen performances, only two of which were in Ithaca.

The Easter concert tour thus took on new proportions with Dann at the helm and travels in 1891 that went as far west as Toledo and Ann Arbor (along with stops in Detroit, Cleveland, and Erie). Other than the weather, which left most of the group sick with colds and several soloists without voices, the tour proved successful artistically and financially. The program included some "compositions of real merit, and the excellent rendition of these songs gave evidence of the real musical ability of the club."[8] The success was repeated in the spring of 1892, when the tour reached Chicago and a local newspaper referred to the concert at Central Music Hall as one of the most successful college club concerts Chicago had ever known. If any doubted the development of the current club from the days of its forefathers, a humorous comparison was proffered in Buffalo, where three original members of the Orpheus Glee Club appeared at a reception and, much to the amusement of the crowd, sang by request. So warm was the response in that city that the audience requested an almost unbelievable thirty-nine encores, and a Michigan headline read, "They Came, They Saw, They Conquered."

A good part of the conquest was the result of student managers working to arrange the tour, and the ever increasing support of alumni in host cities. Manager Lenard Keiffer 1892 made great efforts to notify alumni (it was not yet common practice), and in March 1892 the *Era* reported, "Cornellians are said to be showing an incredible interest in the advent of the clubs." Encouraged to "Give 'the boys' crowded houses, and renew your connection with alma mater in listening to well-rendered college music,"[9] alumni responded. In nearly every city they wined and dined the group, entertaining them at home, securing invitations to dance parties, and hosting receptions, not to mention arranging the details for the concert performances. The newly combined Glee, Banjo, and Mandolin Clubs had arrived and so had widespread support from an alumni family little more than 20 years old, support that would become a mainstay for Cornell and its Glee Club.[10]

About this time concert activity of another sort began to appear more frequently on the Musical Clubs' calendar, with corresponding music. One commentator on American college songs, Franklin Bliss Shaw 1911, observed that the prototypical German college song "deals chiefly with the convivial side of undergraduate days," running over with the theme of wine, women, and song, while the American student "celebrates first and foremost his alma mater and her supremacy in athletic and intellectual achievement."[11] The connection between athletics and music was unquestionably growing, and as song and sports came together in musical verse, so did they in life as well. The 1892 Commencement concert, as with concerts in years past, doubled as a benefit for the crew, and the following spring the clubs participated in a benefit concert for the baseball team.[12] Tour profits also were donated to athletics, and on a rare summer tour taking the men from Richfield Springs, New York, to Narragansett, Rhode Island, during July and August 1892, the Glee Club formed its own baseball nine and won four out of five games played. A new musical intercollegiality also sprang up around athletic events, beginning for the Cornell singers at Thanksgiving 1894 when they performed with the Lehigh Musical Clubs on the eve of the Cornell–Lehigh game. Though the tradition did not take root until the next decade, the collaboration became the first of many joint concerts given on the eve of football games with the two teams as invited guests.

Along with the growth of the Musical Clubs the tie with athletics proved the critical impetus for the groups' first international tour. The first mention of such a trip was made early in 1894, when a tour of Britain, France, and Germany was proposed. As a selling point the *Era* purported, "It would be the first appearance of an American university's musical clubs before an audience in a foreign country."[13] The tour never took shape in that form—seventy-five years passed before Germany heard Cornell-singing, and it took even longer for France. But as the year progressed, the Cornell Crew made it known they would travel to compete in the Henley Regatta during the summer of 1895. That news proved the rallying point, and on April 20, 1895, the official announcement came: "The Glee, Banjo, and Mandolin clubs have decided to make a concert tour through England, Scotland and Ireland. . . . Three concerts will be given in London and then the clubs will go to Henley to witness the race. About twenty concerts will be given in all."[14]

Presumably plans had been in the works for a while (although even with Dann's organizational presence international tours did not benefit from extensive advance planning), and so to account for the timing of the voyage, the usual spring tour was taken over the Christmas holiday instead. The group sang in Scranton on Christmas Eve, eventually traveling south to Washington and Williamsburg and west to Toledo and Cincinnati. In the spring final preparations were made, the touring group was chosen (sixteen from the Glee Club), and the Clubs gave a rousing Senior Week concert, proving on the eve of their departure that "Cornellians have pride in their musical clubs as well in their crews; and the clubs will carry with them the best wishes of every loyal Cornellian."[15]

The full story of what happened is saved for Chapter 7. In short, the Glee Club left for England on June 19 and gave their first concert on July 5 to critical praise. The *St. James's Gazette* reported the Cornell minstrels had performed "with the greatest possible success. Everything was encored," while another account read, "The singers render their simple part songs, mostly of a humorous nature, in perfect time and tune, and their *pianissimo* might well be copied by English glee vocalists who essay higher class music."[16] But after their promising start, the collegiate troubadours were consigned to an inauspicious finish. So was the crew. The Cornell eight were derided in the press for both a supposedly unsportsmanlike victory and their eventual defeat; as a result, the Musical Club men reportedly lost heart. The fragility of the manager's arrangements was laid bare and, as engagements were canceled by the tour's would-be sponsors, the clubs found themselves bankrupt and homeless.

The Savage Club of London, an organization of men who gathered to socialize and entertain each other with their various talents and exploits as musicians, storytellers, actors, and explorers, befriended the Glee Club, extending club privileges to them for the duration of their stay. But the tour was effectively over. The group broke up and the men went their separate ways. Some returned home quickly while others lingered for months, touring the Continent before making the trip back. As someone speaking of the Glee Club's earliest tours once said, "We didn't make any money but we had plenty of fun."[17] Nevertheless the organization that little more than ten years earlier had been wobbling in and out of existence had made an ambitious leap forward in crossing the ocean—insofar as the record shows, no other musical club in the country would get as far for another twenty-five years.

In more than one regard 1895 proved a landmark year for the Glee Club. About the same time as the England tour several local movers and shakers with strong ideas about the organization of the Clubs stepped forth and formed the Musical Clubs Council. Their reasoning was clearly expressed: "The musical clubs have long felt that their organization was defective and that there should be a constitution drawn up and a governing body which should include men of wider experience than the average undergraduate can have. . . . The following constitution . . . promises to give the clubs steady, consistent policy and careful, conservative management." The adopted constitution made specific provisions for the election of five officers: president, secretary, treasurer, business manager, and librarian. It delineated the procedure for selecting new members, as well as the responsibilities of both members and officers. Among the interesting regulations Article V directed the treasurer to collect $5 from each man as a fine deposit. Thereafter lapses in attendance would be punished by a declining balance, the fines being as follows: "For tardiness at rehearsal, twenty-five cents. For absence from rehearsal, one dollar. For tardiness at concert, one dollar. For absence from concert, three dollars." The shrewd Glee Clubber could come late to three concerts and seven rehearsals and still have enough left to buy a cup of coffee and a sandwich. But then again, with tuition at $100, a fine of even $1 was stiff in 1895—equivalent to about $150 today.

More significant, the constitution established an executive council, comprised of the executive committee (the president, business manager, and one additional member from each of the three clubs) and four other members, two from the university faculty and two alumni. At the time the constitution was adopted the elected council included Professors Huffcut and Bristol from the faculty and C. E. Treman 1889 and B. S. Cushman 1893 as alumni representatives. Yet in fall 1895 a report on the Musical Clubs clearly stated that the executive committee was "subject to the advise of an executive council, composed of four members."[18] Hence, while the students were *ipso jure* members of the executive council, it appears the power ultimately lay with the four members outside the group. Dann still retained the power to select new members, and the management the duty (at least ostensibly) of scheduling concerts, but only the executive council could elect the business manager and an assistant manager. Furthermore, Article III, Section 4 stated the executive council was "to select and contract for musical directors; and to decide matters of general policy."

One of the key players in this arrangement was Charles Treman. A member of the Glee Club while a student at Cornell, he had gone on to set up the Treman, King and Company Hardware Store in Ithaca; he also was the head of the Tompkins County Trust Company. In 1902 he became a trustee of the university and over the years took an authoritative interest in many facets of town and gown life. So much so the story is told that Chauncey Depew, the famous orator and solicitor, once asked Liberty Hyde Bailey during a visit to Ithaca, "Do they still run the university out of that hardware store downtown?"[19]

The Musical Clubs were in no way officially associated with or sponsored by the university in 1895, so the creation of the Musical Clubs Council brought distinct advantages, not least of which was the clout of someone like Treman. With the failure of the European tour the group found itself $2,000 in debt and sorely in need of more stable internal leadership. Treman, having previously bailed out athletics when they were in financial need, soon put the Musical Clubs back on sound financial footing. Nevertheless the formation of the council created several dangerous precedents. In a very short period of time several men had established themselves as leaders with the power to hire or fire the director and to oversee the clubs' other activities by means of the managers they elected. They themselves were subject to election every two years (two one year, two the next); ten years later, however, three of the original four members were still serving on the council, and Treman was listed as the permanent treasurer. As long as they had the best interests of the clubs at heart and yielded to the discretion of the musical directors, all would probably be fine. But the executive positions could one day pass to other people who would have the potentially abusable capacity to control a musical organization from a nonmusical position.

Even in a peaceable scenario the wills of the executive council and Dann might forseeably collide, and there is evidence a conflict ensued almost immediately. Early in fall 1895 an *Era* article stated the following about the Musical Clubs: "At the present writing nothing definite can be said in regard to the proposed trips. Director Dann does not favor a Christmas trip, and would prefer to have the clubs postpone their journey until the Easter vacation. The executive committee does not favor Professor Dann's proposition, and it is probable that the clubs will give a series of concerts during the holidays."[20] The relationship was off to an uneasy start, but in this case neither side prevailed—the groups did not tour that Christmas or the following spring other than short February jaunts to Owego, Elmira, and New York, and a later trip to Poughkeepsie. However matters were eventually resolved, mutiny was avoided, and a working peace was established between Dann and the Musical Clubs Council, which continued to influence the affairs of the Glee Club well into the twentieth century.

Meanwhile the students continued to sing, somewhat oblivious to the underlying forces that ran the Glee Club. Enrollment in the group noticeably rose in 1895 for the first time since membership had stabilized under McKenney, and numbers steadily swelled over the next decade. In 1896 the Glee Club recovered resiliently from a larger than usual loss of graduating seniors, and after fall 1897 auditions in the Club rooms at 9 North Tioga Street, membership crossed 30 for the first time. (Membership in the Banjo and Mandolin Clubs had done so a year earlier.) Not all institutions enjoyed the same growth. In November 1897 the *Era* reported "Owing to a lack of material, the Brown University Glee Club will not organize this year."[21] Cornell's numbers remained around 30 until the turn of the century, when they suddenly boomed. Membership surpassed 40 in 1901, 50 in 1903, and 60 the following year, reaching 64 in 1905–1906.

> With the very good material that has been brought forth by the competitions for the Musical Clubs a new problem has presented itself, namely, to keep all new men of ability and yet not have clubs that will be overcrowded or unwieldy. For the first time in Cornell's history there has been a brisk competition for every position except celloist in the Mandolin Club, and this has stimulated the men to greater activity. It has been proposed that a second club be formed to give concerts in the smaller nearby towns, and to act as a feeder for the regular Glee, Banjo, and Mandolin Clubs.[22]

The idea of a second club suggested in this October 1899 editorial must have fallen on deaf ears—in the years that followed Dann apparently decided simply to expand the size of the Glee Club.[23]

Nevertheless, with the cost of transporting so many singers to out-of-town engagements becoming prohibitive, Dann had already begun to send smaller, select groups on the road about the time membership crossed 30. In fall 1897 a quartette was sent to Montreal to take part in a joint concert at McGill University; small groups sang at debating contests both home and away, and a group of about 14 made a trek each of the next few years to sing at alumni banquets in New York City and elsewhere. In February 1897 the Musical Clubs were invited to perform—and a small group was sent—for the Chautauqua Literary and Scientific Circle in lieu of an address by former president Grover Cleveland that was canceled. These groups were often a great hit, and encores were tirelessly requested, with performers compelled to sing themselves "almost to death."

Following the England tour, activity had initially suffered a lull while finances stabilized and the Musical Clubs and council adjusted to each other. Historically, fall was quiet for the early Glee Clubs, and in 1895 and 1896 it's difficult to say what the group was actually up to, if anything. With no tour to prepare for (a proposed Canadian tour for 1896–1897 was canceled) and the Junior Week concert still several months off, rehearsals quite possibly were held only intermittently. Somewhat surprising to more modern Glee Clubbers perhaps, the Glee Club rehearsed the same way during several springs as well, taking weeks off and then cramming music in daily rehearsals immediately preceding upcoming concerts. The effect could not have been ideal, and in 1897 the Glee Club reportedly gave a weak Junior Week performance. They did not reach top form until the Commencement concert.

Matters quickly improved as the Glee Club's schedule began to grow at a pace known before the England tour. After a two-year hiatus a tour was taken through the Great Lakes region during the 1897–1898 Christmas holiday. In addition concert activity began to fill the autumn semester. In 1898, after starting the year with a more rigorous rehearsal schedule, Dann took the Glee Club down to perform at Ithaca High School, where he still spent his days working with the high school singers. During the second week of December, they traveled to the Willard State Hospital near Ovid, New York, to sing for the patients.[24] From then on, each fall generally held something in store for Cornell's singers, particularly with the advent of the football concerts. Following the precedent of the Lehigh concert in 1894, the first of many Thanksgiving concerts with the University of Pennsylvania clubs took place in 1899. Between fifty and sixty members of the Cornell clubs boarded two especially wide, vestibuled cars of the Lehigh Valley Railroad and departed on the self-proclaimed "largest musical club trip that ever left Ithaca." The next of these Cornell–Penn concerts was not till 1907, but for years thereafter they were a reliable fall staple. On occasion students could be found doing double-duty, as for example the Cornell quarterback who played in the Mandolin Club. Joint fall concerts (sometimes two a season) were undertaken also with musical clubs of other gridiron opponents, including Columbia in 1903, Princeton in 1904, Chicago in 1909, and Dartmouth in 1912. Moreover fall was the time to prepare for the Christmas tours, which from 1897–1898 continued with little interruption to the present day. The rest of the year also remained busy; the Junior and Senior Week concerts had grown so popular, auctions were being held for tickets. And there were the spring sports to support with the regatta concerts (often with Harvard, starting in 1907 and continuing for several years in both Cambridge and Ithaca), the baseball concerts, and an unusual program in 1900 combining Cornell songs and instrumental solos with a fencing exhibition.

Cornell was a growing institution. The 1895 venture across the Atlantic had been a bold move, showing a youthful confidence and willingness to step into the arena with the long-established institutions of higher education and European culture.[25] But as with youth, the university's idealism could run aground on reality. Early and by necessity the school had learned to band together to face the outside world. But internally Cornell had its large and little qualms—

some arising from a desire to hold with the status quo, some from a desire to push ahead with a new vision of the future. Among the matters of concern as the century closed and Cornell approached its 35th birthday was the question of school spirit.

At times the issue was raised in reference to becoming behavior. Far more than today the campus concerned itself with the impact of individual actions on the reputation of alma mater. Fans were chided for cheering when the other team was penalized—it was unsportsmanlike and reflected poorly on the school. More seriously, a much-chagrined administration and student body repeatedly lamented the occasional riots between classes or between students and townees that were gracelessly trumpeted across newspaper headlines.

When the issue of school spirit became prevalent on the pages of the *Era*, it was often discussed in terms of music and revolved around "Senior Singing." An 1897 editorial commented,

> It is to be regretted that the suggestion of the president of the Senior class rel-ative to singing on the campus during the spring term should have been re-ceived with so little enthusiasm by the members of Ninety-seven. . . . Will a class which, since its entrance in the University, has been noted for its loyalty to Alma Mater, now allow to go unheeded an opportunity for furthering Cor-nell spirit among the students?

It was suggested the seniors gather two or three times a week for the re-mainder of the semester to sing Cornell songs, and furthermore that "arrange-ments should then be made for securing the Glee, Mandolin, and Banjo clubs to lend their assistance in establishing what from this year should become as firm a tradition at Cornell as is the gathering of the Seniors on the steps of Old Nassau at Princeton." When the seniors did eventually decide to meet, the singing of the Alma Mater moved one writer to remark, "Cornell spirit per-vaded the whole campus last evening."[26]

The issue resurfaced in 1899, when the senior class attempted to reinaugu-rate the custom, and the *Era* commented,

> It is true that conditions here are not such as would favor the natural devel-opment of Senior Singing, and that something more than an acquiescence in the idea and a willingness to help make a noise, is necessary, in order to cre-ate the tradition artificially. It involves some sacrifice for some of us who may have worked hard on the hill all day long and who are therefore more or less loth to haunt at night the scene of our daily labors, to walk up to McGraw just for the purpose of spending a half hour in conversation with our fellows and in the singing of college songs. The sacrifice, however, is thoroughly worth the while. We should be only too glad here at Cornell, where, up to the senior year at least, we are divided off into so many distinct crowds or cliques, and where

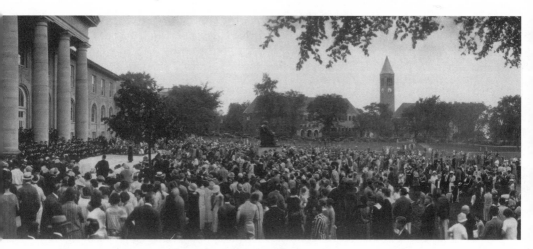

5. Senior Singing on the steps of Goldwin Smith Hall.

our residences are scattered . . ., to foster any custom whatsoever which would at least tend to bring everybody together on a common footing. In this way we shall gradually build up a feeling of unity, in preparation for the time, now not far distant, when we shall have dormitories and an alumni hall—two of the most powerful agents in the creation of a genuine university spirit.[27]

The Glee Club had achieved something with the acquisition of their Club rooms on Tioga Street, but the issue of a home on campus remained for the students at large (except the women students housed in Sage College). Pragmatic sloth began to win out over rugged spirit, and in succeeding years singing took place at the Dutch Kitchen (in the Ithaca Hotel downtown) rather than on campus. But regardless of where it took place, it fostered a sense of school spirit, a warm camaraderie known on the steps of Goldwin Smith or over a mug of beer. Dann once said, "Every great nation is a singing nation." And in a way school spirit was a local brand of nationalism.

By other standards the musical climate on campus had been improving since 1890 when the *Era* wrote, "The attention given to music by Cornell students is noticeable but little outside of the Glee and Banjo Clubs."[28] A faculty concert series was instituted in 1890–1891, subsequently named the Chamber Concert Series, and internationally eminent artists began to pass through Ithaca. In 1892 the great Polish pianist and future statesman Ignacy Paderewski made his first visit, and others, such as Leopold Damrosch and the New York Philharmonic, followed. Also in 1892 the Glee Club sang for the inauguration of President Jacob Gould Schurman. Music at Cornell had just found a new friend. "A university cannot too often present to its students an artist in living body, who shall open the door, if only for an hour, to a world which is dreamt not of in the philosophy of athletics,"[29] the *Era* once said, and clearly Schurman agreed. He began to invite visiting professors to lecture on music, and his purpose was readily apparent in the words of the first of these, Rev. Hugh R. Haweis of London. At the close of his talk Haweis stressed the need for a musical department, saying he had "been told Cornell is the most unmusical place in the world. Those who like music go elsewhere." The following spring (1894) Professor Waldo Pratt spoke on the topic "Music as a University Study." President Schurman personally introduced both speakers and in 1895 issued a statement of policy regarding the organization of the university's musical interests.

The chief consequence was the consolidation of the musical forces into a chorus, orchestra, and military band and, as President Schurman put it, "to show that results can be expected from it, a music festival will be given in the spring."[30] He personally addressed those who assembled at the first interest meeting for the festival, and more than two hundred singers attended the first choral rehearsal. The Grand Music Festival, as it was called, took place on May 29 and 30 in the armory with the University Chorus (in all likelihood Cornell's first mixed ensemble), reinforced by the Geneva Choral Society and assisted by a full orchestra, the Cadet Band, and soloists. Perly Aldrich of Rochester led the ensembles in "The Heavens Are Telling" from Haydn's *Creation*, John Francis Barnett's *Ancient Mariner*, and Brahms's *Song of Destiny*, and with the artistic achievement of the festival Cornell began to show signs of real musical life.

The success of the festival was partly attributable to the contributions of faculty and students from the new Ithaca Conservatory of Music, a welcome addition to the cultural landscape of Ithaca. The conservatory was founded in 1892 by William Grant Egbert, a native of nearby Danby, New York, who had studied in Germany and served as concertmaster and assistant conductor of the Sevcik String Orchestra in Prague. He opened the school with the help of several Ithaca businessmen, of whom three in time were benefactors of Cornell's Glee Club: Charles Treman, Frank Boynton 1917, and Charles Blood.[31] By 1903 the conservatory had twenty members on its faculty and a wide range of course offerings.

With Schurman at the head Cornell likewise was developing its own music curriculum. In 1895 came an announcement, "The faculty has decided that one hour of University credit shall be given to students taking either of the courses of musical instruction controlled by the executive committee of the Choral Union [i.e., the operetta-performing Choral Club]. . . . The students should now evince a greater interest in the acquisition of musical culture."[32] The following year the first two formal courses were offered: one in voice production and vocalization and a second, somewhat more advanced, Anthem Singing and Hymnology, led by Egbert. In 1898–1899 the Sage Chapel Choir grew out of the two-credit Course in Vocal Music, which involved "singing in the morning Chapel service each Sunday and one hour rehearsals each week for studying the hymns and German chorales."[33] George M. Chadwick, organist at Sage Chapel and the conservatory, served as the choir's first director, while Egbert began to conduct the orchestra, offered for two credits as well.

Other ensembles likewise benefited from the newfound leadership of gifted musicians. Cornell's military department appointed Patrick (Patsy) Conway director of the Cadet Band, a post he held from 1895 until 1908. One of the conservatory's first students, he had started an Ithaca band in 1895 which later became the nationally known Conway Band—the group toured the country annually and was considered the equal of Sousa's band. *Daily Sun* comments suggest Conway was not as successful with the student band, but his musicality must have rubbed off on the players, and matters had surely improved from the days when the *Ithaca Daily Journal* had reported that "the Cadet Band played a few strains, but the principal strain was on the audience."[34]

The Banjo and Mandolin Clubs got their first professional director when George Coleman was appointed in 1901. Coleman was born in Titusville, Pennsylvania, across the state from Dann's hometown. His father had taught him several instruments, and when he enrolled as a freshman at Cornell in 1891, he quickly became active in the city's musical life. He was student leader of the Wilgus Opera House Orchestra, played violin with Egbert in the conservatory string quartet, conducted works in which Egbert was soloist, and probably sat in on a few local theater bands with Conway to work his way through school. In 1895 he graduated from Cornell's School of Architecture and entered the profession in Ithaca, practicing until the depression of 1929. He simultaneously kept up his music, and when appointed director of the Banjo and Mandolin Clubs, began a remarkable commitment to Cornell ensembles that lasted forty years. In 1905 he picked up the orchestra from Egbert and in 1917 took over the Cadet Band (renamed the ROTC Band toward the end of World War I) which swelled from 50 to 220 members under his leadership. Thus he headed all of Cornell's instrumental ensembles from 1917 until his retirement in 1941 and still found time for architecture and a partnership with Joseph B. Hickey in Hickey's Music Store, an Ithaca establishment since 1892.

By the time Coleman took over the instrumental clubs at the turn of the century, banjo and mandolin clubs had become a familiar corps of musicians on many college campuses. At Cornell the Banjo Club had been successfully organized in the spring of 1888 after an initial Banjo and Guitar Club from the previous year had fallen apart.[35] The group collaborated with the Glee Club in Ithaca at the Commencement concert of 1888 and was already a favorite with audiences by the next Junior Week concert. In 1889–1890 the group was organized as the Banjo and Guitar Club, and the following year the *Era* announced that A. D. Grover of the Boston Ideal Banjo, Guitar, and Mandolin Clubs had been engaged to select and arrange all the music for the club. By the Easter concert tour of 1891 the groups were collectively referred to as the Glee, Banjo and Mandolin Clubs; under this joint name they were officially incorporated in the

6. Glee, Banjo, and Mandolin Clubs' motif.

first article of the 1895 constitution.[36] The Banjo Club of 1895 included "banjos, banjeurines, banjolins, and guitars," while the Mandolin Club had "mandolins, mandolas, and guitars."

Though they performed together, the Musical Clubs functioned as a glee club and a banjo and mandolin club, auditioning separately, rehearsing separately, and often electing their own officers (who together formed part of the Musical Clubs Council once it was established). Programs were normally split between the groups, but from time to time they collaborated—in spring 1895 the Glee and Mandolin Clubs performed a joint version of "America," in 1900 the "Evening Song." At times they were three independent groups, varying in relative size and strength. In 1890 the Banjo Club performed without the Glee Club at the Commencement concert; in 1902 a Christmas day concert featured the Glee and Mandolin Clubs. Membership during the early 1890s was roughly equal between the Glee Club and the Banjo and Mandolin Clubs combined, each with about 20 men; in 1896–1897 membership in the Banjo and Mandolin Club surpassed the Glee Club's for the first time, and in 1910 the Mandolin Club had more than 80 to the Glee Club's 50.

Until Coleman took over in 1901 the instrumental clubs were run by student leaders, much as the Glee Club had been in its earliest days. And student leaders on occasion directed the Glee Club and the Banjo and Mandolin Clubs long after the arrival of Dann and Coleman. Elected by the ensemble in the same manner as officers, these leaders coached, coaxed, and conducted their peers through the program of songs. The timing of their election, which usually took

7. Banjo and Mandolin Clubs, 1892–1893.

place in December (managers were typically elected in the spring) is noteworthy—soon after being chosen, they often led the group on Christmas tours *without* the assistance of either director. Walter Price 1920 later recalled that Dann met the group halfway through a trip, listened to a special rehearsal, corrected mistakes, and then sat in the audience that evening. The Glee Club leader was "the man in charge of all the concerts."[37]

Admittedly surprising to more recent Glee Clubbers accustomed to professional conductors up front, the use of student leaders might better be understood in historical context.[38] The role of conductor as we know it had emerged only in the nineteenth century and was still evolving. Furthermore, the Glee Club's repertoire was such that a wave of the hand, nod of the head, or foot-tapping count of one-two-three-four often sufficed to get a piece going. From there, with a little guidance from the leader seen standing at the left end of the Club's first row, the music largely ran itself. By most accounts these student leaders acquitted themselves well, upholding the reputation of the ensembles and the musical standard set by the directors, who kept watch when not conducting.

The Musical Clubs might have used student leaders, but Cornell's early days of ragtag ensembles and impromptu student-led minstrels were a thing of the past. Taking stock at the turn of the century, music making at Cornell had shifted little by little from an endeavor driven by the whim and will of the students to a more formalized pursuit guided by local professionals. Together with

Dann, Coleman carried the Musical Clubs well into the next century. But it was Hollis Dann who put Cornell music on the map.

Since his arrival in Ithaca Dann had engaged himself in nearly every aspect of the city's musical life—he was head of music at the high school, sang with and conducted the Choral Club, gave private voice lessons, conducted Cornell's Glee Club, directed the Presbyterian Church Choir, and served on the executive committee of the Ithaca Conservatory. The very fall that Coleman had taken over the Banjo and Mandolin Club, Thomas Tapper published an article in *Musical America* which amounted to a sketch of an ordinary day in the life of Hollis Dann. The morning began at the high school, and Tapper writes, "As we entered the room the students cheered him . . . they sang well as a chorus. Tone, shading, meaning, all had been carefully worked out." Twelve exhausting hours later the day ended when the "man behind the singing, who was doing it all," finished his rehearsal with the Glee Club.[39]

The summers were scarcely different. In 1896 Dann accepted an invitation from Clarence Birchard to join the faculty of the New School of Methods in Public School Music, where he came to the attention of William Tomlins. Tomlins, a noted conductor and teacher in Chicago, was impressed with his voice and felt he could launch Dann on a career as a professional singer. Dann decided to head to Chicago but then changed his mind and returned to Ithaca, renewing his commitment to the Glee Club and the musical life of the city. Birchard later recalled, "I think this early association with Mr. Tomlins laid a foundation which proved a factor in the later growth and achievement of Hollis Dann. I recall one occasion, one morning at the school, when Hollis with great emotion told me how he had been stirred by Mr. Tomlins the evening before, in a recital-lecture Mr. Tomlins gave on Handel's 'Messiah'. Hollis said he had not slept a wink that night, but had been thinking, laughing, and mostly crying all night." Birchard concluded that Dann's decision to return to Ithaca was good "from the success he achieved in the coming years in every phase of music education, and particularly as conductor."[40]

Despite Cornell's growing interest in music and Dann's distinguished résumé, he was not even on the faculty after more than a decade as director of the Glee Club. After thirty-five years of existence Cornell had yet to appoint its first professor of music. When the first music classes were offered for credit in 1896–1897, neither Dann nor any other musical instructor appeared in the Cornell Register's faculty list, although the list of instructors and assistants included Herman Reeve Ryder V.S., demonstrator of anatomy, and Jared van Wagenen Jr. B.S., assistant in butter making. But matters were moving forward. President Schurman asked in 1898, "Who will build and endow a College of Fine Arts from which Architecture, Music, Painting, and Statuary might fling an ideal grace over the strenuous intellectual regimen of our daily lives?" The answer, at least for music, was Hollis Dann, and in 1903 he was appointed instructor in music. As the new head of music at Cornell, he outlined his plans for the university in an *Ithaca Daily Journal* interview: "Naturally, I must blaze my way at first . . . for no one has showed the way, particularly in the University. My general object is to promote an interest in music, and a knowledge and appreciation of the great art . . . not only among the student body but also in the University as a whole and in the City in general." To him the best way to do this was to have as large a number of students as possible participate in choral work by the study and public performance of the best music, to continue weekly organ recitals in Sage Chapel, and to bring the best available musical artists to the city.[41]

To Dann choral singing was the apex of music, and he once claimed, "People become and remain musical largely through group singing."[42] So pursuing his first objective, to engage as many students as possible in choral work, he initiated the Cornell Music Festivals. Nine years earlier, in 1895, Dann had tried to organize a civic performance of Handel's *Messiah* in conjunction with the Choral Club. He assembled and polished a choir of 125, and the concert was given at the Lyceum on June 12, shortly before the Glee Club left for England. Musically it was deemed a success, but the *Ithaca Daily Journal* later recalled (April 18, 1904) that Ithaca, not ready for oratorio, "did not appreciate chorus work." The hall was half empty, and the Choral Club lost several hundred dollars. Now, perhaps remembering the musical conventions of his childhood, Dann conceived a much bolder ambition, saying in the 1903 interview, "There is no reason under the sun why Ithaca and Cornell University should not become the musical center of this part of the State, to which people from surrounding towns and cities will come to hear the best music." He was determined to make it so.

Forming a chorus of more than 150 by combining the forces of the Glee Club, the two curricular choirs (one engaged to sing the morning services, the other the afternoon vespers at Sage), and members of the community, Dann began rehearsing Mendelssohn's *Elijah*. "In rain or shine, on nights of bitter cold and howling wind," the Ithaca newspaper reported, the young men and women of the chorus "were faithful to their work. Their leader was thorough, exacting, severe at times, but they had confidence in him, and his enthusiasm inspired them all."[43]

For the festival Dann brought in the Boston Festival Orchestra and its conductor Emil Mollenhauer, a group of musicians long familiar with the hazards of collaborating with amateur choruses. The players had become masters at holding performances together, frequently covering up mistakes, reining in tempos, or anchoring straying singers to the keys of a piece. When they arrived in Ithaca, the orchestra was pleasantly surprised to find a different state of affairs. The Music Festival opened on April 1, 1904, and the critics responded with overwhelming applause. "Ithaca never heard such a chorus as that which sang in the *Elijah*. . . . From the opening notes of 'Help Lord' to the final 'Amen' of 'And then shall your light,' it sang with an intelligence . . . , an assurance, an enthusiasm, and a volume and quality of tone that were beyond criticism." Like the God of Elijah their voices sounded with "precision and fire" and "the supreme art was attained of making every word seem entirely natural and spontaneous."[44]

At the close of the festival, which included an afternoon orchestra concert between the two performances of *Elijah*, Dann was heartily congratulated by press and public alike for the triumph of his first year in office and his remarkable work with the singers. One journalist commented that the "young men and women of the 'Elijah' chorus of 1904 have helped make a musical epoch in the history of Ithaca and of Cornell University," and speculated, "What the future has for music in Ithaca depends almost entirely upon what the future has for music in Cornell University." That future lay in the hands of Hollis Dann who, officially appointed an assistant professor that fall, had become Cornell's first professor of music.

Under Dann's guidance the Music Festivals continued until 1920, a total of twelve being held in the sixteen-year period. Concerts were announced by a trombone quartet stationed in the bell tower, and after the first year the festival expanded to three days to encompass five concerts—two choral major work concerts, two orchestral performances, and one mixed program (usually featuring soloists and smaller pieces)—in addition to related lectures. Handel's *Messiah* and Rossini's *Stabat Mater* were performed the second year, and in later years, the repertoire included Haydn's *Creation* (1906), Saint-Saëns's *Samson and Delilah* (1907, 1908), Verdi's *Requiem* (1906, 1915) and *Aida* in concert form (1909, 1910, 1920), and Franck's *Beatitudes* (1920). More than one year the entire community took part, as when brothers and sisters joined fathers and mothers in *The Children of Bethlehem* of Gabriel Pierné, performed first in 1909 with a choir of 200 children, and again in 1916 with 300 children. The Boston Festival Orchestra, under Mollenhauer, served as the orchestra through 1911, after which the Chicago Symphony Orchestra and its conductor Frederick Stock performed in the last four festivals (1914, 1915, 1916, and 1920). In 1916 Stock remarked, "Professor Dann's chorus measures up to the finest of its kind in the country, and is unsurpassed in beauty and excellence."[45]

The Glee Club always took part in the festivals, playing a pivotal role in the earliest years according to the *Cornell Alumni News:* "That the chorus should be characterized by those very same qualities which have marked the work of the Cornell Glee club since it has been under Professor Dann's direction was to be expected, for it was the growth and success of the Glee club which alone made it possible to hold the Festivals."[46] After the 1905 performance of *Messiah* reviewers commented that the most striking feature of the chorus was the magnificent showing of the male section, the fine quality of the tenors, and the full rich bass. The Glee Club of course was not responsible for the entire male sound—there were other gifted singers from Cornell, the conservatory, and the community who took part. But in 1906 the *Alumni News* again claimed, such a Festival of Music would be impossible at the University without the Cornell Glee club from which to draw material for the male parts. The double training which those men have had under Professor Dann's direction, in the Glee club and the Chapel choirs, redounds to the advantage of the Festival Chorus, and renders so much simpler the task of training that great organization. Conversely, the experience gained by the men during the five months of steady rehearsing for the Festival is of untold value to them in their Glee club work.[47]

In 1911 an advertisement asked, "Why don't you hear the greatest male chorus ever heard in Ithaca, 100 men including the entire University Glee Club?" That year, the men sang the stirring "Soldiers' Chorus" from the third act of Gounod's *Faust,* storming the air "with a vim and spirit that surpassed anything that had ever been heard on the hill." "The effect was overwhelming, and literally made the audience rise out of their seats." The applause was so insistent, the singers were forced to respond with an encore.[48]

With the first festival Dann accomplished his initial objective to involve the community in music making; by the last he had achieved a reality perhaps tenfold the scope of his initial vision. As early as 1910 the demand for tickets far exceeded the capacity of Sage Chapel and hundreds of listeners contented themselves with purchasing tickets to the final rehearsals. In 1908 Dann had dreamed, "We hope to have an auditorium, provided with a great organ, where thousands of students shall form a mighty chorus singing the songs of Cornell and the matchless chorales of the masters."[49] The dream was realized with Bailey Hall, and for two years (1912, 1913) the festivals were omitted while the 2,249-seat auditorium was built. They resumed in 1914, and in 1915 a *Musical America* headline read, "Ambition of Dr. Hollis Dann, Head of Cornell's Music Department, To Make the University City a Leader in Intelligent Appreciation of the Art Strikingly Realized."[50] In 1920, after another hiatus from 1917 to 1919 caused by World War I, the entire auditorium was sold out by mail-order subscriptions. The audience that year congregated from more than seventy-five cities stretching from Maine to Missouri and witnessed what proved to be the last of the festivals.

Part of the consistent success of the Music Festivals was due to Hollis Dann, businessman. As meticulous as he was in attention to musical detail, Dann had an extraordinary knack for organization and paid scrupulous attention to non-musical details. President Schurman later remembered that although the festivals involved an annual expenditure of thousands of dollars, Dann never asked for a cent from the university or private individuals and by the time he resigned had accumulated a surplus of seven or eight thousand dollars profit. "Professor Dann," Schurman continued, "is the only teacher of art I have ever known who is pre-eminently a business man and a successful financier."[51]

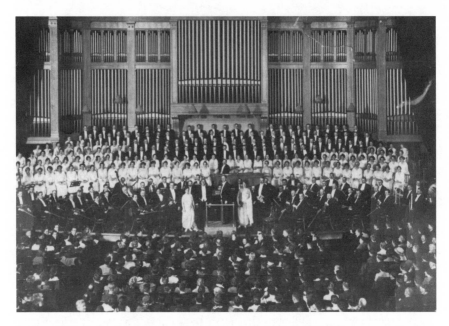

8. Cornell Music Festival performance in Bailey Hall, April 30, 1914 (Dann on podium).

Not that he didn't have a little help along the way. Concerned one year about ticket sales, he approached Comptroller Charles Bostwick about stringing a banner between the University Library and Boardman Hall (which once stood across from Uris). Bostwick reportedly replied, "Dann, nobody can give you that permission except the Trustees and it would take you a year to get it. On the other hand, if you put a banner up there, nobody except me would have authority to order it torn down and, my eyesight not being what it once was, I probably wouldn't see it until after you sold out."[52] And Dann himself could be particularly persuasive. After the 1904 Music Festival several papers reported the chapel's old pipe organ had gone on one of its periodic strikes, being "cajoled into good humor" only for the second performance of *Elijah*. Dann pushed for a replacement and after making his final argument to the committee convened by Schurman, A. D. White was moved to say, "Dann, you should have been a pleading lawyer. For me, the organ matter is settled."

In retrospect the impact of the Music Festivals is difficult to estimate. There is no question that Ithaca's artistic course was remarkably altered and music at Cornell was transformed. Imagining American music at the time without the festivals might perhaps give us a better idea. In the words of *Musical America*, "It is quite probable that no one man has accomplished more within the last twenty years than Dr. Dann toward ... education of the general public to know good music."[53] Dann in an insightfully simple phrase once said, "The highest things cannot be taught. They must be caught, as it were, by contagion."[54] An ebullient epidemic, the Music Festivals he fathered helped scores of people catch the joy of music.

Dann's primary impetus for the festivals had been to educate by exposure. This same principle governed all his work in the Cornell Department of Music. Again and again Dann would say, "The best educator in music is music itself." To ensure that the community's exposure to music was not limited to a weekend oasis sometime in the middle of the spring each year, Dann kept after his second 1903 objective—the weekly concerts at Sage, for which he developed a standing choir of more than a hundred. As for his third objective he established an annual concert series, even though the Musical Festivals already brought first-rate musical artists to Ithaca.[55]

Both directly and indirectly the Glee Club benefited from this musical climate Dann created at Cornell. The festivals gave the ensemble a way to contribute to the larger life of the community, refuting the local complaint that Cornell musicians were interested only in their own clubs. Moreover, the festivals exposed the students to more "serious" works of music by the "master" composers. But the Glee Club still kept up its own autonomous schedule on top of the added commitment from November to April the festivals required.

Let us go back to the Glee Club at the time of the first festival. Retired Cornell president A. D. White had recently returned to Ithaca (having stepped down as U.S. ambassador to Germany), and fall activity was returning to normal after a typhoid epidemic had laid the university low in the spring of 1903. Two rounds of competitions in September brought a harvest of new men, the Cornell–Columbia concert took place in mid-November, and rehearsals began for *Elijah*. The day after Christmas and again during Junior Week, the Musical Clubs gave concerts down at the Lyceum, though they were starting to lose the Banjo part in the Glee, Banjo, and Mandolin title. (That year's *Cornellian* listed no Banjo Club, and the group suffered an unstable existence over the next decade.) On May 27, hot on the heels of their successful part in the debut Music Festival, the Glee Club gave a concert coinciding with the Navy Ball. Success continued in the following year (1904–1905) with a Christmas tour farther south than any Cornell singers had yet reached—Virginia, North Carolina, South Carolina, and Augusta and Savannah, Georgia. By the end of the 1905–1906 season the *Era* boasted without hesitation, "our glee club stands pre-eminent as ever and has gained fresh laurels," while the music festival is unparalleled.[56]

Rowland A. Curry 1907, student leader of the group at the time, offered a clear view of the Glee Club in 1907:

> It is true that the average student looks upon our Glee Club as an organization brought together for a good time, to sing Cornell songs and college swipes, and when it has enough of them prepared, goes for a lark on a Christmas tour. The organization has however a higher purpose, and I shall give a brief description of the work and enumerate the educational advantages offered by

its membership. We begin the collegiate year by calling on candidates for the Clubs. There are between 150 and 200 men who respond to the call, and after each man is tried-out and given an opportunity to show his ability, a possible twenty-five are selected, who are nevertheless uncertain of their position until they have proved their worth. There is no course in the University, whether in the class-room or on the field, in which the rules and regulations are so strict as in the Glee Club. Promptness is sacred with the men, it being an unusual occurance [sic] to see a man late at a rehearsal.

The study of our music is a task which demands more hard work and time than the outsider can realize. The men are required to commit the songs note for note and word for word, and, when put together, the study of expression must be well learned, since, without this, many good songs are ruined and sound cheap. In order to obtain a high standard of perfection, a system . . . requires that every man appear in a quartette and demonstrate that he knows the various songs. If he has not learned them satisfactorily, he is either dropped from the Club or fined.

After the music is learned in this manner, we proceed to put the parts together, so as to make a complete balance of the four divisions. In this way we are drilled until the later part of December, when thirty men are selected for the annual Christmas trip. Four alternates are chosen and held in readiness to be called on, in case of sickness or any misconduct on the part of a chosen member. These thirty men are considered fortunate, and so they are, yet their work is not mere pleasure. They go into a course of training, like the athlete, after a fashion. . . . Unless he is strong physically he is subject to contracting a cold, which makes him useless to the Club on a long and trying tour. . . . These trip men must work hard to get as near perfection as possible. A responsibility is felt by each man and he realizes that he has a part to play in holding up the reputation of his "Alma Mater."

The Educational advantages that are offered are such as cannot be duplicated in any other way. In the four years on the club a man will have traveled over 12,000 miles, visited the largest cities of the Eastern, Central, and Southern States, and will have been entertained by the best people in the land,—Cornell Alumni. He will have visited and been entertained by the undergraduates of the leading Universities . . . and he has helped in this way to secure a closer bond of friendship between the men of these Colleges and our Alma Mater.[57]

The piece paints the portrait of a disciplined, hardworking group, and at least the author is interested in debunking the common impression on campus (which was understandable given the group's history) that the Glee Club was a fun-loving, flippant bunch of serenaders. In his 1901 article on Dann, Tapper had written, "In the evening of that day I heard the College Glee Club sing. They called it a rehearsal. I suppose that is the reason the boys were so much at home between the numbers." The subtle barb may still have been true in 1907, but the seeds of

Dann's work ethic took hold. Another account of the Musical Clubs in 1908 reports: "Rehearsals are held two or three times, and sometimes even four times, a week from the middle of October till the beginning of the Christmas vacation."[58]

That's not to say they weren't having fun. As President Schurman once said, "A man is more than his work," and Curry makes it clear the education of the average Glee Clubber embraced far more than musical experiences. On the 1908–1909 tour, which passed through St. Louis, Erie, Dayton, and Chicago, the men reported that in Louisville they were introduced to "break-in" dances, to their minds a great invention, as they were able to meet so many more young ladies than at an ordinary dance.

While a man might be more than his work, the university began to think it should decide just how much more. A plan put forth in 1910 proposed to strengthen the emphasis on academic work by limiting student involvement in activities. The plan was approved, and extracurricular activities were divided into class A and B; a student could participate in one A activity (such as football) or two Bs at a given time—Glee Club was considered a class B, or "minor activity." (The policy did not stop such people as Leslie Clute 1913, who at one time was both singer in the Glee Club and captain of the baseball team.) Whether the Club's class B ranking adequately reflected the time commitment involved, the group's managerial structure differed then from the current arrangement by which undergraduates are almost entirely responsible for the group's management and could easily earn a class A ranking. Back then the organization included graduate managers (who, being alumni, no longer had to burn the midnight oil on class work), as well as student managers who did not actually sing in the ensemble. Officers were also elected from the singing membership, but the system of graduate management, widely adopted by campus organizations in 1901–1902, freed many undergraduates for other pursuits, including an occasional look at their books.

On the class B activity's calendar, fall of 1909 included two concerts on the eve of football games—one with the University of Chicago, one with Pennsylvania—and in 1910 a concert was again given for the Chicago team. That season had begun, as many did, with concern over the reduced ranks of the organization—the Glee Club had lost its student leader, the entire quartet (a small group employed on various occasions), and all but one of its soloists. But after patient rebuilding the Club set out in December 1910 on its most ambitious domestic tour to that point. Sixty-five members of the Musical Clubs were chosen (roughly thirty from each group), and competition for spots was especially fierce in the Mandolin Club, which by this time was hovering at about eighty members divided among first mandolins, second mandolins, guitars, violins, flutes, clarinets, two cellos, and one bass. Passing through New York, Kansas City, Cincinnati, and Pittsburgh, the tour reached as far west as Omaha, Nebraska, where twelve enthusiastic Cornell alumni met the train.

Proud of such achievements, the students repeatedly praised the work of

Dann and Coleman, attributing the clubs' high reputation among American colleges to them. But these students hadn't been the only ones noticing. Alfred University conferred upon Dann an honorary doctorate of music in 1906, citing his remarkable accomplishments: "You have contributed largely toward taking music from its isolation as a fine art, and placing it upon a pedagogical basis in the public schools and further still in making it take rank in the University curriculum."[59] A year later Dann was promoted by Cornell to professor of music (at the time there was no rank of associate professor), and his educational contribution to the university soon extended to the summer. After having spent more than a decade teaching with the American Book Company summer schools in Boston and Hingham, Massachusetts, and New York City, Dann launched the Cornell Summer Session for the preparation of music supervisors in 1910. (The same year he became chairman of the Music Council of the State of New York.) By the twelfth and final session in 1921 the program had grown from 4 faculty members (including Dann, Tapper, and Laura Bryant, Dann's successor in the Ithaca public schools)[60] and 60 students, to 24 faculty serving 452 students enrolled from thirty-five states and Canada.

By the 1911–1912 year Dann had earned a sabbatical. In February he took leave of the university and set sail with his son for a five-month tour of Europe. (Always the enthusiastic judge he lent his lighter critical side to officiating an ocean liner pillow fight en route.) Dann intended to study the educational methods in foreign schools, conservatories, and universities and planned stops in most of the cultural centers of Italy, Germany, France, and England. He was particularly impressed with the work of Margaret Nicholls at the Farmer Road School in East London, which was said to have the best girls' school choir in the British Empire, and spent a week there alone, collecting new ideas for his singers. He met with other musicians, and attended opera and oratorio performances in the concert halls of Vienna, Berlin, Paris, and London, where he heard the great Nikisch conduct the London Symphony Orchestra.[61] Meanwhile the Glee Club was facing its first director hiatus in more than twenty years. Though members were too young to remember the days when the Glee Club floundered without a director, there was great concern for the health of the organization's season. William Luton Wood was "prevailed upon" to take the place of Dann, however, and the group sang a schedule of concerts that actually was busier than normal. When Dann returned the next year, the Music Festival still awaited the completion of Bailey Hall, but the traditional athletic, Junior, and Senior Week concerts had continued uninterrupted, and Cornellians acknowledged the Glee Club to be "one of the best established institutions here."[62]

Among the established annual events Junior Week had become a trusted tradition with Cornell and the Glee Club. The week was recognized early on as one of Cornell's first customs, and eventually it earned an official position in the school year, recognized as the short break between the first and second term. Unlike anything else of the time, it embodies Cornell culture during the turn-of-the-century period. Every year, in the bare cold of late January or early February, the campus dressed up to welcome visitors and treated them to a host of festivities. Women, who were invited from all over the country (since Cornell was still largely male), arrived by train, where they were met by their hosts and immediately taken on a tour of the campus or a novel ride in an automobile. From there ensued the week of events that had clustered around the original Junior Promenade of 1882—the Ice Carnival (with tobogganing and sleigh riding), the Masque performance, the Musical Clubs' concert, and the Sophomore Cotillion (added in 1892). Barton Hall was done over in white bunting with carnelian ornaments and a blue sky eventually lit by electric stars. Youthful couples in tux and gown whirled to the music of an orchestra playing traditional waltzes and a more hip band (often Patsy Conway's) furnished to handle the "ultra-modern two-step," dancing sometimes lasting till four in the morning. Moreover there were smaller parties, dances, and theatricals presented by fraternities, literary organizations, and others which carried through until dawn, when a breakfast began. After a week of little sleep the night for leave-taking came, and undergraduates had to face up to the books they had escaped for a time.

The Glee Club concerts became the first major addition to the week in 1888, early concerts taking place in the Wilgus Opera House (the site of the first Junior Prom). In 1893 "trains coming into Ithaca Thursday afternoon were crowded with Junior Ball guests who felt that their visit to Cornell would not be complete without the opportunity of hearing the famous musical organizations of the college."[63] The Promenade Concert later moved to the Lyceum, and with "every available seat . . . filled either by a pretty girl or by an admiring man, . . . the highly appreciative audience, not satisfied with the fourteen pieces, raised the total number to more than thirty by their enthusiastic encores."[64] The Glee Club was also doing well financially. That year, 1895–1896, and many following, an auction sale of seats was held for the popular concert. In 1914 the concert moved to Bailey Hall, marking the Glee Club's first appearance there, and the tradition continued into the 1950s.

It is not surprising—with a social event as the mainstay of the year's calendar, and the wining and dining that was part and parcel of tours—that society began to play a larger and larger role in the affairs of the Glee Club. This emphasis was an inevitable reflection of the times, and the tour of 1894–1895 proves a model example of the fin-de-siècle sensibility involved. One newspaper's headlines read:

BRILLIANT SOCIAL EVENT

———

CORNELL GLEE CLUB'S CONCERT AND RECEPTION

———

Who Occupied Boxes and Loges at the Frothingham . . .

Another article, after listing all the guests who attended the reception and concluding "college concerts are the stellar attractions of social seasons," condescended to include just a few words on the actual music in the concert, and went on: "Ladies and gentleman were there in full evening dress, and everything about the place bespoke of it a semi-social holiday affair."[65] While some papers discussed the program before the guests, none failed to mention the social importance. The floral brocades, the color of the ladies' gowns, the color of the programs—everything was promenaded in print.

This trend continued on most tours during the next few decades, the men being treated to an endless run of smokers and balls, celebrated in innumerable toasts, and subjected from time to time to floral showers while onstage. One student made a surprising suggestion following the 1913–1914 tour:

> The Clubs are now not only a representation of the University's musical talent, but are also exemplifying more and more the social element of Cornell. The men have hitherto always been picked solely for their musical ability and have always held up the social end of the trip to advantage. Now that more stress is being laid on the social side of tours by our hosts it might be well to lay a little emphasis on it at this end. A perfect club would be one which, besides making the usual musical hit, which is now always looked for from a Cornell Club, would make an equally good impression at the social functions. This would be the best possible advertisement the University could have.[66]

Imagine then, a Glee Club audition that included tests of social aptitude—perhaps a graded interview on etiquette over a glass of Scotch, perhaps a little demonstration of a waltz step, perhaps a simple assessment of Greco-Roman godliness. Taking into account a presumable shift in the purposes of the Musical Clubs, the author obviously intended for the group to put its best ambassadorial foot forward, in every sense, but the mounting social emphasis must have troubled Dann periodically; he had built a music festival and everything else on the premise of propagating music, not social life. Nevertheless, the next year's report suggests success hinged on "a fortunate coincidence of good voices and particularly good personalities"; the prominent social role of the group was inescapable.

In the midst of the 1914–1915 tour's social fare, the Glee Club passed another distance mark. The tour logged more western miles than any previous tour, reaching Denver, Colorado, and a "light, varied, and unusual program" won over audiences across the country. The initial train trek to Denver, which began on the evening of December 23, was smoothed by the addition of a private library-buffet car (in addition to the usual baggage car and two private Pullmans) and a special Christmas dinner. What the men really needed was sleep. When they disembarked on December 26, the itinerary for the day included a breakfast party (hosted by Denver women), a luncheon, an afternoon tea-dance, a dinner given by alumni, a concert in the 3,300-seat Denver Auditorium, followed by a smoker in honor of the men to cap off the evening. Hearts probably were left behind in Omaha, where the "fair sex" of that city had "a very enviable reputation," but they could always be restored the next day in Kansas City, or the day after in St. Louis. The tour passed through Milwaukee, where the Harvard and Michigan clubs had also made stops that season, and two other cities before concluding with a concert in the ballroom of New York's Waldorf-Astoria Hotel on January 4. Despite the need to cover costs with concert revenues the Club took altruism as well as music on tour, donating proceeds to the athletic associations of Denver schools and contributing in Chicago (at the suggestion of alumni) to a local charity hurt by the diversion of funds to the war in Europe.

In spring 1914 the Music Festivals had resumed where they left off with a reprise of the 1911 *Faust* success, and excerpts from Wagner's *Parsifal, Siegfried,* and *Die Meistersinger.* The following year, performances of Moussorgsky's *Joshua* and Verdi's *Requiem* assured the public the festival was once again a fixture in Ithaca cultural life. Meanwhile, after a year's break, the tradition of the Cornell–Penn Thanksgiving concert was renewed in the 1915–1916 season, a Christmas tour traversed New York and the Great Lakes region, and of course, there was Junior Week.

At the end of that year, a rather remarkable statement appeared in the *Era:* "Cornell has recently become a University with a past."[67] The clean stones had grown weathered with time and tradition, and there were songs and stories now familiar to the green newcomer and seasoned alumnus alike.

Having gained a past, Cornell was about to become an adult in the crucible of World War I. As tumult swept across Europe and the kaiser's U-boats terrorized the seas in the early years of the war, life on the Hill went on much as always. There was talk of the "European conflict," and President Schurman, following President Wilson's injunction to neutrality, refused to let partisan speakers proselytize on campus. One or two bold students had heeded the call and headed for France to become ambulance drivers; but the majority of students kept to their studies, debating matters of more local importance. For a time the war seemed a distant reality. But in fall 1916 the university delayed its opening. When the students finally reassembled, the Glee Club quickly pulled together and was able to give a concert on November 10, followed by the Thanksgiving concert in Philadelphia with Penn. Woodrow Wilson was re-elected to the cry, "My son was not raised to be a soldier," and America huddled in the hands-off advice of its forefathers. The Musical Clubs' Christmas trip went off well, taking the groups from New York City and Louisville to Duluth and St. Paul. Audiences were taken by the novel "stunts" on the program, and in the warmth of backstage and ballroom receptions for the Glee Club the casual observer might conclude all was well with the world.

War was declared on April 6, 1917. The music stopped. The classrooms emptied. Traditions were left unobserved, games unplayed. In the normal springtime thaw, academic interest melted with the snow, and student fervor pitched with the rest of a nation now eager to take up the fight. Young men were given leaves of absence or degrees according to their standing as they hastily left Ithaca for the service. One wrote, "The year was the end of many things for us, and the beginning of much more."[68] When the university opened in fall 1917, enrollment had dropped by more than 1,400 students to 3,859. Most of the men who remained took up some form of military training. Traditionally negligent in this regard, the university had paid more serious attention to military science in recent years, and in 1916 a unit of the Reserve Officers' Training Corps was established. Pup tents went up and down on the quad, roads were trampled beneath the rhythmic marching of student-soldiers, rifles were shot and stacked, and live ammunition was sent hurtling across Cayuga Lake by the artillery. Many tried to maintain a semblance of academic life, but as Bishop writes, "As the campus quivered to the tread of soldiery, classroom morale sank to a new nadir. Few could concentrate on the eternal verities, which seemed very dull, even to their professional devotees, in comparison to the eternal emotions."[69]

There is a conspicuous similarity between the membership of a collegiate glee club and the ranks of those called forth to serve their country, both being groups of young men about age 18 to 22. Now the "Soldiers' Chorus" was being sung across Europe in the key of a bloody war, and many of Cornell's young men did not wait to be called. A group of Cornellians recruited by schoolmate Edward Tinkham left for France as ambulance drivers, war being declared while they were en route. Upon arriving, they were reassigned to drive ammunition trucks to the front line and became the first Americans to carry the Stars and Stripes into battle. Meanwhile, student organizations back home limped along in the wake of the wartime exodus. Whether or not the Glee Club was rehearsing, there was nowhere to sing—their concerts were gone. Junior Week had been canceled, the Music Festival was silenced, Commencement was stripped of its pageantry with only the bare event remaining. Some organizations vanished forever, some were bolstered by an increase in the enrollment of women students; many, like the Glee Club, were essentially dormant. When the year came to an end, a senior who had stayed on summed everything up: "We are now scattered in America and in France. Those who will graduate are but the remnants of what started out so full of hope three years ago."[70]

The situation worsened steadily at the outset of the 1918–1919 academic year. A change in the Selective Service law lowered the draft age to 18, and the War Department engaged universities to prepare future officers through the Students' Army Training Corps. Cornell became a military school with most of its male population in uniform. As the *Era* said, "Everything was 'off.'" The Glee Club could not organize because of the SATC and was further handicapped by the departures of Dann and Coleman for posts with the military. Dann had heard John Carpenter, musical adviser to the War Department, discuss "Music in the Training Camps" at the Music Supervisor's National Conference in April 1918. Carpenter described the effect of hearing the "boys" sing: "You will get a reaction that you never experienced before. The only thing I can liken it to is a surf hitting you on the beach. It is simply overwhelming to hear a regiment of men all singing together with enthusiasm." Dann was moved to apply for the position of Army song leader and in November took up his duties at Camp Zachary Taylor in Louisville, Kentucky, where he remained until the middle of March directing choruses of soldiers and two nurses' choruses. He brought his typical verve to the task and upon returning to Ithaca in the spring was highly commended by the Army for his work.

On November 11, 1918, the armistice was signed. The Glee Club's picture (with Dann seated in the front row) had appeared in the war year *Cornellians* as though nothing had happened. But it took some time before matters returned to normal. Cornell counted its contribution and its casualties—nearly 4,600 Cornellians served as commissioned officers, 2 percent of all officers in the Army, Navy, and Marine Corps; there was one Congressional Medal of Honor, and more than 500 other decorations and citations. Two hundred and sixteen had died in the conflict. And during the last days of the war, Cornell had also lost its patriarch and first leader, A. D. White, on November 4.

By June 1919 the university regrouped to celebrate its semicentennial, a grand family reunion with members of every class returning to campus. The Glee Club was resurrected and for the first time in its history gave a concert in Bailey Hall assisted by alumni. That was on Thursday, June 19. It was announced the Glee Club and members of the Sage Choir would lead informal singing on the campus Sunday evening, the night before Commencement. But perhaps the most memorable singing was in the twilight of Saturday evening, the 21st. A series of addresses had been planned for the alumni at Schoellkopf, who gathered as the sun slanted across the crescent arch of the stadium. But no one had a mind for speeches. Instead, they sang in the still evening air until darkness enveloped the field; the sound carried two miles across the lake to the West Shore where people sat enthralled, listening to the songs. Music had returned to the Hill.

The 1919–1920 year was bright for the Glee Club. People once again made their way to the Lyceum to hear the fall concert, the traditional Thanksgiving performance in Philadelphia with Penn was renewed, and more than 14,000 heard the group on their eight-city tour. In Cincinnati hundreds of alumni crowded to the stage to sing the Alma Mater with the Glee Club. There wasn't any standing room left at the Junior Week concert, the first in three years, and a group of twenty returned to New York City (having been there on tour) to participate in the Spring Lamb Festival at the Hotel Commodore. By the time the Music Festival reappeared in May, Bailey Hall had already seen a full season of concerts, including the memorable Fritz Kreisler event.

The Austrian virtuoso had performed to an enthusiastic crowd in October 1917 and was invited back for the second concert of the 1919–1920 season, to take place on December 10. Knowing the violinist had briefly served in his country's army, the American Legion raised an uproar in town and Ithaca's mayor incited all patriotic citizens to boycott the concert. Cornell on the other hand resolved to fill the hall. When Kreisler took the stage, "Bailey Hall was packed, the front seats being conspicuously occupied by the football team." But a plot was afoot to sabotage the performance, and somewhere near the mid-point of the program, the lights were cut. A group of eighty hoodlums, as they were later described by the *Sun*, tried to storm the hall. Dann however had gotten wind of the plot ahead of time and had the Glee Club policing the doors. The students jumped to their feet to repel the intruders and the battle was joined. "A large band [of people] returning from a basketball game took the invaders in the rear. Kreisler, unperturbed, played on in the din of the Battle of Bailey Hall. President Schurman took his stand beside the performer. A volunteer leaped on the stage with a flashlight for the accompanist. The invaders were magnificently repelled, to the strains of Viotti's Concerto in A minor. No tumult since Nero's time has had such a fine violin accompaniment."[71]

The Music Festival couldn't compete with this dramatic scene, but it brought down the house with a concert version of *Aida* and Percy Fletcher's *Song of Victory*, concluding on May 15 with Elgar's *Dream of Gerontius* and Franck's *Beatitudes*. It was to be the last festival. For those in the know it was becoming clear that Dann was numbering his days at Cornell. He had recently been elected president of MENC (the Music Educators' National Conference), and others had an eye on him to head up musical programs elsewhere. On October 20, 1920, came the official announcement that he would resign from Cornell in the summer and leave Ithaca to become the state director of music for Pennsylvania, ending a tenure of thirty-two years with the Glee Club. In a later letter Kate Wool (an associate in the Ithaca public schools) recalled, "Ithaca and Cornell University experienced a great loss when this man left for larger fields, but we knew that we could not keep him here. His talents were too great and his sphere of usefulness too far flung."[72]

Harold Samuel attributes Dann's departure to a change in college policy. The faculty of Arts and Sciences voted during the 1919–1920 academic year to re-assign credits earned in certain technical and music courses, and the new policy in effect moved much of Dann's program outside the Arts College. But to what extent this was the impetus for his decision is not known. After thirty-two years at Cornell Dann probably was ready for a change, and his dedication to advancing the cause of music education surely put him on the lookout for new opportunities.

Ostensibly the Glee Club's concert season remained much the same, even with Dann gone part of the 1920–1921 year. He had surveyed the Philadelphia schools during the latter part of January and was granted a leave of absence for the spring to tour states farther west, reviewing school music programs, lecturing, and conducting festival choruses. Coleman by now had returned from work as entertainment director for the American Expeditionary Force in the British Isles and could oversee the activities of the clubs. Inevitably the Music Festival had to be canceled, but the Glee Club continued on under its student leaders, singing the Junior Week, Spring Day, and Senior Week concerts.

Despite the regular schedule several shifts were noticeable in the presentations and purpose of the clubs. First, following the 1920–1921 tour it was reported that, "in accordance with the policy started last year, greater emphasis was laid on stunts." Already a part of the program for years, stunts were the humorous, vaudevillelike numbers that often sent audiences rolling with laughter and hooting for encores. Novelties of the 1916–1917 program involved "a talented Saxophone Sextette, a skillful Hawaiian Trio, a soft shoe dancer of unusual cleverness and two soloists of marked ability supported by a well trained chorus."[73] Along with a blackface poker stunt, 1919–1920 had a Chinese marimbaphone trio, a jazz quartet, and a banjo quintet, in addition to the six on sax. Dann undoubtedly was party (and quite possibly parent) to some of these stunts. But given his tastes and aspirations, he probably found this side of the clubs' repertoire increasingly less engaging. In the 1930s, not necessarily referring to the Cornell Glee Club specifically, he said with obvious distaste, "Counterfeit brands of sentiment are everywhere prevalent: cheap, sickly, mawkish sentimentalism that violates every tenet of musicianship; silly horseplay and gross exaggerations by high school and college glee clubs; singers that shock us with all manner of 'croonistic' crimes against propriety and good taste. Cold, *un*emotional singing, *devoid* of feeling, is better than cheap sentimentalism."[74]

Moreover, the social trend evident for some years continued to push the offstage side of the clubs' activities into increasing prominence and may have ensured that Dann's musical interest in the Glee Club was not strong enough to keep him in Ithaca. Whatever his feelings the social phenomenon was a fact. A report of the 1920–1921 tour states that the "attendance of a great number of influential and socially prominent patronesses indicated that the concerts of the Cornell Musical Clubs hold a high position in the season's social calendar. . . . Each year the social part played in the trip becomes more important, and more elaborate entertainment was provided this year than on any previous trip. Luncheons, tea dances, dinners, evening dances, theatre parties, and other forms of amusement characterized the trip."[75] Taking advantage of the changing of the guard perhaps, Club leadership moved to incorporate this social emphasis into the formal policy of the organization. A review of the 1920–1921 season said, "A new policy is to be instituted in the election of members to the Musical Clubs. A membership committee . . . will be formed. This move has as its object a better understanding between the management and the Club members, and the reconstruction of the Musical Clubs into more of a social organization."[76]

In the end we know little of Dann's parting feelings about the Glee Club and music department, and their futures. The verifiable reactions to his leave-taking were almost unanimously positive, and exuberantly so. In spring 1921 Allan H. Treman 1921 (nephew of Charles and then president of the Glee Club) wrote, "In 1889, Professor Dann took charge of the Club and directed it with very great success until the present year, when the Musical Clubs Council, much to their regret, have had to accept his resignation to enable him to take a very important position as Pennsylvania state supervisor of music."[77] Another *Era* article, "A Parting Glimpse at a Prominent Professor," called him the "greatest musical supervisor of graded schools in the country," and continued, "it will be exceedingly difficult to find someone on whom his mantle should fall . . . he has given the students, professors, and the citizens of Ithaca a rare musical education—one which few if any could find fault with and which no one could experience and not feel greatly benefited."[78]

By all accounts, including the Reven DeJarnette biography, Dann was a master technician of sound. In addition to the usual attention to posture and breathing, he used what he called "right thinking" (a series of mental exercises) in his focus on "tone-quality." He was particularly effective in teaching falsetto singing, or *mezza voce* singing as DeJarnette calls it: "His first conspicuous success in developing a beautiful tenor quality with *mezza voce* was with the Cornell University Glee Club." But to Dann technical details were there only to serve the music, not to become well-worn fixations. His attention to diction arose from his conviction that "Singing is the interpretation of two languages." He felt the ebb and flow of the musical phrase corresponded to the demands of natural pronunciation. It is no surprise that someone said, "He was very effective in making the beat materially assist the phrasing and the natural pronunciation of the words"[79]—to him they were the same.

The *Era's* parting article closed with a more personal insight into the conductor, commenting on his "habitual reserve. All through his life he has seemed to wear a mask over real personality. Sometimes it has been a bit difficult for people to penetrate this isolation and come face to face with the real Hollis Dann, yet, it takes but a short acquaintance to perceive that as long as you play square with him and give the best that you can he is one of your truest and most loyal friends."[80]

Dann was a private man, tending to keep a distance between his work and his life at home, between his life within and the life known to the thousands with whom he worked. But reserve did not mask the deeply emotional man, and the *Era's* impression must be weighed with other views of his true personality. Fired by the intensity of his musical convictions, Dann was prone at times to disagree vehemently with others, particularly on matters of educational pedagogy, and more than one account tells of "misunderstandings" at MENC conventions. Hand in hand with his incitations to improve the technical training of musicians, he repeatedly argued for the emotional impact of music making.

"The capacity to respond to emotional stimuli is something to be thankful for, never to be ashamed of. Too often we repress rather than give expression to our emotions," he once said, and he saw music as salvation for the emotional life.[81]

In Dann's words "singing detached from the atmosphere of the song—joy, sorrow, mystery, love, adventure, adoration, fear, play—*any* emotional state, is grossly incomplete—only the skeleton of music—a body without soul. The spiritual element must *dominate* the singing, reversing the present trend, which stresses the mechanical and starves the emotional." And his music making expressed these convictions. After a 1919 MENC program, "A Choral Interpretation of the War with commentary texts selected from the works of Walt Whitman," one singer commented that "Dr. Dann conducts with his heart in his baton" and continued the compliment: "After all is said and done regarding conducting as an art, the art itself is of no avail without the inner life, the true manhood which has something to impart to those under his leadership." In a 1939 memorial address MENC's president stated, "No chorus that he ever conducted can forget the thrill which his own deep response to the music communicated to the singers."[82]

"Never stop the march of a song," Dann used to say. "Always the conductor and singer must keep alive the feeling of motion; . . . the inward urge that inevitably pushes on to the very end."[83] The same was true of his life. From Cornell the nationally renowned leader in public school music went on to make the place of his childhood a "singing State." While in Pennsylvania he continued to pioneer a remarkable trail for American musical education, working to establish music courses in all the grade and high schools, to secure training and minimum standards of certification for music educators, and to improve the lot of community music in the form of an annual, statewide music week. Three years later, at age 63, Dann accepted a post as professor and head of the Department of Music Education at New York University, assuming his duties on February 1, 1925, without a glance at retirement. Over the next eleven years he made his dream of a school for music educators a manifest reality. He continued to conduct, leading the Department of Music Education chorus in critically acclaimed performances of Verdi's *Requiem* at the 1926 Sesquicentennial Exposition in Philadelphia and again in 1932 at Carnegie Hall (the first performance being with the Philadelphia Symphony Orchestra, the latter with the New York Philharmonic). In his ongoing role with MENC he conducted the National Supervisors' Chorus several times and at the 1928 conference conducted the first National High School Chorus (which he led again in 1930 and 1931).

His ever present influence on educational policy was manifest in MENC policies, state policies, and the works he created and compiled for educational use. Having previously published eight volumes of the *Hollis Dann Music Course,* the American Book Company released the five volumes of the *Hollis Dann Song Series* in 1935–1936. Dann also compiled and edited anthologies of song, including volumes of spirituals and anthems and a book of glee club songs. Retiring in 1936, he was named a professor emeritus at NYU, but went on to engagements as guest conductor, adjudicator, and lecturer, opportunities he had previously been forced to decline. At 75 he was keeping a hectic schedule—engagements in ten different states during the two-month period March to May 1937 alone. But age began to take its toll; a performance on his 76th birthday had to be canceled and plans to conduct a tour of European musical centers that summer could not be fulfilled. Eventually confined to his bed, he died on January 3, 1939.

Hollis Dann often claimed that the "stream cannot rise higher than its source."[84] During his life the currents of American choral singing ran high and strong, and Cornell's rose with them. When he left in 1921, Ithaca had risen from "the most unmusical place in the world" to musical mecca. Music had become a department in the university and an art avidly pursued by the student body. In his thirty-two years as director, the Glee Club had more than doubled in membership and begun to tour extensively on an annual basis, establishing a national reputation for itself. The group no longer teetered on the edge of existence; having survived financial disaster, a typhoid epidemic, and a world war, the Club had become a Cornell institution. The traditions built into the year's concert calendar between 1889 and 1921 would support the years ahead, and with the foundation he had helped to build, Dann would remain a profound influence at the base of the Glee Club's history. Now it was time to find a new leader.

3 The Dudley Years, 1921–1942

> The real college man . . . is a versatile person possessing many sides, and unwilling to develop one at the expense of the others; so glee clubs should sing not only classical music but such "college" music as is sincere and valid, the best of its kind.
>
> —Archibald T. Davison, "A New Standard for Glee Clubs"

As the final notes of Handel's *Messiah* drifted up through the rafters of Sage, a thunderous applause broke out in the chapel, and for several minutes the floor vibrated with stamping feet while the nave rang with uproarious cheers. It was the close of the 1905 Music Festival. As the audience finally settled and moved to envelop the musicians in personal congratulations, a member of the festival chorus stepped forward to the side of a smiling Professor Dann. The man carried an engraved cup, a gift from the singers. "Professor Dann," Eric Dudley began, "on behalf of all the members of the Festival chorus, I am requested to present to you this loving cup as a token of our keen appreciation of the splendid work you are doing, not only for the individual members of the chorus themselves but for the cause of music in the city of Ithaca . . . I have, sir, great pleasure in presenting to you this cup of love and friendship."[1] Little did either man know then that some years later the mantle would pass the other way.

Englishman Eric Sydney Dudley was born on April 17, 1874, in the town of Wigan, some miles northeast of Liverpool, and raised in Manchester. Further historical background is hard to come by. By at least one account he was the youngest of fifteen children, and given that he listed a brother as his guarantor on college forms, it is possible that one or both parents died while he was still young. He probably exhibited early talent as a singer and most likely sang in a boys' choir.

He spent his student days at the Royal Academy of Music in London, entering in the Michaelmas term of 1898 and staying for five terms. While there he studied singing, piano, harmony, and elocution, earning a bronze medal in singing and elocution. He was further honored with the Parepa-Rosa Gold Medal, an award still given today to the soprano, alto, tenor, or bass (alternating

9. Eric Dudley, c. 1930.

from one voice part to the next each year) who best performs a set of pieces selected by the prize committee. He graduated following the Lenten term in the
spring of 1900, but the honors didn't stop there. Dudley began an active career
performing in recital, oratorio, and opera; after one of his public appearances
the Hampstead Conservatoire of Music of London awarded him a full scholarship without examination.

Somewhere in the halls of the Royal Academy, or perhaps on a concert stage
in Great Britain, Dudley met Lillian Morgan, a gifted young soprano. Born and
raised in Wales, she later studied in Germany and was also a medal winner at
the academy. The two were married and arrived in the States in 1903 with Sir
Charles Hawtrey's touring theatrical company, which initially engaged Eric in
1901 as music director of the production "A Message from Mars." The show
became an English hit, eventually offering "the Dudleys" (as they became known
to affectionate concert audiences) a chance to tour abroad. Stepping off the train
somewhere along the line, the couple left the company and settled in Ithaca,
taking charge of the Ithaca Conservatory's vocal department. They could not
have chosen a better time. The pair arrived just as Dann acceded to a Cornell
professorship, and they soon became part of his musical extravaganza, singing
as soloists on the Sunday programs at Sage Chapel. With Dann's burgeoning
responsibilities Dudley took over as director of the Presbyterian Church Choir—
a position he held for the next forty-four years.

The Dudleys made two extraordinary contributions to the Cornell Music Festival in its earliest years. On the premiere evening of the first Music Festival,
Friday, April 15, 1904, the *Elijah* performance narrowly avoided disaster. The
soprano singing the Widow had suddenly taken ill. Lillian Dudley came to the
rescue, consenting to sing the role with a mere few hours warning and no pre-

vious knowledge of the part. "It is needless to say that this was a feat which would appall the most experienced musician," the *Ithaca Daily News* wrote. "That she carried it through successfully and even effectively adds another to the many triumphs which she has achieved in Ithaca."[2] Eric followed suit in 1907. One of the festival's major attractions, Dubois's *Seven Last Words of Christ*, was to star "famous baritone Emilio de Gogorza." When Gogorza failed to appear, Dudley stepped in with only a moment's notice. The *Daily News* noted, "The absence of Mr. Gogorza was disappointing for a time, but Mr. Dudley did as well, taking the missing baritone's place and evoking storms of applause." The *Sun* didn't notice Gogorza was missing, and the *Journal* added Dudley "was given an ovation after the Fourth Word."[3]

In 1904 Dudley became musical director of the Ithaca Conservatory, and in that post later became embroiled in more than one financial and political maelstrom. In spring 1906 the conservatory disclosed a deficit and decided to consolidate financial responsibility for the school under the principal teachers, the eighteen stockholders agreeing to transfer their holdings through Trustee Charles E. Treman to Eric Dudley, W. Grant Egbert, and George C. Williams (who taught elocution and drama, before succeeding Egbert as president). The triumvirate, increased to a foursome a year later with the arrival of pianist Herbert Hilliard, assumed entire responsibility for the institution's debt, not to mention its administrative and educational functions. This "tidy oligarchical structure," as John Harcourt calls it in *The Ithaca College Story*, worked fairly well for a time. But then a remarkable series of events unfolded in the spring of 1917. Hilliard had fled under pressure the previous year, and Lillian Dudley was elected to take his place on April 25, 1917. Eric Dudley made an immediate move to oust Williams and Egbert, who in turn resigned. What followed was a ridiculous series of coups and conciliations. Harcourt sums up, "In just over two weeks, the membership of the Board of Directors had changed some thirteen times, with a total cast of only eight persons. Whatever the unrecorded offstage maneuverings, the net result was clear. The Dudleys were out, the Egberts and Williamses in."[4]

Even so, the Dudleys fared well in musical education. Harcourt reports that by about 1910 they had "broken all previous records in the number of local students and had expanded their operations to Owego, Trumansburg, and Candor."[5] Aiding the cause of Hollis Dann, Dudley proved influential in resurrecting and firmly establishing the conservatory's curriculum intended to prepare music educators for work in the public schools. After leaving the conservatory he gave three years to musical service in the military, returning to Ithaca in 1920. He continued with the church choir and privately coached voice students in the studio run jointly with Lillian.

When Dann resigned in 1921, it fell to the Musical Clubs Council to name his successor. A good deal of speculation ensued. Who could uphold the reputation of the Glee Club, not to mention the musical name of the university? Who could succeed a man who, by force of personality, turned out fine choirs "from very raw material"? Dudley had acquitted himself admirably as an Army song leader during the last years of the war, and had, in his work as director of the Presbyterian Church Choir, already proved he could succeed Dann successfully. The Musical Clubs Council decided he was the man. "When the name of Eric Dudley appeared as the new appointee the musical public knew that that problem had been solved."[6] At about the same time another friend of Cornell music had stepped down. President Schurman retired in 1920, and a year's search had uncovered Livingston Farrand to succeed him. Hence, Eric Dudley, second principal director of the Glee Club, entered Cornell simultaneously with Farrand, fourth president of the university.

Dudley's assumption of the post differed substantially from Dann's. When Dann took over, the Glee Club hardly had a tradition, let alone its own governing committee. Dudley inherited a group with a history, an interested (and invested) alumni, and a council, most coming into being during the Dann years. Dann's professorship, however, was not offered to Dudley, who was not listed among the faculty of 1921–1922; his position in the university remained ambiguous for most of his life, becoming an issue particularly at the time of his retirement. Partial responsibility for this situation can be ascribed to the Musical Clubs Council's mode of management; the council operated autonomously, paying the bills and salaries, making the decisions, and sweeping the floors, inevitably keeping the university at arm's length. Few saw any reason for it to be otherwise. Following the appointment of Otto Kinkeldey in 1923 as chairman, the music department moved in an academic direction. Performance was not neglected—indeed Kinkeldey served as university organist and directed the Sage Chapel vespers for several years. But as the future founder of the American Musicological Society, and the man appointed to America's first chair of musicology, he brought greater emphasis to the scholarly side of Cornell music. And neither he nor anyone else in the department saw fit to perpetuate the achievements of Dann's Music Festivals, or a faculty line in choral music.[7]

Departmental appointment or not, there was a Glee Club to run and young men eager to sing. Dudley got right to work, holding practice twice weekly following auditions in the Club's Tioga Street rooms and Barnes Hall. His first concert came on the night of November 23, 1921, in the Bellevue-Stratford Hotel in Philadelphia; the evening's success ensured the interests of the Glee Club were in good hands. The traditional Junior Week, Spring Day, and Senior Week concerts continued with an unusual addition to the concert schedule here and there. In early December of Dudley's first year the Glee Club performed at a benefit for the Welfare Association of Ithaca held at the Lyceum, after which they launched their nine-day Christmas tour. Another novel concert was scheduled for March 1923, booked when the Cornell group agreed to put its reputation on the line against glee clubs from twenty-one other colleges and universities at a competitive concert in New York City. An eleventh-hour snarl with the Committee on Student Affairs and waning student interest, however, caused the Music Clubs Council to reconsider and eventually to back out. We can only wonder if the "We Always Win" slogan of today would have held true seventy years ago.

Second tenor Schuyler Pratt 1925 wrote to his parents on December 3, 1923, to say the Christmas tour was approaching, "containing many unusual opportunities in an instructive and social way. I don't know whether I shall be chosen as one of the eight second tenors or not." Under Dudley, the Christmas tours had remained every bit the musical and social experience that they were under Dann. In his first year Dudley set a precedent by accompanying the group on the entire tour, and Glee Clubbers felt that the "high standard of the concerts was to no small extent due to his presence."[8] Proclaimed the thirtieth annual Christmas tour (it was really only the twenty-sixth or so, seeing as several years had been omitted), the 1923–1924 tour began on the night of December 26 when the men convened in Buffalo, arriving separately from hometown holiday visits.

Schuyler had made the touring group, and wrote letters home almost daily. A December 16 letter from Ithaca contained the schedule, which left "hardly a breathing spell." Once the tour was underway, he wrote from Detroit on December 27 to say they had rehearsed at the station for that evening's concert, taking place in an auditorium seating between two and three thousand people. "A big bill board advertises our concert and in front of the theater are announcements of future appearances of such artists as Heifetz and Paderewski." On the following day came a letter from Chicago relating that the Detroit concert went "fairly smoothly" and was enthusiastically received. "Alumni have only the warmest praise for our concerts. We are being entertained very royally." He added, "There are no fatal illnesses as yet although about a third of the Club seems to have at least a minor cold."

On December 29 he wrote from Des Moines about being entertained at a Wakonda Club luncheon, followed by bridge and a tea dance. The Glee Club, he relates, does all "the entertaining at dinner and luncheons except occasionally when the hotel orchestra furnishes continuous music. Today the entire Glee Club sang Alma Mater, Noah, and Winter Song all of which were roundly applauded. The alumni seemed to make as much noise in the yells as we." Pratt also related that the Chicago concert seemed to be the best given and the best received, but he didn't think it had been broadcast. "We seem to be reaching the peak of our success now and hope we don't get sliding the other way." The following day, from Kansas City this time, he relates that very few are free from sore throats and colds, and wonders how they'll sound by the time they reach Rochester. The concert at Des Moines, he continues, went fairly well but the warmest reception was still the one in Chicago. Most of the audiences were composed of those who regularly heard the best in music, and although the Des

Moines people were not "wildly enthusiastic . . . someone said that Galli-Curci failed to move them. We responded to many encores however."

The men anticipated radio broadcasts in most cities, and even though they often failed to materialize (as in Chicago), the expectation was not far-fetched. On the previous year's tour the Glee Club had been heard nationally in broadcasts from New York City and St. Louis with the aid of powerful radio sets secured especially for the occasion. Ever since Pittsburgh radio station KDKA's broadcast of election returns from the Harding–Cox presidential race on November 2, 1920, the wireless had crept steadily into American households, as it would into the musical life of the Glee Club. On the 1924–1925 tour the final concert in New York City's Town Hall was broadcast courtesy of the Radio Corporation of America. Radio audiences heard the group live the next winter from Chicago's Orchestra Hall, and again from Town Hall over New York's WEAF, with telegrams rolling in from enthusiastic listeners even before the concert had finished.[9] By 1930 radio had become a forum for the public to hear glee clubs, by way of programs specifically designed to present college organizations from around the country. Some groups hesitated to take up radio's offer, being suspicious, uninterested, or barred by university policy; Cornell's Glee Club turned down a 1930 offer for a Columbia (CBS) radio broadcast despite the promoter's promise of a potential audience in the millions, showing if nothing else that they weren't hankering after exposure. But there was no way for glee clubs to ignore the profound impact radio would have on their way of life in the decades ahead.

Roughly concurrent with the advent of radio, and unrelated initially, the Glee Club began to modify its program. Without exaggeration the Dudley years could be termed the revolutionary era of programming. From 1921 to 1942 the group went through about as many radical repertoire changes as Stravinsky did periods as a composer. The initial departure in the early 1920s, which inclined toward a slightly more serious program, was a ripple from a stone dropped more than a decade earlier. Here we need some background.

In 1925 the Harvard Glee Club came to town. An unusual amount of press accompanied their arrival, much of it directed at the group's pioneering choice of repertoire. The *Ithaca Journal* wrote, "Parted from the time-honored custom of including popular songs and vaudeville skits in its program . . . the Harvard Club has gained widespread fame, in both America and Europe, for its singing of classical and choral music—a distinct advance in college glee club performances."[10] Calling the Crimson Glee Club a "Pioneer in Adapting Classical Music for Concerts," the *Daily Sun* explained that the group's performances "are devoted entirely to good music, ancient and modern." The Ithaca program proved a model example, including an Ave Maria, Byrd's "Iustorum Animae," Parry's "Jerusalem," and pieces by Lassus, Morley, Bach, and the emerging Francis Poulenc.[11] Intrigued, Ithaca's musical aficionados lined up at Bailey to hear what proved to be a first-rate concert by this group that "divorced itself from the banjo and mandolin clubs and undertook the experiment of singing classical music."

The experiment had begun some years earlier. In 1911 Archibald T. Davison was appointed to direct the Sunday service at Harvard's Appleton Chapel. Doc Davison, as he was affectionately called, immediately abolished the long-standing boy's choir and installed a chorus of men as replacement. Elliot Forbes in *A History of Music at Harvard to 1972* writes, "A sound new to Harvard, indeed new to America, emerged: sparkling diction, homogeneous tone that was never forced, shaded dynamics, and a fine sense of phrasing and ensemble." Here we might say the sound was merely new to Harvard, as surely Hollis Dann had previously achieved this effect with his singers. But Davison's musical sense did embrace an approach unquestionably new to American male singing. Forbes continues, "Many members of the choir were also in the glee club—at the time a rough and tumble, student-led organization of some forty voices. The contrast in musical effect between the two groups was striking, and the glee club wondered why they could not sound as polished as Doc's ensemble. So they asked for his help."[12] He became a coach to the ensemble in 1912 (eschewing the position of director until he had full charge of what was sung) and began espousing a new approach, eventually achieving what had become a renowned novelty by the group's 1925 appearance in Ithaca.

A few years into the enterprise Davison summed up the Harvard group's progress to date:

> First, by the performance of really good music they have now the approbation of professional musicians and the respect and interest of the public. Instead of the hysterical applause with which the public was wont to greet a new vocal outburst against our New Haven brethren or a vigorous selection in praise of the wine, the audience now first stops to sigh and then begins its applause; for it should be understood that college students are not out of class in attempting really good music; instinctively they recognize its validity. . . . [And] glee clubs should sing not only classical music but such "college" music as is sincere and valid, the best of its kind. It is this sort of adaptability that interests and attracts the audience at a glee club concert. . . . In the case of the Harvard Glee Club concerts the public has been quick to appreciate the compliment bestowed on it by a group of young men who instead of asking their hearers to laugh at an evening of false whiskers and barber-shop chords, assumes that they can enjoy real music and forthwith asks them to listen and to think. The glee club has learned, in the second place, that the average college music does not stand the wear and tear of constant rehearsal. Marked precision is demanded of college glee clubs, a clean attack, clear enunciation, varied dynamic, and in general all the exterior forms of technique common to a well-trained choral society. In order to attain the necessary degree of

proficiency a great deal of rehearsing must be done; . . . before long the members become weary of hearing the same obvious type of music. They find nothing new in the music after the first meeting; there is no mystery about it; they will never discover unsuspected beauties in it, and in the end the performance becomes entirely mechanical. Not so, however, with music which must be studied and felt in order that it may be well performed. This year, for example, the Harvard Glee Club has had the unusual experience of finding its members increasingly enthusiastic over the *music* rather than the *concert,* and at the close of the season the members voted unanimously not to lower the standard, but rather to elevate it still higher. This is simply an application of the truth that intimate association with what is truly great and good generates first respect and then love. . . . The men really love [this type of music] and call for it to the exclusion of music previously considered the only suitable thing for college glee clubs. . . . If the college man's view of music is really broadening so that it permits him to enjoy singing classical music, why should we stand in his light and insist that he sing inferior music simply because in years gone by we were satisfied with less than the best?[13]

This 1915 piece, "A New Standard for Glee Clubs," might be considered a manifesto for glee clubs in the twentieth century. Gradually—in some cases slowly, in others by incisive and abrupt force—most collegiate glee clubs, not to mention other choral organizations, have come to resemble the image of Doc Davison's prototype. Even in this first instance, the change met with resistance from staunch alumni defenders of tradition—the matter was not definitively resolved in Cambridge until 1919, when the first modern American glee club was severed from the instrumental clubs. But Davison's idea had appeal and was developing a following. Other organizations wrote the Harvard club for information regarding their policies, program, and constitution. The demand for compositions sung by the club was so great that Davison began publishing his own arrangements, unusual in that most groups produced arrangements for their exclusive use. Said the *Cornell Daily Sun* on April 24, 1925, "The movement is spreading among other student glee clubs, and a number of colleges are adopting a program of good choral music."

By this time Cornell's Glee Club had already made a move in that direction. The perennial summary of the season reported in 1923–1924 the program of the Glee Club and Mandolin Club "was one which has since attracted most favorable comment because of its variety, including, as it did, not only the college songs familiar to the old grads, but music of wider repute by well-known composers."[14] The banjo quartets and musical antics certainly were not out, but the group prided itself on splendidly rendering a "difficult, and for a college organization, presumptuous program which included many operatic and classical selections as well as the ever popular college songs."[15] Whether by design or default, the Glee Club settled on a hybrid program, combining some of

Harvard's innovation with the humor and sentiment of homegrown tradition. Further advance toward a classical repertory did not occur until the early 1930s, when the wealth of talent in the Musical Clubs made it possible for Dudley and Coleman to depart from standard college fare.

> After the usual Cornell songs, the *Alma Mater* and *Cornell*, the Glee Club gained favor with the classicists with songs by Schumann and Arcadelt, *The Two Grenadiers* and *Ave Maria* [the same Ave Maria that had opened Harvard's 1925 concert—that is, after "Fair Harvard"]. Bruce Boyce 1933 appeared in costume to give a most enjoyable rendition of the prologue from Leoncavallo's opera, *I Pagliacci.* . . .
>
> The Mandolin Club also presented an unusual program, with the rendition of classical and semi-classical numbers, each equally well played by the talented musicians.[16]

The movement toward a serious program might have continued were it not for external pressures that forced change in a new direction. Among these were widening holes in the organization's finances, eventually turned into craters by the Depression. Yet despite the market collapse the decade ended much as it began for the Glee Club, in a relatively untroubled fashion. Surely the 1920s had their postwar disillusion, and there were the dry days of Prohibition, but in contrast to trials past and pending, the decade offered a quiet interlude. If there was any harbinger of problems to come, it was the Glee Club tours. On the face of it they continued steadily through the decade, carrying the songs of Cornell in ever widening circles. In 1924–1925, the year Hollis Dann's son Roger Lewis 1925 was president of the Club, the Christmas tour covered 3,000 miles, many below the Mason–Dixon Line.[17] On the long trip south the men were entertained by a garrulous baggageman who "related endless tales of trains that had run off the numerous curves of the Southern Railroad."[18] The group made it safely, but it wasn't long before the Glee Club's train would be run off the track by financial maladies. Another southern tour in 1927–1928 stretched to Little Rock, Arkansas, and the Lone Star State, where the Glee Club was greeted by the Cornell Club of Northern Texas and performed in Dallas's McFarland Auditorium. It stretched the bank account too far.

Financial expediency dictated a shorter Easter recess trip to nearby states the next year. A managerial letter dated August 1929, still several months before Black Friday, revealed that all these concert tours lose money, a reality since the war. In any given year profits from Junior Week and other home concerts balanced the books, but for some unseen reason attendance was dropping, and solvency had to be given serious thought. Tour audiences were now more likely to be between 600 and 800, a healthy following but nowhere near the crowds of 1,500 to 2,000 in years past. And the Glee Club wasn't getting any help from economic trends. Nor, however, did they immediately crash with the market in

10. George Coleman, c. 1930.

1929. Some harbored the rosy impression that entertainment suffered little during times of relative depression—people presumably wished to escape their troubles. And it proved true amid the whirl of dances, dinners, and concerts on the 1929–1930 tour, reinstated on the Christmas break. The men were well received from Syracuse to Chicago, where they broadcast over the National Broadcasting chain, and few could mind that audiences were a little smaller than in years past. But the Depression was not just relative, and the next Christmas tour was an eye-opening splash of cold water. Anticipating a tight year, and knowing they would need between $1,500 and $1,800 per concert to break even, the Club advised local organizers to cut expenses, noting that entertainment (tea dances, smokers, and the like) was secondary and could not be deducted from gate receipts. The Club later relinquished this request, authorizing at least one city to deduct those costs, and the tour was as musically and socially successful as ever. Only after returning home did they find it had run a deficit of nearly $4,000. The group had already been living off the fat for a few years, and there was no way to keep it up. Graduate Manager Romeyn (Rym) Berry 1904 wrote George Coleman in April 1931 of the serious need for frugality.[19]

Coleman had already written the Musical Clubs Council a few days earlier outlining his ideas for retrenchment. He saw it in architectural terms, advising that tours be budgeted in the way one plans to build a house—so much per cubic foot, or in other words, so many dollars per man per day. He also suggested switching from trains to motor buses, which could be hired at 40 cents a mile. On the other hand he argued that cutting the number who toured was not an option. It would compromise the clubs musically. "I believe it was in 1915," he wrote, "that Mr. C. E. Treman raised the number of travelling instrumentalists from eighteen to twenty-five. Our alumni friends tell us the Cornell concerts are superior in effects because of a fine balance obtained by sufficient numbers."[20]

At the outset of 1931–1932 Rym Berry wrote to Allan Treman (who had been elected earlier that year to the Musical Clubs Council, succeeding his late uncle Charles), "This undergraduate organization has to be financed according to squirrel methods—when you get a nut, hide it."[21] Hoarding was helpful, but the organization knew finances were too thin simply to tighten the belt. A series of policy revisions ensued starting with the tour policy, which was completely rewritten between 1930 and 1934.[22] It was practice for the Glee Club at the turn of the decade to require no guarantee from local organizers—the Club was responsible for all expenses and took all the profits. By 1934 the Musical Clubs Council had codified the policy—contracts for out-of-town concerts stipulated a guarantee be paid to the Glee Club, and the remaining profits split fifty-fifty. The guarantee varied from city to city, depending on the area's drawing power; Washington might be $300, while New York City was usually $500. The expenses became the responsibility of the local presenter (usually a Cornell Club), and with the presumption that local clubs would work harder to promote a concert they stood to lose or gain by, more responsibility was accordingly shifted to them. This outline—namely the guarantee and local responsibility for the concert's promotion and place—remains the basic model for today's tour contracts.

Setting a policy did not guarantee a solution. When managers set out to arrange the 1931–1932 Christmas tour, most cities balked at the guarantees. Times were tough, and communities were hard hit. Toledo had four of its six banks close, and a man from Pittsburgh wrote that it was time to forego fun and pleasure. The tour was postponed until spring, and eventually abandoned altogether. It wasn't merely that local alumni clubs felt financial conditions were too poor to risk sponsoring a tour. The Musical Clubs Council feared the clubs would go bankrupt and might not survive another ground-shaking loss and, voting without the two directors present (Berry said it was better to leave them out of business matters), canceled the trip. The clubs were able to muster up a spring tour to a handful of cities in 1933 and four more in the spring of 1934; New York, Atlantic City, and Baltimore were visited both years. Even in pared-back form the tours lost money, and problems persisted with the new contracts. In 1935 trips were made only as far as Binghamton and Rochester; in the first city the concert was poorly attended, and the local club refused to pay the guarantee despite a signed contract. And as of October 10, more than five months after the second concert, no money had been received from Rochester. As far as touring was concerned, the new policy had answered little—between the spring 1934 and the 1937–1938 tours the Glee Club made only one out-of-state tour—a three-day, three-city trip in spring 1936.

The Glee Club had done its part in scaling down operations and beefing up policy to offset the Depression and increasing losses. Strange it wasn't having more effect, unless ephemeral financial deprivation was masking a deeper problem—something many glee clubs around the country had suspected for some time.

In October 1931, the same year the Cornell Glee Club canceled its tour altogether, a letter addressed to the conductor arrived from the graduate treasurer of Colombia's glee club. He was trying to get some perspective on the glee club landscape, and after describing his group's difficulties in booking concerts and wondering about the reasons, he inquired about Cornell's experience. Rym Berry wrote back that they too had a problem with their Musical Clubs, which after being a highly popular Cornell institution for forty years with well-attended concerts, were finding their popularity fading. A forthright person, Berry did not mince words. When the Musical Clubs Council weighed the risk of a tour against the chances of the Club's survival, he said flat out, "The Glee Club business, in my opinion, is a dying business."[23]

To his way of thinking the Depression wasn't the force driving the clubs toward extinction. When trying to explain the disastrous financial outcome of the 1930–1931 tour and the inability of Ithaca concerts to cover the shortfall, he attributed the main cause to a lack of interest among the undergraduates themselves.[24] The Junior Week ticket sales bore him out. From 1927 when receipts peaked at $2,837, income steadily declined at a rate of about $500 dollars a year until it hit $910 in 1931 and bottomed out at $739 the following year. (Thus, the first $1,000 of decline came before the stock market crashed.) Receipts for Spring Day followed a similar trend, dropping from $2,228 in 1927 to $740 in 1932. Plenty of people were still trying out for the Glee Club, and membership actually increased between 1925 and 1930 from 60 to almost 70, eventually crossing 70 for the first time in 1933–1934. For some reason, though, the student body's general interest in singing was waning.

Commentators with their finger on the pulse of American music had noted a change since World War I. Osborne McConathy's 1939 memorial address in honor of Hollis Dann recalled the halcyon days as it paid homage:

> To one who has followed closely the effects of Dr. Dann's work upon music education, one of his outstanding achievements— perhaps the greatest achievement of his career—would be the part which he played in the revival of interest in choral music at a time when that interest was low indeed. To the younger generation it may be unknown that in Dr. Dann's early years and indeed almost up until the time of the World War, this country was alive with choral interest. . . .
>
> About the time of the World War, however, an unaccountable apathy spread over the face of choral activities, both within the schools and in the community. It was at that time that the tremendous wave of instrumental music began to sweep the country. Under notable leaders this wave of enthu-

siasm for bands and orchestras in our schools grew with leaps and bounds until it overwhelmed the field of vocal music.[25]

McConathy was accurate in sounding the decline of singing tradition, but to what extent was an instrumental boom the primary cause? From a late-twentieth-century point of view, there is no question that instrumental music is the favored sibling to choral music, speaking strictly of so-called serious music.[26] Thinking about New York brings to mind the Yankees, the Knicks, and the New York Philharmonic, not the Ars Nova or the Dessoff Choirs. And in general, scholarly discussion of recent musical periods privileges the instrumental works of instrumental composers, except where the choral and orchestral meet, namely in opera and major choral works with orchestra. True, after Palestrina and Bach, composers such as Haydn and Schumann wrote a great deal more for instruments than for choruses. But the smaller choral works of major composers are consistently neglected, and in today's climate, a primarily choral composer is most likely destined for second-class citizenship. Yet, is it true to say the rise of instrumental music meant the fall of choral music?

In McConathy's view the Glee Club might have been on firm ground—they had the Instrumental Club to go with them. Yet if anything was the case, Instrumental Club membership was dropping—down to about thirty in 1930, and a report in 1933–1934 said in truth that the Mandolin Club had "but one Mandolin."[27] Instrumentalists aside, the Musical Clubs' ticket sales were drooping.

Other causes of the choral decline had yet to be detected, but dealing with the consequences couldn't wait. As ticket sales fell off, one Glee Club tradition after another was questioned. In the spring of 1932, the bottom-of-the-barrel year, thought was given to discontinuing Senior Week. The men were making a sacrifice to stay on the Hill until graduation (in mid-June at this time), and it was hardly worthwhile if audience support continued to decline. Rather than give up the ship, the Club asked Foster Coffin 1912 (for a good number of years a faithful friend to the Glee Club from his university office in Willard Straight, where he served as alumni secretary and later director of the building) to encourage alumni support. Coffin did so with his traditional eloquence, and Senior Week continued.

Spring Day was another matter. Dating from 1901, and usually sporting a carnivalesque atmosphere, the tradition often brought out the more primitive, Bacchanalian side of undergraduate life, making the affair a distant and profligate relative of the current Slope and Dragon Day festivities. Since the early collaborations with Harvard on the eve of crew races, the Spring Day concert had been linked to athletics, and the Musical Clubs had become associated with the Athletic Association, publicity for such concerts as Spring Day being handled out of the athletic office. Approaching the concert in May 1931 Rym Berry wrote to Dudley suggesting that the Musical Clubs would do better to detach themselves.[28] Spring Day itself was losing steam. The 1931 event was snowed out, and the occasion questionably reinstated in 1933 as an aquatic carnival on Beebe Lake, complete with a Donald Duck Derby featuring water fowl racing under such names as the Duck of York, Ducky Strike, and Moby Duck. Many thought it time to get off the boat. After concert income precipitously dropped by $700 in 1932, Berry formally proposed that the Athletic Association and Musical Clubs part company. One final Spring Day concert was given in 1933, declared an artistic success, and then the familiar fixture of thirty-some years was buried for good.

Other traditions had already fallen by the wayside. A letter received in August 1930 suggested reviving the Thanksgiving eve concert with Penn, which had fallen off since Dudley's first concert in 1921. After making the observation that crowds no longer drifted in a day or two before the football game, Berry wrote that he saw no reason for bringing the concert back unless there was great interest shown along with a demand from the Cornell Club of Philadelphia.[29] The custom was not resurrected. Fall grew very quiet after 1924, almost a decade went by without a single concert prior to the Christmas tour activity. (When Berry turned down the radio broadcast in the spring of 1930, it sounded like the Glee Club of old—he claimed rehearsals dropped off for six weeks after Junior Week and restarted in the spring for upcoming concerts.) Even the Savage Club, where upperclass Glee Clubbers traditionally found entertainment and camaraderie during the lulls, was questioned.[30] A member himself, Dudley wrote in October 1930 that there did not seem "any good reason for its continuance. Things and conditions had changed so much since the old times that its usefulness and 'raison d'être' have disappeared."

Was the same true of the Glee Club? Berry, who was middle-aged by the 1930s, loved to talk about the old days as though the Golden Age had passed. "I am pretty dubious about glee clubs anyway," he once confided, though he added that he loved glee club concerts and heard a lot of them. He liked concerts that recalled the "dear, dead days," but these concerts were on the wane. "The old fellows like them for sentimental reasons but they are hard to sell to the kids."[31]

He thought "the kids" in the Club had other interests and said as much in his reply to the 1931 letter from Columbia: "I believe that the better musicians in our Club would prefer to study and sing more serious music and give no more than two or three carefully prepared concerts each year with the social feature secondary. Students are getting middle-aged and it is only the old grads who are youthful."[32]

To Berry and his generation, the glee club purpose as they conceived it was dying out, the songs of college life and sentimental journey losing sway to the more "austere" tastes of the younger crowd.[33] Their complaint, not uncommon at the time, was largely with the proliferation of a "more serious" repertoire—in a way, they wished to see the clubs revert to childhood, though Berry did express a certain contentment with Cornell's hybrid approach. The question arises however, were glee clubs literally dying or was one form of glee club merely going through a metamorphosis? The latter seems more true. The issue of glee club survival was very real; but the intersection at which all roads met, the crux of the debate of the time, was not *would* glee clubs continue, but rather, in what fashion. In other words, what was the appropriate and suitable repertoire for a collegiate group.

The *New York Evening Post* launched a pedantic editorial on the matter in January 1931:

> Now that we have 'cleaned up' football we propose to address our attention to another collegiate matter that needs reform—that is the college Glee Club. . . .
>
> Mr. [Robert A.] Gardner says that his interest in the glee club lies in his hope that its concerts will bring back to him something of the atmosphere of the campus, something that his children will get as significant of the humor and sentiment of undergraduate days. He deposes that he is sick and tired of having his college loyalty called upon to support *alma mater's* singers and then finding that the boys give him mainly highbrow choral music.
>
> We wholly agree with Mr. Gardner. He is opposing the exact thing in college music which we have been opposing in college football. College boys are not professional singers. The Mendelssohn and other choral societies meet a fine public need. But the undergraduate should not be called upon to live up to their standards of excellence. The undergraduate should express and control his own music just as he should express and control his own football.
>
> More than that, the college glee club with college tunes and college humor and college tenderness fills a niche in life that is worth the filling. Perhaps it is all sophomoric, it is all adolescent. But this phase of life exists, and however unimportant it may seem musically, nevertheless it deserves expression.
>
> We don't know what can be done about it. Harvard started this heresy a number of years ago when it tried to lift the undergraduate singer up into abstract musical realms where he does not belong. . . .
>
> As for us, we just simply don't go to glee club concerts any more. They are hybrids. They are artistically wrong. . . . They don't express the life of the college as revealed in music. They are a bore. We suppose that the only thing to do is to wait until time gives us glee club showmen with a more penetrating vision.[34]

The opposite view had its circle of supporters as well. One need only recall Hollis Dann's criticism regarding mawkish sentiment and horseplay in college glee clubs, or the infectious influence of Doc Davison's work. So while Harvard's Glee Club joined Radcliffe and the Boston Symphony Orchestra to perform Stravinsky's *Symphony of Psalms*, other organizations held to the *Evening Post's* idea. The Cornell Glee Club found itself somewhere in the middle, having worked out a compromise in its program between serious and sentimental. Watching the sinking box office returns, the directors and council began to weigh how compromising it actually was to sit on the fence.

The last Spring Day program in 1933 included both Schubert and Sullivan. Time had come to take the Glee Club program definitively in one direction or the other. Over the next few years, most if not all the problems plaguing the Glee Club converged in the resolution of the repertoire question—the unbearably expensive tours and alumni complaints, the loss of student interest in the Junior and Senior Week concerts, the decaying and abandoned frame of tradition, the Club's emaciated bank account, and what I would advance as the most basic problem, the radio. Influenced in some way by all these factors, the Glee Club pulled the brake, posted an about-face, and embarked on a radical departure from their previous tradition.

Even the Glee Club didn't stop on a dime, of course. The program revolution that began in the fall of 1933 took several years. But if the initial question was Franz Schubert or Arthur Sullivan, the overwhelming answer was Sullivan. With no possibility of a 1933–1934 Christmas tour, the Musical Clubs devoted themselves to a collaborative effort with the Women's Glee Club, the Dramatic Club, and the music department—a fully staged rendition of Gilbert and Sullivan's *Mikado*. The show opened Saturday, December 16, in a Bailey Hall transformed into the world of Japanese orchids, kimonos, and moonlight. For a time the English operettists had fallen out of favor, but students had more recently clamored for a Gilbert and Sullivan performance on campus and eagerly responded to the precedent-setting collaboration. Several days before the opening the hall was essentially sold out and a second performance was scheduled for Monday the 18th. Apparently a key to financial woes had been found. Moreover the rave response left quite a wake. "An entertainment dish fit to set before a Mikado was uncovered Saturday night in Bailey Hall, with just about the most brilliant performance by student amateurs which this reviewer has ever witnessed," wrote one critic.[35] The *Cornell Daily Sun* (December 19, 1933) sounded a celebratory note and clamored for a repeat performance during Junior Week. To their mind this was the answer to the Glee Club debate:

> **The Sun** has for several years been completely in favor of substituting the comic opera for the old, time-honored glee and musical club show. The latter has seen its best days and lost its once strong appeal with the college and alumni audience not only at Cornell but elsewhere throughout the country. Gilbert and Sullivan is just the type of thing we've been praying for. And Messrs. Dudley and Weaver and Drummond and Coleman are just the men to answer our prayers.

The operetta was not repeated at Junior Week, though selections such as "A Wandering Minstrel I" and "High Barbary" were included on the noticeably lighter program. Rather than risk an empty-looking Bailey, the concert was given in the Memorial Room of Willard Straight and a dance followed. The *Mikado* triumph had stabilized finances, but it couldn't be taken on tour, and cautious frugality was the watchword—with good reason. After *The Mikado* had rekindled student interest in campus choral music, the Junior Week attendance was low (partially due to bitter cold weather), and the spring tour to Baltimore, Washington, New York City, and Atlantic City rekindled nothing but familiar financial woes and some of the most acrimonious alumni comments to date. One wrote from New York that nothing would improve without a revolution in the Glee Club's program, as the older alumni supporters were "painfully bored and irritated" by serious classical presentations and would not put up with them much longer. He continued,

> I had believed the classical urge was just another prohibition psychosis and that when beer came back, the Club would start scrapping the Olympians— I expected the Club to resume the musical felicitations—giving their regards to Davy, bringing the forgotten wagon back home, and complimenting the graces of the saccharine Adeline—the lamentations of the late Mr. Andrews over his busted fate would also outrank the somber cadences of the Beethoven Funeral March.[36]

There was some truth in this outspoken opinion, and Glee Club leadership recognized it. Dudley favored the more classical program, but both he and Coleman knew there were larger forces at work, and a vital, entertaining club of singing performers was preferable to a sophisticated but dead choral society. The repertory revolution moved ahead with the 1934 Senior Week program. The performance was "in reality a variety show, fully staged and carefully lighted. Avoiding the usual classical programs, the clubs presented a very pleasing group of light airs by Gershwin and Strauss to keep up the spirit of fun and liveliness."[37]

The success of staged Gilbert and Sullivan productions and the novelty of variety shows were precursors to the bolder experiment in programming which shaped the Musical Clubs for the rest of the decade. The first effort in 1934–1935 was another gala Gilbert and Sullivan performance: *H.M.S. Pinafore.* After two December shows and a tidy profit the music department and collaborating directors decided, "If it ain't broke, don't fix it," and staged it a triumphant third time at Junior Week. The Glee Club's creative instincts must have been aroused by all that English operetta wit, and at Senior Week they departed from the usual concert formalities, experimenting with "an entirely new type of show—a burlesque amateur radio show."[38] Hosted by Jay Fassett 1912, one of the men's father and renowned Broadway actor, the "broadcast" included stunts and novelties, Fred Waring airs ("The Song Is You"), the Savage Club Quartet, the treble-voiced Campus Trio, and the inimitable Al Sulla 1929 on banjo.

In spoofing the radio the clubs had turned the heart of their problem to their advantage. For radio, bringing professionals into the parlor and turning every home into a concert hall, had put a damper on the Glee Club's serious repertoire and cut down attendance. With keen insight George Coleman summed up the situation:

> Today, the radio offers to the general public a variety of classical and standard music, played by the best of professional artists. . . . The mere fact that by simply turning a dial, the music-loving public may hear the best compositions given by the greatest talent in the world, may have something to do with the public's desire for lighter collegiate entertainment. I believe that the experiences of some of the Eastern University clubs with serious programs would bear out this point of view.[39]

Perhaps live collegiate concerts weren't dying after all—the public simply wanted a style of collegiate entertainment which complemented radio's offerings. In that light the overwhelming success of staged productions was no mystery. "The radio," Coleman concluded, "handicapped by mechanical limitations, has left open a new field of novel entertainment that utilizes stage effects in its musical presentation. . . . It seems now best for college organizations to entertain the public with the informal spirit of student life as lived in the University." That's precisely what the Clubs elected to do.

The amateur radio hour became a full-blown musical extravaganza in 1935–1936 with the Musical Clubs' production of "Oh, What a Night! or Stranded in Wichita." Imagine Bailey Hall transformed into a cozy tavern with full bar, checkered tablecloths, and the promise, "You'll Like Our Home (on the range) Cooking." The proprietor Eric Dudley walks in and proceeds to decide whether a straggly band of singers from Ithaca might sing for their suppers. (Though rumored to have no previous experience as a proprietor, he acquitted himself well.) One Junior Week press release pledged the Musical Clubs would present "a novel show in a lighter vein which will be completely devoid of the customary heavier musical scores." Allan Treman's suggestion in 1935 "that the clubs turn to more modern orchestral and choral numbers, that there be fewer soloists, and that future concerts be either entirely serious or entirely humorous," must have found sympathetic ears. The student manager later wrote, "The Cornell Musical Clubs no longer give a concert; they give a show, and informality is the key note." Without question. The Glee Club gave up their sharp double-rank crescent formation around the piano and black-tie look for the realistic garb and blocking of the pastiche at hand. When they repeated "Oh, What a Night!" on the 1937–1938 Christmas tour, the men followed a photo-negative dress code—they dressed informally for the concert, and changed into tuxes afterward for the various social engagements. As for any lingering concern about overcoming Prohibition psychoses, the manager requested each city

11. Publicity release for "Oh, What a Night!" in 1936, showing, *left to right*, tenor soloist of the "stranded" troupe, singing waiter, cabaret entertainer, and singer in drag as cigarette girl.

to provide the group with a quarter of beer and a picnic pump for use on stage. "We find that this not only adds color to the show but does wonders for the men's voices."[40]

Publicity for the original "Oh, What a Night!" promised it would be "a novelty in musical entertainment." Each succeeding year introduced an addition to the novel line of Glee Club productions. The 1936 Senior Week brought "Ship Shape" aboard the S.S. Harmony, followed by "Life Begins at Midnight" the next Junior Week, where for $1 one could "see the Clubs run rampant in the most informal midnight dormitory scene that collegiate life has ever produced." The 1937 Senior Week moved from ship to familiar shore with "Rusticana," set in a farmyard and featuring bucolic singers in straw hats and overalls. After the "Oh, What a Night!" revival, "Hell's Bells" (performed at the 1938 Junior Week) burlesqued the nationwide radio program advertising Ipana toothpaste by promoting "Youpana" toothpaste. On that program baritone soloist Thomas Tracy 1931, then assistant to Dudley, directed the ensemble. Further productions included "Trial by Jury" (Senior Week 1939), "In the Red" (1939–1940), "Coediquette" (1940–1941), "Red Rolling" (1941–1942), and the "Reunion Time" heading, used more than once at Senior Week.[41]

With radio shows often the target of Glee Club spoofs (as in "Hell's Bells" and "In the Red"), the musical thespians had a chance to poke fun at the source of recent woes with the university. During the 1930s, the clubs periodically received invitations to perform on radio shows. In December 1935 the Instrumental and Glee Clubs broadcast on succeeding days from campus over WESG and WABG respectively, performing Cornell and other songs. The performances were, with national hookup, broadcast over the CBS network as part of a series on which other collegiate groups, including Yale, Colgate, Penn, and Temple, had appeared. An invitation to broadcast in New York in February 1936 as guests of Benny Goodman and his orchestra on the *Jack Oakie Hour* followed, igniting a conflict with university officials. For some time the Glee Club had been required to clear all performances with the Faculty Committee on Student Activities (alternately called the Committee on Student Affairs). So, letters of permission were perfunctorily submitted and approved until the 1936 radio incident. The Glee Club had gladly accepted the invitation from New York after a request for leaves of absence was initially approved. On February 17, only days before the broadcast performance, the faculty rescinded the permission, claiming the program was a commercial broadcast and therefore unsuitable for a group from Cornell. The men in the group were so outraged, they considered going without the leaves, but the trip was eventually called off by the Glee Club for fear of faculty retribution.

Dubbed by the New York radio promoter as "the sad and brutal story" of the Glee Club, the issue did not rest and resurfaced more than a year later when the University Orchestra and Sage Chapel Choir were to broadcast Beethoven's *Christ on the Mount of Olives* over the Columbia network. A *Cornell Daily Sun* editorial pointed out the faculty committee's inconsistency in permitting the Beethoven and fall football broadcasts while prohibiting the Glee Club's. With a new decision pending regarding the University Band the paper called for a definitive policy:

> Broadcasting, sponsored by commercial producers, is here to stay. Whether a broadcast is commercial or not, Cornellians will listen to it, and appreciate it because it comes from Cornell. And if Cornellians will listen, so will the general public—with no thought of degrading Cornell. . . .

Since the band broadcast is dependent on the committee's action, it is important that its decision be favorable, for on it depends future Cornell broadcasts.

Furthermore, precedent having been broken once in refusing the Glee Club permission to broadcast, the committee should scarcely base its Band decision on "established precedent." That would be a crowning bit of false logic![42]

Eventually the faculty recanted, allowing Cornell organizations to participate in commercial broadcasts.

Notwithstanding coverage in the *Sun*, the Glee Club had its own means of satirizing commercial radio and the faculty and did so in back-to-back years with "In the Red" and "Coediquette." Both created by Richard Lee 1941, the shows marked an improvement in the ingenuity and humor of the clubs, with "Coediquette" particularly notable for its originality. Many of the scripts, from "Oh, What a Night!" to "In the Red," tended to be a canvas for Cornell and other Glee Club songs, weaving a tenuous plot line from one number to the next. Much of the writing was banal, if not outright fatuous. Take for example the following lines from "Oh, What a Night!" in 1936:

[The "Song of the Bayou" has just ended.]
Speaker: That's a swell number of the balmy South, but how about letting us sing you a song of the frozen North?
Proprietor: Oh that's right! You boys came all the way from Ithaca where you have skiing and tobogganing and sleighing—sleighing! Say, do you fellows know the "Sleigh Song"?
Speaker: Sure! [The Glee Club breaks into song.]

Things had improved slightly by "In the Red," where we find the following lines:

Members of our radio audience this is the *ST 54-40 hour.* You have just heard the famed Cornell Musical Clubs render a salute to their *Big Red Team* which crashed through this year's season *undefeated and untied.* (Trumpet salute). Speaking of champions, why don't *you* try *ST 54-40* or fight your own microbes mouthwash. . . . Do not accept substitutes, for no other product will give you that sweet baby's breath, that dangerous alure [sic], or that fly-bait look. . . .

For the benefit of those of you who have just tuned in, this is the *ST 54-40* hour featuring the Cornell Musical Clubs. If you feel you must socially put your foot in your mouth, first disinfect it with our product.

And so on. The show included Dick Lee's original song "In the Red and White," which was sung the night before Junior Week on the nationally broadcast

Chesterfield program by Fred Waring and his Pennsylvanians. The song became a hit with the Glee Club and its audiences and for years had a place on the concert program. Encouraged by this success, Lee undertook a bolder endeavor for the next year, writing both the script and ten original songs for "Coediquette" over the summer of 1940. A soccer player and chimes master in addition to his Musical Clubs activity, Lee composed music all day and poetry all night, apparently with "little opportunity to put in any laboratory work on co-eds."[43] Some sources claimed he was inspired to debunk the overworked line, "Four out of five co-eds are beautiful, and the fifth goes to Cornell." Entirely possible, for he was committed to advancing the position of women on campus, evidenced in 1941 when he and Evelyn Kneeland 1942 (then president of the Women's Glee Club) organized the Carnelian Chorus, a group open to both the men and women of the glee clubs. The plot of "Coediquette," unfolding in a parodical faculty meeting, ran as follows: the men are summarily flunking and the faculty wants to know why. The resulting inquiry reveals coeds are the root of distraction, so the faculty decides to do away with them. A forthright woman (played by a Glee Clubber in drag) steps forward to protest and wins over the malleable teachers. Subsequently the visionary profs reinstate coeds and vote to do away with grades.

Musically styled in the vein of Gilbert and Sullivan (with such song titles as "Flunk! Flunk! Flunk!" and "Chaos Chorus"), the operetta was reminiscent of the popular productions of the 1930s which had since trailed off. After *Pinafore* in 1934, a year was skipped despite calls from musical lovers for another "delectable operetta." *Princess Ida* was given in December 1936, the Ithaca premiere of the lesser-known work. Itself a satire of university life, *Princess Ida* was followed in 1938–1939 by *Trial by Jury*, the last revival of Gilbert and Sullivan staged by the combined forces of the music department, the Men's and Women's Glee Clubs, the Instrumental Club, and the Dramatic Club.[44] After a two-year hiatus, the campus was ready for more and bought up every seat for the 1941 Junior Week performance of "Coediquette."

When "Coediquette" was performed, it took up only the second half of the program. The first half was devoted to Cornell songs and a smattering of other light repertoire. A scant selection by Grieg or Sibelius was the only trace of "serious" repertoire left. Yet in the midst of their repertoire revolution, the Glee Club had found a way to, as the saying goes, "cultivate vocal culture," striking a balance between the light- and heavyweights on the program. The counterbalance to the variety shows was the formal Spring Concert, given annually with the Women's Glee Club beginning in 1934.

The Women's Glee Club had been founded in October 1920 by Lillian Dudley, a year before her husband took over the Men's Glee Club. Giving its first concert on April 29, 1921, the group's membership grew rapidly, crossing the one-hundred mark by 1928–1929.[45] The idea of a concert using both glee clubs was a natural outgrowth of the successful *Mikado* the semester before, and the first collaborative concert was a spectacular success, offering a program that included Gilbert and Sullivan joined by not the fight songs but Gounod, Wagner, Massenet, and Mozart. The next year's program brought "the glamour of the opera" and the "daring of the '90's" to Ithaca with a Floradora Sextet number in full costumes, a dance-duet from Humperdinck's *Hansel and Gretel*, and selections by Bizet, Bach, and Handel.[46]

Spring Concerts usually featured solo arias and duets in addition to the choral works, and more than one celebrated singer graced the Bailey stage in the April performances. Marie Powers, the renowned contralto who sang with the La Scala Opera Company of Philadelphia, joined the groups in the 1937 concert; Arthur Kent 1928, winner of the 1940 Metropolitan Opera Radio auditions, shared the stage for "Spring Fervor," the 1941 Spring Concert. But big-name artists did not have to be imported during those years—there were more than one in the making at Cornell. Both Powers and Kent had been pupils of the Dudleys, who over the years displayed masterful ability in taking in young voices and turning out successful vocal artists. Among those returning to sing with the clubs was Dorothy Sarnoff 1935, who took leading roles in the Gilbert and Sullivan productions and sang under Lillian Dudley in the Women's Glee Club. She went on to perform as soloist with the NBC Symphony Orchestra and Philadelphia Opera Company, later taking the leading role in Strauss's *Rosalinda* (an American adaptation of *Die Fledermaus*) on Broadway. Another Dudley pupil, Marie Maher Walkins of Cortland, made a last-minute substitution at the Metropolitan Opera in 1942 and was immediately signed to a two-year contract. And the Men's Glee Club had the inimitable Bruce Boyce 1933. A student in the Veterinary College who initially didn't know one note from the next, Boyce was encouraged by Dudley to study music when the director discovered the tall baritone in the ranks of the Glee Club. He was the star soloist of the Club through the early 1930s, the kind of singer who could turn Leoncavallo into a Junior Week hit, and in his first decade after graduation Boyce performed as soloist with the Montreal Symphony Orchestra, sang opera in Carnegie Hall, and twice gave recitals in New York's Town Hall.[47]

During the 1930s the famous weren't solely on the stage—they were also listening in the audience. The Baroness Vera von Eul of Holland (who later took Sarnoff back with her to Europe to study music) was in the 1934 audience of *H.M.S. Pinafore* and was completely enthralled with her first visit to an American college. "I have bathed in the Nile; . . . sold a 36-carat emerald for a bottle of water; I have been bear hunting in Alaska; I was the first white woman to enter Tibet; I have listened to the festival of Buddah; I have dined with the highest sheik of Arabia, but I have never been to college. I love your America, and your Cornell impresses me as a place with a future."[48]

Perhaps more impressive was the connection to American "royalty." On

February 18, 1932, the Glee Club performed a program as part of Cornell's Farm and Home Week, usually the territory of the University Orchestra. A letter was later received from the governor of New York, who had been in attendance:

Dear Mr. Dudley:

Mrs. Roosevelt and I were delighted to hear the Glee Club at the Master Farmer's dinner at Ithaca last week. The songs were a very pleasant addition to the program.

Very sincerely yours,
Franklin D. Roosevelt[49]

In May 1933 Bruce Boyce and the well-connected accompanist of the Glee Club William F. Detwiler Jr. were the weekend guests of the President and Mrs. Roosevelt in Washington, where they entertained for a White House lawn party and gave a private recital for the First Couple.[50]

Even when they weren't in the audience, notables somehow found their way onto the Glee Club patroness list, as was the case with the spring trip to Washington in 1936. The patronesses included the First Lady, the wife of the chief justice, Mrs. Charles Evan Hughes, Congressional wives, and the wife of the Chinese ambassador, Mme. Sao Ke Alfred Sze, whose husband happened to be Cornell Class of 1901. The notables even found their way into the scripts, including lines of "In the Red" which directed a few barbs at Eleanor Roosevelt. She probably wasn't on the patroness list for that concert.

Nor was she a patroness for the Christmas tour of 1937–1938, the year the Glee Club took "Oh, What a Night!" and beer on stage. The first Christmas tour in seven years, it almost had taken place a year earlier, but the 1936–1937 tour was initially postponed from Christmas to spring. Apparently the time was not yet right, and the tour folded for good early in March 1937; even so, the organization felt it was one of the most successful seasons since the prosperous 1920s and announced the Musical Clubs were giving a bang-up Senior Week show, "having risen like Phoenix from the troubled ashes of everybody's depression."[51] Economic conditions continued to improve, the change to a staple program of popular melodies with additional antics borrowed from New York reviews had quelled alumni complaints at least for the moment, and attendance at concerts was on the rise. Tour or not, there was a growing sense that a return to long, stably financed tours was near at hand. The 1937–1938 Christmas tour proved this true, taking the men from Buffalo to Chicago, Indianapolis, and Pittsburgh on an eight-city, seven-concert journey. Before it was over, the press wrote, "Debutantes and School Set Rule Society Activities," alumni audiences had joined the boys for a few drinks, and one young man had invited five young women to Junior Week.[52]

A Cornell Club president from Ohio wrote an enthusiastic letter after seeing "that concert, or whatever you call it." Indeed. The Glee Club's program had unquestionably become more of a "whatever you call it," and though response was generally enthusiastic, was the applause for musical excellence, or the old songs and comic antics? Several years later Foster Coffin, who had been elected to the Musical Clubs Council and continued to assist the Glee Club in planning tours, wrote with candor, "I well know that there were several years in there when the clubs were none too good. During the last year or two they have put on shows that have been distinct successes."[53] During the not very good period, perhaps the informal style of program was drawing a different field of auditionees or inviting a relaxed musical standard (membership itself remained constant at 65–70 for most of the decade). The clubs must have sensed all was not well with the keg-on-stage approach, and the program style took yet another turn on its tortuous path. A self-description for the 1938–1939 tour program advertised, "a high class musical show . . . producing a jovial atmosphere that brings back pleasant memories to all Cornellians and thrills those unacquainted with the Hills above Lake Cayuga." Elegance was gradually sneaking back into the program. The men now changed into tuxes during intermission. A joint performance with the Women's Glee Club of *Trial by Jury* at the 1939 Senior Week concert restored some musical integrity to the choice of staged entertainment, and the well-executed and popular Dick Lee productions followed in the next two years. By 1940 the reactionary New York City Cornell Club was still trying to make sure the program would be strictly Cornell songs and no arias. But other cities were looking for reassurance. A managerial letter to Indianapolis (which was visited on the beer-swigging 1937–1938 tour) in April 1941 said, "the show has changed. It is no longer the extremely informal concert. The boys appear in formal attire and through the cooperation of helpful suggestions of Cornell Clubs, before which we have appeared during the last two years we have built up a truely new type of entertainment which has met with enthusiastic approval of all who have seen our shows. . . . We have played to packed houses everywhere in the past two years."[54]

The account of attendance was not inflated. On the short three-city Christmas tour of 1940, all three performances were played to capacity audiences, and a Springfield music critic praised the concert as a brilliant event in the holiday season. Describing the group as an "old-fashioned glee club whose members appear to sing for the fun of it," he related that both the audience and the men had a wonderful time and that applause was long and loud at the finale, with curtain calls for composer Dick Lee and principals.

In those times it would be hard to know exactly what the reviewer meant by an "old-fashioned glee club." The Cornell Glee Club, if it was any indicator, had traveled all over the musical map in the past two decades, getting in turn more serious, more dramatic, more frivolous, and ultimately surviving musically stiff shirts and dangerously loose experiments before settling on a balance between the tradition of collegiate songs and the novelty of dramatic shows. It was at once the old and new, light humor and good glee club work, singing which

12. Audience at a CUGC tour concert, 1940s. Photograph by Erich Kastan.

apparently appealed to radio-age audiences. One time, at a Glee Club tour concert in Detroit, a man reportedly rushed into the lobby late, carrying a hamburger in his gloved hand. That was the Glee Club—they delivered a fairly unpretentious diet with the polish befitting the motets of Lassus or the prayers of Poulenc. And they did so with the unjaded passion of amateurs. For if old-fashioned simply meant ars pro artem, singing for the pure enjoyment of song itself, then Cornell's Glee Club was one of the outstanding and old-fashioned glee clubs in the country, not merely musically but in spirit.

Unfortunately, love of amateur singing was no longer as widespread outside the Glee Club. The general public's interest in singing had never fully recovered from its post–World War I decline. In "Students Twenty Years Ago and Now" Rym Berry compared singing habits along with studying, morality, drinking, and adventuresome spirit:

The masses no longer regard part singing as for the masses. It's a serious business for trained experts. Amateurs and common dubs are expected to chirp in unison if at all. Singing in unison is a deadly thing (beyond the third grade) and in consequence there isn't much general singing.

Twenty years ago nobody but a coward sang the air. Tenor or bass—it didn't make any real difference. One jumped in and took the end where he could be most useful at the moment.[55]

Indeed, impromptu serenading in town on a Friday night no longer existed. Men such as Hollis Dann and Archibald Davison were doing a great deal to cultivate and advance good singing—and in some areas, particularly high school music, teacher training, and opportunities for women, matters had much improved since the 1860s. In 1933 the Cornell Glee Club had taken part in a Rochester glee club festival with five other colleges and the Rochester Civic Orchestra performing works of Mendelssohn, Grieg, Bach, and Wagner; it was hailed as a great advance.[56] But outside the formal practitioners—amateur and professional—widespread interest and participation in singing on the order of the old days were gone, perhaps forever. Dann once said, "In the united singing of a large body of students there is a tremendous latent power which no American university has as yet utilized. The unifying and uplifting power of the music from thousands of students singing together in unison, supported by a great organ, will some day come as a revelation."[57] In America today that power is still unrealized.

Still the Glee Club did much to promote and preserve the traditions lodged in song and to encourage singing on campus. In addition to presenting their own Spring Sing, the Musical Clubs sponsored a song fest in spring 1940 for fraternities who would field a group and compete against each other. In that instance only three groups entered, and the audience was a few short of sparse, but better success was found as the year drew to a close. In those days Commencement and Reunions coincided on a shared weekend in mid-June. Preceding their 1940 Senior Week concert entitled "Reunion Time," the Glee Club arranged a senior-alumni sing on the steps of Goldwin Smith. Letters addressed to "Dear Ol' Glee Clubber" went out inviting former members to join their voices again with the students on the steps of Goldwin Smith an hour and a half before the concert began. Following the reunion of voices the Musical Clubs presented their Senior Week program subtitled "A Cornell Year in Song," which implies the Glee Club was able to make Cornell's tradition of song into a musical yearbook. After the concert seniors danced the night away to the sounds of Duke Ellington and his orchestra.

With graduation the seniors moved into the ranks of the alumni, and the Glee Club looked each fall for new men to fill the spaces. While general interest in singing was declining, interest in the group held fairly steady through the

Depression years. Dudley had each person auditioning fill out a 3 by 5 card asking, in addition to the usual background information, whether or not the candidate read music. One man answered, "I pretend to," while another wrote "Yes," crossed it off and wrote "No," crossed that off, and concluded with another, rather suspect "Yes." Both men made it. As of 1935 policy stated that men were chosen based on "musical and social qualifications" and admitted as associate members. Having taken an active part in the organization for a year, a man could then be elected to full membership. The 1939–1940 *Cornellian* listed 76 members, the peak enrollment to that point, and if the count is to be believed, membership made a tremendous leap to 92 the next year, with 23 first tenors alone. The steep rise and subsequent fall (membership returned to about 75 in 1941–1942) conceivably reflected the popular interest in Dick Lee's creative productions, or perhaps changing university enrollment, which stood at 6,000 in those days; civilian enrollment actually reached 7,315 in 1940–1941 before dropping sharply during the war years.

The music department had also grown significantly since the Dann days. Between his departure and Kinkeldey's arrival in 1923 the department consisted of Coleman and organist James Quarles. It slowly grew to six, and by 1941–1942 there were eleven musicians on staff. That year Roy Harris was appointed Cornell's first composer-in-residence, joining a faculty that included pianist Egon Petri, conductor and violinist Ronald Ingalls, and Max Exner, whose full-time appointment (jointly sponsored by music and rural sociology) was to assist rural churches with their music programs. The country's pioneer graduate program in musicology was joined by a graduate seminar in composition, and class enrollment steadily rose. In addition to the usual orchestras, bands, and choral ensembles, the Sage Chapel Choir kept a workmanlike pace, and university organist Richard Gore founded a coed A Cappella Choir, later renamed the Cornell Chorus (not to be confused with the still later, treble-voiced Cornell Chorus).

One group whose enrollment was not on the rise was the Instrumental Club. Named as such in 1934 when the Banjo and Mandolin Club had three banjos and but one mandolin, the group had undergone the same tumultuous repertoire ride as the Glee Club, adapting in part to accompany the vocalists (as with the Gilbert and Sullivan productions) and in part to the demands peculiar to instrumental music. For a time the Instrumental Club provided music for the postconcert dances; for a time they played such tunes as "Parade of the Wooden Soldiers" and the polka from "The Golden Age" by Shostakovich. Publicity in 1937 claimed the Instrumental Club had "come to be a full-fledged orchestra with a varied repertoire of classic, light, opera, and modern symphonic jazz";[58] that kind of eclecticism was to be expected from a band trying to keep pace with the evolution of music in the Swing Era and performing with a group changing musical clothes as fast as the Glee Club was. For a time, despite its shrinking enrollment and increasingly ambiguous purpose, the group nobly stayed afloat, and by its last year, though the mandolins and banjos had all but disappeared, the ensemble had expanded to include winds, brass, drums, piano, strings, and accordion. But the one thing the Glee Club's partner could not survive was the loss of its director.

George Coleman was forced to step down at the end of the 1940–1941 season because of the university's age regulation—he was about to turn 70. For forty years he had guided the instrumental half of the Musical Clubs, and was single-handedly responsible for the growth of other instrumental ensembles at Cornell, including the Marching Band, the University Orchestra, the Women's Instrumental Club, and the Women's String Ensemble. A valedictory concert was given in Bailey Hall on May 23, 1941, to honor Coleman, and former members of the orchestra returned to participate, including the author, historian, and radio show host Hendrik Willem Van Loon 1905, who had played violin under Coleman's baton when the maestro first took over the ensemble. One man recalled, "Mr. Coleman meant a lot to me when I was in college and . . . made it possible for me to build up some darn fine memories."[59] Cornell music could have said the same.

On August 11, 1941, Glee Club manager T. Crouse Barnum 1942 wrote to his predecessor that the Instrumental Club had folded.[60] Once the "lionized collegiate music-charmers" in the words of George Coleman, the mandolin players and their banjo-strumming associates had gone the way of the theorbo and lyre, and the Instrumental Club had followed.

The Glee Club had lost its companion of fifty years; the Musical Clubs were now just the Glee Club. The group had much to work out, and a lot more was on their minds beyond planning a program without the instrumentalists. War had again engulfed Europe. For several years the Glee Club tour contracts had carried war clauses, forseeing the day when they might be voided in a national emergency. Simultaneously a storm was brewing within the Glee Club. Dudley was approaching his 70th birthday and had only one year left with the group. No one wanted to see the Glee Club follow the Instrumental Club, and few if any felt it was a real possibility. But recent history made it certain that engaging a strong new director in troubled times was of critical importance.

Considerable preliminary discussion took place among then-chairman of the music department Paul Weaver (who also sat on the Musical Clubs Council), other members of the council, Dudley, and the fifth president of the university, Edmund Ezra Day. A series of letters between Dudley and Weaver followed over the summer of 1941, ironing out details of the director's retirement. As a direct result of the earliest correspondence the Musical Clubs Council drew up several resolutions at their meeting June 13 regarding Dudley's future. With the understanding that he would be automatically retired at the end of 1941–1942, and the Department of Music would have a choral specialist on staff in 1942–1943 who would be available to direct the Glee Club, moreover, wishing to recognize Dudley for his "long and distinguished service to the Glee Club," the council resolved that he would be named director emeritus at the close of

1941–1942 and retained for two years (at his present yearly salary of $1,500) to give special vocal instruction to members of the Glee Club. Following that time, he would be fully retired with a lifetime annuity of $900 payable by the council. The council, temporarily yielding its constitutional control over the post, requested the Department of Music provide the Glee Club with a new director in 1942–1943, and instruction for Glee Club members in voice training and production starting in 1944–1945. The council also encouraged what became a separate agreement between Dudley and the university, whereby he was appointed by the Board of Trustees to serve on staff as the university's voice teacher, an appointment terminable only when he was no longer "able to teach effectively." Having handled the matter with some degree of foresight, the Musical Clubs Council momentarily set it aside, and Dudley looked ahead to beginning his last full year as director of the Club.

In the early dawn of December 7, 1941, a young U.S. Army private saw a profusion of light on his radar set. He notified his commanding officer, who told him to ignore it. Still curious, the young man and another private followed the blip and concluded the radar must be broken. A few moments later, the Japanese struck. The next day the U.S. Congress declared war, again plunging the nation into the necessity of international bloodshed.

For a short time the Glee Club, like Cornell, was largely immune to the war. In the rather heavy volume of Glee Club correspondence the first letter even to acknowledge the war was dated December 22. And the scheduled Christmas tour to Buffalo, Pittsburgh, and other cities in the last week of December was not canceled, despite the contractual war clause. Instead it became the first tour since an early 1890s trip to the Midwest on which the Glee Club traveled without its accompanying instrumental friends. (The void was filled by intermittent use of several instruments during the program.) Soon, however, immunity from the war became impossible. The Junior Week and Spring concerts put unnerving thoughts in the background for a few hours, but America was intensifying the draft, mobilizing for large-scale conflict. The spring semester was eventually telescoped, forcing the Glee Club's commitments closer together and making necessary the cancellation of a Rochester concert. Manager Crouse Barnum recalled that in the last war the Glee Club had lost three managers to the call within four months. The foreseeable decline in enrollment and necessary financial belt-tightening caused immediate concern within the Glee Club, and with a period of uncertain leadership just ahead, the exigencies of war intensified the debate surrounding a new director.

A reconstruction of the ensuing political subterfuges suggests two of the polarized players were Weaver and Barnum, at least as Barnum describes it. On February 19, 1942, he wrote manager Ellsworth (Bud) Erb 1943: "I said that I was afraid that Prof. Weaver was after the Musical Clubs. I am sure of it from what I have seen." Barnum, having earned his degree in February and started military training in Syracuse, wanted to keep Dudley. He asked Erb to sound out several members of the Musical Clubs Council on the matter, including Treman, and to consult with Laura Bryant, longtime friend of Cornell choral music who was still serving as supervisor of vocal music in the Ithaca public schools since taking over from Dann in 1905. In a postscript longer than the letter itself Barnum suggested Bryant would work with Erb behind the scenes; according to her, Weaver could not control Dudley and therefore wanted to get a director he could control. Barnum added that through the new director Weaver would try to make more of a choir out of the Club, and to change the concerts from light to formal. After urging Erb to go ahead only if he was in agreement, Barnum wrote: "I must depend upon you to help me. I hope you want to do this. I think that it is in the best interests of the Musical Clubs."[61]

At least ostensibly Barnum's principal reason for pushing Dudley's case was the likely effect of the war. Having been away from school, he had a better idea of the situation abroad and the country's mobilization, which he considered to be very serious. Quite reasonably, he argued the new director would have to be a fairly young man with some experience and a great deal of talent—exactly the kind of man the military would draft, either for musical or other service.[62] Specialists were in demand. If the Musical Clubs Council was already bound to pay Dudley a salary, why not keep him on as director? By such an arrangement the Glee Club would avoid having to look for a replacement should the new director be called away. Moreover, Barnum contended, the university would be facing decreased revenues; income from tuition would decline, and governmental war taxes would injure the dividends on university investments. Keeping Dudley would lighten the financial burden of faculty salaries by approximately $3,000, and the university might then help the Glee Club by shouldering part or all of Dudley's $1,500 salary. Finally, Barnum knew that the war, however long it endured, could threaten the survival of the Glee Club. And he concluded Dudley was the man who would know how to keep a glee club together in such times.

Weaver, on the other hand, felt it was time for new blood and, in looking back several years later, justified his efforts to bring the Glee Club under university control, writing that if the department had not gained control of the two glee clubs and their situations, it could not have interested any choral director of recognized standing and ability in the work available in 1942.[63] Hence the lines were drawn—Barnum and Bryant backing Dudley, with others from the music department and university administration somewhere in or around the Weaver camp. These were anything but openly acknowledged front lines, however, and several players were operating largely from behind the scenes. Barnum wrote to Bryant on February 19, 1942, the same day he wrote to Erb, lamenting how difficult it was to further the affair they had planned without being on the scene. This statement in itself intimates their scheming on the sly, though it simply may indicate a wish to see Dudley continue in his post.

Whether Dudley was actively involved cannot be determined from the existing record; he did have his political past. And his June 1941 letters to Weaver have a distinctly self-aggrandizing tone. But once he made his views known, other people apparently were inclined to carry the ball a good way on their own. Barnum went so far as to write President Day after a visit to Cornell, quite possibly without consulting others in his camp. He contended that he had found a petition had been circulated among the members of the Glee Club and signed by almost all of them asking that the present director be continued in the coming year. President Day wrote back saying he acknowledged with interest Barnum's concerns regarding a new director, but personally felt it would be better for both the Musical Clubs and "the broader musical interest of the University" to continue with the plan outlined by the Musical Clubs Council the previous spring.[64]

Perhaps Barnum got carried away in his support of Dudley and became overzealous and slightly deluded about his role in the matter. But there is evidence that he was not worried about mere wind. At first glance Paul Weaver appears to be a mildly formal faculty musician going about his business and being hampered by the outspoken interests of an uncertain lobby, and maybe that was true. Questioning his intention to change the Glee Club's style of program could on its own be dismissed as mere opinion; a more formal program might warrant some financial concern in light of recent programming history, but it was hardly a contendable point for a chameleon like the Glee Club. Of legitimate concern, however, was Bryant's belief that Weaver wanted control of the group and its director from the outside. Was he interested in taking over as director himself, or was he going to play the puppeteer? There is little documentable evidence aside from the letters exchanged. If anything, Weaver is explicitly on record advocating a continued degree of autonomy for the Musical Clubs Council. Just before their June 13 decision he writes:

> The department ought to concern itself primarily with the artistic and educational aspects of the work of the Club. I consider it highly desirable that the Council continue to function as it has in the past: that is continue in control of policies and finances, continue to select and advise the student officers, and continue to advise the incoming director just as it has advised you [Dudley] over this long period of years.

Of course he was on the council. Moreover, there is a suspicious hint in his letters of an ostensibly inflated way of doing business, which may well have acted as screen to a secret set of intentions.[65] Much of this is speculation, but there is some reason to suppose that Weaver merited cautionary attention as the Glee Club moved to secure a new director.

Whatever the truth, it was open season for politicking, though no one involved wanted to roil the waters too severely. A bloated confrontational battle would shed disrepute on the Glee Club and the university. Barnum wrote that he didn't want to see "a fight of personalities," or punitive measures or any bitterness as a result. He added that the council and sundry other individuals involved should conduct their affairs "in upstanding business ways, and not as personal feuds, or where conditions are used as levers."[66] When the Musical Clubs Council met on April 20, 1942, they came up with a new set of resolutions in diplomatic fashion. The issued statement declared that the council reaffirmed "its desire and intention to adhere in general to the agreement made in June 1941 between the Council, the Department of Music, and the Administration of the University." Furthermore, because Dudley was willing and because the music department had, in light of the state of national emergency, recommended the university administration postpone for one year the planned development of other aspects of the choral field, it was resolved that if the university "finds it unwise or impossible to engage a choral specialist for the year 1942–43, the Council then request Mr. Dudley to continue as director of the Glee Club for that year, in lieu of the arrangement covered in the agreement of June 1941."[67]

Attention then turned back to finishing the war-eclipsed semester, and plans went ahead as though Dudley would retire. A farewell dinner was held, and indeed, it was farewell. Dudley did not return as director the following year. For the rest of his life he held the title of director emeritus and continued to teach voice and conduct the Presbyterian Church Choir. From time to time he would drop in at Glee Club rehearsal, even consent to conduct a few numbers, and in a somewhat serious, somewhat sentimental mood recall the old days. A concert program several years later mentioned, "His was a familiar figure seated in Bailey Hall, silently singing each song with the men."

Those honoring him at the farewell dinner might have recalled him in various moments from his twenty-one-year career as director of the Glee Club. They might remember him in his perennial vest and tie, standing in rather Alfred Hitchcockian profile as he led the group in song. There was that second chin that appeared as he scrunched over and peered down intently through his spectacles at a score, or that bright, spirited look in his eyes as he leaned into the swell of the music or embraced a former student. The Glee Club's rehearsal hours from 7:30 to 9:00 two evenings a week were reportedly "periods of genuine enjoyment, due partly to the genius of Eric Dudley . . . for instructive entertainment and . . . to the natural pleasure of rehearsing with a well trained group"; and his rehearsals were "a distinct pleasure for those who really love good music." Walter Gerould 1944 remembers some of that instructive entertainment. In his first rehearsal with the Club in the fall of 1940 they got as far as "Far above Cayug-" when Dudley "stopped us and in his most curmudgeonly manner gave us a 45-minute lecture on the pronunciation" of the lake.[68] It is not "Far above Ky-yu-ga," (the ky rhyming with sky) but rather "Far above Kay-yu-ga's waters," according to Dudley.

Allan Treman recalled one evening with the Presbyterian Church Choir:

"Dudley was a strict disciplinarian—punctuality included. One time after I had sung four or five years, I was five minutes late for a Thursday evening rehearsal. Dudley stopped the choir, laid his baton down and said, 'Allan, you are five minutes late. There are seventy in the choir tonight. Seventy times five equals three hundred and fifty minutes—about six hours wasted.' Needless to say, I was never late again!"[69]

In auditions, Dudley looked out not so much for experience as a "love of music and a desire to learn to sing." Glee Club members both in and out of rehearsal often received what amounted to "individual instruction in tone quality, reading, phrasing, and color," which drew many first-rate singers to the Club in Dudley's time. In the end his greatest gift was perhaps his skill as a voice teacher. And he had a passion for the profession. He wrote toward the end of his career:

> It takes many long years of experience and study to be an able and *safe* teacher of voice.
>
> The *voice* is the most delicate of all instruments, and it would seem to be the very height of folly for parents to think that *anybody* will do. . . .
>
> Why are these inexperienced teachers allowed to ruin our promising young voices? I have thought very, very much about this. I hope some day it will be legally impossible.[70]

Some anecdotes about his life may not have been known to those who knew him well. While at Camp Upton on Long Island during World War I, Dudley supervised part of the popular soldier show "Yip, Yap, Yaphank," which was later memorialized in the Army's stage and screen hit, "This Is the Army." One of the camp's song leaders also contributed to the show, someone called Irving Berlin. One morning, original manuscript in hand, Berlin came to Dudley to get his opinion on a song called "Oh, How I Hate to Get Up in the Morning." As the story goes, Dudley assured him that it sounded fine, and another Berlin hit was born.

Following World War I, the Dudleys presumed their service had earned them American citizenship, and for more than a decade they enjoyed all the privileges pertaining thereto, including voting. It wasn't until officials pointed out "carrying a tune instead of a gun in time of war" didn't qualify them as citizens that they learned they were still subjects of the king of England. They were officially naturalized on February 24, 1936.

On March 21, 1946, George Coleman died at his home in Tennessee. The faculty necrology read, "To literally hundreds he was the trusted guide, the constant advisor, the intimate and beloved friend."[71] Little more than a year later, his Musical Club colleague of several decades passed away. Hospitalized on April 22, Eric Dudley died on May 21, 1947. He made music until the end, his last major public appearance coming in February of that year, when he led the singing at the Nobel Prize awards dinner. Those who bore his coffin—among them Thomas Tracy and the Savage Club Quartet, including Truman (Trink) Powers and Allan Treman—bespoke the work of his life. Laura Bryant offered the following words as a fitting epitaph:

> With the passing of Eric Dudley, Ithaca loses a great artist and teacher of good singing, and a great choir leader. Our loss is incalculable. His devotion to his art, his uncompromising desire for perfection in singing, his loyalty to and support of all of us in the profession is something that cannot be replaced. His last work with the choir, "The Seven Last Words of Christ" just before Easter with the inspired singing of his devoted pupil, Thomas Tracy, will live forever in the memories of those who heard it—a fitting finale for the music life of Mr. Dudley.[72]

4　The War Years and Thomas Tracy, 1942–1957

> Voices of boys were by the river-side.
> Sleep mothered them; and left the twilight sad.
> ....
> For by my glee might many men have laughed.
>
> —Wilfred Owen (used in Benjamin Britten's *War Requiem*)

While stationed in France as a company commander during World War I, the young Wilfred Owen trained his poetic powers on the spectacle before him:

> Our eyes wept, but our courage didn't writhe.
> He's spat at us with bullets and he's coughed
>   Shrapnel. We chorussed when he sang aloft;
> We whistled while he shaved us with his scythe.
>
> Oh, Death was never enemy of ours!
>   We laughed at him, we leagued with him, old chum.
> No soldier's paid to kick against his powers.
> We laughed, knowing that better men would come,
> And greater wars . . .[1]

Owen was killed at the age of 25 on November 4, 1918, a week short of the Armistice. But within a generation his prediction of "greater wars" proved strikingly prophetic. In September 1942 Washington ordered members of the Army's enlisted reserve "be called to active service at the end of the term in which they should reach selective service age." That age was lowered to 18 in November. The presumption that students could take their degrees before taking up arms had to be abandoned. President Day pledged his university's resources to the national cause, and conceded, "For the duration of the conflict . . . there can be little or no education as usual."[2]

At the outset of the academic year, however, while the draft age was still fixed at 21, the Army could not call every young man. Another organization set up shop in the Willard Straight rehearsal room and recruited five new first tenors, five seconds, five baritones, and six basses. The most notable new recruit was the man running the auditions—John M. Kuypers.

Having come from Hamline University in St. Paul, Minnesota, where he was chairman of the music department, Kuypers was the university's answer to the director debate. His qualifications were formidable. Born on November 15, 1900, in Rotterdam in Holland, he came to the States at the age of 14. He earned his bachelor's degree magna cum laude from Carleton College in three years and became a viola player with the Minneapolis Symphony Orchestra. Kuypers also conducted the orchestra on numerous occasions and in his last three years in Minnesota led the Pro-Musica Sinfonietta, a chamber orchestra drawn from the ranks of the symphony. Meanwhile at Hamline, where he had been hired in 1932 to build up the music program, by final reports more than half the student body was singing regularly in one or more of his choral groups.

Choral director, violist, and orchestral conductor, Kuypers was a wise choice to fulfill the plans of the music department. As Kuypers came in and the Dudleys stepped out, the department intended to consolidate all the campus musical organizations under its umbrella. "Acting Associate Professor of Music" John Kuypers soon found himself conducting not only the Men's and Women's Glee Clubs, but the University Orchestra, the Chamber Music Society (or String Sinfonietta), and the Sage Chapel Choir. In addition, as though five ensembles weren't enough, he also developed the Cornell Chorus (formerly the A Cappella Choir), opening the group to "advanced members" of the glee clubs and choir. The response was so overwhelming, he had to form a Cornell Junior Chorus to accommodate the overflow.

The upswing in Cornell's musical activity looked like a war ending, not one beginning. Nearly 700 students were involved in the campus ensembles, with more than 100 in the Cornell Junior Chorus alone. According to the department's wishes, anyone who wanted the experience of singing or playing had a place.

The Glee Club numbered about 60 as the men settled into the weekly regimen of rehearsals Wednesday and Friday evenings. As they moved forward into the semester, people began to disappear; those remaining kept singing. The tour was canceled; they still kept on. In March the *Sun* announced the annual "Spring Show" for the night of the 19th in Bailey Hall, featuring the glee clubs, the Savage Quartet, and Swing Five, a new vocal group. That evening the men and women combined to perform music of Gilbert and Sullivan; apparently neither group was strong enough to perform on its own. The moving performance of Roy Harris's "Fighting Sons" for brass quintet, kettle drums, and organ stood in for those who could no longer be there. Together the glee clubs now numbered only 80 voices; the *Cornellian* photograph of the men, probably taken months earlier, had shown only 36.

Publicity for the Spring Concert, sounding like Max Detweiler promoting the Trapp Family Singers, had warned Cornellians it was "their final opportunity to hear the renowned campus vocal groups who . . . will not appear together in concerts for the duration . . . unless radical changes are brought about in present plans."[3] Radical change was not forthcoming. On April 22 Paul Weaver wrote to President Day:

> As was inevitable, the membership of the Men's Glee Club has dwindled rapidly since Christmas to the point where there are now just over thirty members left on campus. At the last rehearsal of the club there were only seventeen present, including the director. It has been obvious to Mr. Kuypers and others for some time that the organization should suspend its work for the duration.

Day agreed: "After the war is over, I hope we can get the Men's Glee Club off to a fine new start under Kuypers' direction."[4]

The suspension of Glee Club activity offered little hope for the days ahead and removed whatever shelter musical camaraderie could provide from the worries of war. But there was one small blessing. Political skirmishes that had persisted in the Glee Club came to an end. As Weaver told Day, "the position of Mr. Dudley in respect to the Glee Club has become increasingly awkward since December, and suspension of work solves that difficulty completely." Now Kuypers didn't have to work with someone looking over his shoulder, and Dudley didn't have to worry about the group carrying on somewhere without him. By the time the Glee Club reconvened, well after Allied victory was signed into history on September 2, 1945, more than two years had passed—the longest gap in the group's history since the dry spell of 1881–1883.[5]

Though the hiatus cooled Glee Club politics, the war years saw some housecleaning in the university, exposing a small mess involving Dudley, Weaver, and the administration. In efforts at streamlining, Kuypers and President Day inquired into Dudley's position as instructor in music.[6] Their findings shed some retrospective light on the Glee Club's director debate.

In June 1944, at the request of Dean Robert Ogden, Weaver submitted a record of his correspondence with Dudley concerning the latter's retirement as Glee Club director, and his subsequent appointment as university instructor. After perusing the correspondence, which dates from June 11 to August 3, 1941, the administration concluded Dudley had an unwarranted monopoly on the university's voice students; moreover, even though he was already past the university's retirement age, his appointment seemed unterminable by the university. A memo from President Day reads, "This situation should be cleansed. I never agreed to any monopoly for Mr. Dudley and if such exists, I think it should be broken. How do we proceed?" (According to a Weaver letter of June 17, 1941, Day had agreed—perhaps unwittingly—to the framework for such a monopoly.) Vice President George Sabine replied by memo to Day, "Unless there is something that does not appear in the written record, I'd call this a fast one." Sabine elaborated in a letter of July 3, 1944, claiming Weaver was responsible for Dudley's unprecedented appointment: "Throughout his negotiations with Weaver, Dudley was perfectly explicit and straight-forward. Weaver offered him an exclusive relationship to the Department, Dudley asked Weaver if this was agreed to by the University, and Weaver assured him that it was. Hence we have a kind of moral obligation toward Dudley, though the agreement on both sides was reached by Weaver's deception."[7]

So the administration reached its conclusion, although all this inquiry had little impact on Dudley's position. As for the Glee Club, the only issue directly concerning them at this time was fulfilling the 1941 commitment to a $900 per year annuity for Dudley. Weaver told President Day, "If I understand Mr. Treman correctly, . . . such a purchase [of the lifetime annuity] would more than wipe out the present treasury."[8] Day wrote Treman on July 6, 1944, requesting clarification:

> Perhaps you will be willing to let me know also of the financial resources of the Council, as well as the probable future functioning of the Council now that the directorship of the Glee Club has been taken over by a member of the University staff.
>
> What would you think of the establishment of a University musical board following the precedent of the Board on Physical Education and Athletics? Such a University board could provide for student representatives so that the members of the Glee Club could have a voice in the overall direction of the Glee Club activities.[9]

Treman replied a week later, describing the Musical Clubs Council and indicating he would be very willing to discuss the whole matter. (No such university board ever took shape to govern Glee Club activity.) He further stated, "The 'Cornell Glee, Banjo, and Mandolin Clubs' has on deposit in the Tompkins County Trust Company interest account $7,691.32 as of July 1, 1944. In addition, it has bonds (mostly railroad bonds purchased before I became treasurer) of about $11,000 present value."[10] The book value sounded substantial, but Treman knew the purchase cost of Dudley's annuity would clean out the entire savings account and dip into the bonds, with no ready means of recouping the loss. During wartime, a silent Glee Club meant no revenues. Barring measures that would bankrupt the Club, some way had to be found to honor the group's commitments. Somehow, while the Glee Club was little more than an idea, a memory, and a bank account, people such as Treman and Day saw that it held together.

During this difficult time, numerous members of the Glee Club, past and future, distinguished themselves in service to their country. First Lieutenant

Lucius Donkle 1948, for example, a future Glee Club manager, piloted a 104-foot Army vessel through the war in the South Pacific. And when peace returned in the fall of 1945, student-soldiers returned to civilian life and joined the ranks of academia in droves. Cornell's doors opened in October as students and faculty jammed into housing at close quarters, and the provost and his staff worried about finding enough beds to go around. Student activities, some nobly perpetuated by dedicated women and most reduced to bare existence, were filled with new life by the returning crowds. Glee Clubbers from the prewar days back at Cornell may have been a little intrigued to meet their new director—Paul Weaver. In fact he was director designate of both glee clubs and the Sage Chapel Choir, having switched places by some agency with Kuypers, who was now chairman of the music department.

Paul Weaver, familiar to the reader by now, was born in Reedsburg, Wisconsin, on July 8, 1889. He took his bachelor's degree from the University of Wisconsin in 1911, taught at Racine College, and then was named assistant supervisor of music in the St. Louis public schools. In 1919 he accepted a post as head of the University of North Carolina's music department, staying there for ten years. During the summer of 1929 he taught two courses in music education at Cornell. The administration was by then desperate to find a qualified candidate for the professorship in music, a post vacant since Kinkeldey had resigned in 1927, and appointed Weaver to the position and the department chairmanship, effective that fall. The move surprised some, as he had only a bachelor's degree and training largely in public school music, something unrelated to Cornell's curriculum. But he had university experience, and under his guidance the department slowly began to grow, notably taking on several new faculty members to teach applied music.

During the first decade of his chairmanship, he built the Music Library (probably with support from Kinkeldey, who returned in fall 1930) from ten records and a small collection of piano rolls to some 4,000 records, 300 rolls, and 300 bound scores. He oversaw the enlargement of Sage Chapel, arrangements for the new organ (the same Aeolian Skinner in the chapel today), and the addition of bells to the chimes. He collected and edited a book of Cornell songs released in 1940, and in 1943 Texas Christian University awarded him an honorary doctor of music degree. Nevertheless, his administration was subject to the criticisms invariably leveled in the wake of a leader as efficacious as Hollis Dann. As Harold Samuel writes, "There is no academic subject which is so much everybody's business as music."[11]

Following the war, with Weaver in charge and a little help from the Dudleys (still directors emeriti), the glee clubs reorganized and returned to peacetime singing.[12] The two groups drew about 120 singers between them—approximately 50 in the men's organization, and 70 in the women's. In April, announcements began to appear in the local press for a concert on the afternoon of Sunday, May 19, the first performance of the clubs in over three years. With a glance from student leader George Lewis (Pat) Landon 1948, the men began "Strike up a song to Cornell, and let the swelling chorus rise before us . . ." A tremor ran through the seats in Bailey Hall, a quiet, sweeping thrill of recognition at hearing this old friend from a distant and peaceful time. The Women's Glee Club soon appeared, offering a set of opera choruses. Alternating back and forth, the clubs finally joined to bring the program to its climax in a chorus from Borodin's *Prince Igor,* followed by a special Weaver arrangement of the Alma Mater, including the rarely heard third verse from the original six-verse poem.

In this anomalous year without a fall concert, Junior Week, a tour, or an active student management, the familiar Spring Concert provided a welcome sound for singers and audience alike. So did the Glee Club's annual Senior-Alumni Week concert, billed as "Cornell Sings Again," and preceded by the traditional sing on the steps of Goldwin Smith. Whereas the Spring Concert kept a fairly serious demeanor, the June program let its hair down with the Savage Club Junior Quartet, novelty numbers (including banjo and pantomime), and a healthy dose of the old-time Cornell songs. The audience applause was loud and long. One newspaperman summed up the general feeling: "It is good to hear Cornell's Glee Club singing again after three years of silence."[13]

After World War I a full year passed before Glee Club life settled back into prewar patterns. The post–World War II adjustment would take longer. Membership the first year back fluctuated, mostly downward, leaving a group of only 36 by year's end. When fall came, Weaver spent a long weekend in mid-October auditioning new candidates for the Club. The next morning, Monday, October 14, 1946, he was found dead in his bed, victim of what was thought to be a coronary occlusion. The Glee Club abruptly and sadly found itself without a director before convening for a single rehearsal.

What path the Glee Club's history might have taken had Weaver had a long tenure as director is difficult to say. In all likelihood, however, history would not have proceeded as it did during the next decade. Weaver had written Day in 1943, "The Glee Club show has seen its day." He would soon be proven wrong.

Only just back together the 1946–1947 Glee Club, facing the year ahead without a director, was at a critical juncture. Much remained in the way of postwar rebuilding, and the Glee Club had to take advantage of the influx of veterans. In fall 1945 Cornell had witnessed a small increase from prewar levels to an enrollment of 7,465 civilian students and about 800 Navy men. The 1946–1947 academic year opened with a deluge of 10,560 students, 6,227 of them veterans. The Glee Club's numbers made a parallel leap, climbing from 36 at year's end up to near 80. With no immediate assistance forthcoming from the music department Pat Landon, initially class of 1944 (eventually class of 1948) and student leader under Kuypers, took charge, organized the newly acquired singers, and put the group through its paces. Having served in Europe as a first lieutenant with the 15th Air Force, he brought unique leadership credentials to the

13. Thomas Tracy, c. 1946.

job. R. Selden Brewer 1940, who went by the name "Selly," also lent a hand in keeping the Glee Club solvent as graduate manager. By December 1946 the *Cornell Alumni News* could say "the Musical Clubs have been reborn."[14] Of course they meant the glee clubs, but the reference to days gone by was likewise a presage of days to come.

Also by December the Glee Club had found a new director, appointed by the reconstructed Musical Clubs Council, which now included Kuypers and Brewer. As unlikely as it may seem, the appointee already had a Cornell job as instructor in engineering drawing. And yet he was no stranger to Cornell music—the man of the hour was Thomas Tracy. Familiar for more than a decade to Ithaca audiences as a baritone soloist, Tracy had served as assistant director under Dudley during the 1930s. Now at 38, he made the step up to the directorship, following in the footsteps of his British mentor.

Thomas Tracy was born a few miles from Ithaca in Owego, New York, on April 1, 1908. As a youngster he sang in the choir of St. Paul's Episcopal Church there and was educated in the Owego schools. After high school he enrolled at Annapolis. Perhaps it was in his blood. His grandfather, Benjamin Tracy, was secretary of the Navy under President Benjamin Harrison, earning in the estimation of some the designation "father of the modern Navy." A military career was not in the cards for the grandson, however. After two years at the academy Tom Tracy was honorably discharged for color blindness. Having the requisite background in science, he transferred to Cornell's College of Engineering and continued his studies.

During his undergraduate years he made the weekly commute to serve as organist at St. Paul's in Owego and found time for academic work and singing as a soloist with the Glee Club. In 1931 he graduated from Cornell with a bachelor's degree in mechanical engineering. Following a stint with a chemical company he was appointed instructor at Cornell in 1936, teaching hotel engineering. He also continued to study voice with Eric Dudley.

During the war he taught in the engineering school under the Navy's V-12 program, began his M.M.E. in 1944, and kept his hand in music at the First Presbyterian Church of Ithaca, substituting as both organist and conductor. When the Glee Club was looking for a new director, ties to Dudley, the Glee Club, and the church proved fortunate for Tracy, and he got the nod. Although several alumni have served as acting directors, he remains the only Cornell graduate appointed to the Glee Club directorship.

With his robust figure and booming voice he assumed control of the Club and headed the group not only back on track but back in time. A managerial letter in 1947 asserted that things were gradually getting back to normal at Cornell and that after six months of work the Glee Club was looking and sounding like it did under the direction of Eric Dudley.[15] One has only to recall that Tracy worked with Dudley during the heyday of the variety shows to guess what was in store. The Glee Club came out with "'47 in A-Chord" for the Junior Week concert that year, written and staged with a healthy sampling of Cornell songs intercut by several specialty acts, including tongue-in-cheek tales of life and death, "The Birth of Donald Duck" and "The Shooting of Dan McGrew." The program received strong acclaim, and the Glee Club took the show on tour to Rochester, Utica, Albany, Long Island, and New York over the April recess. A spring concert with the Women's Glee Club followed in May, and the year closed in Bailey with the traditional Senior Week show, dedicated to Eric Dudley. Hence all the prewar traditions were reinstated by the end of Tracy's first season. And the bank book, which showed $22.13 at the outset of the year, closed with an estimated net profit of $1,077.97.

Cut loose from the university by Weaver's death, the Glee Club had once again become an independent, self-supporting organization, responsible for covering the director's salary, the cost of new music, and any other incidental expenses. Financial success thus had been essential, and based on the 1946–1947 achievements, the Musical Clubs Council sent a letter to President Day requesting both glee clubs be kept under the administrative guidance of the council, rather than the university, for an indefinite period. The council argued the year showed a strong revival of activity and interest in the glee clubs, assured the president the current group's work was "entertainment of high caliber," and affirmed the recent spring tour had rendered a valuable goodwill service to the university.

The statement was encouraging, but not everyone thought the matter was settled. In September 1947 two letters passed between Allan Treman and the new chairman of the music department, Donald Jay Grout. Grout, a man of substantial erudition who remains familiar for his classic book *A History of Western Music,* expressed his interest in reestablishing a liaison between the department and the glee clubs, with the result that a director of the glee clubs would be drawn from the music faculty. The tone of the letters suggests the department was looking to relieve Tracy of his duties at the earliest opportunity. Sensing this situation, Tracy or Treman may have encouraged the council to approach President Day; apparent support voiced for Tracy forestalled any immediate departmental action and ensured he would have at least one more year on the podium.

The 1947–1948 year was a full-force return to nationwide exposure for the Glee Club, including a performance on ABC radio's *Tommy Bartlett Hour,* and a full-length Christmas tour ranging from Pittsburgh to Chicago, appropriately entitled "Here We Are Again." One publicity release advertised "Not wine! Not women! But song aplenty," which proved true—the Club survived one preconcert manhattan and martini party and a slew of postconcert dances where the hostesses all arrived with their own dates. And of course they sang, not to mention joked, mimicked, and told stories. By Senior Week the program had turned into a circus, literally. "Come to the Fair," advertised by a pair of managerial compets (competitors for managerial positions) wearing sandwich boards all over campus, came complete with "sideshows, barkers, jugglers, lions, tigers, and elephants." The audience turned out in droves, and with grads young and old singing from their seats, the Glee Club achieved its purpose of the moment—"to bind Cornell together in song."

As to the security of Tracy's position, one of the student managers summed up the year saying, "Mr. Tracy has a remarkably outstanding ability to inspire and fire the group. This [is] coupled with his keen ear and acute knowledge for music . . . he is well liked and very popular with the men."[16] Student support was bolstered by outside opinions from press and alumni, which may have done more to quell the music department's appetite for change. One alumnus called the "Here We Are Again" tour "a credit to the University," and after the program was repeated at Junior Week, the *Ithaca Journal* spoke of the "real artistry of the Club and the careful directing of Thomas Tracy."[17] By the end of 1948 President Day seemed satisfied, writing, "The Club has always been one of our best media of spirit and goodwill, and here on the campus it continues to make a remarkable contribution to the University community."[18]

Tracy now was free to continue implementing his vision of a college glee club or, perhaps more inadvertently the character of the Club came to reflect his feelings about its ideal spirit and style of performance. His approach, though not unfamiliar, was yet another turn in the Glee Club's evolution.

The 1940s had begun with the Dick Lee productions; Dudley's tenure closed with similar-style variety shows. Kuypers steered toward greater seriousness in musical programming but was forced into a corner by the war. When the singers returned, Weaver allowed the Glee Club a fair number of Cornell songs, both at the beginning and the end of the program, alotting more of the serious repertoire to the Women's Glee Club. But he was certainly committed, as other department colleagues were, to encouraging a more ambitious level of programming, and there were no scripts used as framing devices. Then came Tracy and with him a program most akin to Dudley's later clubs, putting the final spin on a tumultuous ten years.

Mary Lou Tracy, who married Tom Tracy in September of 1939, recalls her husband's tastes. "He liked a variety. He liked serious music, but not totally— he thought you'd lose the interest of most of the groups you're singing for. He thought there should be some of it [serious music], and plus he wanted the Club to learn to appreciate it. I think Tom really did feel though, when they took a show on the road, alumni interest was definitely for the lighter stuff. The alumni, they really love light things, much more so than the heavies."[19] So the program included the "Battle Hymn of the Republic," "Loch Lomond," and the ever popular Grieg's "Land-sighting," along with such songs as "The Jolly Beggars," "Hey Diddle Diddle," "Dry Bones," and "Over the Rainbow." A 1950 self-portrait read, "light and serious music [combined] with outstanding college specialty talent in a show providing fine entertainment for non-Cornellians as well Cornellians," a description distinctly resembling that of 1937. The group's appearance on the *Tommy Bartlett Hour* was listed in a Chicago newspaper's entertainment section under "Variety, Comedy, and Drama" rather than "Music," which was indicative in some way. While music was not absent, the program included a rendition of "Casey at the Bat," garbled stories about "Ali Theeva and the Forty Babs" and "The Loose That Gaid the Olden Geggs," juggling, magic, and Scotty Edwards's imitation of Victor Borge's phonetic punctuation skit. "He'd just do sounds," Mary Lou Tracy says, "that you wouldn't believe were possible, or human."[20] Summing up all these skits and sounds, an ad called the Glee Club's program a mix of "music, mirth, and madness."

The programmatic style espoused by Doc Davison by now had many followers, but with Tracy in charge the variety show enjoyed a vogue at Cornell well into the 1950s. The following list shows the diverse production titles for Tracy's programs:

1946–47	'47 in A-Chord	Strike Up a Song
	(Junior Week, Spring Tour)	(Senior Week)
1947–48	Here We Are Again	Come to the Fair (SW)
	(Christmas Tour, JW)	
1948–49	Daze of '49 (ST)	To Hill and Gone (SW)
1949–50	Notes of '50 (JW, ST)	Gullible Travelers (SW)
1950–51	Minor to Major (JW, ST)	Base Cleff (SW)

1951–52	Out of This World (JW)	Total Eclipse (ST)
	Take a Note (SW)	
1952–53	Occidental on Purpose (JW)	(no title, ST, SW)
1953–54	From Far Above (ST)	
1954–55	From Blue Cayuga (ST)	
1955–56	Stand By for Song (ST, SW)	
1956–57	All Hail Cornell (ST)	

In postwar days, bubbling over with nationalistic enthusiasm in any form, Tracy's term was a return to the supremacy of Cornell songs, to the Glee Club as a catalyst and collectible for alumni in search of school spirit. They flew under a crest reading, "Such is the purpose and pleasure of the Cornell Men's Glee Club: to reaffirm the bond between alumni and Cornell."[21] It was a return to the idea of a "college club" à la Rym Berry's "dear dead days," the "college club" advanced by erstwhile proponents in the *New York Evening Post.* And with return came predictable consequences—the revival of concerts with other college clubs revolving around athletic events. The tradition first reappeared in fall 1948, when Cornell's Glee Club shared the stage with Army's. The first fall concert since 1941, it rattled the seats of Bailey when the two ensembles, 180 voices strong, blended to sing "The Battle Hymn of the Republic," "Brothers, Sing On," and the two Alma Maters. Then Dartmouth came to Ithaca in 1950, followed by Michigan in the fall of 1951, renewing intercollegiate goodwill on and off the stage. Both clubs appeared with Cornell in fall 1952, the same fall the Penn tradition was resurrected in Philadelphia (with a concert dubbed "First and Ten"). For the next three years, Thanksgiving was spent with Pennsylvania, in addition to home performances with Columbia, Dartmouth, and again Columbia from 1953 to 1955.

The resurgence of fall activity was but one sign of music flourishing in Ithaca. By any standard the postwar years were a boom for both the Glee Club and the rest of musical life at Cornell. Sped by the enrollment explosion a tremendous interest in music manifested itself on campus. The 1946–1947 Bailey Hall concert series was sold out in the spring of 1946, months before the first notes were played, and the quartet concerts given by the resident Walden String Quartet had to be repeated in toto to please local listeners. The Rochester Philharmonic, already booked for a March concert, was engaged for an additional winter concert. Nor did concerts want for musical excitement. The March RPO concert brought a young Leonard Bernstein to Ithaca for the first time. Only 28 years old, the wunderkind conducted Haydn's *Symphony 102,* Copland's *Danzon Cubano,* his own ballet score *Facsimile,* and Beethoven's *First Piano Concerto* (which he led from the piano). One critic wrote, "It is difficult for this reviewer even to imagine a more sensational evening of music than yesterday's."[22]

A remarkable 40 percent of audiences at these concerts were students, much

14. Tracy and the Glee Club in concert at Bailey Hall.

higher than the level today. Kuypers suggested music's newfound popularity was a nationwide trend, perhaps attributable to the weary effects of war and the joie de vivre people felt having emerged. He added that "students know their symphonies," a positive influence of radio possibly, and in "approaching music from a fresh point of view and with an open mind, their frequently shrewder evaluations are sometimes better than those of people steeped in music."[23]

With such remarkable student interest in music, the Glee Club's cup ran over. The 1949 Junior Week program, "Daze of '49," recalled the days of the 1849 gold rush, and for the Glee Club the gold rush was just beginning. In 1950, not unlike the modern scramble for Big Red hockey tickets, people waited in line all night for Junior Week tickets. The demand to see "Notes of '50" was so great, hundreds had to be turned away, and the show was repeated in Bailey Hall a month later. For the next few years, the Junior Week concert was given on two nights back to back, with the expected box office benefits. The Fall Weekend concert also became a doubleheader, packing Bailey on the eve and evening of game day, and for a year the Glee Club mined five home concerts—two fall, two Junior Week, and one Senior Week. After that high point, with Junior Week having gone the way of the Banjo and Mandolin Clubs in 1954, the remaining three concerts continued to be extremely profitable throughout the 1950s. The 1956 Fall Weekend concerts alone brought in more than $5,000.

The Glee Club's popularity with audiences paralleled expansion within the singing group. Since university enrollment had gone over 10,000 in 1946–1947, the Glee Club had enjoyed a stream of students interested in participating. After ascending to 95 in 1947–48, membership hit a high watermark of 97 in 1948–1949, presuming the *Cornellian* listing can be trusted. Membership showed little sign of decline the next year, but the size was becoming unruly for rehearsal purposes. So in the fall of 1950, Tracy formed the Orpheus Glee Club, resurrecting the name as designation for a junior ensemble. The "embryonic choral group" was "primarily for interested freshman and sophomore warblers," its purpose being "to give more men the opportunity to sing as members of a glee club, as well as to provide each with the more personalized instruction possible only in a small group."[24] In its first year the group took on some fifty singers, leaving about as many to the Glee Club. The young group shared the spotlight at Junior Week and gave several additional concerts on its own, including a spring tour that visited cities close to home.

A year prior to the Orpheus Glee Club's appearance, another group emerged from the ranks of the Glee Club—the Cayuga's Waiters. In what can be considered the advent of a cappella small group singing on Cornell's campus (at least as we know it today), the Waiters made their first public appearance at the 1950 Junior Week concert. Officially a triple quartet (though sometimes a baker's dozen), they enjoyed a meteoric rise to campus fame, singing songs such as "Goodnight Little Girl" and "Blue Moon," mixed in with an array of other popular ballads, spirituals, barbershop harmonies, and specialty numbers such as "Goofus." The group added color to the Glee Club's programs and within a year was keeping a busy schedule of its own, with gigs in and out of town.

As the Glee Club grew, so did other musical clubs. Its members participated in the Octagon Club, founded after the war to produce original musicals and so named because its membership was drawn from the eight colleges then in existence at Cornell. By 1950 their spring musical comedy had a following large enough to warrant consideration of a complementary fall revue. More closely allied to the Glee Club, the Savage Club also found itself popular with a distinguished group of people. Meeting over beer and pretzels in their East Green Street rathskeller, the Savages entertained each other according to only one fixed rule: he who is called upon must rise and perform, or forfeit his membership. In addition to undergraduate Glee Clubbers, those who found themselves defending their membership with a song, story, or other act included Tom Tracy and music department chairman Grout. Even President Deane W. Malott, Cornell's sixth president and successor to Edmund Day, dropped in on occasion. When funds ran low, the meeting was moved to Bailey Hall where, minus the beer and pretzels, the group would demonstrate its multifarious talents for a paying audience. Titles for the public programs were always given in the peculiarity of the Savage tongue, resulting in such names as "Pacsloof ni Segavas." The tie with the Glee Club was so strong during the 1950s, the Savages were invited to stand in for West Point's Glee Club when the cadets couldn't come for a spring 1955 concert with Cornell. That concert, entitled "Songs and Savages," was followed by collaborations in the next two years.

The postwar boom in attention to music, manifest by the mounting numbers in groups and their audiences and reflected in corresponding financial success, brought prosperity to even the greatest of the Glee Club's sinkholes—tours. After a 1949 spring trip had to be scrapped, the Club rebounded in 1950 with a strong spring tour, playing "Notes of '50" to appreciative audiences across the Midwest. With a healthy postwar economy the Glee Club was asking and getting $500, $600, $800 guarantees from local Cornell clubs, on top of which money was still left over for local Cornell scholarship funds from the fifty-fifty split of remaining profits. When the tour grossed a profit in 1947, it must have been a revelation for Treasurer Treman—since the early 1920s, three decades of Glee Club management had struggled with tours that had no prayer of breaking even. By the early 1950s profitable tours were commonplace. The Glee Club could draw up a schedule and, confident of their financial leverage, simply offer dates, knowing most clubs would be inclined to take them.

With everything going so well, at least in the ostensible categories of money and membership, the Glee Club could afford to think more ambitiously. In October 1950 an initial invitation to bring the Glee Club to Brazil was received from the Sociedade de Cultura Artistica. Offering concerts in both Sao Paulo and Rio, along with covering the cost of transportation, the organization wrote, "the friendship between Brasil and America is already an old tradition," one which would be strengthened by such a tour, "provided those on whom, in this crucial hour, depends the world's destiny, don't interfere with our worthy desires and pacific plans."[25] Even as they ran confidential creditability checks on the Sociedade through Cornell contacts, the Glee Club considered the possibility of expanding the tour to include stops in Venezuela, Puerto Rico, and Cuba.

After the Sociedade was initially given a clean bill of health in November, doubts as to their ability to cover the travel expenses arose in early December. Talks went on for months while Glee Club management investigated other sources of funding, including the U.S. Department of State, but queries were answered in the negative; with no additional funds available the idea was abandoned. For the short term ambitions were channeled into domestic tours. In spring 1953 the group toured the northeastern seaboard, stopping in Boston on April 2. Rather remarkably, that performance was the Glee Club's first tour stop in Boston, even though they had reached the West Coast and set foot on British soil before including their New England neighbors on a tour itinerary. (The group had performed previously in Boston with Harvard, but those occasions were always independent trips.) Still, having caught the scent of an international tour, the managers kept their noses to the air for a new opportunity. Late in 1952, months before the Glee Club visited New England, the management had already put plans in motion for a cross-country tour. Still harboring ideas of visiting American neighbors to the south, the group approached Mexico in July 1953, and in August, Mexico City agreed to a concert on March 28, 1954, in the Palacio de Bellas Artes. It was a remarkable opportunity for cultural exchange, and the first chance in more than half a century for the Glee Club to cross international borders.

Helped in part by anticipation of the trip, the Glee Club found itself riding a wave of growing popularity into the 1954 tour. The Waiters, by far the most eminent garçons in town, were booked for a week at Bermuda's Castle Harbor Hotel over the 1953–1954 Christmas break. In a short time they had become the most sought-after entertainers on the Hill, which only added to the Glee Club's popularity in concert. Meanwhile the media spotlight on the entire group intensified as the 1954 tour approached, affording the Glee Club opportunities to step into national prominence before ever setting foot on the plane. As pre-publicity for the journey the Glee Club was booked to be heard on the Mutual Broadcasting System's College Choir and Glee Club series. The prerecorded performance was aired on December 27, 1953, Cornellians across the country tuning in to hear what Mutual commended as "a beautifully planned and executed performance." Adhering to the publicity philosophy of "get all we can," the Glee Club pressed on along other promotional avenues, investigating the possibility of a TV appearance with someone like Ed Sullivan. The coup came when managers secured a spot on the *Perry Como Show.*

Singing on television was not new to the Glee Club. While on tour with the Glee Club in 1951, the Waiters had been seen in many midwestern homes. That same trip, the whole group had made its first television appearance on NBC's *Kate Smith TV Hour.* Mary Lou Tracy recalls the evening: "We didn't even have television, and my friends invited me over. I always remember because they were also passing around Alexander. First time I'd ever had a [Brandy] Alexander in my whole life. I thought it was the most delicious thing. We were sipping Alexanders and listening to the Cornell Glee Club."

Scheduled to appear February 19, 1954, on the nationally broadcast CBS program, the Glee Club arrived that morning at the New York studio and spent the day rehearsing with Como and the Mitchell Ayres orchestra. Uncertain nerves were calmed a bit when the orchestra broke into spontaneous applause at hearing the singers' rendition of the "Evening Song." At precisely 7:45 P.M. the orchestra kicked in with a swell as viewers across the country heard the show's regular announcer, Richard Stark 1934 say, "the Perry Como Show, with all the top tunes on TV, brought to you by Chesterfield . . . and now here's our star, Perry Como."[26] After opening up with a saccharine and swoony rendition of "Heart of My Hearts," Perry Como turned over the stage to Tracy and the Glee Club. This was it—live TV. On a set of stairs beside ivy-draped pillars representing the portico of Goldwin Smith Hall, the Glee Club opened with a verse of the Alma Mater. The clock tower looked on from a distance, set in front of

15. Thomas Tracy and Perry Como exchange pleasantries during the Glee Club's appearance on the *Perry Como Show,* February 19, 1954.

a backdrop of stars in the night sky. As the opening verse graded into a hum, Tracy stepped forward to chat with the host:

> Perry Como: I understand you're just about to go on one of your international tours.
>
> Tom Tracy (hitching his hands on his trouser pockets and starting out in a rather strong voice): Yes we are, Perry. On March 26, in a special Pan American World Airways Clipper, the boys and I take off for Mexico City, Los Angeles, San Francisco, Houston, Denver, Atlanta, Tulsa, Topeka, and Davenport.
>
> PC: You were reading those, you know.
>
> TT (feigning incredulity): Oh, really?

The singing continued with a hand-clapping, knee-slapping barnyard selection, "Cindy," featuring soloist Irving Pettit 1955, followed by the first verse of "Evening Song" to close out the Glee Club's segment of the program. Musically the group sounded top heavy, in part because "Evening Song" was sung in B, a fourth up from its usual key of F# major. But the men appeared to enjoy themselves, and aside from a few eyes tempted from the conductor by the cameras, the performance came off well.

With a wandering manner and distracted eyes Como looked at times as though he didn't know quite what to do with the Glee Club's director. Accepting the host's congratulations on the performance, Tracy nearly shook Como's arm off. But the two followed the ordained script fairly well together, exchanging a few pleasantries before parting ways. Como closed out the show with "Night and Day" from the night-cloaked "campus" of Cornell.

From the publicity point of view the appearance had achieved its goal. Calls came in from Cornellians and non-Cornellians all over the country requesting ticket information for tour performances. Final arrangements were made, passports secured, and bags packed. On March 26, 1954, the men boarded a chartered DC-4 named *Messenger Clipper* and headed for Atlanta accompanied by a five-man crew, the Tracys, the Tremans, the Brewers, and Foster Coffin. The proud sign on the fuselage read, "Cornell University Glee Club 1954 Spring Tour."

Appropriately entitled "From Far Above," the program was flown city to city at an exhausting pace. From March 26 to April 3 the Glee Club gave nine concerts in nine cities, a concert a day. And what days they were—rehearsals, tours, performances, and in one case a flight of 1,750 miles across two time zones. Somehow, the jet-set troubadours summoned enough energy for each concert, perhaps inspired by the fifteen thousand alumni and friends who attended, some driving more than five hundred miles to hear the Club. The critics found no signs of weariness or lapsed concentration. The Los Angeles press wrote, "Their manner was more that of a natty stag at the junior-senior prom than a troupe of haggard travelers," and further commented, "These young men happily hit a midway mark between the too emotional and the too rigid. They have enthusiasm, disciplined skill (not a pair of eyes veer from Conductor Thomas B. Tracy) and proper phrasing." The local alumni, celebrating a "Cornell Glee Club at Last," made it clear they wanted to see the group on "an annual rather than centennial basis." The Glee Club gave joint concerts with the University of California in San Francisco and with Dartmouth in, of all places, Tulsa. In Mexico the government rolled out the red carpet, and the Glee Club responded in kind, closing their program with the Mexican national anthem, sung in Spanish. On the April 4 flight home, the captain circled low over the campus on his way to the Binghamton airport. It seemed like a victory lap; Cornell's Glee Club had returned home safely, enthusiasm running high within the group, and for the group all over the continent.

Having begun the academic year back at the now distant Freshman Activities Fair, the Glee Club closed out 1953–1954 with its Senior Week and Commencement performances. They had logged some 8,000 miles, several LP bands, ten minutes of national TV time, and an audience in the tens of thousands—the peak year of Tracy's directorship. In the next few years the experience of men singing together would continue beneath the veneer of prominent (or not so prominent) performances and tours. But Tracy's last clubs never again achieved the summit of 1953–1954. That is not surprising; a club cannot be expected to repeat that kind of success annually. Nevertheless, related or not, there were gathering signs that all was not as well with Cornell's Glee Club as it could be. A period of adjustment and growing pains was near at hand.

There were some musical concerns. Like many groups the glee clubs of those years had their good and bad concerts, celebrating and suffering the inevitable vicissitudes of performing. After the 1951 Fall Concert with the men of Michigan (which, incidentally, Michigan praised effusively in every sense), one manager wrote, "There has been a good deal of excitement here among the singers, as a result of a rather weak performance over Michigan weekend. All in all, it has done a lot of good; they are really out to do a good job now, and I think that the rest of the shows this year are going to be damn good."[27] Two years later Selly Brewer wrote expressing reluctance over allowing the Glee Club to go to New York during the fall season because of lack of proper preparation, whereas in the spring the group could "put on a performance that would favorably compare with other college groups."

Having accepted a late November engagement in New York nevertheless, he underlines the problem in another letter of that same year, saying that because the Club is not up to its full strength and quality, Tracy would prefer an abbreviated show in some hotel ballroom or similar location rather than a place like Town Hall.[28]

Curiously these letters date from the summer and fall of 1953, the year of peak activity. Why was the Glee Club getting off to a sluggish start? Was it simply too early in the year? Granted, in those days classes did not begin until middle to late September, but fall football concerts often took place in October—late November should have given the Club more than enough time to attain a level comparable to other organizations. Was the insouciant mood of the Glee Club's repertoire sliding over into its rehearsal practices? Were there other musical problems? Mary Lou Tracy offers some insight, referring to the original wave of veterans and its eventual drop-off. "When he [Tracy] took over the Glee Club, those voices he was working with were far more mature than the ones coming out of seventeen year-olds. I recall so clearly, after all those older boys had graduated, the difference in the amount of time he'd have to spend with them to get them shaped up. It made quite a difference." It is true that by 1953 the flood of GIs entering college would have dwindled to almost nothing, and by then the young Club may have sounded a little wet behind the ears.

She also recalled evening prelims creating numerous conflicts, which resulted in a troublesome level of absenteeism. Whatever the causes, and Brewer may have had others in mind, the decreasing number of older students could have been only part of the picture. Most collegiate groups faced the same predicament, and most glee clubs at Cornell never had the advantage of GIs to begin with. Nevertheless, the shift in vocal maturity was an adjustment, and possibly Tracy found more work than he wanted in directing the younger voices.

Along with whatever musical problems attended rehearsal, there was some dissent over the Glee Club's concert style. After the 1952 Senior Week concert, quite a few people from President Malott on down voiced their displeasure about the master of ceremonies (who apparently drew his pitch from the burlesque and saloon); it was in Malott's words "particularly inappropriate to have a lovely religious number introduced with a sexy secretary story."[29] Though many of the skits and introductions were popular, clearly their success was not absolute. Comments registered a year later included a complaint about the MC's grammar: "The masters of ceremonies were nice and clean, but I liked it better when they played it straight and did little more than make the announcement of the next number. Humor seemed a little labored, and the grammar slipped some."[30]

Some of these mishaps of "good taste" may have influenced the Club to change its tone of program slightly, which leads us to the greater growing pain, one that would occupy the rest of the decade: the repertoire question. In fall 1953 the Glee Club had received an invitation to perform Handel's *Messiah* with the women of Wells College. They declined, but not for the expected scheduling reasons. A letter of reply read, "Mr. Tracy feels that the club is not a proper unit for such a rendition."[31] The women of Wells were referred to the Sage Chapel Choir. In an inconspicuous way this response put a new Glee Club position in writing. Dann's, and at times Dudley's glee clubs had once been the proper groups for formal music, but not anymore. Tracy liked oratorios—he had sung in many as a soloist, and felt it worthwhile to expose the students to that repertoire. But he felt that major works, be they oratorios or masses, did not belong in the Club's daily diet. Consequently the usual avenues to performance of those works were not pursued. Even though Tracy had taken over the Women's Glee Club in the early 1950s, relations between the two groups had atrophied, Tracy having kept them separate. And over the next few years several other outside invitations to collaborate were declined on the ground that the proposed style of program was not compatible with the Glee Club's.

Was the Glee Club falling out of step with choral progress? While in California the group gave a joint concert with the University of California Glee Club. Neither club was strictly serious, seeing as the California group gave one number, "Daisy," with burlesque ballet accompaniment. But one critic's observation that 60 percent of the Cornell Glee Club had crew cuts to only 20 percent of the California singers perhaps implied something about the chosen repertoires. Another San Francisco critic wrote:

In short, the University Glee Clubs' joint concert might very well come under the heading of sports. And when it comes to scoring—let's be honest. Cornell walked off with top rating for stage appearance, English diction, and vocal finesse. But U. C. scored by its repertoire, presenting the only serious music of the evening.

Cornell's repertoire was comprised almost entirely of the rhythmic patter type of humorous ditties enjoyed by glee clubs and glee club listeners everywhere. They were splendidly sung, with good tone quality and a diversity of tonal and dynamic effects.

But the only attempt Cornell made in the line of serious music was made in conjunction with the UC singers in Bach's "Now Let Every Tongue Adore Thee" and Handel's "Hallelujah, Amen" from Judas Maccabeus.[32]

The commentary clearly suggests that a more serious repertoire would be appropriate and preferable. The *San Francisco Chronicle* agreed, writing, "These virtues [the Cornell group's technical polish and the like] were exercised on music worthy of them in works of Carissimi, Mozart, and di Lasso; elsewhere the music scarcely measured up to the performance."[33]

Similar thoughts had been voiced after an early 1950s tour performance in Baltimore. Praising the concert, one alumnus nevertheless wrote,

> I asked several people—Cornellians and others—who attended this concert and the one in 1949 for their opinions as to how the two compared. Most of these had the same reaction as I had—that this year's concert, while very good, was not quite as good as the last one, from an overall viewpoint. The general opinion was that this concert was just a bit on the light or frivilous [sic] side and not as well balanced as the previous one. I believe that one or two "heavy" choral numbers that are generally familiar would have been very appropriate and would have achieved the desired balance.[34]

This was from a man who thought Bach too serious for college clubs. In some sense sticking with a program reminiscent of the good ol' college club, the Glee Club was behind the times—or perhaps, myopically fixed to them. Obviously the extent to which they felt attuned with musical culture hinged on the musical climate of the fifties. In America crooned ballads were popular; Perry Como and Bing Crosby were in, and lighter tunes of the musical theater, some of which the Glee Club sang, were among the most popular songs of the day. The songs of school, collegiate Alma Maters and otherwise, somehow befitted the bobby socks, letter sweaters, and be-bop of the time. Record companies even released collections of college songs, including "From Blue Cayuga's Waters" or "High above Cayuga's Waters." Of course, the fifties also brought new developments in jazz (Miles Davis et al.), musical theater (*West Side Story*), and the world in which Stravinsky and Schoenberg (posthumously) reigned, not to overlook the rise of Elvis and rock and roll. But something in the American musical milieu must have supported the Glee Club's style, putting them not so much behind the times as confining them to a pocket of musical practice which though it worked well for the moment could become quickly dated by the next. They were not alone—the clubs at Dartmouth and Penn were still putting on comparable programs. And who could argue with box office success?

Even so, the matter did cross Tracy's mind, reflected in the inclusion of Haydn, Handel, Mozart, Schumann, and Schubert on programs in spring 1955. The academic year had begun with the Fall Weekend concert, at which the group was apparently content to sing a show of spirituals, folk songs, and Broadway hits. The classical and romantic depth was added for a March concert in Batavia, which elicited the following comment from a local critic:

> If there is any doubt as to the remarkable progress vocal music has made in America, it was dispelled by the performance of the Cornell Men's Glee Club at the high school auditorium. . . .
>
> [They] could not only give splendid renditions of songs dear to the heart of Cornellians, but they also gave us samples of the classics, sung in a thrilling manner.[35]

Tracy was apparently finding ways to get a good sound out of the younger singers. But attributing great progress to Cornell's Glee Club at that point, progress premised on commitment to "the classics," may have been a misattribution. During the 1955–1957 years, programs usually held a few numbers that qualified as "serious," but the group in a sense was only paying lip service. The programmed works, rather than exploring the TTBB repertoire, often were SATB choruses revoiced for male chorus and repeated year to year. (The Lacrymosa from the Mozart *Requiem,* which appeared on programs every year from 1954 to 1957 is a good example.) On occasion Glee Club pianists such as Maynard Makman 1955, Leonard Rubin 1959, and John Weaver 1959 would provide interludes with selections by Chopin and others. But in its choral programming the organization showed little more than a surface commitment to the so-called progress represented by "serious" repertoire. Ultimately Tracy liked the Glee Club to ham it up, to sing pieces everyone could "sing in the shower"—which the organization sensed the alumni preferred.

Did "serious" repertoire necessarily mean progress, and precisely what distinguished a true advance in choral presentation? The reviewer in Batavia also wrote, "Not too long ago, a performance by a college glee club meant a program that consisted of old time songs, a liberal quantity of songs traditional in the college and many so-called novelty acts. The 'old Grads' would sit back and revel in reminiscence of bygone days on the campus. True, college glee clubs still sing the nostalgic themes, but the way they sing them has placed them in the class of good music."

Somewhat different from the *San Francisco Chronicle's* view, this statement suggests good music is not what you sing but how you sing it. Were skits and novelty numbers mixed with lighter songs inappropriate? Was there progress perhaps in singing the old, sentimental songs well and pulling off mesmerizing skits? Many found entertaining fun in such Glee Club novelty numbers as "Mountain Melody," a skit involving two hillbillies hamming it up on guitars and carrying on in "mountain accents." And there was still musical value in a good performance of a piece like "Tenor and Baritone"—Doc Davison had argued as much back in 1915. Should there be a group to offer theatrical laughs along with some four-part harmony on popular tunes, and would that be a glee club? Time probably has something still to say on the matter. At that moment Tracy was happy to conduct the Glee Club, and program in that manner. Today perhaps there is an implicit prejudice about what choral groups, specifically college glee clubs, should perform—a prejudice toward "serious" repertoire; yet there are perhaps other programmatic possibilities that in their own right are musically creditable and stimulating.[36]

And yet there were the press comments, suggesting Cornell could program more ambitiously, and there was the question of balance. For with all prejudices aside, the tone of the Tracy Glee Club, however popular it may have been with Cornell students and the Musical Clubs Council, in some choral circles was considered noticeably off the path of musical development. Doc Davison's heirs espoused a balance between seria and buffa, between sacred and secular, between foreign and indigenous, and in some cases, between major works and smaller pieces. And Cornell's Club largely lacked that balance. Tracy may have programmed some "serious" pieces because others complained that Cornell was falling out of step with the choral times, or simply because they were good pieces. Very likely, however, it was not because this was a direction in which he and the group were particularly intent on heading.

Independent of any musical problems the Glee Club might have, its popularity continued to ride a postwar crest during the early fifties. Concerts were well attended, and more than a hundred singers were trying out each year for the group. Cornell was likewise thriving. Morris Bishop once suggested Deane Malott's presidency might be called the "Era of Well-Being," and so it was. Campus building continued at a remarkable pace, notably in the area of dormitories. The West Campus U-halls, Mary Donlon on North Campus, and the law school dorms all went up during the 1950s. The Albert Mann Library opened on the agriculture quad, and a hall named for Anabel Taylor went up next to the law school's Myron Taylor Hall. The university's operating budget grew toward $100,000,000, and sponsored research continued to escalate well into the millions. Cornell's athletic program developed into the largest in the country at the time, and in 1957, the crew beat nearly every other team in the world, including the Russian and Italian champions, and Yale.[37] On the musical scene,

Ralph Vaughan Williams came to Cornell in fall 1954 and, according to Harold Samuel, gave lectures, coached performances of his works, "and generally spent a good deal of time with the students, much to their and his delight."[38]

For the Glee Club the era of well-being did not last the decade. Indications by the mid 1950s were that the prosperity of the years just passed was coming to an end. At the Musical Clubs Council meeting on October 25, 1956, several points were raised: (1) expenses for spring tours had doubled since the end of World War II; (2) the alumni sponsoring organizations therefore were not showing the same enthusiasm; and (3) television, though helpful to the cause once in a while, was hurting college glee clubs a great deal.

Regular television broadcasts had begun in the United States in 1941, and spurred by the war, the industry had developed rapidly, often springing out of existing radio stations. Television's effect on glee clubs, if it could be clearly measured, likely was akin to radio's initial impact. But this time, there was no salvation in stage antics. Anything a glee club could do, TV could do, and probably better. By the fifties, television programs were rife with music, and as people got used to being entertained at home in their living rooms, they grew less interested in going out on cold or rainy nights to hear glee club concerts.

With its financial problems compounded by this revolution in entertainment, the Glee Club drew in the purse strings of post-Mexico tours, along with geographic range. To offset rising costs and waning interest, the Musical Clubs Council recommended lowering the guarantee that local sponsors had to pay, and cutting travel expenses by limiting the tour to an area closer to home. The suggestions were prudent. The 1957 tour brought in a fair profit, visiting Buffalo, Syracuse, Cleveland, Rochester, Jamestown, Wellsville, and Batavia. Any pinings for the East Coast had been satisfied earlier in the year, when the Glee Club traveled to sing at the Waldorf-Astoria in New York City on the occasion of the Ezra Cornell Sesquicentennial Dinner on January 11, 1957, and here was an occasion for which the Glee Club was still better than TV. One can only wonder what Ezra would have thought of television.

Concurrent with the decline in financial prosperity, the Glee Club shouldered the disappointment of the Cayuga's Waiters. The Waiters had enjoyed a steady rise to fame in their first five years, a heady experience on top of the Glee Club's campus popularity. "The memory of an appearance by Cayuga's Waiters brings a smile long after the melody has gone"—at least it did in their minds, seeing as they could count on campus celebrity.[39] So certain were they of their status independent of the Glee Club, the Waiters decided to break from the group in spring 1956—an unprecedented parting of the ways which will be discussed more fully in Chapter 9. Almost immediately the Glee Club formed a new triple quartet, the Sherwoods, and the merry band made their debut at the 1956 fall concert, quickly filling the vacant spot in the Glee Club program.

That same fall the Glee Club appeared at Carnegie Hall with Yale and Brown, under the auspices of the newly formed Ivy League Musical Activities Council

(ILMAC). People had talked for some time of an Ivy League athletic association (which became official in 1956), and Selly Brewer saw no reason why the same ties couldn't be extended to the realm of music. Hence, in addition to the already established Intercollegiate Musical Clubs Council, the ILMAC was formed in 1954–1955, naming among its purposes the prevention "of conflicts among the musical activities of the Ivy League schools," and the organization of a joint concert in Carnegie Hall.[40] In fall 1955 Columbia, Penn, and Dartmouth participated. A year later, on November 30, 1956, Cornell took part. Initially Harvard was supposed to join Yale and Cornell but in the end did not do so, finding fault with the ILMAC. In their opinion the organization should expand its focus beyond the annual New York concert and hold meetings for officers and conductors to discuss aspects of managing and leading glee clubs, as well as form a regional group as part of the Intercollegiate Musical Clubs Council. But other groups felt the New York concert was the chief cohesive force, more so than the suggested joint football concerts. In a meeting of conductors the day after the 1956 concert J. Bailey Harvey of Columbia said, "It seems clear that five legs are supporting, but two or three are not!" (he meant Harvard and Princeton). Fenno Heath of Yale added, "I have no interest in taking part in an organization in which all members don't participate."[41] The directors adjourned still at odds, but agreed to meet in January 1957 to discuss the immediate future of the council—ultimately, it was disbanded.

Back home Cornell's Glee Club had other things to think about, not the least being that home had moved. Back in May 1954 Foster Coffin had informed the Musical Clubs that the Women's Glee Club could use the North Room of Willard Straight Hall for only one more year, and that the Men's Glee Club had the use of Sage Chapel for only one more year, after which they would have to meet elsewhere. The Glee Club, in conjunction with the Savage Club, took it upon themselves to secure new quarters, resulting in a move to the Toboggan Lodge on the south shore of Beebe Lake.

Symbolically the lodge represented new distance between the Glee Club and the university. But in the music department the feeling remained that the Glee Club should eventually come under its aegis again. Donald Grout had thought so for years; all the way back in 1947 he had told Allan Treman that the policy of his predecessors as chairman, much like his own, was "to work constantly towards a liaison between the Music Department and the glee clubs," and that the department envisioned "the possibility of one day having a regular member of the Music Department who would also be satisfactory to the governing bodies of the two glee clubs as director."[42] In a step toward that liaison, Grout actually had served on the Musical Clubs Council during the late 1940s, but the departmental policy had progressed no further, and in 1949 he had stepped down from the chairmanship. When he took up the post again in 1953, he resumed his gradual work toward that goal. Already the bands had become a department activity, completely divorced from the Department of Military Science by the early 1950s. The hope remained the glee clubs could be brought back. The true catalyst was a series of events that began to unfold early in 1957.

The music department had been seeking someone to take charge of the Sage Chapel Choir, University Chorus (a mixed-voice ensemble), and A Cappella Chorus, and the Harvard Glee Club's assistant conductor, Thomas A. Sokol, was offered the position. He accepted in spring 1957. Meanwhile Tracy announced he was planning to step down as director of the Glee Club. Grout could hardly believe the opportunity before him and Sokol was about to learn of the one awaiting him. Having already asked G. Wallace Woodworth at Harvard about the young conductor's qualifications, President Malott called up Sokol and asked "How would you react if you were invited to conduct the Glee Club?" Sokol replied, "If I were invited to conduct, I would react favorably."[43] The council soon extended a formal invitation, and Sokol was true to his word. A new era was about to begin.

Tracy, for his part, was relieved at stepping down, at least in his wife's recollection. She attributes his decision to other commitments, including the Presbyterian Church Choir, family obligations, and work in the Ithaca schools. She also sensed he was weary of training the younger singers. He conducted his final concerts with the Glee Club in June 1957. At the Senior Week concert Howard Greenstein received the Glee Club Award and Charles Stanton the Dudley Award.[44] Then, to paraphrase the Sullivan piece Tracy often programmed, the long day closed.

In fall 1957, already involved with the Ithaca schools at the invitation of the superintendent (who sang in the Presbyterian choir), Tracy began teaching at Boynton Junior High School, where he headed the mathematics department for more than a decade. Summers were spent at the family's second home some miles up the west shore of Cayuga Lake. Set out on a point, the house was Tracy's achievement. "I've done every bit myself," he would say, meaning the electrical work and plumbing in addition to the structure. "The one thing he didn't do," Mary Lou Tracy says, "was dig the hole for the septic tank."[45] While he was still building the house in the 1950s, Glee Club publicity reported that between hammer blows his booming baritone voice could be heard echoing across the lake on many a weekend. The Tracys spent summers there with their neighbors the Brewers for company, and in 1968 moved there permanently.

Tracy was indeed a man of many hats—engineer, singer, organist, conductor, mathematician, golfer, husband, builder, father of five. In his earlier years some thought he should pursue a career as a singer. "I always considered his voice sounded a lot like Lawrence Tibbett," his wife reported with a laugh, "[but] he figured there were just too many baritones in the world and he'd rather take his chances on engineering, which didn't last too long either." The singing did last, though, especially in the memories of those who knew him. "He loved to sing," Deane Malott recalled. People often requested his signature

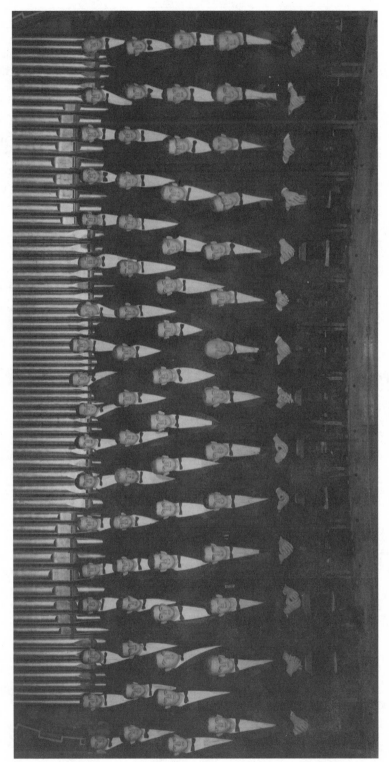

16. The 1956–1957 Glee Club. Photograph by C. Hadley Smith, used with his permission.

renditions of "The Road to Mandalay," and the Toreador Song from Bizet's *Carmen,* but he didn't need requests. "Whenever we would go on trips with the children in the car," Mary Lou Tracy recalled, "he'd drive along, singing at the top of his lungs. He loved to sing driving in the car."[46]

Lou Donkle later remembered his work with the Club. "Under Tracy it was great fun to be in the Glee Club. He had a sense of humor that developed an exceptional esprit de corps in the group. We sang with gusto and enthusiasm. Yet, he demanded perfection. He was a strong leader and sort of a man's man. When you listen to the Glee Club under Tom, the enthusiasm and joy we were having come through in spades. . . . The Glee Club was the high point of my Cornell experience!"[47]

In 1970 Tracy considered retiring from the school system. He still had church choirs and private vocal students to keep him busy, and he looked forward to spending time at the place on the lake. He was talked into staying one more year; it was his last. On March 19, 1971, Tom Tracy was killed in a car accident on his way home from work. Officers from the Tracy years were notified by the Glee Club, and a memorial fund was initiated to pay for vocal training for Club members. In the Glee Club newsletter that spring, his successor Thomas Sokol penned the following tribute:

> Tom Tracy '31 was a beloved member of the Cornell Glee Club family for nearly three decades as a singer, as Assistant Director under Eric Dudley, and for eleven years as Director (1946–1957). Under his tutelage over 700 Cornell men learned the art and joy of making music. In the difficult period following World War II, he provided the leadership for rebuilding the Glee Club, both musically and organizationally, and under his direction concert tours were made to Cornell clubs throughout the United States and Mexico. One need recall the names of only a few of his singers like Heinsius, Sells, Bump, Davis, Douglass, etc. to realize his lasting influence on the life of the Glee Club and its men.
>
> His untimely death . . . on March 19 was a great loss to all generations of Glee Club men. We are fortunate to have had his warm personality and excellent musicianship and we jointly pay tribute to his memory.

5 The Sokol Era,
1957–1995

Together we have made golden moments of music.

—Eugene Ormandy to Thomas Sokol

"Good evening, gentlemen, everyone up—deep breath in . . . and out. In . . . , out. And would you hum a D . . ." Opening words seemingly as familiar as "Once upon a time, and a very good time it was . . . ," they have now served for generations of Glee Clubbers as the invitation to the dance. For thirty-eight years Professor Thomas Sokol took the podium with those words, words that remained constant as podiums changed underfoot, hair graded from dark to gray, and his title settled in as simply "Professor." But now, at the end of Sokol's Cornell career, we must turn back to the beginning.

Early on a chill morning in spring 1957, before the sun had come up, a young man stepped from a taxi and considered his surroundings. He recalls,

> I was coming over to meet with President Malott, this was after I had accepted the department's appointment, and I think we were going to discuss whether or not there would be a relationship between me and the Glee Club. I came on the train to Syracuse from Boston, and I thought I could get a bus down, but at that very early hour, there were no buses. So I thought I would have to take a taxi. I think it was going to cost seventeen dollars or so, a lot of money. I was reluctant to do it, but I had an appointment at eight in the morning with President Malott. We made it as far in the taxi as Lafayette where the taxi driver pulled over and said, "We've got a problem." I don't know, the transmission went out or something of the sort, and we were stranded there. He said that he wouldn't charge me for going that far. But I was there with my overnight suitcase wondering how I was going to get from near Lafayette, in the middle of nowhere, down Route 11 to Ithaca. And so I hitchhiked. I got one ride as far as near where the Elm Tree golf course is now, and that person had to turn off there, and so I hitchhiked again and got a ride with a man who

17. Thomas Sokol, c. 1970.

I recall was working at the Montgomery Ward store in Ithaca. He very kindly dropped me off near the university on the way in. Having such a difficult time even getting here was my first daunting challenge at Cornell. But I did make it for my eight o'clock appointment with President Malott.[1]

And so Thomas Sokol came to Ithaca, the opening of a new chapter in the life of one man and one ensemble.

Thomas Andrew Sokol had come from further than Syracuse, or Boston for that matter. He was born in Beaver Falls, Pennsylvania, on July 28, 1929, and raised farther up the Ohio River in Sewickley, a town of 5,417 outside Pittsburgh. He was educated in Sewickley public schools, a beneficiary of Hollis Dann's work in that state little more than a decade before. Though he took part in bands and choirs, much of his early musical education was outside the classroom. At the age of 10, he began studying trumpet and was soon apprenticed to Almeron Carroll, who kept a music store in town. Carroll had played with several leading swing and jazz ensembles, including the Eddy Duchin and Charlie Spivak bands and the Dorsey Brothers, and continued to sit in with the Pittsburgh Symphony and radio station KDKA's staff orchestra. The boy soon found himself sitting in the middle of the brass section during rehearsals and broadcasts. The lesson, he says, was witnessing Al Carroll perform at a high level under pressure, which taught him the importance of "focus and concentration when it comes to the moment of performance."

When Sokol's choirmaster at St. James Catholic Church had a heart attack, Sokol was asked to take over—he was then only 13 or 14 years old—and he continued to lead the church choir throughout his high school years. The pastor at St. James had done his training at St. Vincent's College outside Pittsburgh and suggested Sokol do some additional study with the Benedictine monks there. At the end of high school and in the year before college (during which he led several dance bands and worked in the steel mills) Sokol commuted to St. Vincent's for music classes at the monastery.

By this time another passion had emerged—football. Having played half-back, tailback, and safety on the Sewickley team, as well as a good deal of sand-lot football where Johnny Unitas or substitute Pittsburgh Steelers might show up on a given weekend, Sokol was offered a scholarship to play football at the Virginia Military Institute. In his first semester he pounded the gridiron, played with a dance band, sang in the choir, and spent time "learning how to deal with an M1 rifle." When the coach left following the season, Sokol decided to transfer to Emory and Henry College in southwest Virginia. There, he continued to rack up impressive statistics—in one game against Maryville College, he intercepted a pass in his own end zone and ran it some 104 or 105 yards for the touchdown. With plays like that the team went to several bowl games, including the Tangerine and Tobacco bowls. At halftime he quickly shed his football uniform and donned a marching band outfit to lead the band in the show.[2]

At Emory and Henry, violinist and faculty member Ludwig Sikorski adopted Sokol as his assistant and guided his studies in theory and composition. In addition Sokol was asked by the Collegians, a male chorus of about twenty, if he would conduct them. He did. Sokol graduated with honors in 1951, taking degrees in music and history, and headed for George Peabody College with a Carnegie Teaching Fellowship in hand. At Peabody (today part of Vanderbilt) he pursued graduate work primarily in composition and musicology, also taking part in the "very high" level of music making on campus. (The composer Roy Harris, briefly at Cornell in the 1940s, had just left Peabody as Sokol arrived, but other composers, including Aaron Copland, Howard Hanson, and Randall Thompson paid visits to campus.) Sokol soon had a church choir, was conducting the Nashville Nurses' Chorus, and eventually was named music supervisor for Davidson County, a responsibility of one high and eight elementary schools.[3] He earned his M.A. in 1952 and had just completed his A exams when he went to spend the summer of 1954 at Harvard, enrolling in G. Wallace Woodworth's conducting class. "Woody," as the latter was familiarly known, took Sokol to Tanglewood with him that summer and then invited him to stay on as his assistant, arranging a Weyman Foundation grant to make it possible. And so finding himself the new assistant conductor of the Harvard Glee Club and Radcliffe Choral Society as well as the assistant choirmaster for the university, Sokol rented a U-Haul and moved his belongings up from Nashville to Cambridge.

This turn of events affirmed music as Sokol's calling. While at Harvard, in addition to being immersed around the clock in music making, he made the acquaintance of Donald Grout (who was a visiting lecturer) and Walter Piston and remet Randall Thompson. Before coming to Harvard, Sokol says, "I hadn't really considered music as a vocation, partly because the people that I knew best in music were recording artists and performers. I really hadn't been involved with any academic musicians. But then I was thrust into the middle of it." Under Woody, whom he considered a "master teacher, absolutely dedicated to his work, and to the music, and to his students," and a man "very respectful of other musicians," Sokol continued to grow and was soon busy with other work. For several years, simultaneous to his appointment at Harvard, he served on faculty at the Newton College of the Sacred Heart and filled in for one year as acting director of choral activities at the New England Conservatory. With several other Bostonians he formed Cambridge Records, Inc., serving as its musical director and vice president. He also served as a standby conductor for the Handel and Haydn Society and at the invitation of President Pusey of Harvard became involved with music at the Belmont Hill School, where Pusey's son was in attendance.

In the meantime Cornell was looking for one person under whom to organize its choral activities. Robert Hull, conductor of the A Cappella Chorus, had left to lead the Fort Worth Symphony, and Grout and John Kirkpatrick (who had the University Chorus and Sage Chapel Choir, respectively) planned to take up other departmental commitments. An associate of Woodworth's, Grout had made an initial inquiry at Harvard, where he had done graduate work with Doc Davison and had been visiting lecturer. Woody recommended Sokol, who was invited for an audition and then offered an appointment as assistant professor and director of choral music.

President Deane Malott, who had served on faculty at the Harvard Business School and remembered the services in Appleton Chapel in the Yard, also had been in touch with Harvard, as we know. Having already accepted the responsibility of the department ensembles, Sokol was asked to meet with the Musical Clubs Council to discuss the Glee Club's future. Following these discussions Allan Treman, on behalf of the council, invited Sokol to conduct the Glee Club.

This was a proposition accepted with reservations on both sides. For one thing, the Musical Clubs Council had provided for the salary of the Glee Club director as part of its normal governance. But Sokol accepted the invitation to lead the Glee Club only "so long as it would be considered a part of my responsibility to the university." In other words he declined the director's salary (some $2,000 at the time), sidestepping any subtle influence on musical matters which might be exerted through the pocketbook. If the council wanted a director, that was fine, but Sokol had ideas of his own, and *he* was going to direct the Glee Club. On their side, the council was clearly not at ease about this. At a May 1957 meeting members voiced concerns about Sokol's "organizational ideas." When Sokol arrived to conduct in fall 1957, some of those ideas took on substantive form, creating a head-on collision between Musical Club traditions and the 28-year-old iconoclast.

The primary engagement for the Glee Club that semester was a joint concert with Columbia on Fall Weekend. Sokol stepped through the door to the low-ceilinged room of the Toboggan Lodge for his first rehearsal and may have been surprised at what he found. Change was swiftly forthcoming. He explains:

Some of the men thought I was a little on the strict side because I wouldn't permit them to smoke cigarettes during rehearsal and also I wouldn't permit them to bring dates to sit with the singers while rehearsing. They thought that was a little too strict, [and] the old phrase was thrown at me a few times, "You're taking the glee out of the Glee Club." But I didn't mind doing that for situations like that because my concept of the glee was a little deeper than that.

The concept of the glee as it related to programmed music was also changing. Whereas glee before might have meant a few novelty acts mixed in with school songs and a good social atmosphere, it now might mean the actual part song, or glee, for which glee clubs were named, or still more "serious" repertoire. The new description under the "program" in the Club's publicity was telling: "The repertoire is usually varied enough to include many different kinds of numbers. Should a particular audience have definite musical tastes, the local sponsoring groups can stress the particular numbers that appeal to such tastes; e.g., if members of a community should have a special fondness for Renaissance motets or contemporary music." This statement seems quite hopeful, expecting widespread audience demand for Renaissance motets, but if nothing else, the hope revealed the group's new musical ambition. The program for the Columbia concert (which included Beethoven, Handel, and Ingegneri),[4] while not radically different from those of previous seasons, nevertheless began to intimate changes that would become more pronounced in the next few semesters. Soon Gregorian chant, Allegri's "Miserere," Tchesnokov's "Spahsyehnyeh" (Salvation Belongeth to Our God), Thompson's "Last Words of David," Lotti's "Crucifixus," and works by Palestrina, Mendelssohn, Copland, and Bernstein joined the college songs in the active repertoire.

Reactions to these changes were not at all favorable in many quarters. Students disenchanted with the change in repertory would launch into "Strike Up a Song" during rehearsal breaks, the symbol of rebel ferment among the old guard. Alums wrote with concern over the changed nature of Glee Club entertainment and clamored for light music. To put things in perspective, Allan Treman remarked to Sokol after one concert, "Well, I don't know how it was where you came from," getting in a dig at Harvard, "but in Ithaca, New York, that's highbrow music," referring to a selection by Gilbert and Sullivan.

Not all reactions were negative, of course. They merely differed wildly, as revealed in opinions solicited after Sokol's first Cornell Day concert (an affair for prefreshmen). One listener wrote that he thought the performance was excellent, the program was the proper length, and each rendition well done. But there were other views: one writer found the concert "*far below* the standard performances of our previous Glee Clubs"; another complaint was that there were too few Cornell songs and too much emphasis on technical performance. Albert Neimuth 1950 wrote: "As an alumnus I love Cornell, am proud of Cornell and do not wish to hear neutralistic songs which I might hear at any concert in New York City or elsewhere in the United States," while another asserted that "if the students can't sing for fun as was the intent of the Glee Club then they should receive college credit for doing such an academic job."[5]

The experience may have influenced Sokol to include more than two Cornell songs on future programs. But refusing to change his vision for the Club's repertory, he stuck to his guns, allowing the power of the music to gradually exert its influence over the students.

Most often the students in the Glee Club both confronted and eventually accepted changes sooner than people outside the ensemble (a process aided by the built-in turnover rate). This was the case with one significant Sokol policy change. Invitation to membership in the Glee Club had been based on the results of a vocal-musical audition along with an assessment of the candidate's perceived compatibility with current members. Not unlike fraternities of the time the group's identity included the notion of being an exclusive club. "I didn't think that was a good basis for having a university musical ensemble so I insisted on inviting anyone to join on the basis of a musical audition," Sokol recounts.

And there was certainly at least one instance when I accepted into membership a Cornell student who was not a caucasian and I believe there were four members of the Glee Club at that time [who] felt that they needed to resign. And they said to me that they felt that I didn't comprehend why the Glee Club was one of the most "looked up to" organizations on the Hill. They said, "We are that because we won't take into membership anyone with whom we wouldn't go into a local bar and have a convivial drink." And I thought, "Well, there's a little difference here so if we have to have a parting of the ways, so be it." And they left and never came back.

Negative reaction to open membership in the Glee Club was also expressed by the Cornell Club of Indianapolis during the 1958 midwestern tour. On Christmas Eve, Sokol had returned to his hotel room after an afternoon rehearsal when he received a message from the local club. They suggested one of the men might go to the movies on the other side of the tracks rather than sing in the concert—they would provide the ticket. The man in question was Fred Parris 1962, an African American who stood in the front row of the bass section. Sokol called the officers together and solicited their opinions as to "whether or not a member of the Glee Club should be asked to not sing on a nonmusical basis." Discussion went around for two or three hours, and the officers concluded that they had come as the Cornell Glee Club and should perform as such, and if the local people chose for them not to perform, they would go on to the next city. "So we sent the message back," Sokol relates, "and when we went to the hotel to perform that evening, at least two of the [Cornell Club] officers and their families waited until we sang our first note, then they stood up and walked out. Among the repercussions to the Indianapolis visit were some letters written back to the president of the university."

Of particular note are three letters that came in the same mail. The first was a stinging rebuke from the president of the Cornell Club of Indianapolis, complaining about nonwhites in the Glee Club. The second was from the Episcopal bishop of Indiana. As it was Christmas, some of the men had gone to a midnight service. According to Sokol,

> At the conclusion of the service, the bishop came around to the entrance and said, "I want to find out who was this group that is making such music in my cathedral, we've never had such glorious singing of these Christmas anthems." And so he talked with the men and he wrote a letter to the president declaring his admiration for them as young men and as singers. And then after that service a number of them went out caroling in the residential area and in one household the family was decorating a tree. [The family] invited them to come in and they serenaded and made the acquaintance of the daughter of the family. It turned out it was [the home of] the governor of Indiana, Governor Handley, and he evidently wrote a letter of great admiration, again to the university. We had the governor and the bishop saying what a wonderful group of students this was, then we had the Cornell Club saying "what a terrible thing" based on the racial issue.[6]

Growing pains of this kind were evident, both in the Glee Club and the society it encountered, as Sokol steered the group away from its 1950s social orientations. For even in the fifties, though the society days of the twenties were gone, the Glee Club was often involved in social functions, particularly on tours, which included dinners and dances. And as Indianapolis suggests, Sokol continues, "as the university became a little more universal in terms of its makeup of student population and these diverse groups might be represented in musical ensembles, not all of them were accepted with open arms in these social environments in various cities around the country." With these important changes, not just in membership but in music, the Glee Club gradually grew more broad-minded as an ensemble. In Sokol's mind "all this was in the context of really doing serious work, rehearsing, trying to sing well, trying to sing representative repertory, still diverse but with an emphasis on music and style that seemed consonant with the purpose of the university."

As Elliot Forbes wrote about the group at Harvard,

> The glee club's fortune in having Doc's selfless catalytic leadership provided a rallying defense against what turned out to be expressions of intense

disapproval from many alumni who saw traditions from the "good old days" being challenged as the club advanced "from a bulldog-on-the-bank reper-tory to masterpieces of the fifteenth- and sixteenth-century polyphony." The struggle ended . . . when a returning group of matured choristers . . . effected a vote in spring 1919 to sever connections with the instrumental clubs and devote their efforts exclusively to preparation of music that Doc selected. And thus he became conductor in the fullest sense; but, in order to secure inde-pendence of action, he insisted that he receive no compensation.[7]

This account, a description of Doc Davison's pioneering work at Harvard and a summation of what Sokol himself refers to as "the change," describes some-thing remarkably similar to the transformation Sokol worked at Cornell nearly forty years later. The instrumental clubs of course had long been disassociated from the Glee Club at Cornell, but the Musical Clubs Council, which originally governed the Glee, Banjo, and Mandolin Clubs, had remained an active vestige. With diplomatic patience Sokol began reforging the Club's relationship with both the council and the university. For the first few years, though he accepted no salary, he used funds provided by the Musical Clubs Council to purchase music and a new tuxedo or two. Beyond that there was little contact, aside from a few volleys exchanged about repertoire and "glee" in the Glee Club; Sokol di-rected the Glee Club, and they quietly kept the books, including all concert revenues. Gradually the council became smaller as long-time members Selly Brewer, Foster Coffin, and Ted Wright (who was a vice president of the univer-sity) stepped down. By 1960 the time seemed right to discuss reorganization of the Glee Club, and an officer's meeting was called in May at the Tau Delta Phi fraternity house. Through the summer and fall efforts dropped off, but another meeting was convened in the spring semester of 1961, with Treman, Brewer, and J. Duncan Sells 1949 representing the Musical Clubs Council. They ac-quainted Glee Club officers with the history of the council, explaining that in their view, their role was a "paternal function of guidance and direction."

In the meantime overtures had been made to include the Glee Club in the university structure. Aside from Sokol the group still had no official connec-tion to Cornell. President Malott recalls, "I thought it was very confusing, be-cause the Glee Club was not under the direction of the president, or any de-partment. It was under some sort of committee, and I thought that was not a good way to run any department of the university, it all ought to be under the president. So, I don't know by what abracadabra I got rid of that committee and got the Glee Club into my hands, but I did, and it functioned very well."[8] Though the magic was not all his doing, Malott took an active role in the Glee Club's reorganization efforts, providing his opinions and support when mat-ters came to a head in 1961. The result was the drafting of a new Glee Club con-stitution, which stated in its preamble, "The Cornell University Glee Club is an authorized activity of the University under the jurisdiction of the Board of

Trustees of the University, acting through the President of the University, and a Director to be appointed in accordance with applicable University regulations," and Article 8 further stating the director was appointable by the Board of Trustees or the president. The document, drawn up by university trustee and Philadelphia lawyer Francis Scheetz, was dated November 20, 1961, and once approved by the university, became retroactively effective from July 1, 1961.[9]

After nearly a hundred years as an independent organization on the Hill, most of those under the paternal, and at times removed governance of a chartered corporation in the state of New York, the Glee Club was officially embraced by Cornell. A letter from Glee Club president William Lathrop 1961 to President Malott read, "We look forward to a happy association with the University," and Malott responded, "I believe that this is a wise and appropriate step which the Glee Club has taken. . . . You will find the fullest cooperation from the University in this new framework and I wish the Glee Club every success in the years ahead."[10]

Between 1957 and 1961 the transitional change in the Glee Club's organizational structure and the gradual dissolution of the Musical Clubs Council was significantly aided by one particular event in the early years of the Sokol era—the Glee Club's 1960–1961 tour of the Soviet Union. With the shift from graduate managers (who were really not graduate students but university staff members) to a more student-centered system of management, Sokol found himself attending to many of the organizational details for the tour. As early as 1958, with the permission of both the Musical Clubs Council and the president, he had begun pursuing contacts in Russia. When final arrangements were secured, Sokol—though he didn't know how much money was in the council's accounts—fully intended that the cost of airfare to and from Moscow on KLM would essentially wipe out the balance. It did, speeding a fiscal transition that corresponded to the organizational transition, and the Glee Club soon after was able to set up its own accounts within the university structure.

The business of clearing the financial decks was eclipsed of course by the overwhelming opportunity for musical and cultural exchange presented by the Russia tour. Not that cultural exchange was initially a sure way through the Iron Curtain. In 1960 Cold War sentiment was rising on both sides of the globe. Khrushchev was banging his shoe at the UN, the Eisenhower administration was sorting out the Powers U-2 incident, and Cuba became an openly Communist country. Culturally, relations had stagnated in issues of questionable reciprocity. Cultural attachés began to count days of cultural visits—if the Bolshoi Ballet visited for so many days, for example, then the U.S.S.R. owed that many to the United States before anyone else could come over—and so on. Against that backdrop arrangements were difficult to make, but after copious calls and correspondence beginning with then U.S. Attorney General William Rogers 1933, J.D. 1936, and leading to the Soviet Committee of Youth Organizations, and Nikolai Novokreshchonov of the Bureau on International Youth Travel, a visit was arranged for late December 1960. Learning of the trip, Cornell friend Keith Falkner, who had just left the Cornell faculty to become director of the Royal College of Music in London, invited the Glee Club to extend the tour to England, rounding out the itinerary which ultimately extended from December 16 to January 5.

During those days the Glee Club gave performances everywhere from the Moscow Conservatory and the University of Leningrad to Westminster Abbey and the Amsterdam airport, in addition to radio broadcasts and appearances on Television Moscow and the BBC network. The response was overwhelming. The Soviet news agency TASS reported, "Shostakovich's 'Song of Peace' made a great hit [as the] Soviets lauded Cornell Choir." Another Moscow musical publication described the ensemble as "excellently trained and disciplined," and the *London Times* wrote not only do they sing "robustly and ardently," they "sing all sorts of music at all brow levels." Falkner, in addition to expressing his own pleasure, reported that Sir Adrian Boult, whom he called "the doyen of English Conductors," wrote him to say the Westminster concert "was a most moving occasion."[11]

Never had the Glee Club attained such international exposure, in the musical world or elsewhere. The *Cornellian* listing for that year began, "HISTORY HAS BEEN MADE." It had. With that tour Cornell's Glee Club became the first university musical group from the United States to give a formal concert in the Soviet Union. The Yale Russian Chorus had previously visited the U.S.S.R., singing informally in parks and meeting the people of the country, but this was the first concert tour given by American students. As such, and given the tense political climate, it attracted a good deal of attention and proved a refreshing moment of cultural détente in the Cold War. As the Soviet Embassy in Washington wrote, "The students of the Moscow University liked the art of their comrades from over the ocean. Naturally, it is better to sing of peace and work, than to prepare for war."[12]

The tour of Russia and England put to rest many of the lingering questions about Sokol's early administration. Success is hard to argue with, and complaints about his musical and organizational ideas rang a little hollow next to the acclaim accorded the tour. Thus, though it was still almost a year until the Glee Club was incorporated into the university, the transitional period could be dated 1957–Russia tour. Moreover, in the context of the early Sokol years, the tour marked a peak in the momentum of the Club's activities. In Sokol's first year the group toured and carried on the usual engagements at home, and also recorded a Christmas program for the Mutual Broadcasting System. In just the second year of Sokol's leadership, the Glee Club had more than thirty performances, including a spring road trip as far as Maryland and the winter midwestern tour, several radio broadcasts (including a CBS Christmas program), and a television appearance. At the end of the year, they found time to record a Songs of Cornell album which came out the following fall, at the start of another full season. During all this activity the music, the rules, the rehearsal venue, and the organizational structure were changing. Membership remained high nonetheless, and with effort equal to ambition Sokol and company carried the vision and activity of this new Glee Club to a definitive high point. After all, a member could not help but be interested in the possibility of singing in Russia, and the public could not help but notice an advertisement promoting a last chance to hear Cornell's Glee Club before they made their historic tour of "the *Soviet Union.*" And it certainly would have been hard to miss the full-page spreads of photos from Russia in the *Ithaca Journal.*

Momentum did not stop with the Russia tour. In the spring following the trip, another ground-breaking event marked the 1960–1961 calendar—a performance of Verdi's *Requiem* with Theodore Bloomfield and the Rochester Philharmonic Orchestra, the Glee Club's first performance of a major work since the days of Hollis Dann. The home concert (performances were given in Ithaca as well as Rochester) was the first live performance of the Verdi Donald Grout and Cornell composer Robert Palmer had ever heard. The occasion marked the same experience for most of the Glee Club. As Sokol remembers it,

> The Verdi *Requiem* was a long piece and I suggested that they [Club members] see the whole process through and after the performance, if they didn't feel this was good for them, I would respect their opinion. We had again a few men who left and I realized that they left as a result of never having performed a piece longer than four or five minutes and certainly not having done pieces in languages other than English. But those who stayed, of course, became sophisticated almost overnight. I thought it was a very productive experience, and really one of the beginnings, once their appetite had been whetted by having the opportunity to perform with a major symphony orchestra under very demanding circumstances. These were golden moments that are rare in life, and these young men experienced it. Some of them in spite of themselves.

Thereafter, performances of major works continued almost without pause. The Verdi was repeated with the Oneonta Symphony in the fall of 1961 and a performance of William Walton's *Belshazzar's Feast,* again with Bloomfield, reportedly shook the chandelier of the Eastman Theater. In spring 1962 the combined Glee Club and Cornell University Chorus had the rare honor of working with Nadia Boulanger. Leonard Bernstein, one of her greatest fans, had invited her to become the first woman to conduct the New York Philharmonic. After her performances in New York she came to Ithaca to lead a performance of Debussy's "Trois Chansons" and the Fauré *Requiem.* Several memories remain from that visit. In one rehearsal of the Debussy she gave one pitch from the piano to begin, and for the entire time that was the only pitch sounded. "She was a quiet powerhouse," Sokol says. "When she said begin here no pitch sounded and they began. I was amazed that the singers responded so well. They were in total concentration, and it was superb." Then there was the first orchestra rehearsal of the Fauré in Bailey Hall. Sokol continues,

> She began and those first few measures are simply orchestral chord, whole note and she went maybe six times over the first measures, saying no, it's not Baaah . . . [beating in a slow four], but it's Baaah . . . [beating in the same slow four]. And all of the players sat there, partly because they were so focused on what she was saying, as though they comprehended what it was she said, when in fact they didn't because what she said was an exact repetition of what was previously done. But it got a magnificent effect in the music. . . . Her approach to the piece was a spiritual approach and it was extraordinary.

She drew audiences with similar magnetism. Bailey Hall was so crowded for the concert that several distinguished members of the faculty tried to sneak in through a window in the men's bathroom and had to be escorted out.

A Boulanger visit would have been enough to sustain anyone for awhile, but 1962 was blessed with not one, but two collaborations with internationally famous musicians. In conjunction with the university's plans to celebrate the construction and opening of the new graduate library, the John M. Olin Library, the possibility of involving the Philadelphia Orchestra was pursued by several intermediaries, including associate librarian Felix Reichmann and G. Ruhland Rebmann, a trustee of both the university and the orchestra. Arrangements were finalized for a celebratory concert in Ithaca on October 10, and two additional performances in Philadelphia's Academy of Music; the program was to be Beethoven's *Consecration of the House Overture* and *Ninth Symphony*, the Cornell University Glee Club and Chorus serving as the chorus. The performances were to be conducted by the orchestra's music director, Eugene Ormandy.

Ormandy sent Sokol a score marked in red pencil (Sokol still has it), and the ensembles set to rehearsing "Seid umschlungen" and "Freude, schöner Götterfunken" according to the maestro's wishes. When he arrived at Sage Chapel to rehearse them, everyone waited anxiously for his verdict. But once certain of his satisfaction with their sound and flexibility, the singers became more relaxed. "That was the rehearsal in the course of which at one moment something went wrong and he stopped and the singers gave one of those Cornell hisses to him. I was sitting right beside him and I thought, 'Oh dear, I'm not sure I want to be here.'" Sokol smiles, "I mean, how is he going to react to this, a world-renowned conductor being hissed by this group of students. There was a brief, absolute silence, and then he looked up, got a huge smile on his face and said, 'You're absolutely right, it was my mistake.' And at that moment their marvelous rapport was reinforced."

With more people than could sneak in a bathroom window wanting to see

18. Eugene Ormandy rehearsing Beethoven's *Ninth* with the Glee Club and Chorus in Sage Chapel, October 1962.

the Ithaca concert, the dress rehearsal on October 9 turned into a performance, with several hundred in attendance. Following the official concerts, including the ones on October 12 and 13 in Philadelphia, the reviews were stunning. "It was an afternoon of superlative music-making," the *Inquirer* wrote. "The Ninth with its choral paean to the Brotherhood of Man added up to one of the most exciting musical experiences of many seasons." And the *Philadelphia Evening Bulletin* read: "Much credit must be accorded the fresh-voiced enthusiastic Cornell University choristers. They sang with remarkable zeal. Their intonation and ability to deal with Beethoven's biggest moments also command respect."[13] Perhaps the best reviews came from Ormandy himself: a letter (shown here) with a reference to making "choral history" and an *Ithaca Journal* interview in which he ranked Sokol as one of the top five choral conductors in the country.

Thus began a close collaboration that stretched through the sixties, one of the great collaborations in the Glee Club's (and the orchestra's) history. In spring 1965 they joined again to perform the Berlioz *Te Deum*. In 1966 a still bigger occasion awaited them. Ormandy invited the Cornell singers to repeat their 1962 Beethoven performance at the opening concert of the Saratoga Performing Arts Center, the new summer home of the Philadelphia Orchestra and the New York City Ballet. Enough singers were somehow brought together in the middle of the summer (the Glee Club and Chorus were also joined by the Capitol Hill Chorale from Albany), and a week of rehearsing preceded the August 4 performance. When the inaugural evening came, the waterfall that ran

The Philadelphia Orchestra Association

EUGENE ORMANDY, MUSIC DIRECTOR

OFFICE OF THE MUSIC DIRECTOR

1405 LOCUST STREET, PHILADELPHIA 2, PENNSYLVANIA
TELEPHONE: KINGSLEY 5-3830   CABLE ADDRESS : PHILAORCH

October 15, 1962

Cornell University Glee Club and Chorus
c/o Mr. Thomas A. Sokol
222 Lincoln Hall
Cornell University
Ithaca, New York

Dear friends:

Now that the unforgetable experience of last week
is a happy memory, I want to send you my heartiest
congratulations on your superb singing with our orchestra,
both at Cornell and in Philadelphia. I do not exaggerate
when I say you made choral history, and I hope sincerely that
before long we can again make music together.

You have an inspiring director in Mr. Sokol, and
the Cornell Choir and Glee Club can expect to reach great
heights under his more than capable leadership.

May I also thank you for the most touching expression
of warmth and friendship in presenting me with the beautiful
gold medal, with the University emblem on one side and
the wonderful inscription on the other. I am deeply
grateful and, as I said to you after Tuesday's concert,
this medal will take its place proudly among the honors I
have received in the course of my long career.

Thank you for singing with us, and thank you for
singing so beautifully and, last but not least, thank you
for giving me a memento of our first, but I hope not our
last, collaboration.

Most cordially yours,

Eugene Ormandy

19. Letter from Eugene Ormandy following performances in Philadelphia and Ithaca of Beethoven's *Ninth*.

down a gorge on one side of the theater was turned off, and a capacity crowd of 5,100—with several thousand more out on the lawns—tuned their ears to the opening chords of Beethoven's *Consecration of the House Overture*. The *Eighth Symphony* followed, marred briefly by a passing freight train off in the distance. Otherwise, the outdoor environment of the hall was unobtrusively enjoyable, and the music carried clearly up the hollow and across the land-scaped countryside, all the way over to the Hall of Springs. The performance of Beethoven's *Ninth* echoed over the grounds, culminating in what the *New York Times* called a "hair-raising . . . mighty last movement." The audience of thousands rose in standing ovation. "This is the most exciting moment in my eight years as Governor of New York," Nelson Rockefeller said.[14]

Thus one of America's finest summer music festivals, perhaps second only to Tanglewood today, was launched with the help of the Cornell ensembles. One manager later wrote that the prolonged ovation following the *Ninth Symphony* marked the occasion as an artistic highlight in the history of CUGC participation in major works. The Glee Club and Chorus joined Ormandy and Philadelphia two more times during the sixties. In 1967 they participated in a performance of choruses from Johann Strauss's *Die Fledermaus* and Richard Strauss's *Der Rosenkavalier*. In the summer of 1969 they returned to Saratoga for a performance of Verdi's *Requiem,* with Maureen Forrester and Martina Arroyo among the soloists. Following the double fugue in the Sanctus, driven with clarity at a horse-race tempo by Ormandy, the audience burst into huge applause—several minutes of applause. The tale of what followed remains one of Sokol's favorite didactic anecdotes.

> The next movement, Agnus Dei, begins with two unaccompanied solo voices singing in octaves. After the five-minute applause interruption, they [the soloists] stood up. And they sang beautifully, but they started a quarter tone sharp. And nobody, neither they, nor the concertmaster, nor Mr. Ormandy really thought to sound a pitch before they began. I knew as soon as they began that there would be a collision when the orchestra entered accompanying the chorus, which repeats exactly the soloists' opening phrase. So the question in my mind flashing by was, should the chorus take the pitch of the soloists or do they make an adjustment of a quarter tone, or what? And that measure where truth comes out, one measure which takes three or four seconds, seemed like an eternity to me. It resolved very quickly, but it was just one of those marvelous examples of nonmusical details that can influence a performance, and that was a spectacular performance.

The 1960s were years ripe with opportunity to collaborate on major works, and beyond Philadelphia, the Glee Club played the field. Major works marked the 1962–1963 academic year: in addition to the Beethoven concerts, the singers performed Prokofiev's cantata *Alexander Nevsky* (reworked from the score to the Eisenstein film) with the Rochester Philharmonic, and Duruflé's *Requiem* in Boston with the women of Newton College of the Sacred Heart. The *Nevsky* performance was Theodore Bloomfield's last with the RPO, and again brought those in attendance to their feet. In 1964–1965 several anniversaries were celebrated through collaborative engagements. In fall 1964 the Glee Club performed Mozart's *Vesperae de Dominica* (K. 321) in Providence with the women of Pembroke College to celebrate the bicentennial of Brown University. The performance was led by the group's director Erich Kunzel, who later became conductor of the Cincinnati Pops and a leader in the pops world. In spring 1965 the Glee Club and Chorus traveled to New York's Lincoln Center to celebrate Cornell's centennial with a performance of Beethoven's *Missa Solemnis*. Composer Karel Husa, then conductor of the Cornell Symphony Orchestra, led the student ensembles in a performance of which the *New York Times* (March 12, 1965) said, "As for Cornell, it did itself proud . . . [Mr. Husa] drew from his forces phrasing and nuance on a professional level without dimming amateur fervor." Almost in preparation for the 1966 Saratoga opening, this concert was the first given in the New York State Theater. A performance the following fall of the Berlioz *Requiem* (called by one reviewer Berlioz's "extravaganza qua mass") again brought the singers and instrumentalists together under Husa, this time in a Bailey Hall with brass players filling almost every corner. Collaborations were also undertaken with the Buffalo Philharmonic Orchestra, including a performance of Janáček's *Slavonic Glagolitic Mass* in April 1968.

Several collaborations involved the Glee Club in premieres of new works. Their first performance with the Buffalo Philharmonic was the world premiere of Juan Orrego-Salas's *Cantata* in May 1966, which coincided with Cornell's Latin American Year. And the 1964 performance with Kunzel in Providence also had involved the world premiere of Ned Rorem's "Laudemus Tempus Actum," commissioned for the anniversary, and with an appropriate text translated as "Let us praise the past by living justly in the future." Earlier that same year, in the spring, the Glee Club gave the world premiere of Cornell professor Robert Palmer's dramatic oratorio, *Nabuchodonosor Rex*. Palmer dedicated the work to the Glee Club who, with the help of the Rochester Symphonic Brass and two soloists, related the tale of the Babylonian king who threw Shadrack and his companions into the fiery furnace. In the context of the 1960s the Old Testament tale took on new resonance as a collision of religious faith and tyranny in a totalitarian framework. The performance, given on April 25, 1964, as part of the Parents' Weekend activities and the Annual Festival of Contemporary Arts, brought plaudits for the Glee Club's promotion and performance of contemporary music. And with Sokol perspiring profusely by the end of the difficult work, no one doubted that the performance, as university organist Rudolph Kremer later put it, was "hot stuff!" Maximilian Albrecht, whose "Exsultet Sanctus" had recently been premiered by the Glee Club, wrote Sokol offering his best "congratulations on your tremendous success! You trained the Glee Club with such a skill and musical knowledge that this Choir has become an outstanding and beautiful instrument."[15]

Repertoire was not all that was new with the Glee Club. In 1963 the university separated Reunion weekend from Commencement, meaning that for the first time, the Glee Club gave a Senior Week concert, followed by a Reunion Week performance two weeks later. Another new concert was introduced that year on October 18 when, with university permission, the Glee Club gave its first Homecoming concert in Statler Auditorium. (At that time the group still performed during Fall Weekend as well, which in 1963 featured the Glee Club one night and Woody Allen the other.) On the a cappella scene the Sherwoods had been dropped from the Glee Club and replaced by the Glee Club Octaves, who had made their first appearance in 1958–1959. And on the nonmusical side the Glee Club was testing its administrative strength. As part of the reorganization efforts in the early 1960s, the group had formed an advisory council. The first members were Sokol, G. Wallace Woodworth, Austin Kiplinger 1939 of the Kiplinger Washington Letter, Bruce Widger 1951, and the Glee Club president at the time. Under their guidance plans were made in 1963 to start a Glee Club Endowment Fund, with an initial goal of $100,000.

Among other noteworthy items of 1963 was Sokol's new position—associate professor. Certainly the tour of Russia stood him in good stead for tenure, not to mention the collaboration with Ormandy and the general tone the Glee Club had taken on in practice, performance, and planning. Some question preceded the promotion, however. Deane Malott recalls Grout came to him and said "I don't think we can promote Tom Sokol this year because he hasn't produced, he's not enough of a scholar." And Malott replied, "'Great, I will then make the Glee Club a department of the public relations of the university, and the head of the Glee Club will report to me.' And that's the last I heard of it," Malott recalls with a laugh. It was hard to argue when such eminent people as Keith Falkner were writing, "Thomas Sokol was an ideal 'ambassador'. His conducting, economy of gesture and the strength and range of expression he drew from the choir were admired by everyone. His impromptu speeches were excellent. He has indeed done sterling work for the University."[16]

Even as the department weighed the tenure question, another tour of England was in the works for the summer of 1963. And it was newly appointed Associate Professor Sokol who led the group overseas to perform in Oxford's Holywell Music Room, Chichester Cathedral, the Harrow School, and St. Paul's Cathedral during the middle of June. Again the reviews were unreservedly positive. A typical response came from the Royal College of Music:

The Cornell Glee Club is a worthy successor to the [tradition of male-voice singing] and their precision in chording and tonal balance is truly remarkable.

The discipline of learning everything by heart is justified by the electric quality of their attack, which by itself would distinguish them from most English
groups of comparable size; but perhaps their most notable feature is purely
American—their sense of rhythm.[17]

Returning to Ithaca on June 27, the Glee Club rested for a few months in
preparation for the fall 1963 semester, which brought change for the Glee Club,
the university, and the course of world history.

Back in 1962 the Ford Foundation had announced that Sokol had been
named one of nine recipients of a foundation grant in the humanities and the
arts. His particular project took him to Russia, England, and Spain during fall
and winter 1963 to study performance styles in those countries. William C.
Holmes, at that time an assistant professor, was named acting director for the
semester, the Glee Club's first sabbatic replacement since Dann's 1912 respite.
Almost as soon as Holmes had begun, the Glee Club performed for the inauguration of a new Cornell president. Deane Malott had stepped down, and in
his place, Cornell's seventh president James A. Perkins took over in Day Hall.
The Glee Club sang "Spirit of Wisdom" and the Alma Mater at the October 4
ceremony, and tacked on an evening concert for the Cornell Council and Trustees. Duly saddened to see Malott go, the Glee Club nevertheless knew they had
a friend for life when the outgoing president wrote them, "The key chain I carry
with me everywhere is the one with the Glee Club medal attached."

Little more than a month later, the nation swore in a new president, Lyndon
B. Johnson, following the assassination of the nation's thirty-fifth president,
John F. Kennedy, on November 22. At that moment, all was set aside for griev-
ing, and the university joined with the rest of the world in expressing its sorrow. The following day, Saturday, November 23, more than 7,500 assembled in
Barton Hall for a memorial service. Honoring the man who once said, "The
artist best serves his nation by serving his vision of the truth," the Glee Club
and Sage Chapel Choir sang the Lacrymosa from Mozart's *Requiem,* Byrd's
"Iustorum Animae," and the National Anthem. A year later, on November 22,
1964, the Glee Club participated in a performance of Beethoven's *Missa Solemnis* dedicated to the memory of Kennedy.

That 1964–1965 season was a remarkably busy one. The *Missa* was repeated
in the spring at Lincoln Center, part of the American Universities and the Arts
Series, which nicely coincided with the Charter Day festivities a month later,
marking Cornell's 100th anniversary. The Rorem "Laudemus Tempus Actum,"
Mozart's *Vesperae de Dominica,* and the Berlioz *Te Deum* were all performed
the same year. And major works were only part of the Glee Club's season—in
addition there were the usual fall and spring concerts, the tour, and the official
university engagements, that is, Convocation, Baccalaureate, and Commencement, not to mention more informal outings, like the quad sings. Years strung

at this high level of activity typified the early Sokol years. But no semester is ever likely to outdo the spring of 1966.

The fall semester that year had been busy enough, with convocations, quad sings, and a December concert that had included the Verdi *Te Deum* (sung with the Cornell Chorus). Then in February, taking the semester off from studies, forty-one Glee Clubbers embarked on a three-month tour of Southeast Asia under the aegis of the U.S. State Department, packing their bags for Ceylon, Singapore, Malaysia, Thailand, the Philippines, Hong Kong, Taiwan, Okinawa (Ryukya Islands), Korea, and Japan. With the Vietnam War escalating, the students were not blind to motivations for the State Department's generosity, but motive mattered little. For these Glee Clubbers, this was a once-in-a-lifetime opportunity for music making, cultural exchange, and travel, not to mention total exhaustion.

The numbers were staggering—49 formal concerts, 38 television and radio appearances, and 50-some informal performances. Not counting travel days, it made an average of almost two performances a day, seven days a week, for three months straight. Some other numbers were also impressive—along with Sokol, Glee Club physician Dr. Alexius Rachun, Donald Smith from the State Department, and the Glee Club men went "55 suitcases, five trunks, 974 pieces of music . . . and several months of anticipation." Tour manager Thomas Cullen 1966 noted preparations had included "150 hours of rehearsal, 217 letters, 18 cables, 45 passports, 450 visas, 421 inoculations, 15 briefings and 36 tourist brochures."[18] As with the best musical performances, beyond the hours of rehearsal and preparation, beyond the number of notes learned and tasks attended to, the true bottom line was best represented by the countless expressions of admiration that poured out from every corner of the Far East. A letter to President Perkins from a Cornellian in the Philippines read, "[They were] the best ambassadors of goodwill that ever came to this country and they have not only sown good public relations, but left good memories and a good image of the country where they come from." One review read, "This was the best male ensemble this reviewer has ever heard and is surely one of the finest in the world."[19] Clearly, the Glee Club had triumphed again in concert and friendship.

One would think a trip of this scope would merit a few months off, but as Sokol might say, "No sir." The troubadours returned to join their colleagues in Ithaca, who had been carrying on as a second Glee Club under the direction of Holmes and, only a week later, gave the world premiere of Juan Orrego-Salas's *Cantata* with the Buffalo Philharmonic Orchestra. By that time some of the touring singers may have been back in the same time zone as the concert. The Senior Week and Reunion concerts followed, which would have marked the end of any normal year. But that was the summer the Glee Club joined the Chorus, the Philadelphia Orchestra, and Ormandy for the opening of Saratoga. There has never been a busier season in the history of the Glee Club.

During his first decade as director Sokol established an increased awareness, within the Glee Club, of the group's history. The 50th and 75th anniversaries of the group (taking 1868 as the starting date) had fallen in wartime, and understandably went unobserved. With the 1960s being a prosperous time for the Glee Club, the 100th anniversary provided a perfect occasion to celebrate the organization and its accomplishments over its first century. Obviously director and group were eager to celebrate—the festivities were planned for fall 1967, the 100th year, but in truth only the 99th birthday. "For that year I had decided and the officers concurred that we should try to do something significant in the way of repertory," Sokol says. He programmed two standout works for male chorus and orchestra—the Brahms *Alto Rhapsody* (on a text by Goethe) and Stravinsky's *Oedipus Rex;* both were performed in a gala concert on November 19, 1967, in Bailey Hall. The Glee Club was joined by the Cornell Symphony Orchestra and a cast of soloists, including Lili Chookasian as contralto in the Brahms, and Woodworth, who came from Boston to be the narrator for the Stravinsky.

Several of the Stravinsky soloists distinguished themselves that evening. John McCollum had been scheduled to sing the tenor part but took ill in Ithaca; he called up David Lloyd, who had previously sung the piece with the Boston Symphony. Lloyd met with Sokol in a Statler Hotel room to go over the score, and with no rehearsal, gave a wonderful performance. Julius Eastman, an African American involved in new music in Buffalo, rendered the bass part, the messenger who reveals Oedipus to be an orphan, not the son of Polybus, as everyone believed. The hall was dark for the Stravinsky, and as the soloists entered, they turned on standlights aimed into their faces. Unknown to anyone Eastman had painted his face silver. When he entered with the messenger's blood-curdling cry, the eerie light on his silver face froze more than a few hearts. "It was quite effective," Sokol recalls. As was the performance of the Glee Club.

The celebration continued with a centennial tour between December 16 and the New Year. Concerts were given from sea to shining sea starting in New Jersey and New York City, passing through Chicago and Milwaukee, and ending up in San Francisco, San Diego, and Los Angeles. In Chicago the Club gathered one day for a performance on WTTW-TV. "The announcer came in," Sokol remembers, "and at our rehearsal which just preceded the actual telecast, he—I think he had been having a little Christmas cheer at the time and he was having a little difficulty reading the names of some of the composers." A minute or so before the performance, which would eventually be broadcast around the country on the Educational Television Network, he approached Sokol: "Professor, would you consider just making the announcements?" "Sure, that's fine," Sokol replied. "God bless you," he said and wobbled off.

Unfortunately the tour plunged the Glee Club into substantial debt. San Diego reneged on their contract, paying the Glee Club only $15, and other income fell well short of covering expenses. The university, which generally provided the

Glee Club no support other than moral, temporarily covered the $6,000 gap while the group went to work to get back in the black.

Back in the fall of 1960, with the Russia tour looming financially, the Glee Club for the first time had sought permission from the university to solicit Glee Club alumni. This fundraising had became more formalized in the early 1960s with the CUGC endowment drive, of which one intent was to put tours on a more independent, stable financial footing. But despite a goal raised from $100,000 to $250,000, the fund was still more than a decade away from six figures; clearly neither the tour nor the endowment drive had succeeded in organizing alumni giving. With the group now in the red, the idea of a Glee Club Alumni Association was put forth. Austin Kiplinger, still a member of the Advisory Council, officially initiated the association with a letter dated October 1969, mailed along with the Glee Club's first newsletter. Citing the Club's precarious "pay-as-you-go way of living," Kiplinger wrote to appeal to the generosity of friends and former singers for the benefit of the Club's "musical, educational, and ambassadorial functions." The association and its new newsletter would "foster a means of contact between the CUGC's alumni and friends and the current Glee Club members." And one could always hope the Glee Club might, as one officer put it, "become a favorite with some wealthy alumni."

The association proved critically helpful at a time when all efforts to secure an annual allocation from the university fell through. Eventually the Club worked itself out of debt, and over time the association prospered. As for the newsletter, there was plenty of material to print in the first few numbers. The 1960s, an extraordinary decade in the history of the Glee Club, closed with a tour to Germany in January 1970. Even in debt, the Club found legs to travel, albeit aided in this instance by the generous support of the Class of 1916. Rhineland performance spots varied from formal concert venues, to less formal U.S. Army bases, to the extremely informal Mathauser beer hall in Munich. To keep the troops fresh and sober, Sokol sent them on eight laps around a youth hostel parking lot one morning and was duly recognized for his exercise regimen several days later when photographs of a few women (au naturel) showed up in one of his scores. Through all the hard work and humor over the course of the two weeks, the group grew close in song and spirit as they visited the Goethe House, inspected antique cars at a Stuttgart museum, gazed in awe at hand-carved beer barrels, and attained a moment of piety singing Gregorian chant in the Kiliankirche of Heilbronn.

The tour melded and affirmed the spirit of the Glee Club, a spirit audible in the symbolic rallying cry of "Io, Io, Io, Io, Io, Io, Io, Io, . . . Io!" from the "In taberna" section of Carl Orff's *Carmina Burana*. But by the late sixties, that spirit was being sorely tested, and the group braced for a period when its popularity would wane. The *Cornell Daily Sun* comment following a performance of the Orff in spring 1970 pointed to this problem: "This reviewer left the hall hoping that the unusually large turnout is a sign of new interest in Cornell's world-travelled and world-travelling Glee Club."[20] *Unusually* large. A semester before, a *Sun* reviewer had written of the Fall Weekend concert, "Would that the audience had been larger; but rather than aim invectives at the Cornell Community for abandoning the choral arts . . . I will only remark that it is disappointing when an auditorium filled with beautiful music is not also filled with listeners."[21] At the Advisory Council meeting that year Sokol explained that formal concerts were less well attended everywhere, and Advisory Council members noted traditional sources of income were in decline. To offset this trend the Glee Club tried giving benefit concerts for several years. Following the idea of a 1968 benefit for the United Way, the Senior Week concerts from 1970 to 1976 served as benefits for the Red Cross, Ken Kunken (a Cornell football player who had been paralyzed), Tompkins County Hospital, the Ithaca High School Music Department, Historic Ithaca, the Ithaca Community Music School, and the Bicentennial Class of 1976. As one manager put it, "The men in the Club thought we ought to be contributing more to the community than just music."[22]

The benefit concerts did aid the community and Glee Club ticket sales, but they were powerless to solve the underlying problems. The late 1960s and early 1970s were troubled times for groups such as the Glee Club, and the causes ran far deeper than competition from rock concerts. To better understand and trace the causes, we should backtrack for a moment.

The Glee Club's 1967 centennial concert, like the 50th and 75th anniversaries, fell during a war. Only this time the war was very different. And as soldiers entered a conflict halfway around the world, Vietnam left the country wrestling with its government and its conscience, a conscience already bowing under the weight of civil rights, nuclear proliferation, and individual freedom. In 1968 two of the nation's finest leaders were gunned down. Robert F. Kennedy often recalled the phrase "Men are not made for safe havens," and he and Martin Luther King Jr. proved how unsafe a haven leadership in America was. It was a time of great upheaval, of change, of rebellion against convention, particularly as embodied in institutions. Glee clubs fell into the category of institutions and, whether they deserved to or not, came under attack. It is an "ambiguous position that an organization like this finds itself in, in a time in many ways unsympathetic to it," the *Ithaca Journal* wrote of Cornell's Glee Club in the early 1970s.

Part of the rub involved what Club president Sanford Shaw, Ph.D. 1975, described as "a tendency among college students recently to become very committed to ideals, goals, and principle, but this has led for many students to a corresponding lack of commitment to any group . . . ; consistent, dedicated group participation has in many cases taken second place to individualism."[23] Perhaps in some sense Glee Club problems didn't run much deeper than competition with rock concerts, insofar as such concerts represented the voice of rebellious individualism. Moreover, as Sokol indicates, "there may have been a tendency for social innovators in that period to look upon the Glee Club or other groups . . . as remnants of the past." Add to these attitudes peaking racial tensions, readily apparent in the highly visible takeover of Willard Straight Hall in 1969, but no less present in countless, more subtle exchanges. Sokol recalls, "Pressure was exerted on students, on black students, to not take part, to not sing. We had a couple of outstanding members who were forced by their own community to withdraw. And that was a period when athletic teams also faced some of these pressures, which were the results of specific segments of the community feeling that they were, or had been, dealt with unfairly and that therefore they should not take part in established activities." Taken cumulatively, these factors thrust the Glee Club into an unpopular position. Campus sentiment—usually readily accepting of such announcements as "Come join the Glee Club and see the world" or "Come hear the Glee Club, the result of months of practice and hundreds of years of composing, like a fine aged brandy"—may have inclined instead toward such thoughts as "Yes, a fine aged brandy, like the authority we're trying to overthrow." Giving the 1968 fall concert "On the Town" off campus at the Ithaca High School probably stemmed from a feeling that the Glee Club had more friends downtown than on the Hill.

Gender issues provided yet another unpopular light for detractors to shine on the Glee Club. In 1969 Yale became a coed institution—a year later, so did its Glee Club. A trend developed when several other schools and their glee clubs admitted women. Cornell, of course, had been coed right along, but the time was ripe to test the Glee Club. In spring 1971, reputedly put up to it by several organizations, a black woman named Gayle Singleton presented herself for an audition. She had been singing some tenor parts in the Sage Chapel Choir, and because of her unusually low voice she thought she should be eligible for the Glee Club. At that time, the Glee Club's constitution read that membership was "open to any male student at the University." Sokol explained the situation, and she agreed to wait while the organization considered the matter and possibly amended the constitution. After "soul-searching and often heated debate," the Club voted twice on an amendment, neither time reaching the necessary two-thirds vote. Meanwhile the case had come to the attention of the university ombudsman, whose office started pressuring the Glee Club to change the vote. Sokol took this to be "an attempt to circumvent the whole constitutional process upon which our democratic system of change is based," and a meeting was called for March 24 with a vice president, three ombudsmen, and the university counsel in attendance.[24] At that meeting the ombudsman's office learned, much to its surprise, that Singleton might not be a bona fide tenor, and an audition was scheduled to find out. "But rather than run the risk of making a biased evaluation, which I felt might be claimed," Sokol recalls, "we arranged for her to be auditioned by objective voice teachers"—two members of the voice faculty at Ithaca College, who were to submit a sealed vocal evaluation to the ombudsman, on which any further decision could be based. The word came back independently from both that, without question, she was a contralto with an underdeveloped top range, not a tenor. And so, some said, the Glee Club "weathered the Gayle."

Even so, the issue resurfaced in the national media when the constitution was amended in the fall of 1972. Sensing they would soon find themselves with an embarrassing and illegal constitution in the face of expected federal and university legislation, Glee Clubbers voted to change the wording to read "membership is open to any student . . ." Corresponding changes were made in two articles to emphasize that the requirement for membership was no longer "male students," but rather "students with male voices (TTBB)," in accordance with the Club's stated purpose, which remained: "the study, practice, performance and promotion of music for male voices (TTBB)." The change was reported on national radio, noted in *Time Magazine,* and found its way onto a back page of the *Atlanta Journal.* "Glee Club Seeks Bassas Profundas," the Sunday *New York Times* (October 1, 1972) read, going on to say that the "Cornell University Glee Club, an exclusive domain of male voices for more than a century, has opened its membership to women—if they can sing like men, that is." Local radio stations added that the September 24 amendment meeting had ended with a rousing chorus of "For She's a Jolly Good Fellow."

In the end no women were taken. One alumnus wrote a letter canceling his association membership, adding, "Let me know when you reclaim your status— *as men!*" On the other side, beyond the gentle satirizing of the press, some probably grumbled that the amendment was merely a clever turn of phrase. The solution adopted by the organization, however, seems just. One must acknowledge the legitimacy of an ensemble based on the demands of the repertoire—the world has string quartets precisely because there is music for string quartets, and likewise has TTBB choruses because there is music for TTBB chorus.

With this debate going on, the Glee Club found the time and energy to organize a tour of Eastern Europe. For twenty days in January 1972, the group made its way through a series of concerts in Germany, Austria, Czechoslovakia, Hungary, and Yugoslavia, quickly learning the word "fabelhaft!" (marvelous!) from those responding to their music making. Anecdotes about the tour abound. There were the border crossings, language barriers, thefts, exchanges with European choirs, the hotel in Prague where to take a bath, one had to find the maid (who spoke only Czech), convince her to unlock the bathroom door, and pay a small fee of 50 cents (more in Chapter 7). Somehow the Glee Club survived the hardships, indulged the high points (which included eating well, particularly when the filet mignon was $2.50 in Belgrade), prospered in concert, and made it back to Ithaca alive.

It was on that trip that Sokol passed definitively into Glee Club legend. The last train ride of the tour was scheduled overnight from Zagreb to Stuttgart aboard the Dalmatia Express, originating in Turkey. Arriving at the station well

20. Sokol leads the group in impromptu singing in the cathedral at Estergom, Hungary, during the 1972 tour of Eastern Europe.

ahead of time to collect their luggage, the men found the unheated lobby sub-merged in a half inch of mud and slush. They dutifully trudged through the grime to Track 2 to await their train, where, with less than fifteen minutes to departure time, they were told their train was actually on Track 1. Luggage in tow, they raced down, under, and up to Track 1, desperately searching for a German-speaking conductor to tell them which car was theirs. The next to last car from the end, they were told, but that proved a red herring—it didn't even have the promised couchettes. At the last moment, tour manager John Nicolls 1972 discovered a second-class coach and began packing the men on as time elapsed. Five men, ten men (plus bags), twenty were on, half the group was on, secretary Jon Kaplan 1973 was just handing his suitcase aboard when the train began to move; he watched in disbelief as his clothes headed for Stuttgart with-out him. Panic quickly spread on both sides of the divide. Those on the plat-form wondered if they would ever meet their comrades again. Those in the dark on the train—it had no lights, no heat, and no couchettes—frantically pointed out the window at Nicolls, who still stood on the platform with *everyone's* ticket and passport in hand. Sokol was assailed with cries of "What do we do?" In the heat of battle, he sat back calmly in his seat and said, "Gentleman, we have the cigars, we have the slivovitz, let's ride on."

A head count was taken—thirty-five aboard. A debate over pulling the emer-gency break had just ensued when, quite on its own, the train ground to a halt. The express backed onto a remote track, paused, lurched forward again, and then returned to Track 1, where the Glee Club was joyfully reunited, and it was discovered the Cornell University Glee Club's coach had been added to the rear of the train.[25] In retrospect Sokol recalls of the incident, "There was a moment of question, but then I thought it was, well it was beyond the moment of panic, 'just relax and we'll go.'" At the time, perhaps he knew something more than the others. Or perhaps he viewed the scene with the breadth of perspective fine leaders often exhibit. Whatever the case, it was that kind of cool, levelheaded leadership that carried the Glee Club through the difficult days of the early 1970s.

Matters would certainly get worse before they improved. In those tumultuous times very few held the university in high esteem. President Perkins resigned in the fallout of the Straight takeover and was succeeded by Dale Corson; of the faculty and students who didn't leave, many grumbled about Cornell. With school spirit at a low the Glee Club—viewed by many as a leading voice of that spirit—suffered an unpopularity inseparable from the university's. "We all know the Glee Club is much more than a Cornelliana music box," some mem-bers protested. But try telling that to a hostile student body. Consequently the 1971 fall concert, which was in fact advertised rather cleverly by the fine-aged brandy ad, included repertoire for the upcoming Eastern European tour, but not a single Cornell song, not even the Alma Mater. And not surprisingly, the spirit within the Club, subjected to much the same defamation accorded the Cornell spirit, fell into decline. An article in the fall 1973 newsletter asked,

"C.U.G.C. Spirit—Is It Alive?" The conclusion was yes, but the 1973–1974 year marked a distinct low point for morale. Requests for inactive status ran high, a tour of the Midwest was canceled, the Club president was replaced by the vice president, and the group lost money. Almost in defiance, that year's annual report stated, "The Club refuses to lower its standards of excellence by either cutting rehearsal time, or by reverting to a lower quality of music."

Financially the pressure was on from all sides. A letter sent out to Glee Club alumni in early 1973 documented the evaporation of resources: on tour fifty years earlier, the group had received a $500 fee when only the previous year, it was $250. In 1963 the Glee Club could sell out Bailey Hall two consecutive nights on Fall Weekend, netting $8,000; now the group made $611.55 from two nights in Barnes. In 1963 the domestic operating budget was $17,000, a decade later the balance was $32. Sources of outside assistance for international touring were also running dry. When the State Department sponsored the Southeast Asia tour in 1966, their cultural budget was $7 million; by 1973 it had been cut back more than 90 percent to $600,000. Then there was the deficit to contend with, which the Club forcibly cleared in 1972–1973 after Day Hall pressured music department chair Don Randel regarding "chaotically financed" musical activities.[26] In response Randel wrote Provost Robert A. Plane, "the Glee Club has always jealously guarded an independence from the Department of Music. . . . And what is worse, the Development Office has aided directly in supporting such activities [tours] without even consulting the Department on whether such use of development funds best contributes to the support of the University's musical activities as a whole." He further argued the Club should be made responsible to the chairman of the department if it wished to retain its financial privileges in the university.[27] Its position and resources under fire, the Glee Club cleaned the financial slate, retaining its independence at the expense of its working capital.

Other groups also suffered as the university tightened its belt. In 1975 the Orchestra announced it would have to curtail collaborations with the choruses after its resources were severely cut. Only two years earlier, the Orchestra, Glee Club, and Chorus had given an extraordinary program together in Carnegie Hall, the Kennedy Center, and Bailey Hall, with Karel Husa conducting. Poulenc's *Gloria*, Beethoven's *Mass in C*, and Bach's *Cantata #4* (which Husa dedicated to Picasso at the Ithaca concert) had all been packed into one evening together with the premiere of Husa's new version of *Apotheosis of This Earth* for chorus and orchestra. Of the *Apotheosis*, one elderly woman in Washington had said, "I feel as though I have just heard a second *Rite of Spring*—such excitement!"[28]

Even though such collaborations were no longer possible, the Glee Club and Chorus could keep up an active schedule of joint concerts with outside organizations. Performances included Shostakovich's *Thirteenth* (on Yevtuchenko poems) and a program of Beethoven (*Opferlied, Calm Seas and Prosperous Voyage,* and the *Ninth Symphony*) with the Buffalo Philharmonic, the latter concert led by Michael Tilson Thomas. The *Buffalo Evening News* (April 21, 1975) reported that following the final chorus of the Beethoven, the audience "stood and shouted, and some of them seemed literally wrung out as they lurched into the lobby with a 'whew' and 'oh boy' in glaze-eyed, smiling wonder." Other 1970s collaborations included Honegger's *Le Roi David* (with Sir Keith Falkner narrating), Mahler's *Second ("Resurrection") Symphony,* Handel's *Messiah,* Bach's *Magnificat,* a performance of the Verdi *Requiem* with the Ithaca College Orchestra, Husa's *An American Te Deum,* and the American premieres of Anton Reicha's *Die Harmonie der Sphären* and *Te Deum.*

The Glee Club's interest in major works was not always keen. In 1968 concern over maintaining a balance between mixed and male voice repertoire resulted in a group vote to add twenty minutes of rehearsal time a week for the TTBB repertoire. During the 1970s alongside already exacerbated gender issues the concern took on a political tone. "You always have a conservative element within that tends to want to preserve what is," Sokol says. "Some felt they wanted to preserve the fraternal aspect of the life of the Glee Club and any watering down of this by having collaborations was somehow going to . . . remove the identity and personality of the Glee Club." For a prolonged period many clamored to sing male voice music almost exclusively, and in 1981 an amendment to the constitution was passed stating that collaborations had to be voted on by the ensemble. An officer wrote, "We need it [the amendment] to keep him [Sokol] in check. The onus rests on the skill of the Glee Club manager and president to use it for bogus collaborations and to steer around it for attractive ones." In 1981–1982 the Glee Club sang no major works, Sokol taking the Cornell Chorale instead to perform the *Missa Solemnis* with the New Haven Symphony. Eventually the sentiment against collaborations eroded with student turnover, the constitution was reamended to relax the stipulation, and the view that "rehearsing with the ladies once a week does excellent things for morale" prevailed.[29] "But there was a little period where I did have to fight against the rather recalcitrant nature of the enterprise," Sokol sums up. "And as I say, sometimes one's patience is taxed."

Collaborations aside, the Glee Club had the opportunity to host a number of international choirs in Ithaca during the late 1970s and early 1980s. Often in the States to participate in Lincoln Center's annual Festival of Choruses, the choirs included the University Chorus of Brno, the Kodály Chorus of Budapest, the Schola Cantorum of Aachen, Germany, the Cambridge University Chamber Choir, and two Polish choirs, the Academic Choir of Szczecin Technical University and the Chorus of the Gdansk Medical Academy. The Club treated them to football games, took them to the dining halls, delighted in their concerts, and sent them off with American currency (despite strict restrictions on foreign exchange). More than once hospitality was enjoyed as a reciprocation, as in the case of the singers from Brno, who had hosted the Glee Club during their 1972 travels through Europe.

As for Europe, after seven uninterrupted years on home soil, the Glee Club found its way back to the Old World with a tour to England in January 1979. The Club sang in several cathedrals, recorded for the BBC, and off the record sent a few notes bouncing off the stones of Stonehenge. Three years later they were back in England for a performance at the King's Lynn Festival. A somewhat shorter stay, spanning a week in the summer of 1982, the tour was highlighted by the performance in St. Nicholas Chapel of Schubert's "Ständchen," Bruckner's "Um Mitternacht," and Max Reger's "Die Weihe der Nacht" with Dame Janet Baker. The concert, rebroadcast on BBC television at Thanksgiving time, was a particular honor, seeing as Dame Janet and Sir Keith had been appointed by Queen Elizabeth II to run the festival.

In 1981 Sokol celebrated his silver anniversary with the Glee Club. Back when he was only 33, Ormandy had ranked him among the five best choral conductors in the country. In 1971 he had won the National Orchestral Association's Conducting Award, and as a result conducted a concert in Carnegie Hall with the Dessoff Choirs and Orchestra. (He served as music director of the Dessoff Choirs for about five years, beginning in 1967.) On this anniversary occasion he accepted the presidency of the IMC;[30] other accolades accorded him over his career from audiences, press, and fellow musicians are too numerous to count. As for the Glee Club members, they had their ways of expressing fondness for his leadership, as shown in the following three songs.

Uncle Tom

Tune: Mickey Mouse Club

Who's the leader of the Club
we know and love so well?
T-H-O, M-A-S, S-O-K-O-L!
Uncle Tom, (toot-too-doo),
Uncle Tom, (toot-too-doo),
Forever shall he lead us all in song, (in so-ng . . .)

Now it's time to say good-bye,
and sing our parting k-nell:
T-H-O, Oh, what a man!
M-A-S ssssssuch a conductor!
S-O-K-O-L![31]

Five Foot Eight

Tune: Five Foot Two

Five foot eight, eyes of slate,
Boy when he conducts we're great!
has anybody seen T S . . .

Glee Club knows, Chorus goes
Into the inactive rolls,
Has anybody seen T S . . .

Now, if you run into a five foot two
Cigar, that's him!
Nose in air, graying hair,
Looks like he's just had a trim:
That's Uncle Tom, Glee Club's Tom
With him our concerts never bomb.
Has anybody seen T S?

George Peabody

Tune: O Tannenbaum

Oh, George Peabody State Teachers' College,
Fountain of our youth and knowledge;
State Teachers' College of George Peabody,
We won't think of you as shoddy.
Your president's a local yokel,
He can't compare with Thomas Sokol.
State Teachers' College of George Peabody,
You will take most anybody.

At Sokol's 25th-anniversary celebration Stan Malinowski, A.M. 1972, Ph.D. 1978, noted in his speech, "Over the years, the Professor has survived through triumph and near-tragedy with equanimity and good humor, realizing, perhaps, that if he didn't have our respect and affection, we would not have developed into such a close-knit musical ensemble, and we might also not have bothered to think of so many ways to try his patience." Manager Stephen Strasser 1984 seconded the thought a year later, saluting Sokol for withstanding "26 years of Glee Club managers and hair-brained schemes." Individually, former Glee Clubbers took time to write thanking him for their experience in the Club, often informing him of their continued involvement in music making. Many had grown to appreciate what was described as his ability in rehearsal to bring singers close to their potential without discouraging them. "He is critical, but sympathetic," a program said of his work, adding that his intention—through the discipline and development of rehearsal—was not only to reach that potential, but to bring students beyond what they imagined it to be.[32]

Certainly many learned from his capacity for self-effacement, which in part explains the way he kept the best musical interests of the Club at heart. One year he was offered an appearance with the Glee Club on the *Ed Sullivan Show*. Sokol expressed interest, but only on the conditions that he choose the music (for whatever duration they wanted) and that the Glee Club be informed of what would directly precede and follow them on the show. After all, he explains, "there was a tendency for it to be a variety show and if you were going to do, for example in the Easter season, some sublime motet and be followed by a seal juggling a ball . . ." The Glee Club never did meet Ed Sullivan.

Even so, each decade brought interesting engagements for the Glee Club, and the early 1980s were no exception. In winter 1982, and for several years following, the group performed in New York at Cornell's annual Medical College benefit.[33] Capable of raising $1 million in an evening the benefit saw the Glee Club headlining with stars such as Raquel Welch, John Barrymore, and Bob Hope. Sometimes the men sang during cocktails, sometimes they performed later in the evening. Whatever the circumstances, the Medical School always sent them off with a check for a few thousand, and box lunches from some place like the Brasserie or Le Picnic for the bus ride home. One year the major producers hired to stage the affair asked Sokol whether the men could dress up in blue jeans and cowboy hats. "I just, you know, I just said, 'No, we don't do that.'" Perhaps such outfits would have been appropriate when the Glee Club sang for the Ag School Round-Up in the fall of 1982, for which they were paid two bushels of apples.[34]

Rather like the train in the Zagreb station, we have to back the narrative up once more to collect a few missed items, starting with the small groups. When last mentioned, the Octaves were the Glee Club's a cappella subset. However, their account was closed in 1966, and the Hangovers were founded in 1968, a hundred years after the first Glee Club. Another group, speciously called the Leftovers, was started and when the Hangovers dissolved in 1971 (mainly due to graduation), the Leftovers soon became the Hangovers and have remained the Glee Club's small group to the present day.

Frank H. T. Rhodes was inaugurated as Cornell's ninth president in the fall of 1977, immediately endearing himself to nearly everyone with his impeccably British style and eloquence. The Chorus and Glee Club joined to perform Husa's "Festive Ode for an Academic Occasion" for the inaugural ceremony, ushering in an age of increased collaboration between the two groups. Starting in 1979, at the university's request, convocations, baccalaureates, and commencements henceforth were to include both the Chorus and the Glee Club, whereas previously only the men had sung. The edict stirred up some introspection in the Glee Club. What about Senior Week? Should the women take part in that as well? With Title IX considerations as a subtext, the 1978–1979 CUGC Annual Report read:

> After much debate internal the Executive Committee recommended to the Club, which accepted the recommendation, that we invite the women to perform a short portion of the concert by themselves . . . a compromise between the camps that are on the extreme sides of the issue (a totally mixed or 50–50 split on men's and women's music, vs. an all male concert).

Although this compromise may seem strange in terms of past efforts to integrate our concerts, the circumstances may be different this time. This does not represent an effort to integrate the Chorus and the Glee Club into one mixed voice ensemble. Instead, we have another campus group of similar purpose who has every intention of becoming as strong and independent as the Glee Club is.

The invitation was extended for one year; meanwhile the Glee Club continued to struggle with the issue, which became subsumed in the question of balancing male versus mixed repertoire concerts. Some pointed to the constitution, which referred to "the study, practice, and performance . . . of music for male voices," and asked if the document was an outdated facade. Others cited the benefit of collaborations. Part of the prejudice, Sokol feels, was societal. "The public was not attracted to treble voice sounds. Pauline Treman [widow of Allan Treman] used to complain, 'I can't stand the screeching sound . . .' You look at audiences from that period, and you would have trouble with most [SSAA] choirs drawing audiences. There was a real social bias, which was manifested in the community as well as within the Glee Club." The opinion is corroborated by one statement on record, which claimed that the average Cornell person would rather hear men sing poorly than women sing well. In the end the Glee Club reextended its Senior Week invitation to the women, and public opinion warmed somewhat to treble voices, particularly in the succeeding decade.

In recent years the Cornell University Chorus has become the Glee Club's closest partner. The Chorus was formed in 1960, tracing a strong antecedent to the Women's Glee Club founded in 1920 by Lillian Dudley (that group had faded away during the late 1950s). Assembled mainly to sing major works with the Glee Club, the Chorus took part in the performances with Boulanger and Ormandy, the opening of Saratoga, the Beethoven at Lincoln Center, the Carnegie Hall/Kennedy Center extravaganza, and numerous other collaborations. They also joined the men for Parents' Weekend concerts (much as the men and women did under the Dudleys), Cornell Day concerts, and annual Christmas concerts in the Willard Straight Memorial Room. On their own they performed once or twice a year on campus but for many years neither toured nor collaborated with other ensembles. To the extent that they functioned independently of the Glee Club, it was a case of "separate and unequal." Thinking back to the activity of the Women's Glee Club in the 1930s, a former president of the group, Gladys McKay wrote, "Actually women's music at Cornell parallels women's experience in other areas of life—we move forward, then are put back and have to do it again."

More recently the Chorus has distinctly moved forward. With the university's inclusive policy regarding official celebrations giving them a greater chance to participate, the group has grown stronger and in 1980 wrote its first constitution. For several years in the late eighties Susan Davenny Wyner led the women, during which time they performed successfully in Ithaca, made short trips, and recorded for CBS. In the early 1990s, with a growing effectiveness in administering organizational affairs and a rising standard of musical performance, they have truly come into their own. The first full-length tour was taken down the East Coast in the winter of 1993, their fall Family Weekend concert (formerly the Parents' Weekend concert that took place in the spring) packed Sage Chapel, and membership grew to eighty. Over the protests of some alumni the Alumni Glee Club (men only) became the Alumni Glee Club and Chorus for Cornelliana Night, and as for Senior Week, beginning in 1988 the women ceased to be the invited guests and became full-fledged participants in the concert, giving half the program themselves.

Issues other than Senior Week occupied the Glee Club at the outset of the 1980s. Officers and other singers expressed concern that the same music was repeated too often on programs year to year—a reality both ruefully and fondly referred to as "the Sokol cycle." And for some years Glee Club for credit was a lively topic for debate. Recent Glee Clubbers, who since the late 1980s have been able to earn one credit a semester for Glee Club, may be surprised to learn that members voted down academic credit several years running. Sokol relates, "There was a strong feeling against it. Some people really felt it would take the glee out of the Glee Club. Again the issue was that this was a first step in having the Glee Club taken over by villainous outside sources, mainly the university." Nowadays some might prefer to earn all their credits from the Club, and a few deserve to, based on the number of hours they spend outside of rehearsal in the basement of Sage Chapel.

Over the years more than a few dedicated students have gotten used to the banging pipes of Sage slaving over Glee Club business. Viewed collectively from the earliest days, the work of student officers and managers constitutes a remarkable, often unsung yet enormously essential contribution to the life of the Club. Members have risked life, limb, and academic careers (not to mention the extreme heat and rodential nightlife of the basement) to ensure the Club's continued smooth running. A member once returned from an IMC convention to say that the musical aspect of the trip was only part of the story—the area in which the group plainly excelled was its organization. Indeed, the great number of selfless individuals who have stepped forward to take responsibility in Glee Club leadership, and the quality of that leadership, remain among the finest tributes to the group and its appeal. More than a few of these individuals have taken the experience and gone on to become managers of orchestras and performing artists, as well as distinguished leaders and administrators in other fields.

One effect of prolonged time in the Sage basement would appear to be a tendency toward writing. The combined output of the Club's managers—

correspondence, annual reports, financial logs, and sundry epistles—is astounding, a mountainous record bound in red folders of the Club's day-to-day life. The Tolstoy of the bunch was undoubtedly Club manager John Nicolls, who in a single year compiled seven red volumes, each one nearly two inches thick with papers. In more recent years (due to computers) the volume has dropped off some. In addition there are the special achievements, smaller pieces that might make an interesting book in themselves. (Alternate song lyrics and an excerpt from a constitution parody can be found in Chapter 10.) Of note is "The Secretary's Report to the Masses," released in 1980 by the Club's correspondence secretary, Robert (Spunky) Lubarsky 1979. A short, entertainingly neurotic work, the report to the masses notes, "Uninformed suppositions merely display the mind of the thinker; they could easily have nothing to do with the Professor." It takes the view the Club has a "history that we remember . . .," migrates into a consideration of the typewriter's keyboard, and concludes, "After having considered a problem or question, how do you leave gracefully?"

In 1982 Sokol became acting chairman of the music department. For the fall semester, David Conte, D.M.A. 1983, served as acting director while Sokol moved downstairs in Lincoln and settled into his administrative post. Dating back to Bill Holmes, the Sokol era Glee Club had worked with several acting directors: David Buttolph, who came from SUNY Binghamton, and William Welker 1973, M.B.A. 1975, David Janower 1974, and Peter Labombarde, A.M. 1983, who were all involved in the Club as singers. Conte was a graduate student in composition, as was Byron Adams, D.M.A. 1984, who served as acting director in the spring of 1984, and for the entire 1985–1986 season. Involvement inspired creativity, and both Conte and Adams wrote pieces specifically for Cornell's choral groups; more than one such work, including Conte's "Canticle," have entered the repertoire of ensembles across the country. More recently Ronald Schiller Jr. 1986 served as acting director in 1992–1993, having already become well acquainted with the group through four years as an undergraduate, and five years (1987–1992) as assistant conductor.

For his part Sokol became the actual chairman in 1985, staying in the position for seven years. Many Glee Clubbers could remember Steinberg's *Nuits de la Foundation Maegt* and the Asian print that hung behind him on the wall, and the actual chair, in which he would lean back, close his eyes, and contemplate justice as it pertained to whatever matter a bumbling undergraduate had just set before him. Not that he didn't get out of the chair. Under his leadership, and that of acting directors, the Club continued to rehearse and perform "hymns, hers, and possibly some motets" as one ad put it. And there were, of course, major works. In 1980 the group collaborated with the New Jersey Symphony Orchestra and its conductor Thomas Michalak in a Carnegie Hall performance of the *Stabat Mater* and the little-known *Harnasie* of Polish composer Karol Szymanowski; the *New York Times* rated it among the top ten concerts of the year.

Also in 1980 the Glee Club performed Mahler's *Das klangende Lied* with the Buffalo Philharmonic and Julius Rudel. Over the next decade and a half the list of major works included Handel's *Te Deum,* Haydn's *Creation,* Mozart's *Mass in C Minor,* Beethoven's *Choral Fantasy,* Berlioz's *L'enfance du Christ,* Bruckner's *Mass in E Minor,* Mahler's *Second Symphony,* Stravinsky's *Symphony of Psalms,* and Bernstein's *Chichester Psalms* (on two occasions, once with the Ithaca College Women's Chorale). In 1988, in conjunction with Ithaca's celebration of its 100th anniversary as a city, Carl St. Clair led a performance of Britten's *War Requiem* involving the Glee Club, the Chorus, the Ithaca Children's Choir, the Cornell Symphony, and the Cayuga Chamber Orchestra.

The one year the Glee Club did not perform a major work (1981–1982) it raised its financial goals. Namely, the endowment campaign was revived and retargeted for $300,000, a bold move, seeing as the original drive had stalled well short of its $100,000 goal. But the Glee Club had beaten the odds before. The Development Office said the group might raise $1,500 at best for the 1979 England tour, to which the Club responded by raising nearly $10,000. A special committee and a phonathon launched the new drive, and Pauline Treman immediately aided the effort with a gift of $10,000. By the mid-1990s the endowment was still short of $300,000, but well past $100,000, and certainly capable of significant growth in the years ahead.[35]

International and domestic tours topped the list of projects slated to benefit from the endowment, and the Club kept the odometer rolling throughout the 1980s. Only six months before the journey to England in the summer of 1982, the group took a ten-day tour to Florida, the most popular Glee Club state during the decade. After a visit to southern California in 1983, they went back down the East Coast to Florida, where the men held the second Fort Myers Bowl and put in a hard day's work at the Tortuga Beach Club on Sanibel Island. They traveled to New England in 1985, the Great Lakes region in 1986, and in 1987 back to Florida. On the way they passed through Macon, Georgia, where they traded in the pigskin for a frisbee. After one match of ultimate frisbee, a Southern belle approached the men. "Who wun the awltimate game?" she asked. "The North," the veritably witty T. P. Enders 1991 responded. A year later the Club voted him president. In the winter of 1988 the Glee Club ventured south again, where the men charmed listeners in Kansas, Arkansas, Texas, and Missouri with (or perhaps in spite of) their Yankee spirit. A 1990 tour to the Pacific Northwest, picking up in San Francisco where the 1983 tour had left off, rounded out the decade.

As for international voyages, in early 1984 managers submitted to university administrators a proposal for a China tour, tentatively slated for January 1986. The idea of visiting China could be traced back at least as far as 1980, but the actual trip to Asia had to be postponed several times while sufficient funds and contacts were secured. The tour was finally set for January 1989, but even before the group could leave, a brouhaha ensued with an Ithaca travel agency and litigation followed.[36] Meanwhile alternate arrangements were made, and after traveling by several circuitous routes, the group convened in Singapore on New Year's Eve. A few performances later, they continued on, giving concerts over the next two weeks in Beijing, Shanghai, and Hong Kong. The schedule was light compared with other tours, but the opportunity for cultural and musical exchange was great, and the Glee Club collaborated with several Asian ensembles, both vocal and instrumental. A Cornell camera crew, following the singers everywhere except into the Forbidden City (the cameras were not allowed), captured the tour in a video entitled "Geographical Fugue," later aired on PBS.

Continuing an inadvertent pattern of international tours—1972, 1979, 1982, 1989—the next followed in January 1992, when the Glee Club spent two-and-a-half weeks in Spain, France, and Switzerland. With a handsome ad of Luciano Pavarotti endorsing American Express on the tour program's back cover, the group made its way from Madrid and the walled worlds of Toledo and Avila to Lyons, Geneva, and Zurich. A collaborative concert with the Lyons Symphony Orchestra, Les Petits Chanteurs de Lyon, and the women of the Geneva University Chorus was given in Lyons and repeated in Geneva's Victoria Hall. The program featured Brahms's *Gesang der Parzen* and *Alto Rhapsody,* as well as Walter Piston's "Carnival Song" with the brass of the Lyons orchestra. For the rest of the tour, the Club was on its own, performing some of the standards of the male repertory, including Poulenc's "Quatre petites prières de St. François d'Assise," Milhaud's "Psaume 121," Biebl's "Ave Maria," and Tchesnokov's "Spahsyehnyeh." The tour recordings were culled and later that year the Glee Club released its first CD, "A Concert of Cathedral Music."

In 1993 the Glee Club turned 125, joining a handful of American glee clubs who have lived to mark the occasion. To celebrate the anniversary, members past and present gathered at Homecoming Weekend that November, spruced up to include a banquet at the Statler (and an impromptu performance with the Chorus for First Lady Hillary Rodham Clinton, whose itinerary brought her through Ithaca the day before the concert) as well as the traditional concert in Sage. The performance that weekend, highlighted by the world premiere of David Conte's *Carmina Juventutis* (Songs of Youth), and bolstered by the voices of dozens of Glee Club alumni in the Cornell Songs, was tremendously moving—one of the truly spectacular Homecoming concerts in the history of the group.

It would prove Sokol's last.[37] He retired from Cornell in spring 1995, a time of great changing of the guard for the university. President Rhodes had just stepped down, together with several members of the senior administration, creating a situation similar to that of 1921, when Hollis Dann and Jacob Gould Schurman had to be replaced simultaneously. Now Cornell's future has been entrusted to its tenth president, Hunter Rawlings III, and the future of the Glee Club to Sokol's successor, Scott Tucker.

21. The Glee Club in song at the ensemble's 125th anniversary celebration.

In April 1995 hundreds of alumni of the Cornell choral groups—the Chorus, Glee Club, Sage Chapel Choir, and Chorale—gathered to pay tribute to Sokol. On the evening of the 29th, the Glee Club and Chorus performed Beethoven's *Missa Solemnis* in Bailey Hall with the Cayuga Chamber Orchestra, led by Heiichiro Ohyama. At the close of the concert, coming out for his bow as chorusmaster, Sokol was greeted by a thunderous standing ovation, recognizing thirty-eight years of service to Cornell, its students, and American choral music. The reception went well into the evening, and the tributes continued at a brunch the following morning for a man who, faced in 1957 with a decision to come to Ithaca, later claimed, "Woody thought it would be a good thing to do, and so I did it . . ."

The Glee Club had its own way of saying farewell and thank you. On June 8 the group held a black tie affair in the Memorial Room of Willard Straight Hall. Again, more than a hundred alumni and three university presidents gathered to honor the captain, in high Glee Club fashion—Cuban cigars, cordials, and complimentary CUGC Apollo head golf balls. Sokol led the Club one last time in the Biebl and Tchesnokov, and at the close of the evening's program, many rose to offer toasts—both humorous and tearfully poignant—to the patriarch of the family.

Sokol had a habit of slipping out after rehearsal down the back stairs of Sage while announcements were being made, doing it in such a way that almost no one ever noticed at what moment he'd left. We cannot let him step out here in the same way, for as the chapter on the Glee Club's most remarkable era to date closes, there is room for one last toast.

The great violinist Isaac Stern once said, "In order to bring out the spiritual content of a work of music, talent must be blended with the artist's humanity and decency and with his whole belief in his art." A man of humility equal to his ability, Sokol exhibited exemplary humanity and graciousness during his years on the podium—and it showed in the music, in the students, and in his respect for both. And he believed in his art—in the process of rehearsal, and the power of performance. Time and again, he underscored the necessity of discipline in attaining true artistic freedom, of focus on details, which in their consummation could become what he referred to as the "golden moments of performance." To him the enjoyment was not distinct from the discipline, but by reason of it, and with patience and perseverance, he pursued the music and this process of educating, by which many were exposed to those high moments of life found in and after great performances.

"One has to accept the fact that perfection in performance is the goal, but it's one that is rarely if ever reached," Sokol has said. "But the process itself . . . of learning and performing is very important, and is almost unique in higher education." To him the university represented a place to work toward "an alliance between the whole enterprise of serious music making and intellectual stimulation." In 1970, sensing the musical side of that alliance was getting the short shrift at Cornell, he spoke out in strong defense of performance:

> *Music* is the heart of musical study; and *musical performance* is the soul of music, just as *scholarship* is its conscience and *composition* is its cutting edge! . . .
> In my opinion it is unacceptable (in fact it is not entirely honest) to relegate performance to an arbitrary position of a sort of respected humanistic hobby, or to leave it to chance, or to subjugate it through neglect or design.[38]

Over the years many benefited from this belief in performance and hands-on experience. Several young musicians had the invaluable opportunity to serve under him as assistant conductors, and like the managers they have made significant contributions to the life of the ensembles during their apprenticeships. Likewise, the "aspiring historians, physicians, engineers, zoologists, architects, lawyers," as the group was once described by the *Sovietskaya Musica,* have had the chance to grow as musicians and people, through the process of making music at a high level with a leader who has been called "one of the most gracious and inspired musicians and teachers in America."[39]

As for Sokol's musicianship, the record of accolades and the vitality of the

Glee Club during his tenure speak for themselves. As a conductor, Sokol might best be described with words that likewise apply to his demeanor off the podium—brilliantly understated. Conducting most often with his hands, he was a master of turning the musical phrase. The declamation of the text, intonation, the acoustic of a hall, and any number of other details all received attention, but in the end few could turn the corner of a motet cadence like he did. On the best of tours, with the flexibility established through memorization and a few timely reminders of "All eyes here," phrases never turned the same way twice.

On and off the podium Sokol personified a phrase Ernest Hemingway once coined: courage is "grace under pressure." Repeatedly his presence of mind carried the Club safely past potential disaster, and his wit prevailed in the face of great odds, musical or otherwise. "That's very nice," he would say, maintaining the general decorum under trying circumstances, and setting an example for his men, who often took heart in his rarely, if ever, expressing despair in public. One need only recall the slivovitz story, or the day when, rehearsing the Husa *Apotheosis* with the Chorus and Glee Club, he came to the moment where the score called for a chord cluster, consisting of nearly every chromatic pitch in the space of an octave. As the singers did their best to find and hold a note in the din, Sokol leaned into the organ, his eyes closed and chin tilted slightly up, and calmly waved a finger at the alto section. "I think we need a little more G-sharp." With this sense of humor and timing came his delight in the music (many will remember the look that would come over his face when the pianists reached the three-against-two rhythm in the four-hand accompaniment to "Fight for Cornell," a place he called perhaps the "finest moment in college songs"), and his collection of favorite anecdotes. He would expound on the mystery of "semiboneless ham," the moment the dove of the Holy Spirit ascended from the rose window in Sage Chapel, or the time "we were singing with Mr. Ormandy, a few years back . . ."—with other stories, they have become part of the canon of the Glee Club's oral tradition, to be retold for some time to come.

Sokol has always been urbane. But for those familiar with him, there is another word, a word in which the musician, the sage, the teacher, and the diplomat all coalesced: "*the* Professor," or "Professor."

Always the gentleman, Professor interpreted the Glee Club's mission with high-mindedness and pursued it with a keen sense of propriety. In nearly four decades together he and the men of the Glee Club achieved a remarkable record: hundreds of successful performances, dozens of major work collaborations, nine international tours with visits to more than twenty countries, domestic tours covering the continental United States, premieres of new works, and—a record that may count highest of all—the education of more than a thousand young men, along with a remarkable number of golden moments.

Henceforth, as with those who worked before and with him, his legacy will stand as a cornerstone for the future of the Glee Club, and of Cornell choral music. Looking to the road ahead, one might borrow the word President Rhodes used so often to close his Commencement address, and say to Professor and the Glee Club he served so well, "Godspeed."

6   The Songs

Lift the Chorus, speed it onward.

—Cornell's Alma Mater

Slowly the mist off the lake rises through wet trees, and settles on the Hill, shrouding the "upstate Gothic" stones of the campus. A lone undergraduate treads up the slope, books on back, as A. D. White looks from his seat out over the valley. It is a quiet hour, with only a murmur of life beginning to spread through the expectant morning air. And then, from up in the tower, the bells peal forth with a sound that hangs for a moment on the mist. "Far above Cayuga's waters . . . ," the notes echo over the land while the next phrase continues, "with its waves of blue." Only it sounds like, "clang, clong-dong bong, clannnggg . . ."

After all, as Broadway composer Jule Styne said, "A song without words is just a piece of music." And since the beginning of the university, well before the bells had a clock tower to hang in, the Glee Club has put words to the music that rings out each day over Ithaca and the surrounding towns. Of course before anyone had a song to sing, someone had to pen the words, and in the case of Cornell's Alma Mater it was two roommates, Archibald Crosswell Weeks 1872 and Wilmot Moses Smith 1874.

They shared lodgings at 60 North Tioga Street (site of the present-day county courthouse), where Weeks took bass and Smith the tenor in duets the pair improvised between studies. Among their particular favorites was the lachrymose ballad "Annie Lisle," which recounted the sad demise of a beautiful, tubercular young woman. Written by Boston minstrel-musician H. S. Thompson in 1857, the air followed a convention in vogue at that time, taking as its title a woman with two syllables in her first name and one syllable in her last. Hence, Annie Lisle was preceded by "Lilly Dale" and joined by "Ellie Rhee," "Ida May," and "Jenny Dale, the sister of Lilly Dale." Jenny and Lilly weren't the only relatives. As Gilbert Chase pointed out, "The maid who dwelt on the lake, or near the lake, and who perished with the autumn's leaf [as they often did in these songs], was first cousin to Poe's 'rare and radiant maiden whom the angels named Lenore.'"[1] Annie Lisle, like Annabel Lee after her, was one such maiden—"Wave, willows; murmur, waters; / Golden sunbeams, smile; / Earthly music cannot waken / Lovely Annie Lisle."

In about 1870, Weeks recalled, "I proposed that we adapt a College Song to the music, and suggested the first two lines of the first verse; [Smith] responded with the third and fourth, I with the fifth and sixth and he with the seventh and eighth. The chorus was the result of mutual suggestion." The result:

> Far above Cayuga's waters
> With its waves of blue,
> Stands our noble Alma Mater,
> Ever free and true.
> Far above the distant humming
> Of the busy town
> Reared against the arch of Heaven,
> Looks she proudly down.
>
> *Chorus*
> Ever rolling, surging onward,
> Glad her praises tell,
> Hail to thee, our Alma Mater,
> Hail to thee Cornell.

The eight lines of verse and four-line chorus followed the structure of "Annie Lisle," though a few slight melodic changes were made, such as the passing note added for "Far *a*-bove" to accommodate the text. Between 1876 and 1900 the words evolved, a good part of the revision likely the work of Colin K. Urquhart, who was listed as author of the Alma Mater in an 1876 edition of *Carmina Collegensia: A Complete Collection of the Songs of the American Colleges.* His version borrowed much from the original, though notably, he changed "Ever free and true" to "Glorious to view," and "distant humming" to "busy humming." Still, his chorus reads:

> Lift the chorus, sped [sic] it homeward,
> Loud her praises tell,
> Hail to thee! oh Alma Mater,
> Hail, all hail, Cornell.

Further revisions obviously were made before the 1900 edition of Cornell songs published by B. F. Lent of Ithaca. In this incarnation the Alma Mater had six verses all told, the first two reading as follows:

> Far above Cayuga's waters,
> With its waves of blue,

Stands our noble Alma Mater,
Glorious to view.

Chorus
Lift the chorus, speed it onward
Loud her praises tell;
Hail to thee, our Alma Mater,
Hail, all hail, Cornell!

Far above the busy humming
Of the bustling town,
Reared against the arch of heaven,
Looks she proudly down.

This remains the standard version sung at Cornell since that time, with the chorus following four rather than eight initial lines of verse.

As to the various authorship debates that ensued in the late nineteenth and early twentieth centuries, it seems safe to name Weeks and Smith as authors, and Urquhart as reviser of the Alma Mater. Several other nameless individuals presumably had a hand in the current version. As for the tune, indisputably Thompson's, it has become the Alma Mater melody for a remarkable number of other colleges and secondary schools, including Syracuse, Lehigh, William and Mary, Swarthmore, Williams, Vanderbilt, Clemson, Indiana, and the Citadel. After a Glee Club concert on the Island of Formosa in 1966, one listener expressed pleasure at hearing Cornell's Alma Mater, as it was the same as his— "and he had graduated some years before from a university on the mainland of China!"[2] Despite the large number of imitators Cornell appears to be the first institution to use "Annie Lisle" as its Alma Mater, though Bowdoin and Trinity College had used it previously for other college songs.

Over time Cornell's Alma Mater has ensconced itself in tradition, and as such, can become the flintstone for fierce debate. The debate, for example, over the proper pronunciation of "Cayuga" is as traditional as the song itself. Other aspects of "performance practice" can likewise provoke alumni to rush to their Alma Mater's defense in an effort to safeguard tradition. At one point Rym Berry chastised the band director for presuming to play the Alma Mater as though it actually were "Annie Lisle." The stanzas are "entirely different from those of 'Annie Lisle' in theme, spirit, and pace," he wrote. "The tempo of the original melody was not at all adapted to expressing the feeling of 'Far above Cayuga's waters,' or to lifting the chorus or speeding it on its way." If there was any question as to how the song should be rendered, he suggested listening to "the accepted interpretation of the 'Alma Mater' as recorded by the Cornell Glee Club before Pearl Harbor and widely distributed by the Alumni Association. There is nothing funeral about that," he said. "The pace is gay and joyous, as befits the lyric. The music takes the chorus and lifts it indeed!"[3]

If the Alma Mater is one bookend to the Cornell songs, the other is the "Evening Song." According to the 1907–1908 student handbook, they were the most popular, songs "every student should know by heart before he has been here two weeks." With such poetic lyrics as "Music with the twilight falls / O'er the dreaming lake and dell / 'Tis an echo from the walls / Of our own, our fair Cornell" and its soft musical hues, "Evening Song" beautifully evokes the glow of twilight over the western hill. The song first appeared in the *Cornell Era* in 1877, attributed simply to T., and was to be sung to the music of the German carol "O Tannenbaum." The author—since unveiled—was Henry Tyrell of the Class of 1880; the song became almost immediately "an especial favorite," which it has remained to this day.

Neither of these however was the first song sung by the Glee Club. As will be recalled from Chapter 1, the first Cornell song sung, and probably the first written, was "The Chimes," penned by Judge Francis Miles Finch to George F. Root's Civil War air "Tramp! Tramp! Tramp! the Soldiers Are Marching":

> To the busy morning light,
> To the slumbers of the night,
> To the labor and the lessons of the hour,
> With a ringing, rhythmic tone,
> O'er the lake and valley blown,
> Call the voices, watching, waking in the tower.
>
> *Chorus*
> Cling, clang, cling, the bells are ringing,
> Hope and help their chiming tells;
> Through the Cascadilla dell,
> 'Neath the arches of Cornell,
> Float the melody and music of the bells.

Three more verses followed the chorus, making reference more than once to "our angel in the tower." Finch, who also wrote words for "Smoking Song" and "Founder's Hymn," had written "The Chimes" at the request of Jennie McGraw, who certainly qualified as that angel. Perhaps it was appropriate the Glee Club opened its singing career with a tribute to the school's omnipresent musical voice, its chimes, and their eventual home in what has become Cornell's central icon—McGraw Tower.

The 1900 edition of Cornell songs quotes an 1874 *Cornell Review* as picking two songs, one of them "The Chimes," as "probably the best yet contributed towards the future Carmina Cornelliana." The other song was "Cornell." Published in an 1869 *Cornell Era* shortly after the Glee Club aired "The Chimes,"

"Cornell" came from the pen of George Kingsley Birge, who was listed in the first *Cornelian* as the Orpheus Glee Club's poet. Following a conceit of "X loves Y, U loves V," and so forth, the first verse ends: "The sailor loves his haven's pier, / The shadow loves the dell, / The student holds no name so dear / As thy good name, Cornell." Also called "The Soldier's Song," "Cornell" confirms that Birge attained some level of lyrical achievement during his short term in poetic office. Regarding the song's melody, some have listed it as "My Last Cigar," others as "'Twas Off the Blue Canaries," and still others as "Dearest Mae," a "ballad from the Catawba region of North Carolina that was composed by James Power in 1847."[4]

Thus far we have heard only from Cornell lyricists, not Cornell composers. "The practice of adapting new texts to popular tunes was very common during the latter nineteenth century and through the first decade of this century," Sokol writes, "especially in American colleges and universities."[5] In the early years of the university, such publications as the *Era* were filled with Cornell songs written by students on borrowed tunes. An 1876 edition of *Carmina Collegensia* already listed twenty Cornell songs, almost all in the format "Title," "Author," and "Air." Most of their words and melodies are forgotten, along with their titles, "Tell Me, Maiden," "The Good Old Cornell Times," "The Ship," "The Girls of Ithaca," "The Owl Song," and "Ye Gallant Sophomore." Eventually several homegrown tunesmiths emerged. One of the first was C. W. Raymond 1875, a member of the Collegensia Quintette, who arranged the "Training Song." Another was Archibald Weeks of Alma Mater fame, who devised the music for "1875: The Cornell Cheer," with its chorus, "Cornell I yell, yell, yell, Cornell!" Lyricist Kenneth Roberts 1908 joined forces with Theodore J. Lindorff 1907 to produce "Carnelian and White," and "Fight for Cornell." Roberts later wrote that the two had conceived the former song during geology lectures. "As first evolved, it rhymed and scanned; but when Mr. Lindorff hummed the words and scrawled musical notes where his geology notes should have been, he couldn't quite feel for my line endings. Yet he liked his own tune so much that I couldn't hold out against his urgings to accommodate the words to his music."[6] The best poets on Tin Pan Alley could have sympathized.

Creating musical Cornelliana was not a pastime limited to students. In addition to Finch other "grown-ups" got into the act. University organist James Quarles wrote the music to the "Cornell Hymn" ("Lo, at her feet"), and Morris Bishop 1914, the words to "Tales of Old Cornell." In 1921 Acting President Albert Smith 1878 penned the words to "The Hill" as a reunion invitation to alumni. George Pond 1910 set them to music, along with another Smith poem, "Hail Thou in Majesty, Cornell," which Pond arranged for the "use of the Cornell Glee Club." Outside composers also contributed to Cornell's tradition in song. Will A. Dillon, who wrote the popular song "I Want a Girl Just Like the Girl That Married Dear Old Dad," wrote the words and music to "My Old Cornell." And in 1900 William Luton Wood, composer of "Smoking Song," set melodies to "Alumni Song," and "Crew Song," which had existed as poems since the early 1890s.[7] His music for the phrase "And for fame of Alma Mater" in "Crew Song" epitomizes the soaring, at times nostalgic sound of school spirit.

As in the case of the numerous rowing songs, such as "1875," which recalled the crew's historic victory at Saratoga that year, many Cornell songs either celebrated or encouraged athletic achievement (a distinct aspect of American college songs discussed in Chapter 2). Aside from an Alma Mater, American schools are most likely to have a fight song in their musical history. And of these the majority will focus on football, the archetypal college sport, which at least in the Northeast seems to go along with the autumn that graces many campus quadrangles.[8] In the Cornell collection "The Big Red Team" remains one of the preeminent favorites, often sung by the Glee Club in tandem with "Fight for Cornell" in a version spruced up by creative four-hand piano accompaniment. Rym Berry wrote the words to the song in 1905, the year after he graduated, reputedly inspired by a cheerleader announcing a prize of twenty-five dollars for "a Cornell football song indigenous in words and music." He later wrote,

> I was told by the cheerleader not to make the words boastful, bumptious, or vainglorious because the prospects looked pretty punk for the team. I wrote the lyrics of THE BIG RED TEAM that afternoon and produced them at dinner. Charles E. Tourison '05 (degree in '06), then leader of the Glee Club, wrote the music after dinner, and by ten p.m. the brothers were singing the thing repeatedly and with zest. To the best of my knowledge and belief the appellation "Big Red Team" was never used before that. . . . The song won the prize and was sung and played by the band at a football game about two weeks later.[9]

Not all Cornell songs have such creative histories, but more than one has a story to tell. When Charles Tourison turned lyricist (likely with help from his Beta Theta Pi brothers W. L. Umstad and Bill Forbes), he burlesqued George M. Cohan's music to come up with "Give My Regards to Davy," the tale of a hapless undergraduate "busted" by David F. Hoy 1891. Hoy was university registrar and thus had the power to eject any undergraduate not up to snuff as far as Cornell academic standards were concerned. Another Cornell song printed in the 1900 edition, the "Bustonian Chorus," laments:

> An' my bloomin' heart is achin'
> 'cause I cannot stay no more
> In these stately 'alls o' learnin',
> Far above Cayuga's shore . . .
>
> Cornell Universitee an' its bloomin' facultee
> Where old Davy raises thunder up in Morrill, No. 3 . . .

22. The legendary pair of "Give My Regards to Davy," *left,* Dean T. F. Crane, *right,* Registrar David Hoy.

> Far away from dear Cornell,
> Never more to hear the yell—
> Oh, a sad an' dreary story is this tale I have to tell![10]

"Davy's" protagonist is more recalcitrant, confident that:

> We'll all have drinks
> at Theodore Zinck's
> when I get back next fall.

In the "Song of the Classes," the story of student life is put forth in a more programmatic fashion. Year by year, the triumphs and travails of Cornell are recounted till the senior steps out and waxes down to a low F singing:

> Oh, I am the senior tormented with doubt,
> My time at Cornell has almost run out;
> The world situation has me quite annoy'd,
> I'm *magna cum laude,* but still unemployed.

Like "The Big Red Team," which for awhile could be used to keep track of the school's size ("Three thousand strong, we march, march along . . ." when it was first written, 5,000 in 1916, 9,000 in 1949, 10,000 since then), the "Song of the Classes" has evolved with the times. The original version, written in 1890 by Frank A. Abbott 1890, has a sophomore who "sports 'round town with the boys of his age, and makes frequent calls on the coeds at Sage." Likewise, the junior's "mood mellows out over lager and tripe," and the seniors "go to the theatre and cut quite a swell."[11] Since then, women's, alumni, and veteran's verses have been introduced, along with countless variations on the original four. The 1960s brought: "Oh, I am the junior, a-smoking my pot; / My mind is expanding and starting to rot . . ." Who can say what the song's students will be up to in the future.

Cornell's first students pressed for school songs to speed the university—by way of tradition—from yearling to legend. At first any songs would do, but over time students strove to amass a repertoire whose value advanced the fame of alma mater. In those years the *Era* complained, "It is true we do have our college songs, but in character they are below those of Europe, and they are especially behind the latter in the frequency of their use."[12] Students envisioned "a procession of students going home from one of their places of assembly in full song," with the leader of the basses shouting "Bass here!" and the tenor, "Tenor here!" to organize the forces, or a community akin to the German gymnasia, "where students and professors met for social confab, to eat, sing and play."[13] Even so, despite complaints about Cornell's musical climate, considerable attention was afforded the school songs. And singing in some form became an observed tradition, as in the case of senior singing, described on 1873's class day as, "The class then gathered around the fountain and smoked the calumet of peace, entertaining the audiences by the singing of their college songs."[14]

In the 1990s when many students graduate with no idea of their school's Alma Mater, the Glee Club—along with the Chorus, the Chimes, and the Big Red Band—is largely responsible for the perpetuation of Cornell's musical heritage. No class has sung as a whole for decades (the very idea would surprise most undergraduates), and no student newspapers clamor for new Cornell songs, or for upholding the old. The tradition is carried on in different ways. The Glee Club has held annual quad sings to teach the songs, and usually closes most programs with a few Cornell selections, culminating in the audience rising for the Alma Mater. Certainly such university functions as convocations and commencements remain occasions for singing Cornell songs, and between performances and parties (not to mention in between them), the Glee Club at some time or another has probably sung nearly every Cornell song ever written. In these ways, though the *Era's* editors might shake their heads to see the state of student singing, the songs once hummed by all who tread the Hill will continue to live.

Like the chimes, on which one might hear Liszt's "Second Hungarian Rhapsody," "Penny Lane" of the Beatles, or the Irish song "Danny Boy" on any given day, the Glee Club's program has included far more than Cornell songs over the years. Pieces performed have encompassed a wide variety of styles, periods, and topics, not to mention languages ranging from Russian, Czech, and Chinese to Hebrew, Yoruba, and Latin. Let us consider a representative sampling of that repertoire.

In 1883 the Glee Club gave a program to which one reviewer responded that the "awkward and frightened appearance of several will undoubtedly be remedied after they become more used to facing such audiences as listened to their music."[15] Nerves were to be expected—it was the Glee Club's first performance entirely on its own. Up to that point singing shared the stage with gymnastics, juggling, "heart-rending" tragedy, or instrumental solos performed by artists outside the group, as in the case of the 1876 and 1877 Musical Association programs. The group typically had sung no more than two or three selections on each half of these programs, which in the 1870s included such non-Cornell songs as "Sailor Boy," "Banish, O Maiden," "O Tempora, O Mores," "Wanderer's Return," "The Parting Day," "What Beam So Bright," and "Integer Vitae," a hymn tune by Friedrich Flemming which F. Dana Burnet 1911 eventually outfitted with new words—"Spirit of wisdom, like an altar burning"—to create the "Song for Cornell," better known as "Spirit of Wisdom."

As the Glee Club took responsibility for a full program, necessarily increasing the number and variety of songs, their exposure to criticism increased as well. "No part of our college life shows greater change and generally vacillating tendency than the class and quality of our songs," the *Era* lamented, speaking not of Cornell songs but of those beyond them to which the Glee Club had ventured.

> The gradual change from the purely "college song," the one dealing alone with the incidents of college life,—has been certain. . . . It is a matter to be regretted that to-day we delight in the somewhat questionable songs of the negro minstrel stage and the cheap variety show. . . . We cannot think we have made any marked advance in our musical tastes while we suffer such substitutes for our legitimate college music.[16]

In other words the ivory tower should insist on its own musical representation, somehow indigenous in style and subject, rather than panning off its American contexts.

This attitude was taken overboard however in the argument that an audience was "willing to overlook all defects in listening to rollicking college songs," with the accompanying assumption that this was reason enough not to include anything else. Such an attitude came clear in criticism of Hollis Dann's programming for the 1890–1891 season. One review said, "It is to be regretted that so many sentimental songs found their way onto the program," and an editorial on the same subject argued, "let them give an evening of *college song,* not love sick ballads, and not grand opera." The main objection here was not degradation, but a perceived "elevation of musical culture." A 1892 review made it quite clear what would keep the critics happy: "What made the concert so entertaining was the fact that no attempt was made to render classical music; all the pieces were popular airs, and as the concert closed with the familiar strains of 'Far above Cayuga's waters,' everyone felt he had been listening to a characteristic college entertainment."[17]

Despite some criticisms of repertory, the Glee Club's performances were by and large popular. At this time audience enthusiasm mandated a repertoire of encores, and it was entirely possible that "of a program of seventeen selections, eleven were encored and half of these encored twice over."[18] On a program from early 1896 shown here one listener penciled in the additional titles, revealing selections and encores typical to a turn-of-the-century Glee Club performance. The printed program often told less than half the evening's story. Also we see selections by the Banjo and Mandolin Clubs, who had joined Glee Club programs in the early 1890s. Their presence took some pressure off the singers, spiced up the program, and offered the possibility of collaboration, which appealed to many: "The 'Tinker's Chorus' [from De Koven's *Robin Hood*] by the Glee Club with mandolin accompaniment was by far the most taking thing that has been given by a Cornell club in years."[19]

Collaboration of another kind was attempted in 1895, the year Dann first tried to mount a music festival. As the *Ithaca Daily Journal* later confessed, "Ithaca

PROGRAMME

PART FIRST

1. *a*—ALMA MATER . . . . *Carm. Cor.*

FAR above Cayuga's waters,
With its waves of blue,
Stands our noble Alma Mater
Glorious to view.

Far above the busy humming
Of the bustling town,
Reared against the arch of Heaven,
Looks she proudly down.

CHORUS:
Lift the chorus, speed it onward,
Loud her praises tell,
Hail to thee, our Alma Mater!
Hail, all hail, Cornell!

b—CORNELL
Beauty's eyes. SOLO BY MR. STURDEVANT

2. KRINOLIN TWO-STEP . . . . *Norris*

BANJO CLUB

PART FIRST (CONTINUED)

3. I'LL SING THEE SONGS OF ARABY . . . . *Clay*
(1) Grandma.
(2) Old folks at home. MR. CLINTON
4. SEGUIDILLA . . . . *Holst*

MANDOLIN CLUB

5. THE LITTLE PEACH . . . . *Neidlinger*
(1) The Farmer.
(2) The Boy in apple Tree
6. THE MERRY MILLER . . . . *De Koven*
(1) Singer's Patrol GLEE AND MANDOLIN CLUBS

PART SECOND

1. LULLABY . . . . *Kjerulf*
(1) My mother's Songs MR. RAMSBURG
2. CATASTROPHE . . . . *Sprague*
(1) Simple Simon
(2) Monkey & Chimporzee
3. AQUILENA . . . . *Paul Eno*

BANJO CLUB

4. MEDLEY *'95* . . . . *Arr. for the Club by H. E. Dann*
(2) Mrs. Winslow (3) They kissed
5. SLUMBER SONG . . . . *Newcomb*

MANDOLIN CLUB

6. TOPICAL SONG, with original verses . . . . *Hawley*
(2, Barnyard Serenade. (1) Song of all nations
(3) Out of sight (4) Ducks MR. FUERTES
7. EVENING SONG . . . . *Carm. Cornell*

WHEN the sun fades far away,
In the crimson of the west,
And the voices of the day
Murmer low and sink to rest.

Life is joyous when the hours
Move in melody along,
All its happiness is ours,
While we join the vesper song.

CHORUS:
Music with the twilight falls,
O'er the dreaming lake and dell;
'Tis an echo from the walls
Of our own, our fair Cornell.

Welcome night, and welcome rest,
Fading music, fare thee well;
Joy to all we love the best,—
Love to thee, our fair Cornell!

23. Program from 1896 with encores penciled in.

was not ready." Here again the pioneering Dann encountered resistance to elevating musical culture, the same strain Davison would find at Harvard twenty-five years later. But Dann's musical vision eventually led to a quiet revolution in both public opinion and the public's exposure to good music. In 1904 the Glee Club sang in Mendelssohn's *Elijah*, launching an association with major works that would continue through the 1920 Music Festival. Those years saw performances of Verdi's *Requiem*, Haydn's *Creation*, and Handel's *Messiah*, which remain staples in today's repertory, in addition to several works now unfamiliar to most ears: Elgar's *Dream of Gerontius*, Coleridge–Taylor's *Hiawatha's Wedding Feast*, Moussorgsky's *Joshua*, Dubois's *Seven Last Words of Christ*, and Gounod's *By Babylon's Wave*.

As for the Glee Club's own program in the early twentieth century, Robert Doyle 1915 later recalled, "the repertoire of the club was largely in the ballad and upper class music of the then popular period, although at times we used some of the lighter classics." Walter Price 1920 remembered singing "Old Man Noah," "It's a Long Way to Tipperary," "Napolean," and "Hannah" ("There was a young woman named Hannah / Who trod on a piece of banana / A slip and a slide / and more stars she espied / Than there are on the Star-Spangled Banner"). He noted the music for the programs was divided into groups, the Alma Mater starting the first group. Groups were separated by the playing of the Mandolin Club and generally "consisted of a 'sober song' followed by a 'light' or humorous one."[20]

Eric Dudley took over in 1921 and during the first decade of his leadership the Glee Club's own program grew in musical ambition—some went so far as to call it presumption—while retaining the light-hearted stunts popular in postwar years. In 1929 one member wrote, "The program itself sounds highbrow, but the encore numbers usually are the opposite. I think there will be two or three comedy stunts."[21] During these years Gilbert and Sullivan began to appear regularly on programs, and "Going Home," with lyrics set to the Largo from Dvorak's *New World Symphony*, became a favorite for Senior Week. The music festivals had of course disappeared, but with the advent of the Women's Glee Club and a rich harvest of vocal talent, the men and women collaborated in opera excerpts and eventually full-scale operettas. During the 1930s audiences heard choruses from *Carmen* and *The Merry Widow* and saw staged performances of *The Mikado*, *Pinafore*, and *Princess Ida*.

The staged operetta was joined by the staged variety show as the Glee Club began to adapt to the effect of radio. A 1937 letter read, "The capable singing and playing of favorite melodies will remain the basis of the program, but this year the concert will steal some tricks from Metropolitan reviews . . . more specialties and stunt numbers, namely quartets, instrumental novelties, and tap dances," and later that same year, "Our performance consists of a fine selection of vocal and instrumental numbers tied together in an informal way with a clever plot and dialogue supplemented by numerous novelties."[22] George Coleman's dictum to college groups "to entertain the public with the informal spirit of student life as lived in the University" took on metafictional aspects in 1938, when the Glee Club presented "Shifting Scenes," a year in the life of "Our Clubs." After an introduction (the school song "Cornell Victorious") the drama unfolded with scene 1: Rehearsal, scene 2: Junior Week Show, scene 3: Rehearsal, scene 4: En Route (including "Keep in the Middle of the Road," arranged by Marshall Bartholomew), scene 5: Operetta (Sullivan's one-act *Cox and Box*), and scene 6: Formal Concert. These musical extravaganzas had begun in 1935–1936 with "Oh, What a Night!" and at times even the printed program imitated "novelty in musical entertainment." The "menu" (shown here) was served up in the Bailey Tavern of Wichita, Eric Dudley, proprietor.

The variety show reached a higher level of cohesion and urbanity with Richard Lee's one-act operetta, "Coediquette," premiered in 1940 and promised as the "best in Cornell music plus the latest campus capers." Set at Cornell, the operetta followed the "art imitates life" motto that had led students back in 1914–1915 to jokingly propose a comic opera on tension between townies and collegians. In this case, as the denouement of "Coediquette" brought the elimination of grades, the students may have wished for Nabokov's argument "life imitates art" to be borne out. The operetta so impressed tour audiences that one paper wrote, "It won't be surprising if one of the songs, 'Dry Away the Tears,' is heard on the air one of these days."[23]

Lee's Cornell song "In the Red and White" had already been heard nationwide courtesy of the Fred Waring singers and as part of the Glee Club's 1939 tour program, of which it was the title song. With an accompaniment modestly more interesting than the normal fare, the song was released on a 12-inch record with Alma Mater and "Evening Song," one of two Glee Club records advertised for sale in 1940.[24] (The other recording included "Cornell," "Alumni Song," "Carnelian and White," and "March on, Cornell.") Lee's next effort in Cornell songwriting, "Strike Up a Song," has remained in the active repertory to this day, its opening arpeggio somehow reminiscent of Edvard Grieg's "Brothers, Sing On," whose chorus

> Come and let our swelling song
> Mount like the whirling wind,
> As it meets our singing throng,
> So blithe of heart and mind.
>
> Care and sorrow now be gone,
> Brothers in song, sing on!
> Brothers, sing on, sing on!

has become to some, like Samuel Webbe's "Glorious Apollo" in days past, a theme song for male choruses in America.

BAILEY TAVERN

*Special Dinner

FEBRUARY 7, 1936

Two Guitars Cocktail

—::—

Song of the Bayou Consommé

—::—

Rantin' Rovin' Robin en Casserole

Winter Song au Dartmouth

—::—

Sweet Potatoes Ocharine   Annies Laurie

—::—

Sleigh Salad

—::—

Pizzicato Polka Parfait

—::—

BEVERAGES

Laughing Song Burgundy   Border Ballad Scotch

Song of Fellowship Cordial

You'll Like Our Home (on the range) Cooking

24. "Oh, What a Night!" program from 1936.

In the brief interim during which Kuypers and Weaver led the Glee Club, the repertoire tended toward "long-haired" music and away from the variety show. Weaver's spring program in 1946 included the women singing Liszt and Gibbons, the men singing Bach and Morley, and the two groups joining in choruses from Borodin's *Prince Igor* and Moussorgsky's *Boris Godunov.*

"Here We Are Again" the program read in 1947, referring to both title and repertoire. Songs from the Dudley years reappeared in force, including "Tenor and Baritone," of which Tom Tracy had sung the baritone half as an undergraduate in the early 1930s. Howard Heinsius 1950 and Duncan Sells were the new duo, a pairing equivalent in Glee Club terms to perhaps Abbott and Costello. The change from a "'stiff shirt' concert to a more lively production fashioned after a musical comedy" was elsewhere evident in everything from the mix of Cornell songs and comic recitations to changes in Duncan Sells's solo listings.[25] In spring 1946 the program read:

Arias for Baritone
Joseph D. Sells

Wher'er You Walk, from Semele .... George Frederick Handel
Vision Fugitive, from Hérodiade .... Jules Massenet

The next spring it became:

Captain Strattons Fancy .... Taylor
Duncan Sells

One part of the program not "here again" from prewar days was the presence of the instrumental clubs, though one alumnus awaited their resurrection, writing that the combined Glee, Banjo, and Mandolin Club show provided more diversification.[26] The absence of the instrumentalists precluded the possibility of operetta in the Dudley fashion, but the variety-style presentation—or "a ninety minute show with over ninety voices featuring favorite Cornell selections, rousing English ballads, and numerous skits interspersed with music, mirth, and madness," as the Glee Club called it in publicity—suited the Club's resources and the tastes of Tracy and the times. Of particular note were the specialty acts—Casey at the Bat in 1947, a pair of jugglers in 1949, Selly Brewer's magic and fur-clad cossacks in 1951, and two years later "German Double Talk" followed immediately by Bach's "Now Let Every Tongue Adore Thee" (a program that also included "Old Mother Hubbard" in the style of Handel). In 1952 one soloist produced a genuine pug, which wore a "dude collar and acted very much frightened." In Tracy's last years as director these novelty acts were kept to a minimum and preference was given to the singing, as indicated in the comment that the group's program did not include anything "bordering on slapstick comedy."

As for the songs themselves, the 1947 Senior Week program "Strike Up a Song" (shown here) offers a cross-section of the Glee Club's repertory during Tracy's

PROGRAM

PART I

Strike Up A Song ....*Lee* '41

Crew Song ....*Wood*

Tenor and Baritone ....*Wilson*
Howard Heinsius and Duncan Sells

The Jolly Beggars ....*Levridge*

The Laughing Song ....*Abt*

Casey At The Bat
David Bancel

Quartette Selections
Haberl, Landon, Wood, Sells

Drinking Song ....*Romberg*

Shenandoah ....*Trad.*

Brothers Sing On ....*Grieg*

INTERMISSION

PART II

Cornell ....*Songs of Cornell*

Alumni Song ....*Songs of Cornell*
Howard Heinsius and The Glee Club

Phonetic Punctuation
Scott Edwards

25. "Strike Up a Song" program from 1947.

Rolling Down to Rio ....*German*

The Rangers Song ....*Tierney*
             Duncan Sells and Glee Club

Quartette Selections

The Song of The Classes ....Songs of Cornell
        Priester, Davis, Blatt, Heinsius, Simkins, Sells

Goin' Home ....*Dvorak*
   Incidental Solos   Erwin Davis and John Chapin

Alma Mater ....Songs of Cornell

25. *Continued*

tenure. Other songs such as "Begin the Beguine," "I Ride an Old Paint," "Dry Bones," and "In My Arms" appeared in the decade that followed, along with Handel's "Hallelujah, Amen," Haydn's "Great and Glorious," and Bach's "Now Praise We Great and Famous Men." Almost without fail Tracy programs opened either with "Strike Up a Song," "March on, Cornell," or "Cornell Victorious." Obviously he found value in constancy rather than change; the Glee Club programs evolved slowly, often containing repeated numbers year to year. Programs in 1954, 1955, and 1956 opened with the same two Cornell songs, and all included Mozart's Lacrymosa, which appeared on the program again in 1956–1957. The 1954 and 1955 programs also included "Black Is the Color of My True Love's Hair" and "Down in the Valley," already on the 1953 program.

Tracy's years were not noted for programmatic ambition. Perhaps propriety would have been offended anyway had too many master composers been forced to share the stage with a pug. But for those concerned that the Glee Club's repertoire was not equal to its musical ability and for those who eschewed involvement in major works, the hour of change was at hand. Sokol took over in 1957 and began to put more depth into the musical lineup. In the early years he followed the tradition of opening with Cornell songs, but was likely to segue into Allegri's "Miserere" or a Mode 1 chant. Ruffling some feathers at the outset, this became an accepted tradition with time. Even in Sokol's first year, one critic wrote, "Musically, with respect to program and technical perfection, it seemed to be an improvement over the concerts given this past year."[27]

With the ensuing tours abroad, national flavors often pervaded the program. Traveling to Russia in 1960, the Glee Club took Tchesnokov's "Spahsyehnyeh" and Shostakovich's "P, ésn,a M,íra" (Song of Peace) and "Taská pa rod,in,i" (Longing for Homeland). The group found that every time they came to a particular phrase in the last song, their Soviet audiences would laugh. Finally the group inquired if there was a problem, to which a native replied that Soviets were enjoying the irony of hearing Americans sing, "Russia is the most beautiful land in the world." Fearing this could become unfortunate propaganda in the wrong hands, Sokol sustained and won a last-minute argument with Moscow television officials, and the Glee Club did not perform the piece on live television. The song remained a hit with concert audiences throughout the tour, however.

Holst's "Turn Back, O Man" and Byrd's "Iustorum Animae" were taken to England in 1963, and "Arirang" (a Korean folk song) and "Sri Lanka Matha" went with the group to East Asia in 1966. The latter was recorded for use by Radio Ceylon, and as far as anyone knows, the sound of the Cornell University Glee Club may still open their broadcast day. In 1970 Mendelssohn, Distler, and Orff were sung in Germany; in 1972 Bartók's "Huszarnota" was performed in Budapest, Janáček's Three Male Part Songs in Prague, and Schubert's "Wiederspruch" and "Gesang der Geister über den Wassern" in Munich. In China in 1989 the group performed the unison folk song "Lao Yeh Wung," which conveys the thoughts of a Chinese fisherman. And in 1992 the Glee Club sang Milhaud's "Psaume 121" and two of Poulenc's "Quatre petites prières de St. François d'Assise" in the old Lyons cathedral. Standing beneath the towering vault that would soon echo with the power and mysterious majesty of French organ music, Sokol explained the way he would like a phrase in the Poulenc to go. "When you come to the text 'par amour,' bring it out," he said. And with a gleam in his eye he added, "And I know that's right, because Poulenc told me so."

In addition to representing the music of other nations the Glee Club has taken a good sampling of American music abroad with them. Copland's "Simple Gifts" or another piece from his Old American Songs collection, Bernstein's "Gee, Officer Krupke," or a few selections from *Candide* often proved favorites, along with African American spirituals, or a work by Randall Thompson.

International tours often afforded opportunities to collect new music from other countries. In Germany in 1970 the Glee Club was scheduled to record a program for the Frankfurt Radio Network. During the session a voice made repeated intelligent comments over the loudspeaker about intonation and phrasing, and according to Sokol "what he was saying was absolutely correct." When the session ended, the man came out of the booth to introduce himself—Franz Biebl, music director of the network. He gave Sokol some of his own music to look over, which included an arrangement of Hungarian folk songs the Glee Club performed two years later in Budapest, and an Ave Maria. Today, several decades after Sokol brought the piece to the States, few male choristers in America need further introduction to Biebl's "Ave Maria."

Back at home the Glee Club could advertise programs containing the music of fourteen countries (as they did after the 1972 tour), though most years programs were slightly less international. Still, the number of foreign languages

CORNELL UNIVERSITY GLEE CLUB

October 29, 1977

PROGRAM

Domine salvum fac . . . . *Charles Gounod*
(1818–1893)

Kyrie eleison (Mode I) . . . . *Gregorian Chant*
Twelfth Century

Peccata mea, Domine . . . . *Jean Mouton*
(*ca.* 1470–1522)

The Heavens Proclaim Him . . . . *Beethoven*
(1770–1827)

Mailied (1876; Op. 13, No. 3) . . . . . . *Hugo Wolf*
Text by Goethe (1860–1903)

Widerspruch (Op. 105, No. 1) . . . . . . *Schubert*
Text by Johann Seidl (1797–1828)

Carnival Song (1938) . . . . *Walter Piston*
Text by Lorenzo de'Medici (1894–1976)
Howard Pollack, James Parakilas, *Pianists*

INTERMISSION

The Turtle Dove . . . . *English Folk Song*
Arranged by Ralph Vaughan Williams
Soloists: James Gordon, Peter Chatel, Ted Snedden

Old Folks at Home . . . . *Stephen Foster*
Arranged by Ralph Vaughan Williams (1826–1864)
Soloist: Don Reaves

Little Innocent Lamb . . . . *American Spiritual*
Arranged by Marshall Bartholomew
Soloists: James Gordon, Ted Snedden,
Peter Chatel, Robert Menes

Soon I Will be Done . . . . *American Spiritual*
Arranged by William Dawson

Selections by the HANGOVERS
Cornell Songs
The Big Red Team
Fight for Cornell
Give my Regards to Davy
Alumni Song
Song of the Classes
Evening Song
Alma Mater

26. Fall concert program from 1977.

usually ranged from four to seven on any given Sokol program, which over the years came to have a recognizable signature. Though an early Sokol program (1962) opened with "Spirit of Wisdom" and had Mendelssohn, Schubert, Debussy, and Bach all on the second half, the reverse became true in more recent years. A standard Sokol program often began with Gregorian chant and then moved into several sacred pieces, followed by secular works by such composers as Mendelssohn, Schubert, or Debussy. The first half usually ended with a "ripsnorter," like Piston's "Carnival Song," selections from Orff's *Carmina Burana,* or more recently a spiritual from the Wendell Whalum series like "Betelehemu." Catches, glees, folk songs, spirituals, and Gilbert and Sullivan were usually found in the second half, along with an appearance by the small group, and a set of Cornell songs to close the program. Encores as they once existed were gone, with the exception of a single encore, which Sokol offered on more than one occasion as a "chaser" following the Alma Mater.

During Sokol's directorship Glee Club programs occasionally offered the attraction of a premiere. Several works by Maximilian Albrecht were given first performances, including his "Exsultet Sanctus" in 1962. The Czech composer Bohuslav Martinu's *Prophecy of Isaiah* received its first American performance by the Glee Club in 1968, followed by a premiere of his *Field Mass* in 1970. Robert Palmer's *Nabuchodonosor* was given its world premiere in 1964, and joining with the Chorus the Glee Club gave the American premieres of Anton Reicha's *Te Deum* and *Die Harmonie der Sphären* a decade later. The Glee Club frequently performed the music of Karel Husa, including the first hearing of the revised version of his *Apotheosis of This Earth.* And numerous premieres of assistant conductors' works have been given, among them "Tenebrae Facta Sunt" by Duane Heller, D.M.A. 1990, and several David Conte pieces now published by E. C. Schirmer.

Over the years the Glee Club has logged many miles through the standards of the major work repertoire, from the Cherubini *Requiem* and Stravinsky's *Oedipus Rex,* to Beethoven's *Choral Fantasy* (on the occasion of the composer's 200th birthday) and *Ninth Symphony.* In 1995 the 1962 performance of the *Ninth* with Ormandy and the Philadelphia Orchestra was remastered and released on CD. Then too the Glee Club brought infrequently heard major works before the public, such as Janáček's *Slavonic Glagolitic Mass* with the Buffalo Philharmonic Orchestra in 1968 and Karol Szymanowski's *Stabat Mater* and *Harnasie* with the New Jersey Symphony in 1980.

Programs in Sokol's time featured other novelties, such as "Crux Fidelis" by John IV, king of Portugal from 1640 to 1656 (on the 1971 Senior Week program), and William Billing's "Modern Music" (printed in 1781) with its text: "And now we address you as Friends to the cause . . . 'tis the part of the Hearers to clap their Applause." One of the more unusual pieces performed by the Glee Club was Ernst Toch's "Fuge aus der Geographie" (from his 1930 work *Gesprochene Musik*) which begins with the text: "Ratibor, / und der Fluss Mississippi und die Stadt Honolulu, und der See Titicaca. / Der Popocatepetl liegt nicht in Canada, / sondern in Mexico, Mexico, Mexico / Canada, Malaga, Rimini, Brindisi . . ."[28]

There are no notes, only the spoken exclamation "Ratibor!" repeatedly launching the fugue theme, and the sixteenth-note triplets of "Canada, Malaga, Rimini, Brindisi."

The piece was slated to be the Commencement anthem in 1970, a year when university officials were concerned that "students then actively protesting the Viet Nam war might attempt to stage a demonstration. . . . Precautions had been taken to minimize the disturbance that such an outburst might create," John Nicolls remembers, and then

> It happened. Right after, as I recall, President Corson's address to graduating students, David Burack charged the stage and attempted to take control of the podium. It is widely, *and falsely,* believed that Blanchard [Rideout, the university marshal and secretary of the university, who had accompanied the Glee Club to Germany that January] took hold of the University Mace and attempted to use it to subdue Burack. In fact, the defensive act was performed by the University Mace Bearer Morris Bishop, then University Historian Emeritus.
>
> By plan, the podium mike was turned off, but the crowd (students) started chanting. As it was time for our anthem, Sokol commanded our attention—we let out our opening line—RATIBOR . . . The crowd apparently thought we were joining them and shut up—after all we had the benefit of the PA System! It's the only time I know of that the Club shouted down a public demonstration![29]

Novelties aside, the standards were the trademark of programs during the Sokol years, and many were repeated. Not entirely like Tracy, who carried pieces through several adjoining years, Sokol's form of repetition, dubbed the "Sokol cycle," worked over three or four years. The obvious disadvantage was minimal student and audience exposure to the repertoire excluded from the cycle. On the other hand the repetition created a body of songs familiar to current members and alums from thirty years ago when the two came together to sing. And that continuity can create something special when during a round of "Tancuj," the Biebl, "Spahsyehnyeh," "Loch Lomond," or "Ride the Chariot" a freshman realizes, as an alumnus sings the same part next to him, that he belongs to a tradition much larger than himself.

After all that is the greatest song the Glee Club sings—not an air about fair young maidens or a drunken abbot; not a ballad from deep valleys or far seas, not a discordant battle cry or the melody of peace, but the song behind the song that all these conjure up. The song of a community, extending across generations and joined to make music—as "Glorious Apollo" says:

> Thus then combining,
> Hands and hearts joining,
> Sing we, in harmony, Apollo's praise.
>
> Thus then combining,
> Hands and hearts joining,
> Long may continue our unity and joy.

Back at the turn of the century a story was told about several Cornellians who took a camping trip in Wyoming. As evening neared, the group fixed their camp on the bank of a river and sat to enjoy the scene, at which point someone struck into "Evening Song."

The others joined, and in the clear evening air, their voices rang out across the river, awaking the echoes, far and near. When they reached the last stanza:

> "Welcome night, and welcome rest,
>   Fading music, fare thee well;
> Joy to all we love the best,
>   Love to thee, our fair Cornell!"

White grasped my hand and I could see, in the twilight, that his eyes, like my own, were misty with tears. It was foolish, I know, but then, boys, the time and place seemed to make our feelings more pronounced. The melody, which had so stirred our hearts, reached the ears of some young men camping just across the river, and soon we were surprised to hear them singing, "We'll honor thee, Cornell;" whereupon my daughter, turning to me, exclaimed:

"They must be Cornellians!"

"They are evidently answering our song," observed White's son, and then he suggested that we sing Alma Mater, and see if they answered that. When the young men had finished their song, they gave the well-known Cornell yell, which out there in the far West fairly set our hearts on fire, and it was with most intense enthusiasm that we began to sing that song, so dear to us all. Scarcely had the first words left our lips when we saw, in the deepening twilight, those four young men launching their boat, and as they rowed rapidly across the river, they sang with us the dear old song. As their boat approached the shore, they shouted, as with one voice:—

"Are you from Cornell, *too?*"

We needed no introductions, we could have none so satisfactory as that little word "*too.*"[30]

Those who have been a part of the Glee Club know the feeling. There is nothing quite like it, nothing quite like coming into the place in the midst of a song where people truly meet and may say afterward, "et in arcadia ego."

7   The Odysseys

Ithaca has given you the beautiful voyage.

—C. P. Cavafy, "Ithaca"

"There are ships in plenty / here in seagirt Ithaca . . . / and I will look them over for you to find out the best one, / and soon we shall stow our gear and put out onto the wide sea." So writes Homer in the *Odyssey*. Many years later, a group of young men have packed their bags and set out from a different Ithaca, halfway around the world. When they departed, perhaps they sought the experience Greek poet Constantine Cavafy describes in his poem "Ithaca":

> When you start on your journey to Ithaca,
>   then pray that the road is long,
>   full of adventure, full of knowledge.[1]

For the thousands who have traveled on concert tours with the Cornell University Glee Club, it has been such a journey.

The first Cornell ensemble to venture out from Ithaca did not travel far. "The first appearance of any Cornell musical organization before the outside world seems to have taken place in 1873," the *Cornell Era* later wrote, "when there was an organization known as the Cascadilla Operatic Troupe, a sort of minstrel society with 'Abie Doodle as leader, assisted by thirteen specialists,' as their announcements state. This 'troupe' gave an entertainment in Cortland, and scored a great success."[2] Cortland, only twenty-five miles away, became the Glee Club's first port of call three years later, following a morale-boosting concert in Ithaca. Back then one could reach Cortland by a combination of walking and riding a train and/or tallyho. The group took a train and surely some Glee Clubbers never forgot their trip, as several musicians found themselves in a cattle car, serenading "a few aborigines of both sexes." The concert, given by the whole Musical Association, came off on May 5, 1876, and though unlucrative scored another musical success for Cornell. The university with one foot in the cow pasture and the other in the concert hall had taken its show on the road.

As Cortland was an isolated trip, called a "one-nighter" these days, the travels of 1880 might be considered the first Glee Club "concert tour." Between May 24 and 29 the group performed in Trumansburg, Auburn, and Syracuse—again not far afield but a step forward for a young band of students traveling by train and steamboat to expand their role as wandering minstrels. That role was set aside during much of the decade while the Glee Club decided whether it was going to exist, until the late 1880s when trips were taken to Cazenovia, Binghamton, and the one-time home of Mark Twain, Elmira. Then came the trip to Owego, which abundantly demonstrates the informality of arrangements surrounding out-of-town performances in those years.

Early in the afternoon of February 1, 1888, the group set out for that small town to the south, arriving only to find "no posters had been put up, no notices put in the papers, and no arrangements made for the concert." With fine emotion, "the Club proceeded at once to procure a four-in-hand and do the town. With a red and white flag waving, large posters covering the front and back of the sleigh, and a gong ringing they tried hard to dispose of the seats." By concert time, the house was full (the audience already familiar with the young men's efforts), and "the concert itself was a grand success."[3]

After Hollis Dann became director in 1889, the Glee Club began to show more direction in its travels. During his first year they traveled in February to Utica, Albany, and Troy, from which they returned to Ithaca by the short route (as opposed to the *Odyssey*'s ten-year journey).[4] Because of inadequate advertising the trip was a financial failure, but the group did have the chance to call on the governor in Albany. In Dann's second year the Glee Club performed outside New York State for the first time, visiting Auburn, Syracuse, Rochester, Buffalo, Detroit, Toledo, Ann Arbor, Cleveland, and Erie over the Easter recess of 1891. That trip, spanning more than a week, marked a tremendous leap in the Club's touring ambition, the first of many tours to fill a university vacation with a formidable itinerary of cities. Dann's crew proved their first major tour was no fluke when they reached Chicago a year later, having revisited several cities, including Buffalo, Cleveland, Detroit, and Toledo along the way. Chicago's *Inter Ocean* was enthusiastic:

> The concert at Central Music Hall was one of the most successful college club concerts Chicago has ever known. The weather which stormed in every key could not keep the people away, and the result was that Central Music Hall held the largest and most fashionable audience it has known for months. For once there was novelty in a college concert. For once the chestnut was roasted in the background and not brought to view. For once a college club concert pleased everybody.[5]

The year 1893 brought the group to Milwaukee and St. Paul, 1894 to Cincinnati and St. Louis. The Christmas holiday of 1894–1895 marked the first win-

27. The Glee Club on tour in the Midwest, April 1894.

ter tour, during which the Glee Club performed for the first time in the nation's capital. The *Washington Times* wrote: "The affair was given under distinguished patronage, and was one of the most successful musical events of what has been an auspicious season."[6] Each tour, big-town papers noted the "fashionable" audiences attending the Glee Club concerts, while back home the *Era* recognized the numerous alumni hosting the Club. The innovation of 1891 had by the middle of the decade become a tradition: American cities could anticipate Cornell Glee Club concerts, and because of recent successes, alumni felt justified in throwing their weight behind the necessary preparations. With a growing confidence in touring and perhaps a slight feeling of wanderlust, the Glee Club looked toward the horizon and the shores of the Old World.

Someone in the know once said of the early tours, "We were always careful to take along money enough to pay our way back."[7] Nothing could have been more apropos of the Glee Club's 1895 tour to England. Back on that 1888 afternoon in Owego, one can imagine a few men nervously fingering their empty pockets when the audience had yet to be corralled. But the prospect of hitchhiking home from Owego did not compare with the daunting proposition of getting back from England.

The tour did not start with such ominous thoughts—the group set out, hoping to second the efforts of the Cornell Crew at the Henley Regatta. Much of the university turned out at the Lehigh Valley train station (on West Buffalo Street, site of a restaurant today) to see the Cornellians off, giving a rousing Cornell yell for the navy; on June 19 the Musical Clubs sailed for Europe aboard one of the most famous ocean liners of the time, the *City of Paris*. Upon arrival they were treated to a celebratory dinner at the American Club of London, it being one hundred and nineteen years to the day that a bunch of New World rebels had declared their independence from the British Empire. The clubs gave their first official concert the next night, July 5, in London's St. James's Hall. The American ambassador to England was not in attendance that night, though the U.S. ambassador to Italy was, along with a contingent of Cornell and University of Pennsylvania students who sat in the center of the house, waving a huge American flag whenever the audience applauded. They applauded long and often, calling for double and triple encores, which apparently miffed many London critics. Dann reported one newspaperman had told him, "Nothing so disgruntles the English critics as a very enthusiastic reception of any concert or piece." Before the evening was over he had confided to Dann that the critics were all sour. "They could not understand why [you] should be given so many encores."[8]

That might explain some befuddled reviews: "A performance of a curious and unconventional character was given yesterday evening . . .," and the dismissive account in the next day's *Times:*

> The entertainment given in St. James's hall last night . . . if rather depressing, was not entirely devoid of interest. With the exception of some negro melodies, sung in the approved style by the Misses Leech, and some student songs and glees capitally given by the Glee Club, the long programme—prolonged to an altogether absurd length by the number of encores—consisted of banjo and mandolin pieces. These . . . exercised a most exhilarating effect upon the audience, and it cannot be denied that the players did all that was humanly possible with their rather characterless instruments. The music selected calls for no special mention; neither it nor the various composers are known in England, or, if known, they are quite unimportant.

Well, there it is. Nevertheless, whether out of courtesy or sincere conviction the overwhelming critical response was extremely positive. Noting Cornell's "go-ahead qualities which characterize our American cousins," one review stated that the "instrumentalists played with skill and expression, but the best feature of the entertainment was the glee singing, some of the numbers being extremely humorous and exceedingly well sung."[9] The encore "Mrs. Winslow's Soothing Syrup," with its waltzing refrain "It soothes the child and softens the gums," was a special favorite, and Dann had to be pleased with one critic's suggestion that the English could learn something from the musicianship of the Americans.

The American troubadours continued on their way, heading for a July 10 concert at St. Mary's Hall of Henley, where seats were advertised at two shillings for the gallery, and four shillings for the stalls. The concert was scheduled to coincide with the regatta, but misfortune struck the Cornell Crew. In the first race against Leander the umpire queried if Cornell was ready, they replied yes, and when Leander apparently replied in the affirmative, Cornell's oarsmen set out with a strong stroke. The Leander shell began uncertainly and then stopped dead in the water. Cornell paused, but the umpire signaled the race was on, so they continued on to the finish at a leisurely pace. Leander argued they had not been ready and had said so to the umpire, but the race remained Cornell's. After the Americans lost to Trinity the next day, the press derided them both for the shortness of their stroke (not noticing the new sliding board they employed), and their unsportsmanlike victory.

Upon his return Dann compared Cornell's athletic and musical reception in England: "The English critics were very fair with us, but we ran against the same prejudice and trouble that the crew experienced—the utter failure of the Britons to acknowledge the worth of anything new. The Glee Club was a new departure to them, and the critics frankly said that when invited to attend the concert they were at a loss whether to treat it from a professional standpoint or as an amateur affair."

The connection between the Glee Club and the crew went beyond innovation—their fates were inextricably tied. "Previous to the race I had received many letters requesting dates for concerts of the Cornell Glee Club, and many bookings had been made in different parts of Great Britain," A. L. Puente, the Glee Club's manager related. "Since the race I have received letters and telegrams canceling those engagements. Nothing could have been more unfortunate for us than the result of the race that the umpire gave to Cornell. . . . The members of the Glee Club lost heart as the result of that race and the comments of the English press and the English people upon the matter and it was resolved at a meeting to abandon the tour."

Dann saw it a little differently:

Much of the failure of the trip is due to the professional manager [Puente] we had with us. We found out too late that he cared more for a nice summer trip and meeting the various London managers to further some private enterprise of his own, than he did for the success of the club, and after our arrival he made no effort to arrange dates for us. We were simply at his mercy and he took advantage of it. It was just as well, however, for after the race the boys were sick at heart and did not care to sing.[10]

Dann returned home with only seven of the touring Glee Clubbers—the rest dispersed throughout Europe, many heading to France and Switzerland, some not returning until August. The entire group was to have returned in August, having given more than twenty concerts in England, Ireland, and Scotland. Concert revenues, expected to exceed touring expenses, were to be donated to

Cornell's athletic clubs. Instead the tour's abrupt end left the Glee Club bankrupt and homeless, dependent upon the good graces of the London Savage Club.[11] (Cornell professor H. Morse Stephens, who according to Rym Berry timed his saunter to school each morning to the length of his cigar, was a member and had sent a letter of introduction with the Club.) To their credit, the Cornellians did give six concerts in all. And more significantly, though Harvard speciously claimed for years their 1921 tour of Europe was the first by an American glee club, this 1895 tour is as far as the record shows the first international tour by an American collegiate ensemble.

Following the England tour the Glee Club did not tour again until 1896–1897. Touring during the succeeding years can be best understood, however, by taking a trip constructed, step by step, as a pastiche of actual journies.

In Stephen Sondheim's *Merrily We Roll Along* the familiar query arises, "Which comes first, the music or the words?" "The contract," a worldly wise character replies. So too with the Glee Club. Before the group set out on the road, months of advanced planning were required, which looked something like this in 1907–1908:

> After the route of the trip has been decided on by the graduate manager and the Musical Clubs Council, the business manager must go over the entire route as advance agent. He, with the graduate manager, must arrange for the theatre and advertising in each town. From the Ithaca office an alumni committee is then gotten together in each city where the clubs play, to take charge in working up the concert and entertainments in such cities.[12]

The decision of actual route alone could take some time, and itineraries typically evolved, on occasion up to the last minute. In 1916, for example, the Musical Clubs forecast a southern trip to Savannah, Atlanta, Birmingham, Mobile, New Orleans, Memphis, St. Louis, Chicago, and Columbus. The Christmas trip they actually took less than a year later went to Rochester, New York, Dayton, Louisville, St. Louis, Davenport, Duluth, St. Paul, Chicago, and Syracuse. Only St. Louis and Chicago were held over from the original itinerary.

With the route established, bags packed, and schedules checked, the group eventually set out from the Lehigh Valley station. Rehearsals were not necessarily held immediately prior to the tour though.[13] Hence, members sometimes departed from different cities, where they were at home visiting family, and met up with their fellow singers at the first hotel for rehearsal. From there the group traveled the road together, which in 1910–1911 stretched to Omaha, Nebraska, and to Denver, Colorado, in 1914–1915. In the former city, even though the Omaha Alumni Association numbered only twelve, the musicians' long ride was rewarded by a warm welcome: "All twelve [had] waited three hours at the station for a train that pulled in at eight o'clock in the morning, and gave a 'Long Yell' for the Clubs as the Cornell Special arrived."[14]

The men often relied on alumni and undergraduates to transport them and their bags to their hotel, which was no small task. Following one arrival in 1906–1907, the hotel-lobby soon had "probably a hundred suit-cases, hat boxes, etc., strewn over the floor." On other occasions the group slept in berths as the train carried them through the night to their next destination.

When the men returned to Omaha in 1914, they arrived early on a Monday morning, having left Denver the previous afternoon. Their schedule for the day, after a long and conceivably sleepless train ride: a luncheon, an afternoon tea dance (with dinner and a possible rehearsal squeezed somewhere in the schedule), an evening concert at the American Theatre, and a large ball to follow. Some said it was doubtful that "the Clubs can make their special train to Kansas City at 3:00 A.M. without many hearts having been left behind altogether, or at least slightly damaged; for authentic reports have given the fair sex of this city a very enviable reputation."[15] On a southern states tour several years earlier (1908–1909) "Louisville was the first place to influence some of the members of the clubs to stay over and miss the train. 'Tis rumored that one member even condescended to come up to Indianapolis in time for the concert, only to return to Louisville again in the 'wee small hours' of the morning after the concert, so enamored was he with that city."[16] More likely the young women of the city.

As mentioned before, the early twentieth century tours were often more social occasions than musical ventures. So much so that after a snowstorm delayed the Glee Club on the 1898–1899 tour, "it was necessary to run as a special train in order to arrive in Franklin in time for a reception."[17] By 1921, Dann's last year, the "great number of influential and socially prominent patronesses indicated that the concerts of the Cornell Musical Clubs hold a high position in the season's social calendar."[18] The men were treated to rounds of luncheons, dinners, receptions, theater parties, smokers at the University Club, thés dansants, coasting parties, and debutante balls. "Every man was made to feel at home from the time he stepped off the train until he left."[19]

Somewhere in the midst of all these social happenings was the concert—the center around which all else revolved, though at times it was in danger of being completely eclipsed by the exciting travel and social whirl. After all, what was the dance without the concert—certainly the men stood a better chance of impressing their dates precisely because they were going to perform or had just done so. And yet, important though the concerts were, less can be said about them than the surrounding events. Concerts were almost unanimously well received, and the men made many friends through their music. Still the music had to suffer from the wearying schedule. For a week or more at a time the men would board the train sometimes after one in the morning, arrive at the next city, be surfeited, give a concert, and again board the train hoping to catch a little sleep en route to the next stop. With so little sleep and the cold weather, colds were common, and some men were unable to sing. At best they were sleepwalking by the end of the tour.

28. The Glee Club caught in pajamas outside their tour train, January 1921, a repeat of the 1909 incident. From *Cornell Era*, 1920–1921.

Weary or not, they did maintain their sense of humor. At a 1909 concert in Dayton, a clarinet player in the Mandolin Club discovered only too late his solo had been sabotaged. According to one eyewitness, when the time came to play, "no sound issued forth. 'Pat' blew and blew, but there was nothing doing. On taking the clarionet [sic] apart he discovered a cork firmly wedged in the end." These days, such a "tour burn" is almost always directed at the director, but back then, men in the group seemed to be the brunt of the jokes. On that same tour the entire group was humbled by one of the finest tour burns of the early years; according to the same eyewitness,

> It was customary on the trip to have our special baggage car next to our sleep-ers. Before going to bed we all went into the baggage car, dressed for the night, and "peeraded" through to the sleepers, leaving our clothes behind us. But for some unforeseen reasons, twice on getting up in the morning we discovered that the trainmen had played a joke on us and had put several day coaches, filled with people, between us and our baggage car. Of course we thought that a great idea and at the next station you might have seen a long line of bath-robes and pajamas "beating it" up the side of the train to the much coveted car. In the mean time, cameras owned by different people on the train were working overtime trying to catch the great "peerade" up the track; the people probably thought that we had just escaped from some mad-house.[20]

With jokes, miles, and concerts in common the Glee Club returned to Ithaca, and for some days could content themselves with the memories of wooded hills and small, winter towns rushing by the window, of people joyful at their presence and moved by their music. And they could rest for a moment in the purposefulness of their recent days. As the *Era* said, "probably no other student organization does more to advertise and extend the fame of Cornell than do the glee clubs on their tours."[21] As their travels extended further and further across the country, the Glee Club brought the name of Cornell to those who had never laid eyes on Ithaca, and the sound of Cornell to those who recognized it from years spent on the Hill.

On his voyage, Odysseus encountered adversity in a host of forms ranging from the wrath of gods to the ferocious Cyclopes. The Glee Club has never met these on tour, but members have faced their modern brethren—fierce weather, financial depression, disabled transportation, and angry alumni. Looking at the Dudley year tours, of which we already know something, we can study some of these trials.

One of the first pressures on any Musical Club man was to make the tour group. In the years when there was no fall concert an entire semester of rehearsing came down to the decision as to who went and who stayed home. Any active member was eligible and the criteria were identified as "musical and social qualifications," no one being "given preference over any other because of his class year." Witness the difference between this and Sokol's formula, which determined tour eligibility through musical qualifications, longevity (that is, length of membership), and seniority (seniors were picked before juniors, and so forth), in that order. Clearly the organization in Dudley's years viewed the anticipated balls, smokers, and tea dances as much a performance as the concerts, and admitted as much: "[On tour] there is more than a musical function to perform. . . . There is a social side to the picture . . . and we are convinced that there are plenty of men with musical ability at Cornell who would also be social assets to the Clubs."[22] Thus the social mandate of tour went so far as to influence admission into the Glee Club itself—little did all the Enrico Carusos know that, because of the Glee Club's social calendar in New York and Chicago, it was just as well they were Cary Grants.

The cut being made, the real adventures began. In 1924 sixty out of one hundred men were chosen and set out Christmas night on a 3,000-mile journey through the South. They had barely crossed into Pennsylvania when someone discovered the baggage car had a broken axle. The assistant manager somehow requisitioned a new baggage car, and with the help of another man, described as the "official guardian of the marimbaphone . . . performed the Herculean task of shifting some thirty trunks and assorted articles of clothing to the new car" (every two men were required to share a trunk). On the thirty-hour trek from Wilmington to Birmingham, the dining car "developed an unexpected hot box," delaying dinner. The men finally pulled into Birmingham, after viewing "red clay roads, cottonless cotton fields, scrub pines, and negro shanties," for three days of drizzling rain. On their way back, they hit a snowstorm that knocked out the electric system and were forced to dress for the evening in Pullmans illuminated by flickering candlelight.[23] The tour group had a good time despite these tribulations, visiting a New Year's reception at the White House and giving concerts everywhere from Town Hall to a New Jersey state prison, "where the prisoners were entertained with songs and stunts."[24]

Other problems were less easily shaken than broken-down baggage cars and bad weather. After the war the cost of transportation rose enough to make tours a "break even" proposition instead of a profitable enterprise. Following the 1924–1925 southern tour the trips began to lose money steadily, forcing the Club to cut into its surplus—by 1931 solvency was a serious issue. Meanwhile, attendance was dropping, at least in part because of radio's growing popularity. On the 1919–1920 tour the average attendance for the eight concerts was over 1,600, with several bringing in more than 2,000 people. A decade later such numbers were no longer the rule, and the group began performing in high school auditoriums in between the larger halls and ballrooms. With the onset of the Great Depression (though it was not the sole factor), the situation worsened immeasurably. Tours continued for two years with disastrous results, making 1931 the self-declared year of retrenchment. The Christmas tour was put off in favor of a shorter spring tour, and manager Brainard Prescott 1932 tenderly wrote to a one-time tour contact: "We hope that we may talk to you about a concert without causing you any undue mental anguish. . . . This year is one of retrenchment for us; we must make the trip pay for itself." The tour was ultimately canceled altogether, leaving the Club plenty of time to sit home, searching for the means for traveling and a program that would sell.

The Glee Club back then—as it still is today—was a Cornell missionary, carrying its name and the university's throughout the country. "Few people realize the importance of this trip to Cornell," the 1928 *Cornellian* stated. "Known far and wide, the Musical Clubs are undoubtedly the University's biggest publicity investment, making many new friends for Cornell each year in different parts of the country."[25] As often as not, however, the chief target of these missions was the converted, the alumni family who were encouraged to attend Glee Club concerts on the grounds it "stimulates one's pride in Cornell . . . and re-establishes contact with one's youth."[26] As the financial picture worsened in the late 1920s, Glee Club tours began to depend heavily on the support of alumni patrons. The situation became unhealthy when alumni began to exert undue pressure on the group's musical matters.

As an example, Thomas Ludlam, manager of the Cornell Club in New York City, wrote several times to express his views, usually voiced from a marketing perspective. He felt the concert was a salable article and (like other merchandise) if it was not satisfactory, the customer would not always buy it. To his mind, alumni were not interested in high-brow music and the Club's level of musical perfection; they wanted to hear the old tunes, which he complained were appearing less and less over the years. So, Ludlam contended, alumni dutifully sat through these concerts and, disappointed by the sales item, did not come back the next time. In conclusion he wrote:

> The Musical Clubs Organization could be made one of the best advertising mediums of Cornell University, and should be considered as such, and built up as such. Music teachers, proper, are not capable of the job, and should not necessarily establish the programs. . . . We buy it. We should have what we want.[27]

To its credit the Glee Club did not uniformly buckle in to such demands. But was it any accident that a Broadway showman headed up the 1936 Senior Week program, the program became lighter (to the point of beer on stage), and serious composers disappeared in favor of Cornell songs? Had the financial situation been better, the 1930s might have sounded different musically. Fraught as they were with problems of the Depression, radio, and tour demands, those years saw the Glee Club using pseudonyms to evade the financial Cyclops, not so much out of shrewdness as the necessity of getting them off the Glee Club's back.

Between 1931 and 1937 no Christmas tours were taken; spring trips, when they occurred, were brief and close to home. Coleman had once scoffed at the suggestion that the Clubs return to their musical childhood, and rightly so, but the short trips to Binghamton, Auburn, and Rochester in the spring of 1935 looked like the Glee Club of the 1870s. Each represented what the Club called an "inexpensive, economical trip in tune with the times," and that same spring the management stated that the "Clubs are keen to do their part in keeping Cornell 'on the map,' but know from sharp experience that the days of carefree expensive trips with a Pullman train, lavish hotel accommodations, etc., are over— probably for all time."[28] Allan Treman had once said occasional trips were vital to the Clubs for keeping up group morale. At the time of the 1934 spring tour some felt that if the tour was a failure, it would be a matter of only a few years before the Clubs went out of existence. When plans for a 1936–1937 winter tour fell through, many began to think the few years were up.

In 1937–1938 however the Glee Club launched its first real tour in almost a decade, a trip bound for Buffalo, Cleveland, Chicago, and other points west. The urge to tour had grown feverish in one individual—after the train left Ithaca, a stowaway was discovered on board. Perhaps one of those passed over for want of social graces, he was kindly allowed to remain, his dedication winning him a place among the chosen.

Dudley's chosen continued to take Christmas tours until he retired in 1942. With the helpful suggestions of some alumni, the Musical Clubs jettisoned the informal dress and beer on stage in favor of tuxedos and a classier program. By the early years of World War II, finances were on the mend, and the groups could count on packed houses. The trips were not always extensive—in December 1940 the Clubs visited only three cities—but they brought memorable moments to the members. One afternoon the groups stopped for lunch at the Union Restaurant in Grand Central Station. The manager recalls, "New Yorkers were quite surprised to see seventy-five boys troop in all at once. However, they were entertained as the Clubs sang all the way through the meal. Such fine applause was received . . . the boys felt very encouraged and when the meal was over, all stood and sang the Alma Mater."[29] In 1941–1942 the Glee Club took its first solo tour since the formation of the Banjo and Mandolin Clubs, after which many of the men traded tours for military duty overseas.

The one Christmas tour taken during the Tracy years was the 1947–1948 "Here We Are Again" trip through the Midwest. That tour Toledo organizers made the mistake of throwing a manhattan and martini party just before the concert, and the hostesses in most cities brought their own dates to the dances. The following year the tour was scrapped, and the other Tracy tours were taken over the spring break. In the early 1950s managers considered the possibility of a tour to South America; it fell through. The eventual replacement was the 1954 tour of the continental United States and Mexico.

Prefaced by the appearance on the *Perry Como Show,* the tour began on March 26, when the Glee Club took off from the Binghamton airport aboard a DC-4 Clipper headed for Atlanta. Despite competition from the Dartmouth Glee Club, a night baseball game between Atlanta and Milwaukee, and the opening of *South Pacific* in town, the concert attracted 1,200. Raymond Kruse 1941, a former student director of the Club and chair of the Atlanta committee, was in the audience. In a move probably unprecedented in Glee Club history, Tracy let him lead several numbers in the concert. The next morning the group was off for Houston, Texas, where Tracy was presented with a ten-gallon hat by the president of the local Cornell Club. Meanwhile Cornellians were gathering from all over Texas, as well as Louisiana and Mississippi, some reportedly driving five hundred miles to hear the Glee Club. The concert on the University of Houston campus was successful—one alumnus wrote the *Cornell Alumni News,* calling it a thoroughly high-grade show.

En route to Mexico on Sunday the 28th, the pilots took a detour over the Aztec pyramids for the benefit of the passengers. Few could have complained about the sight-seeing from the air—the entourage was later treated to the Golden Gate Bridge on the way into San Francisco, Pike's Peak on the way from Denver to Tulsa, and Cornell University on the way back to Binghamton. But the daily flights were wearing, and the hop over the Mexican border turned turbulent. "Never seen so many green people in my life," Mary Lou Tracy later said.[30] Touching down in Mexico City about noon, the queasy Glee Club was welcomed by a Mexican band and a police escort to accompany their air-conditioned buses around town. That afternoon the Palacio de Bellas Artes was filled to capacity.

29. The Glee Club on tour in Mexico, with police escort, March 1954.

The Mexicans enthusiastically demanded a second singing of "Cielito Lindo" and cheered wildly as the Glee Club closed the program with the Mexican national anthem, sung in Spanish. A reception and dinner dance arranged by Cornellians followed, which must have seemed a pleasant dream when the bleary-eyed Glee Clubbers arose at 5 A.M. the next morning for the flight to Los Angeles. Crossing two time zones and 1,750 miles, the group arrived with enough time for rehearsal and a dinner party at the Biltmore Hotel, followed by a concert at Philharmonic Auditorium. After eighty-five years, the Glee Club had finally realized its manifest destiny, reaching from New York to the Pacific Ocean. The concert was a moving one, particularly for the alums overjoyed at hearing a familiar song so far away from their alma mater. The "Evening Song" brought tears to their eyes, and one recalled a tingle ran down his spine as soon as Dick Bump 1955 sang the first notes of "Cornell." Alumni and reviewers alike enjoyed such other numbers as the Lavender Cowboy lament with guitar accompaniment, the hand-clapping "Sourwood Mountain," the peaceful "Down in the Valley," and the pair "Paul Revere's Ride" and "Concord Hymn," in which by one account the Club sounded like "a great organ resounding and swelling its paeans."[31]

Then it was on to San Francisco, where Cornell joined the University of

California Glee Club (directed by Ithaca College graduate Robert Comman-
day), followed by Denver, and Tulsa, Oklahoma, where the group stayed at a
familiar place on tours—a hotel run by a Cornellian. In Tulsa the Glee Club
made an afternoon television broadcast from station KCEB, and then joined
Dartmouth for an evening concert, to avoid competing as they did in Atlanta.
After the concert Tracy and Dartmouth's director Paul Zeller were inducted
into the Osage Nation and presented with authentic Native American garb. Tracy
was given the name "TA-KA-HE-KAH" or "Deer Chief," and Zeller the name
"WAH-TOH-NA-SHE" or "Standing and Looking."

The next day, April 2, graduate manager Selly Brewer, Allan Treman, their
wives, and Foster Coffin, who had all accompanied the Glee Club on the journey, paid a visit to the University of Kansas, familiar territory to Deane Malott,
while the Glee Club rehearsed for its concert in Topeka. The following day the
group gave its final performance in Davenport, Iowa, where the captain of the
chartered plane, E. N. Park, Colgate 1925, and his crew of four men were called
up on stage. In recognition of their many kindnesses during the trip Brewer
presented them with certificates naming them honorary lifetime members of
the Cornell Glee Club.[32]

One of the great pleasures of touring is homecoming, and when Captain
Park landed the plane in Binghamton on April 4, there must have been a sigh
of relief at the prospect of an evening off. The group had given nine concerts
in nine days, covering two countries and nearly 8,000 miles in the spare moments. They had seen much of the country on far and away the longest tour
the Glee Club had ever taken. Thinking back to the birth of Glee Club touring
and the early trips to Cortland and Syracuse, one person speculated, "It is
doubtful these early travellers ever imagined that their successors would one
day make tours covering thousands of miles each year."[33] Indeed, it is doubtful that those on the Mexico tour ever imagined how far the Glee Club would
travel in the next two decades.

Three years later Sokol was named the director, and the remarkable run of
international tours began with the 1960–1961 trip to the Soviet Union and
England. The idea of a Soviet tour had been germinating for nearly two years,
sparked by conversations between Sokol and President Malott following the
latter's visit to the Soviet Union with other American university presidents. The
matter was pursued through Attorney General Rogers, who referred Sokol to
Ambassador William Lacey in the State Department, who referred the matter
to the East-West Contacts Staff. Late in 1959 the State Department suggested
Sokol contact the Council on Student Travel, who arranged the tour in conjunction with the Soviet Committee of Youth Organizations (CYO) and the
Bureau on International Youth Travel. Meanwhile, the Musical Clubs Council
approved expending its entire $20,000 bank account on the trip. On April 8,
1960, word came down the pipeline that the tour had been approved—four-

teen days, seven in Moscow, seven in Leningrad, with four concerts in each city and additional sight-seeing, all covered by a cost of $80 a person.

Several times in the next few months the tour was almost derailed. In May, Sokol called the Council on Student Travel "to inquire about the effect of the imminent collapse of the Paris Conference on the C.U.G.C. proposed Russian tour. Reply: If Mr. Kruschev so desires he will send a directive down the line to suspend cultural exchanges for a while. We should know in a week."[34] Two weeks later the State Department reported that East-West exchange, excepting government exchanges, would continue. Barring further international upset the tour was on. In November the passports and visa applications were submitted to the Soviet Embassy, and at the suggestion of Valentina Titova, vice chair of the CYO, Sokol visited the Soviet Embassy in Washington. He was promised visas within ten days, but by the second week of December, the embassy had received no confirmation from Moscow. Finally on December 10, only six days before the group was to leave, a telegraph reported the Soviet Ministry of Foreign Affairs had approved the visit. But would the passports arrive from Washington in time? Rather than take the chance, Glee Club secretary Bill Lathrop 1961 and associate manager Tom White 1962 drove to the capital through a blizzard on the 13th, all planes being grounded. On the 14th they returned triumphant to Ithaca, passports and visas in hand.

On the evening of Friday the 16th, the group gathered to board the bus to Syracuse. Joining the Glee Club for the trip were Dr. Alexius Rachun of the university infirmary, Richard Leed of the modern languages department, and Lowell George, university proctor. The seventy-five singers had been chosen by a complex, one-hundred-point system involving seniority, longevity, attendance, musicianship (judged by a special audition), a rating by the officers, and a director's rating. Once chosen, the men were lectured in Soviet relations and culture, tutored in Russian, and inoculated against diseases for the trip and for immunization certificates required to reenter the United States. The entourage embarked with the best wishes of the university and President Malott, and strong encouragement from the State Department to register at the American Embassy in Moscow as soon as they arrived. And they embarked knowing they would represent not just Cornell and its Glee Club, but the United States to thousands of Western European and Soviet people. As officer John Fleischauer 1961 said, "The importance of this enterprise is self-evident; it will be up to us to make the best of our opportunity to share our art and customs with the Russians."[35]

The group arrived shortly before 9 P.M. at the Syracuse airport, to find no KLM plane—it had been held up en route from Amsterdam by storms. Thus began the unplanned 1960 tour that preceded the intended one. The group was advised to spend the night at the Airways Motel, a far cry from the Tourist Hotel in Moscow, but its dining room made do for rehearsal the next morning. The plane *Yellow Sea* arrived at 1 P.M. the next day and by 4:55, the Glee Club was airborne for Amsterdam, enjoying the cuisine de luxe peppered with Russian lessons from Leed. They arrived in Amsterdam Sunday morning, already nearly a day behind, only to find the next leg to Moscow would have to wait till the storm-beleaguered airports to the east reopened. Again the Glee Club registered in a hotel at hand and held afternoon rehearsal in the ballroom. On Monday morning the 19th they left Amsterdam aboard the *Sea of Japan* expecting to make Moscow in about five hours via the northern corridor (Copenhagen and Riga). Only a half hour from Moscow, low ceilings forced the captain to turn around and head back along the southern corridor toward Warsaw, the nearest airport with good weather. A hasty shift from Leed's Russian lecture to Dr. Rachun's Polish tutorial ensued.

Sokol's journal of the journey picks up the story:[36]

5:45 P.M., arrived at the Warsaw airport. Not having Polish visas, we were restricted to the rather drab terminal building. For nearly an hour there was anxious shuffling inside, from tables to the window, to the small gift counter, while outside little gasoline trucks scurried around the huge DC-7C. The atmosphere was tense. Then, after clearing a corner of the waiting room, the Glee Club formed a semi-circle and began singing most of the program of our first concert, scheduled for that very hour in Moscow. As the men sang, fifty or sixty clerks, custodians, crewmen and soldiers crowded into the room and hallway and their faces lit up. Glancing out the window, I saw two old men, who had been sweeping the outer walk, and who seemed embarrassed to come in, leaning with their ears cupped against the window to catch every note. After this impromptu concert, the whole terminal seemed to open its heart to us. But since the airport had no lodging, we left at 9:40 P.M. for Copenhagen, where we arrived 11:30 P.M. and stayed at the Hotel Imperial.

Tue., 20—our flight to Moscow was again delayed by bad weather until the next day. 5 P.M., impromptu concert in the hotel.

So the tour continued. The Glee Club finally landed at the Sheremetjevo airport on the 21st, where they were greeted by delegates from the government, the Bureau of International Youth Travel, and the Moscow State University. They met their nine interpreters and had just enough time to pass through customs, check in at the Hotel Tourist, change, and get back to the State University campus on Lenin Hill for their concert. The Sokol diary continues,

8 P.M., concert in the Univ. auditorium (1000 seats, and the concert had been over-subscribed by 2000), the audience extremely enthusiastic and demonstrative. Afterwards, on the stage, Prof. Serafim Popov presented us with a collection of songs from his choir's repertory, and the Student President gave us a magnificent book of pictures of Moscow . . .

A review of this concert in *Sovyetskaya Cultura* reads: "The stage of the

House of Culture of the Moscow State University has had opportunities to see representatives of virtually all nationalities. The only exception, perhaps was the Americans. It is not surprising, therefore, that great interest was aroused here by the performance of the Choir of the Cornell University (from the city of Ithaca in the State of New York) . . .

"Shostakovich's 'Song of Peace' from the film *Meeting on the Elbe* was prepared especially for performances in the Soviet Union.

"For the students of the Moscow University, the artistry of their comrades from across the ocean spoke straight to the heart. And this is understandable; congenially to the soul, it is better to sing of peace and work, than to prepare for war."

Thu., 22—9 A.M., tour of the Kremlin, including the four cathedrals (now museums) and the "Armory" (the State Museum), and, outside the Kremlin, the Red Square and the Lenin mausoleum. We visited none of the government buildings, the Supreme Soviet being in session.

2 P.M., visit to the Moscow Conservatory, where we were cordially welcomed by the Director, Prof. Sveshnikov. We sang three motets, and heard a rehearsal of the Moscow Philharmonic Orch., with Kondrashin preparing the first performance of the 1st symphony by Nikolayev, a recent graduate of the Conservatory.

8 P.M., we were guests of the CYO at the Bolshoi Ballet, to see the premiere of *Shuralee* by the late Tartar composer, Yarullin. During intermissions we met with members of the troupe and with Mr. Preobrazhenskii, Director of the Bolshoi Theatre, who expressed his pleasure in receiving us, and remarked that they would soon like to visit the U.S. again.

Fri., 23—10 A.M., visit to the "Friendship House," where Tikhon Krennikov, Chairman of the Union of Soviet Composers, lectured about contemporary Soviet music and answered questions from the men. . . . Then he asked us to sing for him and we sang some motets including Tchesnokov's "Salvation Belongeth To Our God," after which he exclaimed: "Wonderful sonority! I have not heard such Russian basses for twenty years!"

That afternoon Sokol and the Glee Club officers were engaged with Russian officials in "a frank discussion of Russian and American university life . . ., occasionally cooled with bottles of lemonade and piva (Russian beer)." They returned to the Hotel Tourist to give an open rehearsal for the staff (more than a hundred attended) and then gave an evening concert at the Moscow Power Engineering Institute, followed by a gala reception. On Saturday morning, they returned to the conservatory where gifts were exchanged (the Glee Club's consisting of copies of two of Donald Grout's books) and the Cornellians heard David Oistrakh and the Philharmonic Orchestra rehearse a Bartók violin concerto. Later that day, following a rehearsal and telecast at the studio of Television Moscow, the chronicle continues:

> 9:45 P.M., we left Moscow for Leningrad, on the crack train "Red Arrow," accompanied by Mr. Bazhanov [the group's government attaché] and most of our interpreters. Two of them, Natasha and Boris, were clearly falling in love, but they were both shy, and the men had been trying to offer discreet encouragement. Boris, who was not going with us, came to say goodbye to Natasha and to see us off.
>
> It was a clear moonlit night, making sight-seeing more attractive than sleep, especially with endless glasses of Russian tea, provided by the "little old lady" attached to each railroad coach.

> Sun., 25, Christmas morning—8:20 A.M., we arrived in Leningrad where we stayed at the Hotel Druzhba. It was snowing for the first time since we left Ithaca. Some of the men found churches and attended services. 6 P.M., the men visited the Cinerama. 8:30 P.M., Christmas party at the Hotel Astoria, where we sang carols and had a holiday banquet. This occasion provided each of us with an opportunity for both contemplation (home, family, Christmas) and celebration (complete with decorated tree).

Over the next few days, the Club visited the Smolny Institute ("birthplace of the revolution"), the Hermitage (palace of Peter the Great), and many other sights including libraries, exhibitions, and a musical instrument factory. On Tuesday the 27th, Sokol recounts:

> 3 P.M., the men visited the "Wedding Palace," designed to provide young couples with an atmosphere of secular solemnity with a slight touch of pomp. A couple being married asked the men if they would sing. After a hasty discussion about what might be appropriate, they sang the Cornell song, "Spirit of Wisdom." 7:30 P.M., we were guests of the Leningrad Youth Culture Palace at a New Year's Dance. There was a large and very good dance band, playing mostly American jazz of the '40's.

Concerts continued on December 26 with a performance at the Leningrad State University, given jointly with the 115-voice University of Leningrad Academic Choir. On the 28th Sokol writes: "7:30 P.M., concert for the Worker's Club of the Food Industry of Leningrad, in the new 'Palace of Culture.' Before the concert an official of Radio Leningrad asked our permission to record it for broadcast on New Year's Day (their most festive holiday) as a special greeting from the Cornell University Glee Club to the people of Leningrad." The 29th, the last day in Leningrad, brought the following entry:

30. Warming up for a December 1960 performance at Leningrad State University in the Soviet Union (statue of Lenin in background).

11:30 A.M., we enjoyed an informal visit to Public Boarding School No. 3. We sat in on classes, saw the library and infirmary, and heard the elementary school chorus. There was a free interchange of questions back and forth, and we received deeply touching gifts from some of the schoolboys—a collection of match-box covers, a hoe and a caliper made in metal-working class. . . .

Returning to the hotel, Tom White asked Mr. Bazhanov which interpreters would go back to Moscow with us; when it appeared that Natasha would remain home in Leningrad, Tom insisted, "But we've got to have Natasha," to which Bazhanov immediately agreed "Okeh." Later on, Natasha confided her thanks to Tom and told him that this meant that she and Boris could have the New Year's holiday together.

On the 30th, the men made their good-byes (Nina, one of the interpreters, surprised several by asking them if they looked on her with disfavor because she was a Communist). Sokol thanked Bazhanov and others for the free and informal exchanges allowed between the singers and Soviet citizens, and everyone boarded the *Caribbean Sea* headed for London. Keith Falkner and Major D. G. Walker of Ibbs & Tillett Ltd. met the Glee Club at the airport and packed them off to the Berners Hotel for a good night's rest and a much welcome day off. Many of them spent New Year's Eve watching *La Bohème* at Covent Garden. Falkner took Sokol to Sandwich to play the prince's golf course, and while the Club slept in the next morning the two were back on the links for another round.

Having rehearsed at the Royal College of Music (RCM) both Saturday and Sunday, the singers were in fine form when the concerts resumed on Monday:

> Mon., 2—1 P.M., at the RCM convocation opening the winter term, after Keith's eloquent address to his faculty and students, we sang a short program. 1:30 P.M., we were all guests of the RCM at a luncheon party at the Royal Albert Hall, the guest of honor being Sir Adrian Boult. 3 P.M., rehearsal at Westminster Abbey.
>
> 6 P.M., concert in Westminster Abbey. We sang clustered around the organ console in the elevated choir loft. It was one of the most memorable experiences in the whole trip.

Accustomed to concerts focusing on one period or composer, the English were deeply impressed by the variety of the Glee Club's program. The next day the *Daily Telegraph* read, "The programme . . . was interestingly planned with contemporary music cheek by jowl with Bach, Gregorio Allegri and Michael Praetorius," under the caption "Poulenc jostles Bach." The *London Times* later ran an editorial, citing the Glee Club's program as "an illustration of the wide-ranging variety used in U.S. music education." Their description of a program given at the RCM shows their surprise: "the Cornell University Glee Club, having delivered Allegri and Vaughan Williams and Praetorius, broke without a trace of apology or embarrassment into a number from *West Side Story*." Following the Westminster Abbey concert, the Dean of the Abbey entertained the men at a reception, after which Sokol had dinner in Sir William and Lady McKie's apartment in the Abbey close, together with the Falkners, and Sir Adrian and Lady Boult.

The next day several Glee Clubbers paid a visit to an old, old friend when they lunched at the London Savage Club. That evening the group christened the auditorium of the new U.S. Embassy building. The acoustic was decidedly less attractive than Westminster Abbey's, but the occasion was significantly brightened by the presence of the widow of composer Ralph Vaughan Williams. By good fortune (no one knew she would attend), Sokol had programmed her husband's "Let Us Now Praise Famous Men" and two arrangements, "The Turtle Dove" and "Wassail Song," providing a fitting tribute to her and to his memory. At the end of the concert Sokol invited all Cornellians present to join the Glee Club on stage for the Alma Mater, to which Falkner, Cornell government professor Clinton Rossiter, and about ten others responded. He had issued the same invitation in Moscow, and at one concert two men had come up on stage. "I don't know what they were doing there," Sokol later said.

Wednesday, the 4th, the Glee Club spent the morning rehearsing and taping a concert at the BBC studios for the "Music for You" hour. The *Dublin Evening Press* later said of the broadcast, "The Cornell University Glee Club added a 'cool' note to the normally 'square' 'Music for You' Program." That evening they gave their final performance in the RCM auditorium for the annual conference of the Incorporated Society of Musicians. Shortly after midnight Falkner bid them bon voyage, and they boarded the *Black Sea* headed for home. One last impromptu concert was given in the Shannon airport shortly after 2 A.M., and the troubadours arrived in Ithaca about 4:30 that afternoon (local time), where they were greeted by family and friends at a reception in the Willard Straight Memorial Room.

Anyone who has been on a good tour (and is still speaking to fellow travelers) knows the afterglow that lasts for a short time, the unspoken camaraderie that abides among members of the group following the journey. After the joyful reunion in Ithaca the Glee Club savored the warm feelings for a while, like the echo of their sound in Westminster Abbey. Passing one another on the Hill, Glee Clubbers could exchange a glance that said, all at once, "singing for the Russian newlyweds, being the honored guests of Keith Falkner, running into a whole group of people you recognize on streets more than five thousand miles from home, yes . . ." In a world where most experience is undertaken and understood alone, or perhaps on occasion with a few close companions, powerful feelings arise from these rare times in which the shape of one's experience is held in common with a large number of people. The afterglow, like the echo, does not last forever—sooner or later new experience intervenes, classes resume, the scenery ceases to change radically day to day. But, in the same way Leonard Bernstein marks over the last quiet chord of *Chichester Psalms* "lunga poss." (lunga possibile), one savors that brief solidarity as long as possible. After that, when the piece has ended and the afterglow has faded, another piece or another journey begins.

Soon, the Glee Club embarked on a return voyage to England. Before they had said good-bye in early 1961, Falkner had urged Sokol to bring the Glee Club back "as soon as possible." In June 1963 the Club was back aboard a KLM plane headed for London. Already the new men were tour veterans, having just taken a nine-day, twenty-two-performance tour of New England secondary schools three months earlier. Aboard the plane the mood was carpe diem, and carpe brolly for the English weather in store.

The flight took nearly twelve hours, but this time the group avoided a lengthy pretour tour and arrived in London to the welcome of old friends. Major Walker met them at the airport, and again he and Falkner proved to have handled all the tour arrangements brilliantly. Over the next two weeks the Club spoked out from their headquarters in London to give concerts across the wet English countryside. The first took place in Oxford's Holywell Music Room, the oldest university concert hall in Europe; before the concert the men had spent the day examining the architectural masterpieces of Sir Christopher Wren and other treasures of the world's oldest university. Musical exchange was supplemented with cultural exchange when, as then President George Ecker 1964 recalls, "our guides indicated that Oxford's older generation is as much dismayed by the 'sloppy' attire of some of the university students as are old Cornellians who return to Ithaca and are confronted with our shaggier representatives. Cornell alumni may now be either alarmed or comforted by the knowledge that what we may term 'informal' attire is an international phenomenon, if not an international problem!" As for the Glee Club's wardrobe on the trip, "Tweed coats and caps became a sort of uniform—weight, shagginess, and abrasiveness being the criteria for approval. No prizes were offered, but the man with the biggest, roughest coat was top of the heap until replaced by the owner of one bigger and rougher."[37]

Succeeding days brought concerts at other institutions—the Highgate School in London, Harrow School, the Royal College of Music, Southampton University, and Eton College, where the high spirited Etonians received the Club with enthusiastic stamping and clapping. By this time most were getting used to seeing their bus head past Dual Carriage Way and Way Out signs. At Harrow School, founded nearly three hundred years before Cornell and numbering Winston Churchill among its distinguished alumni, the group sang two anthems at Evensong in the school chapel, followed by a full-blown concert. The next edition of the student newspaper, the Harrovian, printed an account, sandwiched between an article on spiders and another on cricket, indicating that the Alma Mater sentiment "Hail, all hail Cornell" would be "echoing round the School for a long time." Meanwhile at the RCM, with the composer in the audience, the Club gave a sneak preview of one movement from Palmer's *Nabuchodonosor,* which they were to premiere the next spring.

On their days off, the singers could be found as far afield as Paris and the Edinburgh pubs, and one underclassman tried out his rhetoric with the Sunday orators on Hyde Park corner. The highlight of the trip, however, was the opportunity to perform in several of England's finest cathedrals. The first visit was to Chichester Cathedral on the south coast, the cathedral that two years later celebrated its 1965 music festival with *Chichester Psalms,* commissioned from Bernstein for the occasion. Prior to the concert the men were having afternoon tea in the town hall when they were invited to an upstairs room. There a wedding party was in full swing, and they watched the bridegroom and others perform a traditional sword dance. In an echo of the Moscow wedding palace the

Club returned the favor with an English drinking song and the English glee, "Amo, Amas, I Love a Lass," much to the delight of the newlyweds. A concert at Hereford Cathedral followed on Wednesday of the next week, and two days later the Glee Club was rehearsing in St. Paul's Cathedral, the same day they taped a radio show for the BBC. The concert beneath the magnificent dome of St. Paul's the next Monday was "a fitting climax" to the Glee Club's stay in London—particularly at the moment when, in the midst of Holst's "Turn Back, O Man," a beam of evening sun broke through a cathedral window, bathing the group in light. Having thus seen many of England's finest sights and a little sun, the Glee Club bid farewell to Walker and Falkner, presenting the former with a tie, the latter with a Glee Club medallion. Within twelve hours the group was back in the States, on Central New York soil.

The next three years were exceptionally busy for the Glee Club, and for the country as it edged closer to racial equality and became embroiled in the Vietnam War. Unknown to all but a few, the nexus between Glee Club and country took a seat at the 1965 Senior Week concert in the person of Charles Ellison, from the U.S. Department of State. He liked what he heard, and in July Sokol wrote to the Glee Club president: "Since our Advisory Council meeting this past Spring there has been an extraordinary development in the Glee Club's plans for 1965–66. . . . The Cultural Presentations Office of the Department of State has invited the Cornell Glee Club to represent the United States' Cultural program in the Far East—a twelve week tour." Rarely does one find an exclamation point in the writings of Thomas Sokol, but he ended the letter with one when he indicated that all costs—transportation, food, and lodging, for three months—would be underwritten by the State Department.

The singers soon learned that Uncle Sam was sending the Glee Club around the world in eighty days. There was general astonishment, though the more cynical in the bunch mused, "They [the State Department] are going to send you only where there is trouble and the American image needs some bolstering, not where it would be fun to go." Even so, each hoped he would be among the forty-one selected to make the trip, and manager Don Weadon 1968 launched the 1965–1966 year waxing prophetic: "The upcoming year brings the promise of fame, glory, and drudgery."[38] The drudgery came first. Cornell and the State Department worked to hammer out a contract satisfactory to both sides, rehearsals began in earnest, and the chosen men were sooner or later subjected to an intensive round of inoculations. Ironically, the stickiest point was assuring the men on tour immunity from the draft. The tour was slated for February, March, and April of 1966, requiring that the men take the semester off and abandon their student deferment status. With the inscrutable workings of the government the State Department could or would not cut a deal with the Selective Service, and a colonel in the New York State division declared though the men *might* be exempt from the draft while on tour, they would certainly be ordered to take their pre-induction physicals immediately upon return to Ithaca.

The university intervened, allowing the travelers to register as full-time students "in abstentia" and thereby retain their II-S status. Meanwhile the contract, held up by negotiations over student debts, insurance, and liability, was finally signed in early January. By then the business of passports, press releases, visas, cultural briefings, and wrong notes was largely resolved, and the Glee Club set out on a "farewell tour" along the Eastern seaboard.

"Then pray that the road is long." For the Glee Club it had never been longer. The group weathered 37,000 miles, forty-nine concerts and as many informal performances, thirty-some radio and television broadcasts, innumerable handshakes, smiles, and embraces of goodwill—all in a span of eighty-six days.

It all began on a cold Thursday morning in Ithaca, with snow piled several feet high around the men lining up with their luggage. Two days later, having flown through Paris, Rome, Cairo, and Karachi, the group found itself on the steaming tarmac of the Katunayaka airport, on the island of Ceylon (Sri Lanka today). From the air the lush groves of palm, banana, and coconut trees cast a rich green to contrast the deep blue of the Indian Ocean. On the ground, where the temperature was a cool 99°, the overdressed hastily shed their topcoats as they were garlanded with floral leis. Greeted by media and U.S. officials, the group was soon spirited away to its first hotel, Colombo's Galle Face, which Club president H. Michael Newman 1964 described as "a rambling remnant of British Colonialism, which, with its slowly rotating ceiling fans, staff of semi-clad barefoot boys, and snake charmers, looked like the perfect setting for a Rudyard Kipling adventure."[39] Almost as soon as they had dropped their bags, they were on a candlelit lawn for their first formal reception, given by the U.S. Ambassador to Ceylon. The next day they dug in on the concert schedule with a performance at the Ladies College Hall in Colombo, appearing somewhat semiformal in long-sleeved shirts and Glee Club ties. The trunks carrying their tuxedos and dinner jackets had forgotten which tour this was and had ended up in London.

Two days later the group was performing in a huge gymnasium at the Ceylon Army Headquarters in Panagoda when a tremendous din broke out on the roof above. The Glee Club was not being shot at—a torrential downpour had erupted, creating a kettle drum out of the gym's corrugated tin roof, and drowning out the singing. The public address system was of little avail, and as the four thousand listeners strained to hear, the singers dropped the program and cut to the Alma Mater. The day was not a total loss, however, as the Glee Club had made a big hit at its first concert singing the Ceylonese national anthem, "Sri Lanka Matha," in Sinhalese. Their success was such that they were asked to record it for the English-speaking Radio Ceylon, which they did the same day as the Panagoda concert. For years after, the Cornell Glee Club opened and closed Radio Ceylon's broadcast day. The anthem became a hit with the Glee Club as well. "So much so that it was probably sung at least once or twice a day

31. Lined up outside Sage Chapel to depart on 1966 East Asia tour. From *Cornell Alumni News*, November 1966. Photograph by Thomas P. Cullen 1966.

for the remainder of the tour," Newman recalled, "and eventually came to be accepted as the 'tour song.'"

The next stop was Singapore, where the men ensconced themselves at the esteemed Raffles Hotel. They were just sitting down to drink Singapore Slings in the courtyard when the air erupted in a rapid succession of explosions. Several turned in alarm, knowing this wasn't rain on a tin roof, but it was no more than an introduction to the Chinese custom of firecrackers to accompany a wedding ceremony. The next evening, happily reunited with their tuxedos, the men opened their concert with Singapore's anthem, "Maju-Lah Singapura," and were

32. East Asia tour, 1966. Soloist Arthur Neal 1969, *foreground,* and other Glee Clubbers, *left to right,* William Moore 1968, William Besgen 1968, John Douglas, Grad, Jon Siegel 1966, Tom Willis 1966, and Adam Perl 1967, prior to a performance on Television Singapura. From *Cornell Alumni News,* November 1966. Photograph by Thomas P. Cullen 1966.

pleasantly surprised afterward when they were greeted backstage by Tanya, one of the translators from the Russia tour. She had no word on Boris and Natasha. Singapore also brought the first television broadcast and the first lecture clinic, given for the Singapore Peoples' Association, which Sokol described as being very interested in developing a choral program for the public. The Singaporeans and Americans sang for each other, after which everyone sat to a magnificent, two-and-a-half-hour Chinese dinner. The men were honored by being served "century eggs," hundred-year-old eggs reserved for special, festive occasions. The singers later described them as looking like "dark green wedges of cheese" and tasting unlike anything they had ever tried before.[40]

On to Malaysia and Kuala Lumpur, where the group was received by Ambassador James Bell. Interspersed with engagements at the Malayan Teachers College, performances on Malaysian radio and television, and a benefit concert in Ipoh, the Glee Club had a day or two off. They spent time visiting tin plants and rubber plantations, and at least half the group, pursuing the rumor that Kuala Lumpur had an A & W Root Beer stand, convened for a feast of milkshakes and cheeseburgers. The men also found time and opportunity to demonstrate their athletic prowess. At the teachers college, Newman recalls, "They showed us the campus and several of our six-foot basketball enthusiasts showed them their skills." While on the beautiful Malaysian island of Penang, the Glee Club was engaged to play a game against the Penang Women's Field Hockey Champs. Always good sports, the men—most of whom had never held a field hockey stick—sallied forth into battle. For a while the whistle blew repeatedly as the neophytes used the illegal side of the stick to hit the ball, but by halftime the score was tied at 1–1. The second half was a defensive battle. Sensing a draw the Glee Force—now more competitive than gracious—rallied in the closing moments to score the winning goal. That evening the two teams met again, "this time, in groups of two and four and above the sound of dance music and clinking glasses, the game was replayed in detail."

Once called the pearl of the British colonies, Penang proved an idyllic paradise in more than one regard. "Then pray," Cavafy writes, "That the summer mornings are many, / that you will enter ports seen for the first time / with such pleasure, with such joy!" From their hotel the men could watch junks make their way along the Straits of Malacca. One Cornell alumnus offered members the use of his coastline beach house for a day. After a second concert at the Penang Chinese Girl's High School Hall the performers were swamped with requests for autographs. The next day they were amazed to see some of the same girls waiting in the hotel lobby, hoping to get some more autographs. In this foreign land Glee Club autographs were coming to resemble trading cards, and some wanted to collect all forty-two. The girls weren't the only Glee Club fans in Penang—the city's *Sunday Gazette* (February 20, 1966) had the following to say: "This was the best male ensemble this reviewer has ever heard and is surely one of the finest in the world."

A week in Thailand was next on the itinerary, and as the tour neared the end of its first month, some men soothed their aching muscles with a bath and massage at one of Bangkok's massage parlors. Many purchased tropical fruits from floating markets with Baht, the Thai currency. The concert itinerary in Thailand centered around institutions of higher education: the Glee Club sang at Thammasat, Chulalongkorn, and Kasetsart Universities and also performed for the American University Alumni Association. At Kasetsart, a leading agricultural school, no less than thirty-four rose from the crowd of twelve hundred to join in singing the Alma Mater. The group also encountered some alumni of NASA. On the last day in Thailand Glee Club intelligence learned astronauts Walter Schirra and Frank Borman were due in at the airport that night just before the Club was scheduled to depart for Manila. When the pair entered the terminal, the Cornell singers met them with a modified version of "Spirit of Wisdom": "Spirit of wisdom, like a comet burning, / High o'er this darkling world, vexed with little learning, / Let thine enkindling ray, round about the

33. On the East Asia tour in 1966 Glee Clubbers William Moore 1968 and Alan Racker 1967 are welcomed with leis in the Philippines. From *Cornell Alumni News,* November 1966. Photograph by Thomas P. Cullen 1966.

nations fall, / Lighting the way for all." Television and radio broadcast the moment, and the astronauts were duly pleased to meet fellow Americans also on a goodwill tour.

The Glee Club flew over Vietnam without incident and was soon in the Philippines, where the Cornell Club rolled out the red carpet with impeccable style. To this point arrangements handled by the U.S. government had been impressive, but those done by the Cornell Club of the Philippines were extraordinary. As the singers stepped off the plane, each was greeted by name by Cornell alumna Joy Simpliciano, who had memorized the pictures and biographies included in the pretour publicity. At the Hotel Mabuhay each man found a handwritten note of welcome (mabuhay means welcome), a barong tagalog (or Filipino dress shirt), and a six-pack of San Miguel beer. On the first day of actual performances the Club was slated for three television appearances—two taped and one live—including a spot on the remarkably popular *An Evening with Pelita* show. (The group was also later seen on *Dance Time with Chito.*) A brief jaunt to Bacolod followed, where the Glee Club noticed a brass band outside the plane. As the first man stepped off the plane onto the red carpet, the band burst into the Alma Mater, leaving the entire group at a loss for words.

The next week was spent performing in Manila, and on campuses of the University of the Philippines in Los Baños and Quezon City. At the first Manila

34. Glee Clubbers Adam Perl 1967, Nicholas Altenbernd 1968, and Brian Little 1967 with thoughts of extending the 1966 East Asia tour into Red China. From *Cornell Alumni News*, November 1966. Photograph by Thomas P. Cullen 1966.

concert, in the Philamlife Auditorium, the Glee Club came out for the second half in their barong tagalogs, much to the delight of the audience. The final Manila concert was shared with the chorus of St. Paul's College, who joined the Glee Club for selections from Handel's *Messiah*. The sisters of the college had on several occasions provided the men with refreshments after rehearsals at the campus facilities, and their superior, Sister Marie Vincent, later wrote, "May you bring as much joy and beauty to other lands and peoples as you have brought to us."[41] The Glee Club then departed from the Philippines, which many, like soloist Arthur Neal 1969, later ranked as the tour's high point. He might have been thinking of the day the group shot the rapids of the Pagsanjan River in dugout canoes, or the evenings when people swooned to his rendition of "Ang Dalagang Filipina," the beloved Filipino love song.

Back in Ithaca it was just about time for spring break when the Glee Club arrived in Hong Kong. The group got its own break, giving just two live concerts in the next week. The singers caught up on their sleep at the Empress Hotel, managed by a Cornell graduate, and secretary of the Hong Kong Music Society Maple Quon attended well to hospitality.

The next stop was Taipei, Taiwan, where the Glee Club again performed the collaborative work of choice, Handel's *Messiah*, this time with the Taiwan Normal University Chorus and the Taiwan Symphony Orchestra. The concert in the Taipei International House was conducted the first night by David Tai, director

35. During 1966 East Asia tour school children in rural Taiwan singing "Old MacDonald Had a Farm" (in English) to Glee Clubbers who had just sung a Chinese folk song, "Lao Yeh Wung" ("The Old Fisherman"), in Chinese. From *Cornell Alumni News,* November 1966. Photograph by Thomas P. Cullen 1966.

of the two Taiwanese ensembles. The second night, Sokol conducted the same program, again before a standing room only crowd. Newman recalls that the "big surprise came when, on the third consecutive night, we performed our own men's repertory in the same hall, in the same city, again to a full house!" Clearly the Taiwanese were lovers of good music, and to Sokol's mind, "extremely open-armed to what you might call the mainstream of Western music—very anxious to develop their singing and playing."[42] They were very dedicated to listening also, as the Glee Club poignantly learned in Taichung. Making their way from a rehearsal building to the auditorium through the rain one night, the group encountered several hundred onlookers who, not able to get a seat inside, were according to Newman "prepared to stand in the drizzle for the opportunity to hear what they could through the louvered slats surrounding the hall."

The Glee Club got to do some listening of its own in Taiwan, namely to several children's choirs. At a rural school near Taipei the men sang "Lao Yeh Wung" in Chinese to the students. The children quickly responded with "Old MacDonald Had a Farm" in English. "I think it reflects a little about the future vitality of musical life," Sokol said. Another group of boys, about ten according to the *Cornell Alumni News,* missed seeing the Glee Club at their airport arrival, "but did manage to locate their hotel later. After getting an approval from the hotel manager, they appeared outside the Cornellians' rooms one evening—

singing a song they had learned in English. They also brought a huge banner and Chinese pastries for the travelers from the United States."[43]

The group's accompanist Richard Bull 1967 later said the last concert in Taiwan easily stood out as the most unusual experience during the tour. Since Taichung, the Glee Club had visited Tunghai University (which owed its existence to former Glee Clubber Leslie Severinghaus 1921), Tainan, and the Naval Academy at Kaohsiung, but they would never see anything again in their lives quite like the island fortress of Quemoy. Positioned just a thousand yards off the Chinese mainland, the island, not on the original itinerary, was included by special arrangement after the island commander saw the group on television and suggested they come perform for his troops. Leaving at a time and place classified up till the last moment, the Glee Club flew in a Nationalist Chinese Air Force transport plane, a C-119 "flying boxcar," surrounded by a fighter escort. The men, seated in lengthwise rows on unpadded seats, hung on and tried not to turn green while the plane lumbered over the waves at an altitude of about two hundred feet to avoid Communist radar. Once on the island, they regained their land legs for a tour of the installation and joined the commander for shots of sorghum wine, drunk with the customary cry of "Gombai" (bottoms up). The concert was given in a cavernous underground auditorium before a thousand or more troops.

The group returned to Taipei, then flew on to Naha, Okinawa. At a reception at the Teahouse of the August Moon the Cornellians were served beer and sukiyaki, accompanied by demonstrations of karate and Okinawan folk dances. After three days of concerts, two in Naha and one in Koza, it was on to Korea. Here, in just seven formal concerts, nearly 17,000 people heard the Glee Club. In Seoul two concerts at Ewha University, at the time one of the world's largest schools for women, brought in 4,000 people each night. (The crowd made up for the want of heat—performing in the very same hall, Helen Hayes dubbed it the "world's largest icebox.") In addition many more heard the group on Korean radio and television. While in the country, the Glee Club had opportunities to witness Korean music and dance, sleep on floor mats, and visit Panmunjom, the site of ongoing armistice negotiations. Newman's account paints a stark picture of the demilitarized zone:

> The Joint Security Area, as it is called, consists of a small compound of several low, barrack-like buildings, the green ones belonging to the Communists and the blue ones to the United Nations. The military demarcation line runs through the tiny area from north to south, actually bisecting the buildings and conference tables. Thus, the Communist negotiators can sit in the east and look toward the west, a privilege which, according to legend, is reserved for the superior powers.

Not all boundaries were so strictly drawn. One of the most touching experiences of the tour occurred in the Korean town of Pusan, just prior to a concert at the Dong-A University. The men were relaxing in their tuxedos outside the concert hall when, as Newman recalls, "To pass the time we tried saying 'hello,' 'good evening,' or whatever phrases we could muster in Korean. At first the children ran away, but soon they returned with their friends. Since most of the Korean words we knew were the lyrics to the folk song 'Arirang,' we decided to try that." The Glee Club gathered around in a semicircle to sing.

> It seemed to have an almost magical effect and pretty soon the kids assembled in a little group, the braver ones in front, and the more timid in the rear. . . . Then we decided to teach them the western gesture of shaking hands. At first no one would accept the offer. Finally one brave little boy decided that it probably couldn't hurt too much since we had demonstrated the technique to them among ourselves. After that, they all wanted to try and before we were called to line up for the concert, they had all learned how to shake hands and say "hello" and "how do you do?"

From the "Land of the Morning Calm," the Glee Club headed to Japan, "Land of the Rising Sun." By then it was mid-April and the group had reached the last country on the itinerary. The tour was far from over however—two weeks were scheduled in Japan, with eight formal concerts, media engagements, and numerous informal entertainments, easily the equivalent of a full-length domestic Glee Club tour. Upon arriving the group met Ambassador Edwin Reischauer and members of the Cornell Alumni Association and later had opportunity for exchange with Tokyo composers and conductors. "The interest in choral music is extremely intense throughout Japan," Sokol later commented, also noting Tokyo alone had three major symphony orchestras.[44] After initial performances in Tokyo, which included a television appearance with a top female vocalist on a program viewed by more than ten million nationwide, the Glee Club gave concerts in Kobe, Takamatsu, Hiroshima, Fukuoka, Nagoya, and Sapporo. Glee Clubbers were occasionally stopped on streets by people who recognized them from the program.

April 19 was a day for reflection, and many looked intent as they arrived in Hiroshima little more than twenty years after an American bomb had blossomed over the city in nuclear fury. The Glee Club paused by the Atomic Bomb Peace Memorial, where a silent prayer and a wreath for victims of the war were offered, followed by the singing of William Byrd's motet "Iustorum Animae"— "The souls of the righteous are in the hands of God."

Other stops included a visit to Kyoto's shrines and museums accompanied by members of the Kwansei Gakuin Glee Club, who had recently toured the United States. In Fukuoka the local Rotary Club gave a luncheon, where the men were well equipped to answer Rotarian questions about Fukuoka's "sister city" in the United States: Ithaca, New York. Ithaca again came to mind in Sapporo, where the temperature was low enough for snow to stay on the ground. The road wound back to Tokyo, where the Cornellians took a last fling at the city's high culture and high prices. A transportation strike did not stop 2,400 people from filling Tokyo's Hibiya Hall for the Glee Club's final Far East concert, and many singers felt it was one of their best. After a send-off party at the Imperial Hotel the group bid farewell to their Japanese friends and the tour of a lifetime and boarded a plane for home.

Visions of Mt. Fuji gave way by the dawn's early light to the snow-capped mountains of Alaska, and the plane filled with the sound of "The Star-Spangled Banner" and "America the Beautiful." Landing in the forty-ninth state, the Glee Club gave its forty-ninth formal concert in Anchorage and rose the next day to make all speed for Ithaca.

To date, several hundred thousand people have graduated from Cornell, and they have traversed the globe to take part in every sphere of life. But in so short a time no Cornell organization has ever touched so many people's lives as the Glee Club on its 1966 tour of the Far East. It was estimated more than 100 million people heard the group during those three months, and the bonds formed remained for lifetimes. The impression the tour left on the world, and on the Glee Club, was evident in the simplest and most beautiful ways. There was the little boy in Tokyo, for example, who came backstage with his mother during intermission at the Glee Club's last concert. The mother explained that her son didn't speak English but would appreciate the men accepting his small gift. The gift was a book filled with Japanese stamps, and inside was an inscription that read, "It was nice to have you this evening. Here's something for you. This is my collection."

Perhaps Cecil Lyon, ambassador to Ceylon, had such moments in mind when he wrote to President Perkins:

> I thought you would like to know the extent to which their visit contributed to improving Ceylonese-American relations. In a climate where Americans are too often looked upon with suspicion, the visit gave us a welcome opportunity to present a side of America which this group illustrated so naturally and effectively. Your fine, friendly young men, under the crisp leadership of Dr. Sokol made contact with Ceylonese in a way which is not easy for members of my staff to do.

Richard Arndt, a U.S. cultural affairs officer at the Ceylon embassy, also wrote to say: "The Cornell University Glee Club has come and gone. I am writing you to attempt, in a poor way, to describe in words their success here. . . . As a group they were impressive; as individuals, they were friendly and communicative. As musicians, they were amazing."[45]

Having returned from one of the remarkable tours in male chorus history, rich with experience, with gifts given and received which defied repayment, the

Glee Clubbers may have found life in Ithaca poor for a while. There were no more autograph seekers, no more five star hotels or brass bands at the airport, no more Singapore Slings. Some men didn't even have a place to live. Others wondered how to explain to their roommates what they'd been doing for the last three months, explain about concerts in bunkers and stamp collections. But there was little time to dwell on such matters—there was more singing to be done. The premiere of the Orrego-Salas *Cantata* with the Buffalo Philharmonic followed just a week after the Club's return, and that summer they had the honor of christening the Saratoga Performing Arts Center with Beethoven's *Ninth Symphony.*

In the time between this international touring the Glee Club continued to tour domestically. Vermont, Connecticut, Massachusetts, Rhode Island, Pennsylvania, New Jersey, Illinois, and Ohio all received visits between 1960 and 1966, and in 1967–1968, the organization decided to celebrate its 100th birthday with a coast-to-coast tour. From New York to Los Angeles ten concerts were given between December 16 and 30, along with four television performances. (A performance for educational TV in Chicago was later broadcast in cities across the country.) In Milwaukee, where the Cornellians sang with their Yale counterparts, Charles Holden 1900, aged 91, was in the audience to hear the group he once sang with. He recalled touring back in his day: "Each young man had his own leather hatbox to carry his silk hat for afternoon receptions and his opera hat for evenings. At their concerts and parties held afterward they wore white tie and tails but they also needed a frock coat for formal afternoon wear at receptions."[46] The current men got a taste of old time touring on the trip's long train rides. At the railroad station in Clovis, New Mexico, they sang a concert for an audience of four and celebrated the holidays with drinks aboard the Santa Fe Chief's dome cars.

Out in California the Glee Club had several memorable experiences. A Christmas Day performance in San Francisco's Grace Cathedral saw them attempt unintentionally, and unsuccessfully, to sing an antiphonal Ave Maria in two unrelated keys. A few days after Christmas the men sang for soldiers at Camp Pendleton, a difficult concert with the audience a mix of veterans back from Vietnam and men still facing imminent assignment to the war overseas.

Then there was the concert in San Francisco's Auditorium of the Scottish Rite. During the tour Sokol had been giving his customary lecture on "Annie Lisle," in the course of which he explained how the piece could be performed with either two guitars or piano. Each evening, as though he were making his mind up on the spot, he would conclude, "Tonight, I think we will do it with ... piano." Only in San Francisco he turned to find two Glee Clubbers stepping forth, guitars in hand. The burn got no further—Sokol quickly dismissed them, "You, leave," pointed at the accompanist, "You, play," and then turned to the group, "You, sing"—which they did quite well for the remainder of the tour.

When the Glee Club first announced the 1895 tour to Europe, the original intent was to visit England, Germany, and France. It took until 1970 for the group to make it to Germany. The tour, assembled in a short period of time, came off with the financial assistance of the Class of 1916, and the sometimes helpful, sometimes hindering Institute of European Studies. Because the institute was not as well connected or equipped to handle a tour as the managers expected, the group ended up relying on the U.S. Army for housing and concert venues. Many American servicemen enjoyed the music, but a Glee Club officer noted, "In general the facilities provided in the Army entertainment halls were of poor quality and not conductive to the highest level of performance"—which is to say the German tour was like most others in ranging from the sublime to the silly.[47] During their two weeks in southern Germany the men stayed in a castle and they stayed in barracks; they sang Gregorian chant in Frankfurt's restored cathedral and "My Darling Clementine" over dishes in the kitchen of a Frankfurt youth hostel; they bought souvenir opera glasses and decorated beer steins.

The tour of sacred song and gemütlichkeit began in mid-January 1970 with the first stop in Frankfurt. The Glee Club sang at an Army base, as they did in Heidelberg, Augsburg, Stuttgart, and Würzburg. At Frankfurt's Hessischer Rundfunk they made the acquaintance of Franz Biebl, music director of the network. Out on the street for a sight-seeing tour, the group encountered a student demonstration in front of Frankfurt's opera house. The students were protesting the hall's renovation, which was apparently draining funds needed for campus construction and professors' salaries. Not thinking this might represent a conflict of interest, the Glee Club broke into song, soon befriending their German peers. While in Frankfurt, they also got in the traditional tour wedding serenade, surprising a bride and groom with Schubert's "Liebe." Only a few singers might remember the moment, the *Ithaca Journal* (February 2, 1970) said, "but it is certain that the newlyweds will tell their grandchildren about it."

The Glee Club continued on to see the legendary Heidelberg University, founded in 1386, the prince bishop's residence in Würzburg, and the Palace of Justice, site of the Nuremberg trials. Formal (non-Army) concerts were given in Heilbronn, Munich, and Nuremberg, and several more programs recorded for regional radio, Radio Free Europe, and Munich television. Another formal concert was to have taken place at Heidelberg University, but the political climate grew too hot. A Black Panther speech was scheduled for the same night, and when a bomb threat was received, officials canceled the concert. Locals still made it to a performance given at the Army base instead, and during a post-concert reception, Erich Huebner, director of Heidelberg's Bach Choir, warmly toasted "die Chor der Cornell-Universität." After Heidelberg came the "smash hit" concert in the packed "Amerikahaus" of the Festsaal Harmonie in Heilbronn. Throughout the tour the Club pleased German audiences with the works of Schubert, Mendelssohn, Orff, and Hugo Distler and were praised more than once for their accent-free German. But in Heilbronn, "something especially nice happened," according to one critic. Just before the concert Fritz Werner, aged 71, director of Germany's Schütz Choir and world renowned for his Bach recordings, gave Sokol a canon he had written for the group—

"Wiedersehen ist ein schönes Wort." During the ten-minute intermission, the Club memorized the piece, and after giving Mozart's "Bona Nox" as a first encore, gave the Werner canon as the second. The audience went wild with enthusiasm.

The Glee Club was still celebrating the triumph when they arrived in Munich, where a local choral society threw a postconcert party for the group at the Mathauser beer hall. At the time the Mathauser seated 10,000 on its three floors, making it the world's largest beer hall. The evening brought drinking songs to vivid life, and the Glee Club offered a rousing mix of German lieder and Cornell songs over the noise of the hall. Clearly the occasion was an immediate inductee into the Glee Club's Party Hall of Fame. Afterward several men (including the director) still dressed in tuxedo arrived at their Munich hotel to find they had missed the 11:30 curfew—when the proprietor could not be roused to open the door, they had to set out in search of alternate lodgings.

Beyond concerts and receptions the tour also brought high points of another sort. In Heidelberg a group of men climbed to the castle on the hill sometime after midnight, "and serenaded the town . . . in the clear crystal air of the courtyard of the beautiful Princess Elizabeth." On another day half the group took a cable car to the snow-capped peak of the Zugspitze, the highest point in the German Alps. From the summit they sang the Alma Mater as they looked out at the "Alps in Austria and Italy with a backdrop of azure blue sky."[48] At tour's end one Glee Clubber concluded, "It has been entirely incredible. . . . For two weeks I have lived a dream," and another wrote, "A Glee Club tour is, after all, the only way to travel!"[49]

In the Glee Club's German entourage, which included Blanchard Rideout and Barlow Ware (from the university Development Office), was the Reverend William (Peter) Weigle 1917. He later wrote, "One Glee Club concert wins more people to the 'good life,'" and was so impressed by the deportment of the young men and the impact of their music on others that he immediately pledged $20,000 from the Class of 1917 for the next international tour.[50] Initial discussions considered South America as a possible destination, but those plans were scrapped, largely due to political concerns. Plans soon focused on Eastern Europe, and on New Year's Day 1972 the Glee Club set out for West Germany, Czechoslovakia, Austria, Hungary, and Yugoslavia. They left well rehearsed, having added a third rehearsal during the first semester, and presumably well packed—one sees why manager John Nicolls earned the nickname "Mother" when reading his meticulous and lengthy treatise entitled "Recommended (and Required) Clothing List."

The tour began in Munich and by the first night looked as though no time had passed since the 1970 German tour. Several blocks from their luxurious lodgings at the Vier Jahreszeiten, some Glee Clubbers discovered the renowned Hofbräuhaus. German students were soon enjoying some Cornell songs in between the oom-pah-pah of the house band, which played great works from the

Germanic repertoire such as "Auld Lang Syne" and "Deep in the Heart of Texas." The next day the group gathered at the Bayerischer Rundfunk (Bavarian Radio Network) to record a concert. "Fabelhaft," Heinz Schnauffer, the network's music director said after he heard the Byrd motet, "Fabelhaft," after the Schubert, and after a spiritual, "Fabelhaft, fabelhaft!" The next evening a similar reception greeted the Glee Club's concert in Munich's Amerika-Haus.

As mentioned in Chapter 5 the 1972 tour ranks as one of the richest in anecdotes. The real adventure began en route to Prague, aboard a double-decker bus which drew many amused looks from those along the roadside. At the Czech border the Glee Club got into an argument with the border guards over the accuracy of certain passports and visas. One journal picks up the story:

> Thursday, Jan. 6 The Czech border guards look really strong— with the kind of fat on their faces that represent long periods of duty in the cold. . . . There were complications which made our stay at the border rather extensive. While most people's passport and visa photographs matched, my pictures and those of five others were altered by various growths of hair. My passport photo was taken during the days of my vandyke beard with a goatee and a moustache, and my hair was quite trimly cropped. My visa photo shows my presently scraggly self—always disheveled. The major of 5 stars on shoulder wanted to make the six of us go back to Germany and get a haircut so that we would resemble our passport photos but our colleague who spoke German and our driver pulled it off somehow. It cost Mike Newman some sweat and George some cigarettes.[51]

By the time the guards finally relented and allowed the group into the country, more than two and a half hours had passed. The bus made haste for the concert, but its size forced several detours, and by the time the Club reached Prague's Dvořák Hall, they were an hour late for their own concert. Though exhausted, they filed off the bus and immediately on the stage to sing the first half of the concert. At intermission, they changed into their tuxedos and, "excited and defiant because of [the] ordeal," concluded one of the tour's finest concerts with a spirited Alma Mater encore.

The Prague of those days, choked with smoke and soot from burning heating coal, dark at night save for a few low lights, and lined with "Edwardian" apartment houses along "mucky cobblestone streets," produced little to improve upon first impressions. Many found the historically beautiful city on the hill the worse for wear under Communist rule. For the Glee Club the beauty of Czechoslovakia instead proved to be contact with other choral organizations. In Prague the men met the Prague Men's Choir, a professional ensemble with an average age of forty and a rich sound. After they sang some Czech folk songs the two groups joined in Orlando di Lasso's "Echo Song," in which the young Cornellians took the echo part. In Brno the Glee Club sang at the university,

36. Hungarian man pausing to peruse advertisements for a 1972 Glee Club concert in Budapest.

and after the concert had a reception with the Brno University Choir. One Brno reviewer wrote that the group "presented a rich and colorful program. . . . The guests introduced themselves sympathetically by interpreting two of Janáček's choruses . . . truly à la Janáček."[52]

On to Vienna, the City of Emperors, where the Club had some free time in between a concert at the Musikverein and a performance of a Josquin des Prez mass at the Franziskaner Convent. Ambassador Humes had the men over to his residence for an evening of conversation and cocktails, and some captured the essence of life far above the Danube with orders of Sachertorte and coffee at Demel's. From the land of whipped cream and Strauss waltzes it was on to another jewel of the Habsburg Empire, Budapest. The visits to both Czechoslovakia and Hungary were of great interest to the U.S. State Department, which looked for any relaxation in the strained cultural relations with Eastern Europe. There was a note of hope in the agreement of state concert agencies in both countries to sponsor the Glee Club, particularly in Hungary, where it became the first American choral group allowed to perform in more than two years. After the Budapest concert a State Department telegram read: "Cornell University Glee Club made excellent impression." The audience that evening in the Eotvos Lorand University auditorium took particular delight in Biebl's "Rhapsody on Hungarian Folk Songs" and the selections by Kodály and Bartók, responding with lengthy stretches of rhythmic applause.

Yugoslavia, the tour's last stop, was the most unkind to the Glee Club. The singers should have known that all was not well when the temperature dropped twenty degrees as they headed south, and one man had his glasses stolen right off his face in front of their hotel in Belgrade. As consolation the concert in the student center there went quite well, and the entire audience (including the group's host choir) joined in for a moving rendition of "Gaudeamus Igitur." The Belgrade choir sang for the Cornellians after the concert, having already made arrangements for the men to see Serbo-Croatian productions of *Hair* and *Porgy and Bess*. The next morning the group departed for Maribor with a tour guide aboard their bus, a grubby looking fellow named Geronimo. They checked into the hotel and left for their concert, only returning to find that Geronimo had been an imposter and that a passport, an expensive camera, and tour photographer George Gull's twenty-five rolls of exposed film were all missing. (The camera and ten rolls of film were later found, making the whole theft seem all the more suspicious.) On top of that the Maribor reviewer slammed the concert, saying that the first half was "rather long and . . . relatively boring. With such out-of-tune tenors and weak basses, the chorus would have been better off choosing a different program."[53] The next day, the itinerary offered little choice for the men but to drown their sorrows during a free day in Zagreb.

We already know what happened next as the Glee Club tried to entrain in Zagreb for Stuttgart, where their flight would depart the next morning for New York. Several times during the tour the group had used trains, but if the role of railroads had been graphed, it would have shown one steady line heading downhill at a steep angle. From Vienna to Budapest the Club enjoyed first-class coaches, and a menu of goulash and paprika schnitzel. From Budapest to Belgrade, the group was split between first- and second-class compartments because the Hungarian railroad failed to reserve enough space. Just as they settled in for the ride, those in one car found it had no heat and were forced to make a backward exodus through half a dozen cars. When the train entered Yugoslavia and a horde of new passengers boarded, one Glee Clubber noticed fate had landed an attractive young woman next to him. By eyewitness account the man "was not able to utter a single word that the girl understood, even though he tried phrases from every language he could think of, including those in our special tour repertory. For an hour they shared friendly glances and Hungarian candy, but little more."[54]

The language barrier worsened on the platform in Zagreb, as the Glee Club scrambled to find its train to Stuttgart. The Club was taking the overnight train only as a measure to cut costs—in reckoning tour accounts the Class of 1917 had been able to come up with only $13,000 of its initial pledge. Had the purse been richer, the Glee Club might never have had the adventure of the cigars and slivovitz. As the train rolled out of the station for the second time—this time with all the men, passports, and luggage on board—the Yugoslav ordeal continued. Water from muddy suitcases began to drip down on the couchettes, and the floors of the train looked like the floors of the station, a bath of mud and slush. Rather quickly everyone realized there was no dining car and, what was worse, though the temperature outside was near zero, the cars had no heat. As the Dalmatia Express passed through the Alps, the water in the rear toilet froze, and ice two or three inches thick formed between the cars. Huddled under coats the hungry Glee Club rationed out what little food they had, and then convinced a porter to part with his stash of watery Yugoslav beer for eight dinars (about 50 cents). During the night the heat came on, turning the train into a suffocating sauna. The erstwhile shivering singers ended up sweating out the rest of the night in ill humor. "A near riot was averted about 1 A.M. when the conductor, who only then found himself short two ticket stubs, was convinced that if he tried to awaken everyone to find those elusive tickets, he might be taking his life in his own hands."[55] The bus ride home from JFK never seemed so good.

Having taken five international tours in just twelve years, concluding with the adventures in Eastern Europe, the Glee Club stayed in the States for most of the remaining decade. They did not have to leave the country to find the temperature extremities of their Yugoslav train. On the hot side the group visited Florida in 1973 and again in 1975, making East Coast stops along the way. The Fort Myers press called the 1973 visit "a feast of fascinating concertizing," and benefit concerts in Clearwater and Winter Haven raised nearly $10,000 for various causes. The trip in 1975 saw the disastrous moment when the singers began "The Hill" a fourth high, mistaking the tonic note sounded on the piano for the starting note. The tenors were pushed against the ceiling of the firmament, but everyone survived. The men were pleasantly surprised by a lively party with the "retired folk" in Leesburg, while a church in St. Petersburg praised the Glee Club as "an instrument of God's work." On the cold side the tours of 1976 and 1978 offered little escape from winter. The 1976 excursion to the Northeast witnessed two concerts canceled by a snowstorm and a debacle with the bus, resolved only when a tow truck pulled the frozen vehicle down the Long Island Expressway until it got started. In 1978 the snow followed the group from Buffalo, to Cleveland, to Cincinnati, where the men sang at a benefit dinner-Superbowl party for the Children's Dental Association, raising the spirits of despondent Bengals fans. For a few days they escaped severe weather in Nashville, Jacksonville (Alabama), and Chattanooga, but an ice storm caught up with them in Raleigh, plunging a dinner party into a blackout. Just as the *Era* encouraged "ye tuneful" to do in 1871, the Glee Club devoted itself "to the making of darkness melodious."[56]

Then came 1979 and the first in a pair of tours to England. Funding international tours had become expensive since the heyday of the 1960s, which is largely why it took most of the 1970s to get another one off the ground. In fall 1976, the year a tour to Hawaii had been canceled, the managerial staff had begun to eye 1979 for a possible tour to southeastern Europe or China. That they eventually made it as far as England owed much to the alumni of previous international tours, who responded generously to a special solicitation. Building thus on the foundation of its past, the Glee Club started by way of New York City for the Old World. The Manhattan itinerary was a small tour in itself. On the evening of January 5 the men performed from a staircase at the Metropolitan Club on the upper East Side. From this "stairway to heaven" they went the next night to the Sloane House and a concert that some took for a revivalist meeting—apparently more than one of the uninhibited listeners had a religious experience listening to the Glee Club. As could be expected, the singers also appeared in impromptu concerts in Penn and Grand Central stations. Shades of Yugoslavia were evoked when one member had his passport stolen and was detained in New York before he could join the group in England.

After checking in at the Hotel Russell in London, first stop was Coventry Cathedral, where the group performed on January 9. Reconstructed after World War II to combine the old bombed-out shell with the new cathedral, Coventry was site of the 1962 world premiere of Benjamin Britten's *War Requiem,* and a moving place to sing Palestrina and Poulenc. After a day of recording for the BBC in a London church it was on to Bristol Cathedral, where two chronic tour problems first emerged—cold buildings, and strikes. "In the 15th century they didn't have the same knowledge about heating buildings that we do now," Glee Clubber David Jones 1980 wrote, "and so . . . it was D on 'fog' instead of D on 'oo.'"[57] A newspaper strike hurt publicity and consequently attendance at the performance.

For the next week and a half, bus driver Bob (Bub) Halliday chauffeured the Club around to the Cranbourne Chase School for Girls, the University of Reading, the RCM, Westminster Abbey, and the University of Selford. Fish and chips were the order of the day, but in Manchester there was no water to wash them down—this time the water filterers were on strike. The men fortunately were returned each night to the hotel and had established a good line of credit at Peter's Bar at the Grand Hotel. The tour concluded with a return visit to the Harrow School, proclaimed "the coldest concert yet"—as they sang, many not only heard but just as well saw the music of Vaughan Williams as it turned into vapor.

In the summer of 1982 it was back to England. Sir Keith Falkner invited the Glee Club over to take part with Dame Janet Baker in the July concert series at the King's Lynn Festival. Having recently given one of her acclaimed performances of Mahler's *Das Lied von der Erde,* Dame Janet later confided she preferred her King's Lynn performance of Max Reger's "Die Weihe der Nacht" with the Glee Club. The Club's festival performance in St. Nicholas Chapel, which President Frank Rhodes and his wife, Rosa, attended, also included Gregorian chant, English glees, sea chanteys, and spirituals.

Various fiascos affected the group's bed and breakfast accommodations, as well as their flights, forcing them to spend two extra days in London—the tour manager admitted, after many calls and consultations, he had "even more frequent consulations [sic] with my bottle of Johnnie Walker Black." But the week abroad was well spent, and several other concerts were given in Horsham, West Sussex (at the members' restaurant of the Zoological Society of London), and St. James's Hall in Picadilly, the site of the Glee Club's first European concert eighty-seven years earlier. After the visit Jean Marchant, secretary at Nutford House on Brown Street in London, wrote to say:

> We have enjoyed having you all stay with us here and I loved your concert on Thursday evening. I am still basking in the glow of this—it was a definite highlight in my normally dull existence. You all have such beautiful voices and sing in perfect harmony. And as well you are all so well dressed, handsome and masculine! . . .
>
> I understand Cornell is situated in beautiful surroundings. Being a disliker-of-cities, how I envy you all. If you ever need an Assistant Bursar/Secretary and could stand the British accent do bear me in mind. . . .
>
> I will never give away the record you have given to me—not even for £1,000! . . . this record presented to me by the Cornell Glee Club is my proudest possession.[58]

Traveling to England didn't prevent the Club from traversing the States during the same year. Six months earlier the road had run to Florida and a harried occasion in Clearwater when the piano and the Glee Club had arrived simultaneously, just ten minutes before the concert was to begin. Six months later, January 1983, the Glee Club traveled to California, apparently cashing in on a computer airfare that existed for only three hours. The real story of the tour, however, was the conducting problem, or rather, the "Conte calamity." David Conte, who had been serving as acting director for the fall term, took ill just before the scheduled departure. Sokol was unavailable. Biting their nails, the managers convened an emergency session to discuss the situation. Meanwhile Bill Welker was on the West Coast making final arrangements for the group's visit, "unaware that in the subterranean office of the Cornell Glee Club, he was being given the command of the Club once again."[59] Learning the music in approximately one day (here the advantages of the Sokol cycle become obvious), Welker led the Club in a series of successful concerts, marred only by an ill-fated rendition of the "Crew Song." (He called it as an encore, only to discover midsong that a frightening number of the members didn't know the words.) The men likewise rose to the occasion, even giving the unlikely "Cornell Glee Club Concert and Dessert Show" in Santa Barbara, put on by the hotel and restaurant management people and topped off with eclairs, chocolate mousse, fruit ambrosia, cream puffs, petits fours, and a lemon yellow ice carving of the Eiffel Tower. All were devoured by the Glee Club. The tour could be best summed up in the now famous phrase Welker coined on the 1982 England tour and unwittingly demonstrated to perfection less than a year later: "Yet another fine example of the supreme sacrifices which Glee Clubbers are frequently called upon to make. Amen"—more often seen as "This is, as always, y.a.f.e.o.t.s.s.w.g.c.a.f.c.u.t.m. Amen."[60]

In 1985 the Glee Club performed in Boston's Old North Church on tour in the Northeast, and in 1987 and 1988 tried their songs to the south, visiting Arkansas, Texas, Kansas, Missouri, and Georgia. Even before they had left for Boston, however, plans were underway for a tour of Asia, and in January 1989, having figured out the way to finance a tour with a price tag of well over $200,000, the Glee Club headed west for the Far East.[61] The China tour is captured in the PBS video "Geographical Fugue," which earned its name as much from travel arrangements as from Ernst Toch. A scant few weeks before they were to depart, managers learned Singapore Airlines had "lost" the reservation for the Cornell group. Although this seems hard to believe, we should recall that the Glee Club had switched travel agencies and had ended up in a lawsuit with their first agency. Passage was booked on seemingly every available flight headed toward Asia, and split into small groups, the Glee Club executed a complex geographical fugue with counterpoint that took some as far afield as Bali, Biak, and Guam. All the singers made it to Singapore in time for a New Year's Eve reception; so did some of their bags.

Following an initial appearance in St. Andrew's Cathedral, the first full concert took place in Singapore's Victoria Concert Hall on January 3. After a tour of the aircraft carrier *U.S.S. Nimitz,* a few meals from the hawker stalls, and a workshop with the Singapore Youth Choir, the group continued on to the People's Republic of China, arriving in Beijing with the first snowfall the city had seen in several years. With the inclement weather a trip to the Great Wall was traded for visits to the Forbidden City, the Temple of Heaven, Mao's tomb, and Tiananmen Square.[62] The cuisine varied wildly, ranging from the Colonel's Kentucky-fried chicken to Peking Duck. As for international relations, a cold war of sorts ensued between several Glee Clubbers and Chinese nationals when they engaged in a friendly snowball fight.

As on the 1982 England tour the Glee Club traveled with several alumni singers, who bolstered the group's sound and pocketbook. Among other Cornellians who met the group in Asia was a remarkable man who had sung in the

Club under Dann and Dudley, gone to Peking immediately following graduation, and over the years become closely involved in Chinese affairs—Leslie Severinghaus. He introduced the Glee Club to the audience at the Beijing Music Hall, endearing them when, after starting in English, he switched into fluent Mandarin. While in Beijing the group also met Yang Hsien-tong, A.M. 1935, Ph.D. 1937, who at one time had served as China's deputy commissioner of agriculture. On behalf of the Cornell Club of China he told the singers, "All Cornellians in the world are one family. Therefore, you are not in a foreign country but in your Chinese family, meeting and enjoying your brothers, sisters, uncles and aunts."[63]

The tour continued over the next ten days to Shanghai and Hong Kong, where the Glee Club made numerous friends beyond the Cornell family. Collaborating at the Shanghai Conservatory with the school's orchestra, the group performed Mozart's *Eine kleine Freimauer-Kantate* (Freemasons' Cantata). The audience enthusiastically demanded an encore, and when the performers began to repeat the opening chorus—"Laut verkünde uns're Freude" (Loudly proclaim our joy)—they were suddenly surprised and moved by the clapping and stomping of the audience to the music. The work was repeated in Hong Kong in a festival concert at the Hong Kong Academy for Performing Arts. Joined by orchestras and choruses from five local institutions, the Glee Club closed its Asia tour with performances of "The Heavens Are Telling" and "Achieved Is the Glorious Work" from Haydn's *Creation*.

The next year, 1990, the Glee Club set out for the Pacific Northwest, starting in California and making its first visits to Oregon and Washington. The tour booklet passed out to each member contained an itinerary and the following instructions: "If captured by the enemy, it is critical that you destroy all sensitive information by humming a D and sing the bass line of Tancuj backwards in French; this booklet will instantly self-destruct in the aura of your mellifluous timbre!" Most Glee Club missions have remained free of politics and espionage, and even in Red China, with Tiananmen Square only six months away, the tour's political overtones had stayed low key. (One argument did ensue outside the Forbidden City between several Chinese and the Cornell camera crew, who were forbidden to take anything but camcorders inside.) Glee Club tours, domestic tours included, however, can intersect with a larger sphere from time to time. In Chicago in 1981 the Glee Club was scheduled to give a concert on January 21 in the mayor's noontime concert series. Instead the concert was canceled, and the Glee Club sang at a televised civic ceremony led by Mayor Byrne commemorating the release of the hostages from Iran.

A decade later, Glee Clubbers again found themselves intersecting with political history. During the northeastern tour the Glee Club arrived in Washington, D.C., on January 12, 1991. After concerts at Georgetown with the Washington Men's Camerata and in the newly completed National Cathedral, the group checked into the Sheraton Carlton, courtesy of general manager Michel Ducamp 1975, a Glee Club alumnus and Sokol's son-in-law. The hotel was two blocks from the White House, and on the night of the 14th, the eve of President George Bush's deadline with Iraq over events in the Persian Gulf, several Glee Clubbers went over to join the peace protest. Most had never seen anything like it. Thousands of people lined Pennsylvania Avenue, forming a throng lit by streetlights, candles, and the intermittent glare of media cameras. Drums pounded constantly from the curbside, while law enforcement agents milled through the crowd. Meanwhile the White House stood behind the fence, illuminated from the outside and offering no clue as to the fate of nations. The group of Glee Clubbers sang for a while, joined in the chants of the crowd, and eventually returned home to bed to wonder. The next morning the group was scheduled for tours of the White House and Capitol Building. After one Club member was threatened with arrest trying to bring the protest inside the Capitol, the tours proceeded quietly, and at the conclusion the group found itself standing on the steps of the White House, facing out at the protesters. Several raised their hands to signal peace. Later that afternoon the group moved on to Albany and, after serendipitously singing for Governor Mario Cuomo in his office, prepared for the final evening concert.

In 1972 one member wrote in his journal about the Glee Club's concert in Prague: "We sing a song, the last song before intermission, called 'Peace,' by Russell Woollen using text of a poem by Gerard Hopkins. . . . I felt the plight and the repression of the Czechs, the tanks, the soldiers; I was pretty choked up during the concert, this song is superlative . . ."[64] "Peace" was again on the program that night in Albany, and many of the men sensed a deeper meaning as they sang,

> When will you ever, Peace, wild wood-dove, shy wings shut
> Your round me roaming end, and under be my boughs?
> When, when, Peace, will you, Peace,
> When, when will you, Peace?

As everyone gathered backstage after the concert, bus driver Mike Haggerty stepped forward. "Gentleman, I have some bad news," he said. "Tonight at 7 o'clock our time, U.S. planes attacked Iraq." There was a moment of silence. The ride home to Ithaca that night was emotional—some drank, some cried, some stared out into the darkness, wondering if the path of the Persian Gulf War would touch them or their friends on that bus.

A year later, the Glee Club was in the Musée de la Croix Rouge, not far from the United Nations buildings in Geneva, when a tour guide pointed out a statue of a nurse helping a general. There are breaks in the stone, she said, symbolizing the broken and incomplete dream of peace. Still there was enough stone for a statue. By that time the war with Iraq was long over.

The 1992 European tour was conceived in part to take advantage of possible funding available in conjunction with the 500th anniversary of the discovery of the American continents. No such money materialized, but the tour did, fitting the last missing piece to the 1895 tour puzzle—France. Spain and Switzerland rounded out the itinerary, all three countries being visited by the Club for the first time. After celebrating "Bonne Année" with the crew aboard Air France and seeing the sun rise on the new year from an altitude of more than 30,000 feet, the group arrived in Madrid, giving the first concert at Los Geronimos on January 2. After visits to the Prado, the Guernica museum, and Madrid's stylish nightlife, they continued on to Toledo. All roads in the town seemed to lead to the immense cathedral, making it appear not only the center, but the divine fountainhead of Toledo's life. Not surprisingly, the city began a string of stops where the religious images of the day began to express themselves in the music making at night.

The Glee Club continued on to Avila where at sunset they gave an outstanding rendition of Biebl's "Ave Maria" within the walls of the town at St. Theresa's Church. Concerts followed in Cáceras, coincident with the Spanish celebration of Reyes Magos, and Bilboa. On the way to Barcelona the entire Glee Club took the cable car up the mountain to the abbey of Montserrat. Sokol and a few others met with the superior, who produced a guest book that Sokol had signed nearly three decades earlier. In the evening the group gave a concert in Barcelona, after which some made a midnight pilgrimage to Gaudi's unfinished cathedral, La Sagrada Familia. The next day the two-bus caravan stopped at the 1992 Summer Olympic facilities, also unfinished, before making a Dramamine journey through the Pyrenees and across France to Lyons.

Les Petits Chanteurs de Lyon and their families hosted the Glee Club, and the two ensembles shared performances in the Lyons cathedral, and the newer Basilique de Notre-Dame de Fourvière, labeled "l'éléphant" by the locals. The concert at the basilica also featured a collaboration with the Lyons Symphony Orchestra and the women's section of the Geneva University Chorus. Repeated in Geneva, the program gave the Glee Club the opportunity to perform Walter Piston's "Carnival Song" in the original scoring for ten brass players. Sokol, having by now conducted collaborative efforts in several countries where he did not speak the language, was unphased by working with the French players. In the Lyons performance, however, one player (conspicuously someone different from the one playing the same part in rehearsal) entered early and cut against the grain for a while before finding his place. Sokol later commented, "That wasn't a language problem, that was a counting problem." The Glee Club also gave a concert of its own at the UN in Geneva before leaving for the cities of Neuchâtel, where the concert at the Temple du Bas was well received, and picturesque Lucerne, with its wooden bridges across the lake inlet. The final concert was given in Zurich at the resonant Fraumünster church.

Like the 1979 tour of England the Glee Club encountered cold cathedrals, and accommodations ranged from the sublime to the absurd. From five-star hotels in Madrid the group moved to a youth hostel in Cáceras with no hot water and little heat, and on to Geneva, where many of the singers spent two nights

37. The Glee Club in concert in Madrid, Spain, January 1992. Photograph by George Gull 1972.

in a bomb shelter. Nothing fostered camaraderie like being holed up in an underground facility with forty beds per room, metal washroom troughs, and enough supplies to sustain several hundred for months. And the rates couldn't be beat. Graffiti spray painted on the outside wall said, "Yankee Go Home." Eventually the Glee Club did, through substantial jet-stream turbulence. When the ride settled, everyone could ascertain that the Glee Club had not only weathered the trip, but had prospered on its tenth international tour of the century.

The next tour, covering the Great Lakes area after the Senior Week of 1993, may or may not qualify as the eleventh but it did visit Toronto, probably (and almost unbelievably) the first Glee Club performance in Canada since an octet visited Montreal in 1897. In January 1994 the Glee Club traveled south, making stops in Nashville and Memphis, Augusta and Atlanta, North Carolina and several Florida towns—Ponte Vedra, Fort Lauderdale, Fort Myers, and St. Petersburg, where the Glee Force played yet another of its hotly contested Florida bowl games. While near Tampa the group paid a special visit to the home of Les Severinghaus, by that time well into his nineties and in failing health. It was his last wish to hear the Glee Club, so the young men gathered in the Severinghaus backyard around the elderly man in the wheelchair, this oldest of living Glee Club alums, and sang for him. His head perked up during the Cornell songs, and there were few dry eyes during the spiritual "Precious Lord." For the few remaining months of his life, it was said, he played the videotape of the backyard performance once or twice each day.

In 1995, honoring Professor Sokol's last year at Cornell, the Chorus and Glee Club took a special joint tour, the first in either group's history. Visiting cities in New York and Connecticut, the January tour closed out a remarkable era of Glee Club travel. During Sokol's years the men had performed from New York to Los Angeles, Leningrad to London, Tokyo to Anchorage. They had sung Vaughan Williams in Westminster Abbey and Shostakovich in the Moscow Conservatory, brought Bernstein to Malaysia and Copland to Switzerland. Far from the days of those first tentative trips to Owego and Syracuse, by 1995 the Glee Club had become an organization with more than twenty countries stamped on its passport.

Regardless of where Glee Club members tour in the future, they very likely will continue to serve as ambassadors of Cornell, of music, and of youth. And to the extent that they exemplify each, as a group and as individuals, they will continue to make a significant difference in the lives of others. After the Cornell Crew's legendary first-place finish at Saratoga in 1875, President White proudly claimed the victory "had done more to tell the world about Cornell than the trustees could have done by spending $100,000."[65] One hundred and twenty years later the same could be said a thousandfold of the Cornell University Glee Club.

As for those in the group who actually make these odysseys, a member once said he had learned the most as a Cornell student while away from Cornell—studying abroad and taking Glee Club tours. For each generation of Glee Clubbers tours have provided a way of seeing more of the world and experience than one can comprehend from one's desk. There is the musical experience of giving a program ten or twelve days in a row, where by the third day nerves have evaporated, and by the tenth each performer has discovered the heights an ensemble can attain when its members have truly moved inside the music. There is the wider educational impact and wisdom of the experience. And there is the joy that runs though those days, and the afterglow that follows. "Behold how good, / And how pleasant it is, / For brethren to dwell / Together in unity," the text that ends Bernstein's *Chichester Psalms* translates. People become fast friends singing together behind the Iron Curtain or stranded in airports, weathering storms on interstate highways or bumming around foreign cities between concerts. That experience is, in part, why the Glee Club so often returns home a Club. To there, and to all these places the Glee Club travels, to harbor *lunga poss.*

8   Haec Est Domus

Mid pleasures and palaces though we may roam,
Be it ever so humble, there's no place like home.

—"Home, Sweet Home," from John H. Payne's 1823 opera *Clari,*
or, The Maid of Milan

One easy way to chart the growth of Cornell is through its buildings—when and where they went up, their cost, their major donors, their function, their architecture, and their secrets. According to Morris Bishop the early campus represented two distinct styles—the romantic, upstate gothic of Sage Chapel, Sage Hall, Franklin (Tjaden) Hall, and the president's house, matched by the sturdy, economical style of Cascadilla, Morrill, McGraw, White, and the first version of Sibley. Over time other edifices appeared on the lands once part of Simeon DeWitt's farm. The University Library and clock tower were dedicated in 1891, Goldwin Smith Hall closed the quadrangle in 1906, and Willard Straight Hall was finished in 1925; Glee Club alumnus Myron Taylor 1894 and his wife Anabel were immortalized side by side in the decades that followed.

Now, more than a century after ground was first broken, time and technology have wrought a campus as diverse as the subjects taught within Cornell's walls. There is the postmodern Center for Theatre Arts, the 1960s utopian decorum of Olin Library, the chameleon law school addition, and the invisible transept of the underground Kroch Library. The campus overall has retained an arresting beauty, offering quadrangles bounded by the natural splendors of gorges, waterfalls, and the view off East Hill.

Touring Glee Clubbers eventually return home to Ithaca, and this place Cornell. Home in a specific sense, however, has changed as many times for the Glee Club as it did for Vladimir Nabokov, who moved every year of his decade or so in Ithaca. From its origins to the present day, the group has used a surprising number of buildings for rehearsal, performance, or partying. They make not only an interesting tour of Ithaca and the Cornell campus, but of CUGC history, for as the university can be read through its buildings, so the Glee Club can be read through its various and multifarious addresses.

In the university's earliest years the Glee Club rehearsed in both Cascadilla, which had a piano, and Morrill, which had nearly everything else, including for a time the university's chapel and library, as well as some dorm rooms. Rehearsal of course was a loose word in those days; the men sang indoors when they weren't out in the open air, "racking the nervous system of all who have to listen by their 'melodious discords.'"[1] In any case these buildings were no more intended for rehearsal than Cascadilla was intended to be a residence hall. Originally built as a water cure establishment, the "generously windowed fort" was only later adapted as living quarters for the young university. Professor Goldwin Smith, who lived there for a time, once commented the building was "so ill-ventilated that as many patients would probably have been killed by the air as would have been saved by the water."[2] Somehow the Glee Club survived Cascadilla to work on their own airs. During their first twenty years the group also availed themselves of the Ithaca Quartette rooms and Leo's parlors, where they met every Friday evening for rehearsal during the 1884–1885 year.

The Orpheus Glee Club's first performance took place in Library Hall, the 800-seat auditorium of the Cornell Public Library, which stood on the southeast corner of Seneca and Tioga streets. For a time Cornell and his family lived across the way, where the Ithaca Savings Bank building eventually was put up. Library Hall was site to the university's inaugural ceremony, numerous Cornell commencements (the first one on campus was held in the Old Armory in 1883), and lectures by such luminaries as Mark Twain, Susan B. Anthony, James Russell Lowell, and Louis Agassiz.

For many years the Glee Club also performed in the Wilgus Opera House and the Lyceum Theater. Officially named the Atheneum, the Wilgus Opera House occupied the third and fourth floors of a building built in 1868 by brothers John and Henry Wilgus, who kept a dry goods store on the ground floor. The building stood on the southwest corner of State and Tioga Streets by the turn-track for the trolleys, a site that is now the heart of the Ithaca Commons. The theater had a beautifully arched ceiling and seats for 1,600. According to Bishop it was

> brilliantly illumined by sixty-four gas jets under a central reflector. A brass rail separated the front row from the stage. Fashion decreed that the occupants of the front row should slouch to the horizontal and put their feet up on the rail. On one occasion eight students chalked large letters on their shoe soles during the intermission; and when the curtain rose the actors read the message: THIS SHOW IS ROTTEN.

On another occasion critical undergraduates actually broke up a traveling show in the Wilgus Opera House, and the ensuing battle with townspeople was carried out into the street.[3]

When the opera house was taken over by the Ithaca Conservatory in 1894, "the Lyceum, with its moving floor, became the favorite theatre for vaudeville

38. Exterior of Ithaca's Lyceum Theater in 1922.

and more serious entertainment downtown."[4] Built in 1893, about the time some Ithaca streets were first paved, the Lyceum had a porticoed entrance at 113 South Cayuga and ran in an L-shape behind several Cayuga Street buildings toward Green Street.[5] Features included "its parterre, an Ithaca social club on theatre nights, and . . . its steep gallery with its hard curving undusted wooden benches."[6] The theater was christened with a performance of Verdi's *Il Trovatore,* after which a new show was presented every second or third night. According to *Ithaca Then and Now,* "the theatre became established as a tryout center for New York City shows, hosting performances by John Barrymore, Sarah Bernhardt and Lillian Russell."[7] The Lyceum could, like the Wilgus, be unkind; audiences commented candidly with boos, stamping, coins, potatoes, and eggs. This kind of reception did not greet the efforts of local musicians. Hollis Dann's first Music Festival took place there in 1895, and the theater remained a home to many Glee Club performances for the next thirty years.

By the time Ithaca was ready for music festivals in 1904, so was Sage Chapel. A year earlier the northeast transept had been extended, according to Dann's recommendations, to accommodate the organ, a choir loft, and room for an orchestra—the third expansion of the building since it was first completed in May 1875. The work of Cornell's first architecture professor Charles Babcock, Sage Chapel was originally just that, a modest chapel. Ezra Cornell had pushed

39. Interior of the Lyceum Theater, c. 1900.

for something on a larger scale, but A. D. White and Henry Sage had held firm, and the red brick chapel took shape as a single east-west nave with room for four hundred, a south transept seating an additional hundred, and a tower under which the organ room was located. The Memorial Antechapel was added in 1883, and beneath it, the crypt in which lie the remains of Ezra and Mary Cornell, Andrew and Mary White, John McGraw, Jennie McGraw Fiske, Willard Fiske, Alonzo Cornell, and Edmund Ezra Day. Those who have surreptitiously sung there while Hiram Sibley's bust looked on know one of the campus's most interesting acoustics.

The chapel was almost completely rebuilt in 1898; the tower and south transept came down, the nave was extended, new north-south transepts were built, and the Sage Memorial Apse with its allegorical mosaic was added. The aforementioned additions followed in 1903, at which time the ceiling was adorned with its elaborate decorations, including a lattice of vines in which appear ecclesiastical emblems, and the sky-blue latin cross filled with "gilded sunbursts and stars."[8] In 1940 the nave was expanded westward to make room for a new organ and choir loft. The Aeolian Skinner organ was installed, with a parapet of golden pipes (many of them purely for visual effect) lining the back of the loft. Behind them the Apostles' rose window remains from the original chapel, often lighting the room with a prism sunset.

40. The interior of Sage Chapel, c. 1905.

While the choir loft was still in the northeast transept, the Glee Club used it each spring from 1904 until 1911 when they took part in the annual music festivals. Before then they had not performed regularly on campus. The Mozart Club had used Morrill or the Sage Hall parlor, the Sage Choir sang in the chapel, and others performed in Barnes Hall, where the Glee Club did sing at a benefit in 1891–1892. Most often the Glee, Banjo, and Mandolin Clubs were found downtown at the Lyceum, where they continued to give their own concerts through the music festival years.

In 1913 the Agricultural Auditorium was opened for use, with seating for just over 2,000. The building was named for Liberty Hyde Bailey, director of the College of Agriculture and the driving force in that school's expansion from 1903 to 1913. The character of Cornell is perhaps reflected in its main auditorium being named for a man whose work includes sixty-three books and five encyclopedias on horticulture, agriculture, farm crops, and farm animals.[9] Originally the upstage wall of Bailey Hall held pipes for the organ given by Andrew Carnegie to A. D. White on his 80th birthday. An accident one year sent water from a flooded blower coursing through the pipes, ruining the organ and resulting in the current wood-paneled back wall. Allan Treman later recalled some of the boards from the organ stops were put into service as shelves in the Ag School. Otherwise the hall has remained much the same as it was in 1913—a big room with a small feel (especially if one has been sitting in the seats for a few hours), a mercurial acoustic in turn lauded and lamented, and an outside brick wall that looks as though someone cut off the rest of the building (or the funding) at that particular spot.

Even before the first Music Festival was held in Bailey, the Glee Club gave its annual Junior Week concert there on February 4, 1914: "The Musical Clubs christened the new Agricultural Auditorium in the evening; the beautiful building and the delightful concert each honoring the other."[10] From then on the group used Bailey and the Lyceum intermittently until the latter closed (conceding to the increasingly popular cinemas), at which point Eric Dudley moved his troops onto campus for all their home concerts. Bailey was home to Junior and Senior Week concerts, Gilbert and Sullivan operettas, and "Oh, What a Night!" in which it became the Bailey Tavern.

Dudley also moved other Club activities onto campus. From about 1897 until the 1920s, Glee Club tryouts had taken place in the Club rooms on Tioga Street. Allan Treman fixes that location as the third floor of 111 North Tioga, a building once housing the Masonic Temple and quite possibly, the former Ithaca Quartette rooms.[11] With many of the men lodging downtown, and frequent performances at the Lyceum, the location was convenient for rehearsal and hanging out. But as performances moved up on the Hill and dormitories began to be built on campus, the meeting place moved too. In the 1930s the Glee Club took advantage of the new student union, Willard Straight Hall, for auditions, rehearsals, and performances. (Named for Willard Straight 1901, who for a time represented the U.S. State Department in the Far East, the union largely realized A. D. White's dream of a great meeting hall for alumni and students.) The North Room was used for rehearsal, and the 1934 Junior Week concert (with a dance to follow) was given in the high-ceilinged Memorial Room.

The Straight remained the Club's address and their principal rehearsal site through Dudley's final years, through Kuypers and Weaver, and well into Tracy's time. Only in 1954 did Foster Coffin write to tell the Men's and Women's Glee Clubs he "could no longer feel justified in allotting exclusive and guaranteed use of the North Room."[12] For a year the men rehearsed in Sage Chapel and then moved their headquarters to the newly acquired Toboggan Lodge on the shore of Beebe Lake.

The toboggan house, as it was also known, was built in the early 1930s by the Athletic Association, using stone left over from work on Balch Hall and the War Memorial on West Campus.[13] According to Treman, "One end of this building was the warming room for frozen tobogganers and the other end was the toboggan storage area."[14] (The old toboggan slide had originally stood nearby on the south shore.) Although the Glee Club had had no official connection with the Athletic Association for some years (stationery in the 1930s had given the Schoellkopf Memorial Building as well as the Straight as addresses), they were able to secure the lodge for use. The men moved in, the piano was reconditioned, and the public was invited to "stroll by Beebe Lake Lodge some

Wednesday or Friday evening. Besides seeing a superb musical ensemble at work, you'll be treating yourself to a free concert."[15]

Sokol's first rehearsal with the Glee Club took place in the Toboggan Lodge. He cleared the air by putting an end to smoking, but even then the place was not ideal. So he and the Glee Club set out in search of new lodgings. Over the next few years they touched down in Risley, Willard Straight, Statler, Stone, the Veterinary School, and an engineering building or two. Sokol later reflected that they probably rehearsed at one time or another in almost every building on the campus. In 1959 Room B of Goldwin Smith was approved for rehearsal. A year or so later the Glee Club moved into Sage Chapel with the permission of President Deane Malott. Here at last was home.

One morning soon after the move Sokol was sitting in the basement at a little table that served as his desk, and Deane Malott happened to walk in. "Is this the best Cornell University can do for you?" the president asked, incredulous to find this was the choral director's office. Within a day the head of the buildings and properties division was over to size up the situation, and soon workers were hammering and sawing away, resulting in the little director's office and the Glee Club's basement headquarters next door. "As of September 1961, Sage Chapel Office Number One . . . has become the quarters of the Cornell University Glee Club," Sokol wrote.[16] The group moved its music over from the lodge, and managers began to break in the office for the generations to follow.

The long subterranean hallway lined with cupboards full of music, the miscellaneous cabinets jammed with CUGC artifacts, the old Steinway on which students bang at all hours of the day and night, and the door to the Glee Club office have become familiar friends to many Cornell students since then. And the air has been full with animated conversations, the chapel's silence, and the sound of the squeaky door leading up the back stairs to the choir loft. Upstairs in the chapel the solemn beauty of the setting continues to rub off on the music making, having framed many a fall concert since the first one there on Homecoming Weekend of 1973. And many a student has had the chance to look up and consider the words "Mind," "Soul," and "Love" as they appear in the frieze running around the perimeter. Here in Sage Chapel and the basement below, inconspicuously tucked in the heart of campus, the Glee Club carries on its daily life.

For every home the Glee Club has had a hangout, and to discuss Sage Chapel and Bailey Hall without mentioning a few other locales would be like presenting someone the living room and the study without showing them the backroom bar and pool table. Here are some of the places formative in making a club out of the Glee Club.

From the beginning there was the Ithaca Hotel, which used to stand downtown on the southwest corner of State and Aurora Streets. The hotel first earned its fame during Ithaca's stagecoach days, when it was a stop on the Catskill Turnpike. In 1898 the Dutch Kitchen was added during a renovation overseen by William Henry Miller, architect for the clock tower and Uris Library. The "Dutch" quickly became a favorite with students, and the class of 1900 pioneered its use for senior singing. By the 1940s Cornellians were calling it "our oldest pub," and in 1948 the Glee Club was still meeting there for spirits and song. About that time Rym Berry wrote that the

> Ithaca Hotel continues to get the bulk, if not the cream, of the student trade. The Dutch Kitchen is now a regular restaurant and the student department has been moved out back near the bar where it is less in the public eye; and ear. . . .
>
> The ladies are not allowed to sit on the bar or even stand up to it. They must use the tables hard by and have the stuff fetched to them in the prim tradition of stagecoach days.[17]

By this time the price of a "short beer" was up to 10 cents, but the stagecoach image lingered. On one of his first trips to Ithaca in 1957, Sokol said, "I remember pulling up near the Ithaca Hotel and at that time downtown Ithaca looked more like a Western community, the kind you see in the movies, and I had some thought about whether or not this seemed to be quite the urban center, cultural center that I thought it might be. . . . It used to be a little bit on the rugged looking side."[18]

Along the street from the Dutch Kitchen stood the Lager Beer Saloon and Restaurant opened in 1880 by Prussian immigrant Theodore Zinck. The watering hole celebrated in "Give My Regards to Davy" probably was the Glee Club's first real hangout. Officially known as the Hotel Brunswick, Zinck's was located on the west side of North Aurora Street. There the cook played student orders *con amore*, and the proprietor might condescend on occasion "to explain the difference between bock beer and the regular brew." Berry continues,

> This man was no clown. . . . [Zinck] was not a person to inspire affection or invite intimacy. It was his sole mission through two decades to provide a university town . . . with an immaculate inn which maintained a respectful, old-world attitude toward good food and drink and stressed the amenities to be observed in consumption of the same. . . . The night he liked best was Wednesday, when, after their rehearsal in the Blood Block, a group from the Glee Club would drop in and sing for another hour over two or three glasses of beer. He'd beam with complete happiness when, for his special gratification, the choristers would render *Gaudeamus Igitur* in dubious Latin and impeccable harmony.[19]

Even if Zinck was aloof at times in his day, the *Era* maintained that in the succeeding years before World War I

41. Zinck's and the Ithaca Hotel on Aurora Street in downtown Ithaca, c. 1965.

Cornellians who finished off the academic week with a seminar at the Dutch, Zinck's, or any of the other local fountains of youth were well acquainted with the bar-tenders in their favorite spots. They usually knew them as well as they did their professors; sometimes better. Red, for instance, who has been vice-president in charge of wassail at "the Dutch" since 1902, is regularly greeted by returning alumni.[20]

That was the situation partly because, until the Straight opened, students didn't have a union that served beer. But as campus and Collegetown developed over the next few decades, activity gradually moved up the Hill, prompting Berry to say in 1947 "Ithaca and Cornell aren't seeing so much of each other as they once did."[21] Zinck's moved several times following the death of its founder in 1903, ending up next to the Dutch Kitchen; it closed in 1967. A year later the Ithaca Hotel was torn down, and panels from the Dutch were salvaged for the present Holiday Inn on South Cayuga Street.

By then the Glee Club was gathering up at Johnny's Big Red Grill, just east of the College Avenue and Dryden Road intersection. Known for its cheap beer and daily special, Johnny's was the scene of numerous Glee Club "fellowship" sessions throughout the 1970s. When it closed—the place has been in and out of business numerous times, and at present writing is again open—the Glee Club moved to Vinnie's Italian Kitchen at 410 Eddy Street, the hangout for much of the 1980s. Vinnie Agresti knew cooking like Verdi knew Italian and used to import his tomatoes from Pianconi, outside Naples. "They come from where I come from," he would say. Many Glee Clubbers remember the checkered tablecloths, brick walls, and pizza from the annual New Man Dinner, or Sokol and Carl St. Clair toasting each other after a Cornell–CCO performance. In 1989 Vinnie's closed, the Agresti family headed for a vacation in Italy, and 410 Eddy Street became Little Joe's.

The Glee Club moved up the block and underground to 420 Eddy Street—The Chariot. In the mid-1990s the group was still convening there, on a dais in the back past the bar and TV, for evenings of song and laughter. Though the tomatoes may not be imported, pizzas can disappear in less than ten seconds, leaving the rough wooden stools free to be used as percussion instruments. Occasionally someone ill-advisedly tries to swing from the wooden matrix suspended from the ceiling or is left grabbing for a picture after accidentally knocking it off the wall. But the rathskeller is always left standing, somewhat richer for the visit, and when the last pitcher is dry, everyone moves upstairs to form a circle and sing Alma Mater and "Evening Song" out in the fresh night air.

There are addresses as yet unknown which the Glee Club will one day call homes and hangouts. For now, nothing conveys the marriage of hell-bent and heaven that is the Glee Club like visits to the subterranean Chariot to hear the men sing "Ride the Chariot" and to Sage Chapel, while the emblazoned rafters echo with Maximilian Albrecht's "Haec Est Domus Domini."

9 The Small Groups

"Skee doo bi ya'n doo da didit doo wa, ba ba dee ya'n doo da"
—Scat riff from the Hangover's version of "'Round Midnight"

Two-thirds of the way through a typical Glee Club concert, occasionally to the surprise of the newest men in the group, the director sits down and a few singers step forward to form a crescent moon. A pitch sounds and they launch into backgrounds of "do-dooo" or "bop ba-da," or "bom-bom-bom-bom." Soloists enter the fray and someone pantomimes percussion instruments, while the singers throb and sway, swing and jump around. The audience ripples with sentiment, cracks up with laughter, and by the end often screams with approval. And then, almost as quickly as all this began, the singers have melted back into the ranks of the Glee Club. The small group has struck again, but who is this group, and where did it come from?

Any consideration of small groups begins with the Orpheus Glee Club—after all, the vocalists in this original glee club could be counted on one hand. Small groups such as the Collegensia Quintette, the Ithaca Quartette, and the quartets in residence at fraternities were the order of the day. Only as the Glee Club grew did the notion of a subset group become more defined. An 1883 editorial on Sage Chapel singing suggested a quartet from the Glee Club lead the music. In 1895 quartets were listed as part of the England tour repertory, and in 1897 an octet from the group traveled to Montreal to take part in a concert at McGill University (at the time normal Glee Club touring size was sixteen singers).

Soon after 1910 a group of students approached Dann about forming a new quartet (or more likely a replacement for a prior quartet depleted due to graduation) to sing in Club concerts. At that time quartet singing was very popular in the country, and Robert Doyle remembers, "After hearing us, he gave us permission.... Some of the songs the quartet sang [including "Lou" and "Honey"] were taken from one of the leading quartets of that day ... and were very well received."[1] By the 1920s, with the Glee Club numbering about sixty, programs designated octets and less frequently, sextets. Subsets had become a formalized part of the organization.

These octets and sextets were trimmed back to quartets in Dudley's later years, years when the Glee Club Quartet, the Sophomore Quartet, and the Savage Club Quartet appeared on the program. The Glee Club Quartet included Dick Lee and Ray Kruse, while the Savage Club's fab four included Trink Powers, Allan Treman, and his Cornell classmate C. Wesley Thomas, a tenor soloist in Dudley's Presbyterian Church Choir. The latter group also masqueraded as the Cornell Alumni Quartet, and though not official members of the Glee Club, they appeared with the group in Ithaca and on tour. After the war Tracy reserved a place on the program for quartet selections, a billing filled by both the Glee Club Quartet and the Junior Savage Club Quartet (a younger version of the alumni foursome). Then too the soloists for "Song of the Classes" formed a natural foursome, requiring several additional harmonizers for the postsenior verses.

Tracy liked the quartets, but he had a mind to try something new, and in 1949 a triple quartet was formed from the ranks of the Glee Club. The founders, wishing to invoke Cornell without actually naming it, called the group Cayuga's Waiters, punning on the opening line of the Alma Mater. According to one account the ensemble "was born in a dark corner during a fraternity party when twelve members of the Cornell Men's Glee Club found themselves in a singing mood. They proceeded to sing the night away and have kept on singing ever since." Another picturesque version has it that,

> early one Friday evening in the cold dreary October of 1949, as a dozen or so equally dreary students sat in scattered fashion around the worn tables at Zinck's, one of the obviously unhappy drinkers began humming a frail chorus of "Davy'" into his glass of beer. In no less than ten minutes, the other eleven had picked up the tune, putting it into modern harmony; and in less than an hour, all twelve were grouped around a table, their voices blended in joyful comraderie [sic].[2]

According to Erwin (Rusty) Chapin Davis 1950, a member of the Glee Club Quartet and one of the original Waiters, Tom Tracy simply gave him the idea and a list of talented Glee Clubbers to cull in forming a new triple quartet. Davis pulled a group together (which soon included classmate John (Tim) Timmerman, author of the song "Cornell Champions" and the Waiters' first business manager), and they debuted at the Glee Club's 1950 Junior Week concert, "Notes of '50." The group's wardrobe signature was a towel draped over the arm of their Glee Club tux; bypassing the wine list, they presented "Mood Indigo," "Mandy," "Everytime We Say Good-bye," and "Lord, If I Get My Ticket." By 1951 they had "become very popular around campus singing at various smokers and other meetings. They also met with great applause on the [Glee Club] tour."[3]

In the context of Cornell's small singing group history, the Waiters were distinguished by the degree of autonomous activity they undertook and, in

42. The first Cayuga's Waiters, 1950, *far right,* Rusty Davis.

comparison with their Glee Club predecessors, the strength of identity they established independent of the Glee Club. Prior to the Waiters the regimen of small group singing, traveling, and recording, completely familiar today, did not exist at Cornell. Not realizing they were pioneers, the new triple quartet set out by accepting local engagements on top of their Glee Club duties and soon found their popularity and activity were snowballing. They began to tour on their own in 1953, accepting an invitation to perform at Bermuda's Harbor Castle Hotel over the Christmas holidays. The same year, they cut their first record "to meet the demand of their fame."[4] They also made inroads into the national small group scene, singing with similar groups from eight colleges in a 1955 concert held at St. Lawrence University. Some of these groups, the Waiters included, soon banded to form a loose confederation known as the Collegiate Choraleers.

In five short years the Waiters' stock had gone up considerably, and it continued to rise through the mid-1950s. It probably went to their heads. In the spring of 1956 the Waiters made it known they were disassociating from the Glee Club, effective immediately, and at least ostensibly because "their feeling is that they don't have sufficient rehearsal time and that they have been out sung by other comparable groups."[5] Other small a cappella groups had sprung up on campus, and at least one, the coed Cornellaires, had once stated that their purpose was "to prove that anything Cayuga's Waiters can sing, Cornellaires can sing better."[6] Perhaps the Waiters felt their celebrity rivaled. More likely,

43. The Sherwoods. From *Cornellian*, 1957.

they may have felt they had outgrown the Glee Club. After all, their stated purpose was "to embarrass the coed in the front row," and they could do that on their own. The Waiters' unprecedented autonomy thus was followed by an unprecedented rift between the Glee Club and its small group, a parting of the ways that left its mark on both sides. The Glee Club moved "that no group be taken on Glee Club tours unless its members are members of the Glee Club. Also it was recognized that the name 'Cayuga's Waiters' does not belong to the present waiters, as it was conceived by Mr. Tracy, and the rights to that name belong to him. Likewise, the physical assets of the Waiters do not belong to them."[7]

The name rights proved an academic point. The Waiters continued to perform, entirely independent of the Glee Club, and can still be heard on campus today. Their style has changed to include guitar playing, informal dress, and beer, and recent repertoire has included such tailor-made songs as "If I Were Not a Waiter," and "We Didn't Go to Harvard" (after Billy Joel's "We Didn't Start the Fire"). Their numbers have remained high (they are often a quadruple quartet, if not larger) and they have maintained a certain popularity.

With the departure of the Waiters the Glee Club created a new triple quartet, the Sherwoods, who were first heard at the Glee Club's 1956 fall concert and soon revealed their specialty in the "Barbershop-Belafonte repertoire." Rather quickly their name came to mean more than Robin Hood's forest home; noted for their "ad lib" style, the group often responded to the impromptu invitation, "Would you like to sing," with the answer, "sure would," at which point they launched into "Let's Do It," "Zoombie Jamboree," or "I Talk to the Trees." Colloquially known as the "Woods," the men appeared attired in ties and green jackets and soon found their popularity on the rise, disproving the Waiters' 1957 motto: "We can't be replaced." Barely one year old, the Sherwoods took an impressive tour in summer 1957 through Hawaii and the Far East, entertaining the U.S. Armed Forces stationed there. Over the next few years they spent holidays visiting what have become traditional a cappella hangouts: Bermuda, the Virgin Islands, and Jamaica. And by 1960 they had already released their third recording, "The Sherwoods at Zinck's," which was aired nationally.

Popularity once again led to conflict with the parent Glee Club, however. The Sherwoods were in great demand at weekly fraternity parties, and Sokol recalls, "It really became intoxicating for them." When they began to miss Glee Club rehearsals, he talked with them at length, trying to hold the large and small groups together and making it clear attendance was mandatory. But when in fall 1958 they informed him they had an engagement the same evening as a Glee Club performance, he realized that was it. "So I dropped them and lost twelve of my best singers. It was very hard to do but we had to do that. It was very important."[8]

And so another small group cut itself off from the Glee Club, the second in a decade to organize and break away. The Sherwoods continued to sing and travel throughout the 1960s, celebrating their achievements in poetry and prose by Robin Q. Hood IV. One highlight of those years was basso profundo Bozo Chagnon 1974 singing "House of the Rising Sun," not far from the Half Moon Hotel in Jamaica. But the group's popularity waned, and they appeared in the *Cornellian* for the last time in 1973. These days, the Sherwoods reconvene each June to sing at Reunions Weekend, when they are heard around campus giving impromptu concerts and appear late Saturday night in Goldwin Smith, following Cornelliana Night, to sing with other groups in what has become a reunion a cappella tradition.

Once again the Glee Club spawned another new small group to replace the departing one. First appearing under the title The Glee Club Eight on the 1958–1959 winter tour, the Glee Club Octaves had become the official small group by the spring 1959 Parents' Weekend concert. Unlike the Waiters and Sherwoods the Octaves never achieved fame worthy of mention in the *Cornellian,* nor a level of wanderlust necessitating a leave from the Glee Club. Instead the group closed up shop in 1966. Still, for seven years their renditions of ballads, folk songs, and new and old favorites added to Glee Club performances, and they represented one more musical pun in Cornell's a cappella names, which include the Noteables, the Touchtones, the Class Notes, and Nothing But Treble.

In 1968, after a two-year a cappella hiatus, Glee Clubber Rick Dehmel 1969 founded the Hangovers. Although the obvious connotation implies excessive drinking, the name recalls the traditional Cornell term for those students who, willfully or otherwise, spent more than four years at Cornell. Arthur Parsons Hibbard 1930 inadvertently became one such hangover when he contracted typhoid fever and was forced to finish his degree a semester late. A member of Theta Delta Chi, he recalled, "At the same time a number of fraternity brothers ... were also back for a number of reasons. ... We naturally graduated into a 'Hangover' group within the Fraternity. It was the custom at that time to do a lot of singing during the meals. ... One of the songs, of course, was the 'Song of the Classes,' so we thought we ought to have our own verse." The hangover verse Hibbard penned went as follows:

> We are the Hangovers, we hang over here,
> The freshman are lousy, the sophomores are queer,
> We don't give a damn for the whole junior class,
> And as for the Seniors, we hope they all pass![9]

Over time, "hangover" became an official designation for fifth-year architecture and engineering students, and for a while the Glee Club's "Hangovers" were the designated group who sang this "hangover" verse, or its variations, in concert. In 1968 these informal "Hangovers" noticed they sounded pretty good together and began to sing outside of rehearsal, most notably outside Balch dorm, where they serenaded the women residents. Encouraged by audience response, they soon became the Hangovers (known as the Hangs for short). An octet at the outset, they started to accept gigs on and off campus, frequently making the rounds of Cornell's fraternities and sororities. Beyond their Greek travels, they visited Germany with the Glee Club in January 1970 and made their first solo journey to Bermuda the next winter. About the same time they recorded their first album, "The Hangovers of the Cornell University Glee Club." By 1971 the *Cornellian* reported: "To alumni they're almost a tradition, since for the past two years Cornell has called upon them to perform during Alumni Week. And thanks to a steady stream of local dates and the record they recently cut, they're equally well known to the Cornell community."[10]

The 1971 Senior Week concert featured two small groups—the Hangovers and the Leftovers. The Hangs closed their set that evening with a satirical rendition of "Teen Angel," accompanied by electric guitar. The audience went wild, and as the last notes faded away, the group crossed into Glee Club history. Dehmel was leaving, as were several others, and the ensemble was disbanding. In the fall the remaining Hangs were absorbed into the Leftovers, ironically a group started by the Club's assistant director Stan Malinowski as an alternative. Seeing as they were no longer leftover from anything, the small ensem (as Sokol has often called it) changed its name back to the Hangovers in 1972 and has remained the Glee Club's a cappella subset ever since.

The Hangs continued to sing through the 1970s, at times facing the vicissitudes of infrequent performance opportunities, irregular rehearsals, internal

44. The Hangovers touring Bermuda on motorcycles, 1971. From *Cornellian,* 1971.

strife, and student turnover, though this last was mitigated by the participation of true-to-life "hangovers."[11] On the other hand, potential tension between the small group and the Glee Club was largely diffused with the Hangs director serving simultaneously as assistant director of the Glee Club during most of the decade. By 1978, having become the longest-standing subset of the Club, the group had grown to thirteen, a size comparable to the Sherwood and Waiters groups of past years. In 1979–1980, the group released a record memento of the 1970s, "The Hangovers: Slightly Sober," and more than doubled its performances.

In fall 1980 the Hangovers resurrected Fall Tonic, a concert originated by the Sherwoods. Back in 1959–1960 the Woods had sponsored a song festival, which brought other collegiate a cappella groups to campus to join them in concert. In 1960–1961, they presented two of these festivals, and by 1962 the concerts were known as Fall and Spring Tonic. Fall Tonic emerged as the annual tradition, packing Bailey Hall throughout the 1960s. Whether the Sherwoods chose the name to convey the "mixer" atmosphere of a concert with several guest groups is not known, but the musical and alcoholic double entendre was more than appropriate for an a cappella group called the Hangovers. Just add Yale's Proof of the Pudding, the University of Rochester Yellowjackets, and Nothing But Treble (then a subset of the Cornell Chorus), the Hangovers' guest groups at their first Fall Tonic.

Held in the Statler Auditorium, the 1980 Fall Tonic was conceived and managed by Phil Hess 1982. The concert lost money, but worked wonders for the Hangovers' exposure on and off campus. They got a much needed chance to break into the a cappella circuit—bringing small groups to Ithaca resulted in reciprocal invitations to sing in similar jamborees at other colleges. More notably, the highlight of the 1980 evening, indeed perhaps its raison d'être, was the world premiere of Hess's original song "Facetime":

> Have you noticed yet there's a game at Cornell?
> It's played at all the campus parties and in class as well.
> You do a lot of talking and it's lots of fun,
> You meet a lot of people but you don't get much done.

> It's called facetime (at Cornell)
> Baggin' classes, hangin' out, actin' cool (actin' cool)
> It's a wonder that we're still in school (you know)
> It's all for Facetime
> It's the number one course at Cornell . . .

> Have you ever been to parties where the facetime is max,
> And everybody's prepped out and they're talking fast?
> You never talk to anybody very long,
> That way you can make the rounds
> You can't go wrong.
> Then everybody knows your face,
> They know who you are . . .

The song continues for several stanzas, ending with the Hangovers singing:

> Baggin' classes, hangin' out, actin' cool (actin' cool),
> It's a wonder that we're still in school.
> Ezra founded an institution where

> Far above Cayuga's waters,
> There's facetime (facetime).

Filled with allusions to Cornell and current culture—Topsiders, khakis, the Temple of Zeus, the Alfalfa Room, alligator shirts, hockey, Psych 101, the Fishbowl, the Dustbowl, and the Straight—the song brought the Fall Tonic audience to their feet. The next spring the Hangs released "Facetime" as a single and rode its skyrocketing success into the campus limelight. The public affairs office developed a slide show to go with it, Yale Daily News's *Guide to Selective Colleges* mentioned the song in their Cornell account, the *Cornell Alumni News* ran a "Facetime" cover story, and in 1982 alumni returned in droves asking to hear the hit live. Within a few months the Hangovers of the Cornell University Glee Club were the most eminent group on campus. Eventually the piece became the cornerstone of their third album, "Facetime with the Hangovers," which on its jacket clearly defined the Cornell pastime in question: "**Noun.** 1. The social act of seeing and being seen at Cornell University, Ithaca, New York. 2. A valuable social commodity, measured in facetime units (f.t.u.) [to catch *face-time*]. 3. Theme song of the Hangovers."

The album also bore a dedication:

> Although we mourn the passing of Theodore Zinck's, freshman beanies, the Ostrander elms, and national football championships, we hail the emergence of a new era of social Machiavellianism, cut-throat pre-professionalism, interpersonal superficiality, and designer jeans. We therefore dedicate this album to the students of Cornell for their unwavering persistence in the quest for facetime. Ezra would've wanted it that way.

Thus the Hangovers satirized Cornell life, advanced their capitalist agenda, and earned a huge number of facetime units.

As for Fall Tonic, the second concert in 1981 proved a financial as well as a musical success, netting about $600 for the Hangovers' brand new university account. By 1984 the group could claim that "Fall Tonic has become a true tradition."[12] Fall Tonics between 1982 and 1984 all but sold out the Statler's thousand seats in advance, meriting a move in 1985 to Bailey Hall, where the concert has taken place ever since. In 1993, the Hangovers celebrated their 25th anniversary at Fall Tonic XIV, welcoming back a huge number of their alumni, and making short work of a "Methusalem" bottle of champagne nearly two feet high and six inches in diameter.[13] Fall Tonic XV followed the next year; at last reports the concert was grossing nearly $9,000—not bad for an evening's singing.

In 1993 the Hangovers renamed their spring concert and gave their first annual Happy Hour. Held each year in Sage Chapel, the concert has already secured a standing-room-only audience, and continues the run of liquor puns echoed in the titles of more recent Hangover recordings: "Cheers," "Behind Bars," and "The Hangovers—On the Rocks." "Behind Bars" in particular deserves mention for its remarkably clever name, a triple entendre title (jailbirds aside) putting the Hangs behind the music, behind the nearest watering hole, and behind their traditional, broad-striped polo shirts. "On the Rocks," the seventh Hangover recording and their first CD, comes with colorful pictures of the Easter Island rocks dressed in appropriate concert attire. The Hangs haven't been to Easter Island yet but they have taken Cornell music abroad on their own as well as with the Glee Club. Back in the early 1970s, a quartet of Hangovers entertained travelers aboard the *S.S. France* cruise ship. (The spree was arranged by Blanchard Rideout, professor of Romance Studies and a friend of the Glee Club.)

Since then, the group has repeatedly traveled to Bermuda, Jamaica, and, most recently, to Japan over the 1995 spring break. While in Japan, they performed at Tokyo Disneyland and lived up to their reputation as minstrels of charity, donating half their profits to the Kobe Earthquake Relief Fund.

Like the Glee Club the Hangovers have had the opportunity to perform for international dignitaries, including financier John D. Rockefeller, German chancellor Helmut Schmidt, the widow of Egyptian leader Anwar Sadat, French president Valéry Giscard d'Estaing, U.S. president Gerald Ford, and Secretary of State Henry Kissinger. This is not surprising, since by at least one account, the "Hangovers were established in 1969 in an attempt by the Nixon Administration to contain the spread of communism worldwide through song. Thus far they have succeeded in saving only Fredonia, New York."[14] Other accomplishments have been duly noted in subsequent *Cornellians*. In 1983: "The Hangovers pride themselves on their myriad of accomplishments, . . . their slick polished sound, and their healthy teeth and gums. . . . This year the group represents 18 different states, 11 different families, and one Glee Club." In 1985: "The Hangovers are as diverse as the university, and between them have taken every course offered at Cornell today." And in 1987: "The Hangovers' newest album, Cheers, has incorporated the fun and excitement of bowling and the precision of male a cappella singing. . . . The Hangs bowl at sororities, fraternities . . . and occasionally play some ten-pin in Balch Arch."[15]

The Hangovers' repertoire has varied from classic rock, to covers of the latest pop songs, to covers of the latest Glee Club folk song, to songs earning the singers the title of "close harmony" group, touching on Van Morrison, the Beatles, and the Nylons along the way. Standards have included "Night and Day," "Mack the Knife," "Brown-Eyed Girl," "Southern Cross," "Teddy Bear," and the encore of choice, "Up the Ladder to the Roof." Former Hangover Jon Wardner observes in his history of the group that "the repertory pendulum has swung so far toward 'devinylization' of pop tunes, that 'traditional' close harmony singing has been lost." Perhaps not lost, but there is indeed a trend among current small groups to give the pop hits a lot of airtime.

The program of the small group involves far more than music. The article on "Facetime" in the *Alumni News* acknowledged that "in the absence of a student humor magazine . . ., the job of mirroring campus social life and patois falls to its student singing groups."[16] The job is undertaken with zeal. Humor has become an anticipated part of any a cappella concert, manifesting itself in the introductions to songs, the songs themselves, and the full-blown skits presented between numbers. A blurb on the Sherwoods once noted, "A common, and at times, welcome sight at fraternities and sororities, as well as at the Straight and the girls' dorms (not always in that order), these little green gremlins are always ready with a song and a bit of irreverent humor, which is one of their virtues, if any."[17] In the midst of their concerts the Hangovers dutifully satirize everything from campus construction and regulations to movies and

45. The Hangovers. From *Cornellian*, 1986.

game shows. Their 25th-anniversary performance included "Waiting for Hillary," a Godot-like spoof (complete with small tree) of the First Lady's visit to campus (and her much delayed speech) earlier that month. By definition the humor of these skits is often parochial, and almost always dreamed up within a day or two of the concert, if not onstage. And like the musical arrangements these groups perform, humor is almost always the product of members within the ensemble.

With the homespun music and homegrown humor, the sold-out concerts and the satirical outtakes, we have the defining ingredients of a cappella subculture, and for a moment we should consider this milieu to which small groups belong. As Hangover Jake White 1988 wrote in the *Cornellian*, "You can run, you can hide, but you just can't escape a cappella singing at Cornell."[18] From the freshman and senior Cornell Nights, to Fall Tonic, the Waiters' Spring Fever, and the Cornell Jamboree (begun in 1985 to feature all of Cornell's a cappella groups), not to mention countless other concerts by the groups, a cappella concerts are arguably the most visible and popular Cornell events on campus (hockey and football excepted). A good soloist can achieve campus notoriety exceeding that of the football quarterback (partly because singing facetime is not impeded by a helmet), and members might find a few fans trailing them from formal concerts to informal arch sings. In concert, groups have been known to hypnotize crowds with the pulsing of a slow arrangement or send them into a Dionysian frenzy with a raucous rendition of a pop song. According to one commentator, "Nothing can extract more wild cheers and uncontrolled emotions from a crowd than a performance by one of the many campus a cappella singing groups."[19] At times the a cappella scene resembles rock culture on a small scale—the group sings, people cheer wildly, followings develop, singers are propositioned, everyone goes to a party. At times, it is simply a combination of hard rehearsing, long hours on the road, and enjoyment of the animated bond formed as a small group of friends, bodies swaying, eyes meeting, stand enveloped in song.

Cornell is not unique in its a cappella subculture. In recent times colleges and universities have seen groups of all shapes and voice parts, small troupes of vocal satirists running around, pitch pipe in hand, to sing their next gig. The phenomenon is particularly noticeable in the Northeast, where some campuses have as many as fifteen of these groups (Yale comes to mind, offering everything from the Alley Cats to the Whiffenpoofs), usually numbering from a quartet to somewhat more than a baker's dozen. Part of the attraction—indeed part of the wonder of these groups—is the amount of talent involved. While some a cappella singers are qualified to sing duets with Sarah Vaughn, most possess more moderate talent, certainly not capable on its own of filling a hall with two thousand screaming fans. Yet in a collegiate context, and by the magical synergism of these groups, such singers can band to together to make good music and earn campus fame in the process. Wonderment at the phenomenon continues when previously unmusical or uncreative members start churning out complex, ten-part arrangements, or coming up with comic skits worthy of the *Tonight Show.*

The names of college a cappella groups, ranging from the Tigerlillies and Beelzebubs to the Jabberwocks, Bandersnatchers, and Footnotes often play off the musical, literary, or institutional with a certain cleverness. Other times they are more straightforward, as in the Colgate Thirteen. Most often the names do not refer to an affiliation with a larger ensemble, setting the Hangovers and After Eight (the Chorus's current subset) apart from many of their counterparts in this regard. The Hangs to be sure have had a benevolent, at times ambivalent, and occasionally tense relationship with the Glee Club. But in the end the relationship has been symbiotic. The small group has benefited from the musical experience and added rehearsal time of the Glee Club, not to mention the large group's university and international prominence and its pool of talent.

The Glee Club likewise has gained from the presence of the small group. Given the popularity of small group singing, the subset has been able to generate added publicity for the Glee Club and attract singers who otherwise would look elsewhere. (More than once a gifted singer has joined the Glee Club simply because it was requisite to singing with the Hangovers and has discovered by junior year the experience of Glee Club was equally if not more enjoyable.) The small group, being more flexible and mobile, also has been able to take jobs the Glee Club would have had to decline. In recent years the Hang-overs have sung numerous times for official university functions, alumni classes, and the annual Tower Club dinner in New York City. And there is no doubt the small group can add a great deal of color and levity to the Glee Club's program.

At times the levity has come as a surprise to the Glee Club's director. On one occasion in 1975 the Hangovers decided to spoof Sokol's "Annie Lisle" lecture, a lecture that typically disseminated much of the historical information men-tioned in Chapter 6—"I should say just a word about the next piece," he would say, concluding "we do now the original version of 'Annie Lisle.'" Later in the concert the Hangs stepped down for their set, and Donald Juceam 1977 launched into the following monologue:

> I should say just a word about the next song. Most of you probably have heard of the great flood of Biblical times. Unfortunately, a great deal of misinfor-mation has been spread about this event. In an effort to find the truth, we searched the Glee Club archives at Cornell University and came up with a song that tells the real story. The ballad, reminiscent of the yicky poetry of H.S. Thompson, was arranged by Marshall Bartholomew, Jim Bennett of the Glee Club, and Mark Clifford of the Glee Club, and they were all writers in New Haven of minstrel songs. Now this song is one of a genre of pieces about fa-mous historical figures with double names, no doubt, the first of which had two syllables and the second, one. Such as—Ghengis . . . Khan, Vida . . . Blue, Rin-tin . . . tin. And of course the ever popular Edna St. Vincent Mil . . . lay.
>
> Now you may ask why the Hangovers are interested in this song. Well, we were the first group to adopt this melody as our theme music and official drink-ing song. Subsequently, some 400, or 500, or 700, or some such number of barbershop quartets, Cub Scout troops, and bridge foursomes have followed suit. Now the original music, preserved through the efforts of Dr. Sokol, in-dicates that the piece can be done a cappella or with one hundred piece sym-phony orchestra. Since we don't have the symphony orchestra we will do it . . . a cappella. . . . We do it for you now . . .[20]

The reader may have noticed by now that many of the small group's charac-teristics—humorous skits, light repertoire, fanatic followings—bear a striking resemblance to the Glee Club itself in its earlier days. In the context of Glee Club history the small group could be interpreted as a living museum of another time, when glee club shows typically offered skits, costumes, magic, and the lat-est popular songs of the day. With the formation of subsets that activity has been channeled inward into a smaller area, continuing there while different ac-tivity has filled the larger Glee Club frame.

Hence in the small group the Glee Club carries within itself the memory of its past. And there, liberated to a life of its own, the subset has continued to evolve with a cappella subculture. As for the Hangovers, so far they have survived as an integral part of the Glee Club, wearing their khakis, singing romantic tunes in soft light, and occasionally ending with their group huddle, from which they emerge with the yell, "Yo, Hangs!" And when the evening draws to its end, they often close singing, "Softly—I will leave you softly . . ."

10 The Club

Io, Io, Io, Io, Io, Io, Io, Io . . . Io!

—"In Taberna," Carl Orff's *Carmina Burana*

"**W**e have several new men here tonight whom we should introduce." Rehearsal is over, and one of the officers is up in front making announcements. "In the tenor section, we welcome Carl Doe."

"Speech, speech," the group choruses as they turn to the new man, waving their hands upward in exaggerated fashion. Uncertain whether he is being invited to an impromptu address or the lion's den, the new singer slowly rises to his feet. The group grows silent.

". . . Uh"

"YAAHH . . . !"—the group bursts into wild cheers and whistles at the first peep. Warmly applauded, the new man sits down with a bewildered smile.

Welcome to the Club.

For each of us born into this world, years go by before we begin to discover we have entered into something far greater than ourselves, something that, hard as it is to imagine, was going on in years before our own. This same experience is repeated in miniature for a new man in the Glee Club, who only gradually discovers he belongs to something far larger than himself. The clues, however, begin to come almost immediately.

It's two o'clock on Sunday afternoon, and from all over the campus, one hundred and twenty men are converging on Sage Chapel. From fraternities and freshman dorms, from graduate centers and the libraries, from Collegetown apartments and from downtown Ithaca, Cornell's Glee Club gathers.

Before going upstairs to rehearsal, some of the men stop in the basement to pick up brown manilla folders of music piled high on a table between silver and brass plates from Malaysia and Korea. Buried underneath lies a two-foot square, wood-mounted picture of grinning Cornellians and Philippinos taken in the Cornell Club of the Philippines. A poster from the Army and

46. Clubbers lifting their steins to join Robert Mecklenberger 1971.

Navy Club of Manila hangs on the wall, advertising a Glee Club performance. . . . A few travel posters dangle on the walls too, but most lie [tucked
away] . . . in a corner of the room, along with Japanese banners, Korean teak
boxes, dolls from Taiwan, and many, many scrapbooks and photographs collected by Glee Club men.[1]

In time the new man begins to discover the photo album of the family he has stumbled upon, but at his very first rehearsal, he may have other things on his mind: being on time, finding the group's musicality to his liking, singing in such a way as to show there was no mistake at the audition and that he really does belong in this group. Musical interest after all is the first thing to compel students in the direction of the Glee Club. And it is usually the first thing to capture their attention. Each year there is that moment when the newest member, standing amid near strangers, or coming up the creaking back stairs of Sage Chapel, hears for the first time the sound of the Cornell Glee Club. He may never hear it in quite the same way again—by the time he is a senior, he will have developed a more acute ear for intonation, a more subtle sense of balance and color. But there will always be the sound of that first sonority—unexpected, incomparable—and its beauty will keep him coming back for more.

During his first rehearsal the new man also may get the impression that he has arrived in medias res. As the group makes its way through the repertoire, he discovers some of the men already singing pieces without their music. He wonders how this can this be, as it is just the first rehearsal. And yet soon he too will sing without the music—not just the songs, but the history, the oral tradition of the Glee Club. At his second rehearsal he already has joined his brothers in clamoring for a speech the moment a new man is introduced.

As the first few weeks of the semester pass, the new man begins to learn his music and learn names for some of the faces pictured in the "Rogue's Gallery" (the Club's photo directory that hangs in the basement of Sage). And he begins to discover that like any family, the Glee Club has its history, its traditions and habits, its inside jokes, its daily bread (the music making), and its trademarks. In the early years of the university though, the CUGC could mean two things: the Cornell University Gun Club and the Cornell University Glee Club. Like the university itself, neither group possessed any tradition to speak of, nor any clear sense of what lay ahead. In time the Gun Club became defunct. The other CUGC gradually developed a history, a standard of excellence, and like any organization with a strong sense of identity, a set of hallmarks—catch phrases, rites of passage, slogans, emblems, songs, apparel—which a hundred and twenty-five years later now number in the hundreds. Some of these are readily apparent, others are more subtle, unrecorded anywhere but in the memory of oral history. All of them conspire to make a club out of the Glee Club, and this chapter will shed light on their meaning and effect. Certainly they begin to have meaning for our new man, whom we shall continue to follow through the course of a Glee Club year.

The New Man Dinner, held each fall and spring over pizza and drinks at the Club's current hangout, officially welcomes each new member with a brief, occasionally embarrassing rite of passage. Each new man in turn must stand on a chair before the assemblage, introduce himself, and sing a selection, most often his high school Alma Mater. If the performance is deemed unsatisfactory, the singer remains up until the masses are appeased, and if no particular song comes to mind, the new man is offered a choice of standards ranging from "I'm a little teapot . . ." (with choreography) to the words of "Amazing Grace" sung to the tune of TV's *Gilligan's Island*. The pompous are brought low, while the nervous do not flounder for long before the benevolent group of strangers jumps in to harmonize. Upon sitting back down, the new man finds himself between a grad student in chemistry who sings tenor and a fellow baritone who leans in to teach him his part on the Cornell songs. Singing carries on well into the evening and before it is over, he has learned about drink breaks and "The Itsy, Bitsy Spider," and he has discovered a sense of camaraderie in what for him may still be a town of strangers.

That camaraderie, along with the instilled discipline of rehearsal, carries over to the first concert. Having purchased his tux and memorized his scores (except the few places where he may be obliged to mouth "watermelon, watermelon . . ."), our new man enters Cornell's concert history. If the performance happens to be a fall concert like Homecoming, the experience will be particularly memorable. Sage Chapel—austere, mysterious, and silent at the previous evening's dress rehearsal—is transformed by the noise and size of the crowd. In front of that audience he first realizes the group's knack for taking everything a notch higher in performance and for the first time, he may share with another that glance of "Et in arcadia ego." Near the end of the concert the current Glee Club is joined on stage by several dozen alumni who step from the crowd, men who once stood in a new man's shoes and now demonstrate by their return how much the group has meant to them and how worthwhile they feel its ongoing activity to be. The concert closes with the moving sound of sixty-five young men joined by thirty or forty of their elder brothers in song, the current group feeling like a river must feel when enveloped by a wide sea. Following the applause the singing continues almost without interruption at the reception, and often afterward out on the town or in the cool night air. Quickly our new man is learning that this group means far more to its members than a few hours of weekly rehearsal.

Once the afterglow of the first concert begins to fade, the Glee Club looks ahead to the next performance and, depending on the schedule of the year, a possible winter tour. With any luck the new man will be chosen for the tour group and will set out with his newfound comrades for Europe or Florida or perhaps Elmira. Be the road long or short he likely will find tour puts the capital C in Club; as an officer once said, "Touring is instrumental in making the Glee Club what it is musically and spiritually."[2] Repetition can engender a special camaraderie, and a tour offers repetition in abundance: not only the chance to perform a program eight or ten times, but the reality of meeting on the bus each morning the same people you performed with the night before, the same people you will see tomorrow at a roadside McDonald's, and the same people you will find beside you still the next day as you push your bus out of a snowbank.

Indeed these are the same people seen back in Ithaca the previous week when the first repetitive regimen began—intensive tour rehearsals. After the music was honed and sculpted by day, the evening offered time for solitude or social festivities, and a chance for the men to get to know each other. "These five days set the tone for the kinds of spirit and fellowship which Glee Club tours tend to foster among the men," a member wrote in 1978.[3]

Thus better acquainted, tour members devoted to good music and a good time set out and soon find themselves on adventures of which oral traditions are made. During the long bus rides time is passed playing cards, reading, sleeping, philosophizing, and singing—not only favorites from the concert repertoire, but also the secret repertoire of bus songs. Occasionally everyone takes a moment to calculate and compare their potato quotient (weight in pounds divided by height in inches), a contest the bus invariably wins. Then, in the words of one tour, it's "off the bus, sing, eat, sleep, on the bus, off the bus, sing . . ."

Traveling city to city, the young men form and renew friendships with the Club's wider families: Glee Club alumni, Cornell alumni, and a host of non-Cornell friends who make up the extended family. The new man, impressed with the number of alums returning at a fall concert like Homecoming, may be even more struck by the number of alums turning up on tour. At a concert one year in Washington, D.C., "the Professor asked all Glee Club alumni to join on stage with the men for the singing of the Alma Mater. As it turned out, the alumni practically outnumbered the present-day Glee Clubbers, . . . [making for] a rendition of the Alma Mater 'heard all the way to New Haven.'"[4] On the 1981 tour through the Midwest—as on many tours—Glee Clubbers "shared food, home-brewed ale, song, and stories of tours past with alumni." And every so often members could hear about Cornell and Glee Club folklore from an elder who knew the Hill in the days of Hollis Dann and Jacob Gould Schurman. As Sokol said of the 1968 centennial tour, "It was very impressive to me to encompass within an arm's length a member of the Class of '03 and some of our Freshman singers, members of the Class of '71."[5]

Beyond alumni of the Glee Club, there have been friends who have secured significant funding for tours and there continue to be loyal Cornellians—Glee Club alums and otherwise—whose offers of accommodations, food, sponsorship, and hospitality pave the path of tours in the States and abroad. In 1994 Cornell alumnus Richard Erali 1969, who barely sang a note as an undergraduate, put up the necessary money to bring the Glee Club to Memphis. He later wrote, "To hear them [the Glee Club] is almost a religious experience, to befriend them is truly an emotional event. . . . It is an organization that epitomizes the concept of tradition; from the songs that are sung to the honorable and the respectful way they greet their alumni."[6]

The greatest pleasure of tour friendships is the bond itself, however long or brief it may be. After the Glee Club's 1966 tour to Southeast Asia, Sokol related the following anecdote:

We were on a train, going from Hiroshima to Fukuoka for a concert, and one of the cars of the train was filled with elderly Japanese ladies taking some sort of holiday trip. Half a dozen or so of the Glee Club members became acquainted with the women and began to sing Japanese songs to them—in Japanese. Then they sang songs from other lands and later some American songs. Well, the number of men kept increasing and at the same time the tempo of the whole get-together kept picking up.... When we got off the train at our destination, all the ladies shook hands with each of the men to express their appreciation for the songs and the friendliness. It was a very warm and touching occasion. It made me proud to be with such a group.[7]

As with any club there must be a reason for people wanting to belong and an abiding sense among members that membership carries honor together with certain coveted privileges. If the ostensible privilege of touring is the chance to see the world, the hidden privileges become apparent in the course of the journey. The new man likely returns to Ithaca from his first tour with a newfound pride in the musical achievements of the Club, in the group's offstage esprit de corps, and in the extended family the Glee Club and Cornell draw together around themselves.

When the new semester begins, auditions are held again and a new man dinner follows, where the first semester new man is now able to teach someone else his part in the song. And so it carries on. Spring brings a major work and perhaps a concert collaboration at a women's college,[8] along with a few Glee Force intramural outings, the election of officers, and some group socializing when classes allow.

In a chapter entitled "The Club," a little more should be said about Glee Club socializing. From the beginning of the year, with the "Meet the Glee Club" reception and the New Man Dinner—or as in past years, when the group held fall picnics and "Glendi's" (gatherings over food and beverage held to teach the new men Cornell songs)—the Club's social activity fosters a sense of brotherhood which inevitably spills over onto the concert stage. No less is true of the socializing on other occasions, be it a CUGC tailgate party at Homecoming, a postconcert tour reception, or a party to celebrate new officers, recalling the days when the winners of Glee Club managerial competitions were announced at a beer party in the Dutch Kitchen. But the simple fact remains, young men and parties get on well together—all the better if the young men like to sing. Indeed there is a reason the male chorus repertoire includes a healthy number of drinking songs, and annual CUGC reports have included sections entitled "Glee Club Parties We Have Known." The Glee Club has not shied away from the pursuit of "epicurean bacchanalianism," to borrow a phrase from basso profundo Barry (B. J.) Jacobson 1970, be it within the familiar walls of Zinck's or the Chariot, or half a world away in Bavaria's Hofbräuhaus. With the overflow

47. The Club in song, *center,* B. J. Jacobson 1970; *right,* Michael Klein 1972.

of emotion following a successful tour concert, receptions have been known to go three or more hours—twice as long as the concert.

To return to the year and our new man, Senior Week follows on the heels of spring exams, ending the year as it began back at Orientation—with a week of intensive rehearsals, culminating this time in a weekend of performances. After performing together in the Senior Week concert Saturday night, the Glee Club and Chorus join together again the next morning to sing for the Baccalaureate Service and Commencement. If the new man—and for that matter new Chorus woman—has not yet come to understand the significant role of music in university occasions, he and she will gain unique insight as they rouse themselves at an ungodly hour to make the 7 A.M. rehearsal.

Senior Week is also a time to observe several long-standing traditions of the Club. First the legendary Tenor-Bass softball game, once played at the fall picnic and now played during Senior Week in the spring. Over the years the balance of power has shifted from one side to the other and back again. At the 1980 fall picnic the basses ended a half-decade of tenor dominance with a decisive victory; one tenor complained, "the only reason they won is because the Basses weren't loaded this year." On another occasion Thomas (Babe Ruth) Sokol turned to the catcher. "You see that right fielder—he's not paying attention"; he then proceeded to slug it over the fielder's head.[9] In the days of the fall picnic, the Wog II—donated to the Club by Melzar Richards 1967—was a symbol of softball dominance, awarded to the winning team. Now, in the days of spring softball, the curious wooden statuette is more appropriately awarded to the losing team. Archaeologists are still searching for the Wog I.

The other event of Senior Week is the traditional Dudley Dinner, an occasion perhaps more influential than any other in perpetuating the oral tradition of the CUGC. Officers and new men are presented with shingles (certificates) to recognize their contributions to the Club, and seniors (those with the Club for at least six semesters and two tours) are honored with Dudley medals. In turn all the graduates rise to request their favorite song and recount their most memorable and embarrassing moments in the Club. As the songs and stories of the past few years are recollected, the group passes on to its younger members a sense of history, a sense that what they do matters not only for the moment but for the record of collective memory. And as Senior Week closes, though the Glee Club will not have become home to every new man, most will look to the years ahead with anticipation, and some will already sense "haec est domus."

The Glee Club's year comes to an end with Reunions Weekend, where more stories will change hands and the solidarity of song will be renewed among the new men of twenty-five and fifty years ago. After the first Alumni Glee Club gathered to perform at the 1969 Reunions, Howard Heinsius 1950 wrote:

We may be a bit balder, slightly grayer—our middles aren't as trim as they were when we climbed up Thurston Avenue—but for one thrilling hour we were back where we belong—on the stage of Bailey Hall presenting our Glee Club show. . . . There's the same electric excitement just before curtain time, the same "frogs in throats," the same guys who were late for shows in '49 were late again in '69—but we were back. . . . It is almost impossible to convey the happy nostalgia one feels when singing with the Alumni Glee Club. Through no other activity do I feel so close to Cornell. The bond of singing together is strong, if not stronger, to me than any other association I personally had at Cornell.[10]

With that occasion the line of past-present-future is drawn full circle. And as past members representing more than fifty years of Cornellians return to sing together, the weekend confirms something the new man has been learning all year—there are many musical ensembles in this country, and good ones too, but far fewer are such families as the Cornell University Glee Club.

No one can say exactly when or how this sense of family first emerged. Considering the unifying power of music, any ensemble proud of its achievements and reasonably stable in membership enjoys some form of camaraderie. And insofar as this camaraderie is tangible, the Glee Club's sense of "club" can be traced well back. In his 1924 book *Concerning Cornell* O. D. von Engeln wrote that membership in the Glee and Mandolin Clubs was held in high esteem, in part owing to the pride members took in the annual tours. Even earlier the *Era* noted in 1892, "The new watch charms, the distinctive mark of the Glee Club, are now worn by its members. The charm consists of an open gold scroll, having on one side the music of Alma Mater in which is set the enamel, red, and white letters, C.U.G.C., and on the other the name of the bearer, his fraternity, if any, and class."[11] Shingles were given as early as 1896, and an 1899 *Era* talks about classic Glee Club phrases.

While these sentiments and symbols suggest an organization with an identity, somewhere along the way a broader sense of family emerged. One starting point perhaps was the postwar Reunion celebration in June 1919, when the Glee Club gave a concert in Bailey Hall and were assisted by alumni. As at no time before, past members were restored to an active sense of belonging in the organization's present. Since then, in the context of a university where alumni return and take part, the Glee Club has become a home to its alumni, an extended family in which one feels, "once a member, always a member." In 1969 the Glee Club Alumni Association formalized this family, and alums returned that June to take part in the Alumni Glee Club, which has performed at Cornelliana Night of Reunions every year since. More recently alumni were invited to take part in an international Glee Club tour in 1982, an invitation renewed for the two subsequent tours abroad. As one Washington alumnus put it, "I know of no other organization at Cornell where alumni are more intimately involved in the enterprise itself than the Cornell Glee Club."[12]

In 1976–1977 the Glee Club published an alumni directory and the *Cornel-*

lian reported there were "more than 1,700 Glee Club alumni living in every state of the Union and in about twenty-five countries."[13] These alumni have gone on in nearly all walks of life, many of them with great distinction, as, for example, former accompanist and assistant director Layton (Skip) James, A.M. 1967, who became the resident keyboardist for the St. Paul Chamber Orchestra, and former singer Alan Keyes who ran for the Republican presidential nomination. Wherever they have gone, many of the assistant directors, elected officers, managers, accompanists, and singers in the CUGC who once felt it deserving of their dedication continue to show their tremendous love and support for this organization. And they continue to demonstrate, as the *Era* once said, "that a valuable and lasting part of a collegiate education, springs from the friendship engendered while at college among college men."[14]

The CUGC family even so extends well beyond the friendships that grow within the ranks. Whether at home or on tour, whether Cornell alumni or not, many nonmembers have befriended—or been adopted by—the Glee Club and found the experience inspired in them devotion to the group and the enterprise it represents. The catalogue of names is extensive, from such university officials as Deane Malott to secretaries, bus drivers, and concert-goers on three continents, to Jimmy the mailman and Floyd O'Grady, the custodian of Sage Chapel for more than thirty years who was featured on the cover of a Glee Club newsletter. If munificence is any testament to these friendships, they are strong indeed. A few years back the widow of Glee Club alumnus Leslie Clute saw that the group got new recording equipment. Advisory Council member Victor Grohmann (a university trustee) outfitted the group with a new set of risers. In 1972 Thomas Swart 1927 wrote to confess that though he received the newsletters, he had never sung in the Glee Club; even so he made contributions to the Glee Club Association. And in the early 1990s, shortly before his death, Advisory Council member Robert Engel (also a university trustee) started the Thomas A. Sokol Endowment for Choral Music. Taken together with the countless other contributions of alumni and friends, these gifts mark an inspired spirit of generosity and loyalty.

Cornell University, like any institution, has its symbols—the clock tower or the statues of Andrew White and Ezra Cornell, the melody of the Alma Mater or the colors carnelian and white, the Big Red Bear or the motto "I would found an institution. . . ." On their own, none of these really is Cornell, but each in some way distinguishes Cornell from other universities. Likewise there are emblems that distinguish Cornell's Glee Club from the Morehouse and Harvard Glee Clubs, or for that matter the Rotary Club and the N.Y. Yankees.

The best known (and in fact official) symbol of the Glee Club is the Apollo head seal. Like the seal of the Harvard Glee Club, with its slogan "Cantantes Licet Usque Eamus" (roughly, "Let us go singing"), it appears on the group's letterhead, newsletters, banners, and programs. Adopted in the early years of Sokol's tenure, the seal recalls the founding of the Orpheus Glee Club and the official song of the world's first glee club, Samuel Webbe's "Glorious Apollo," along with other early glees such as the "Adelphi Club Glee":

> Let brother to brother good fellowship proffer;
> Apollo invites us, come bow at his shrine;
> The Glee and the Catch are the incense we offer,
> The bond that unites us is Music divine.

Symbolizing as he does the efforts of the CUGC, the Greek god of music and poetry appears on more than just paper. As with the watch charms of the 1890s, the Glee Club of the 1990s possesses a whole line of apparel, usually advertised in the "L. L. Glee" section of the newsletter. The logo appears on the Glee Club sweatshirt, the Glee Club mug, the Glee Club golf ball, and the always appropriate Glee Club field watch, as well as the CUGC emblems that specifically recognize achievement: the shingles and the Dudley medals.

There is one item of Glee Club apparel on which the wreathed god head does not currently appear—the Glee Club tie. "Available in bow and traditional four-in-hand styles," this "timeless symbol of sophistication and impeccable taste" is made officially for the CUGC and has been spotted on the likes of President Bill Clinton and NBC news anchor Tom Brokaw (did they borrow them, perhaps?). The tie, worn at daytime concerts, was created in 1960 with the help of Cornell president Deane Malott. "I had not realized Mrs. Malott and I had the responsibility for the Cornell 'red' but at any rate I am happy to give you any advice I can," the president wrote, graciously distinguishing between Wine 89, Red 1, and Red 3, and further pointing out Red 3 "is actually a crimson—nearly corresponding to the Harvard crimson—and heaven forbid we couldn't be confused with that!"[15] Like the 1918 U.S. airmail stamp printed with the plane upside down, there is even a rare edition tie, accidentally created when the diagonal stripes were printed the wrong way.

Among other CUGC trademarks are the verbal idiosyncrasies. It is never the "Glee Club" but the "Glee Force" that sallies forth into athletic combat. And there are the slogans "Yet another fine example of the supreme sacrifice..." and "We always win" (also rendered as "We never lose") which for years have colored members' speech amid the other phrases that go in and out of vogue. There are even gestures that the discerning anthropologist would include in a study of the Glee Club, among them the group's tendency to express approbation by snapping their fingers rather than clapping their hands.

The symbols, the sayings, the gestures all point to the suggestion that the Club, as a composite of its current membership and collective memory, has an actual personality. On his twentieth anniversary with the group, Sokol acknowledged the great joy he had derived from working with more than a thousand Glee

Club singers, paid tribute to the high spirit they had struck, and listed "those qualities in the respective generations of Glee Club men which have given the Glee Club its distinctive personality: intelligence, musicality, capacity for hard work, organizational initiative, sense of responsibility, concern for the art of musical performance, wit."

Conspicuous among these is wit. How else could members survive the misadventures that have befallen them—the dubious accommodations, the conflicts with border officials, the less-than-ideal concert venues, the endless bus rides—unless their characters included the fearless ability to laugh, and laugh at themselves? And how else could the Glee Club have perpetrated so much fun? Truly, nothing has added as much color to the group's personality, or its oral history as its collective sense of humor.

And so, somewhere in the middle of nowhere, a bus travels along filled with the sound of young men singing. But the songs aren't those mentioned in Chapter 6, or found on any official Glee Club recordings for that matter. If they were recorded and released, the best title would be "The Cornell University Glee Club—Off the Record." As that recording probably is not forthcoming, we shall listen to what's going on inside the bus:

> The Itsy, Bitsy spider went up the water spout
> Down came the rain and washed the spider out
> Out came the sun and dried up all the rain
> and the god d—- son-of-a-b—— went up the spout again.

> Oh Harvard's run by Wellesley and Wellesley's run by Yale
> Yale's run by Vassar and Vassar's run by ——
> Princeton's for the pretty boys and drunkards go to Penn
> but far above Cayuga there's a race of hairy men.

> Oh we are the race of
> [thunk with fist on chest] hairy-chested men,
> [thunk] hairy-chested men,
> [thunk] hairy-chested men
> Oh we are the race of
> [thunk] hairy-chested men,
> and we are from Cornell.

> "Don't send my boy to Hahvahd,"
> the dying mother said,
> "Don't send my boy to Syracu . . . sssssssssssse
> I'd rather see him dead,
> But send my boy to Princeton,

or better still Cornell
[the harmony expands into a large, sustained chord
that rings for a moment before the singers continue]
And as for Penn-syl-vain-i-ayyyy
I'd see him first in hell."

To hell, to hell with Pennsylvania
To hell, to hell with Pennsylvania
To hell, to hell with Pennsylvania
To hell with U of P (pee-yew!)

[pianissimo] We were only, only foolin'
We were only, only foolin'
We were only, only foolin'
[forte] The hell we were, Pee-yew!

So far as anyone knows, the "Itsy, Bitsy Spider" has never been heard in a Glee Club rehearsal. And yet not a year goes by that it isn't heard sung down at the Chariot after rehearsal or on the tour bus, testament to the oral tradition learned and then perpetuated by each year's members. The song is only one of many in the Glee Club's "Off the Record" collection of course, and as soon as laughter has settled on the bus, the group launches into a spoken chant:

Peaches and cream, peaches and cream
Let's have a cheer for the Hahvahd team
"We're not tough, and we're not strong
But boy can we crochet"

Knit one, pearl two
Hahvahd boys, yoo-hoo!
[everyone waves his handkerchief in the air]

That's H-A-Ah, H-A-Ah
H-A-Ah with a V
V-A-Ah, V-A-Ah
V-A-Ah with a D
Hahvahd, Hahvahd, rah . . .

There is a brief pause, and then someone sings out, "Oh it's Paul, Paul, Paul, whose high notes always stall in the halls (in the halls), in the halls (in the halls) . . ." at which point the whole group enters:

Oh it's Paul, Paul, Paul, whose high notes always stall
in the halls of Michigan.

> My eyes are dim
> I cannot see
> I have
> not
> brought my specs with me,
> I have not brought my specs with me.
>
> Oh it's Doe, Doe, Doe
> who's always in the john, in the halls . . .

And the song continues, with individual members improvising verses to poke fun at each other, while the group carries the refrain "My eyes are dim . . ." accompanied by the counterrefrain "a,b,c,d,e,f,g . . ." sung to the same melody.

There are other songs—"Passengers upon the Train," the song of Princess Papuli, the Mr. Rogers spoof "In Your Neighborhood," the "So-and-so is a real nice guy" refrain (and its variants), and director songs such as the Sokol/Mickey Mouse Club parody.

Richard Reuss makes an interesting note on the historical tradition of this kind of singing: "These songs are rendered by students of their own volition during moments of informality and relaxation without external coercive pressure or stimulus from any outside or superior authority, and are seldom heard in the presence of dignitaries, guests, elders, and—on formal occasions—sweethearts."[16] The presence of directors (and occasionally sweethearts) notwithstanding, the statement accurately describes part of the Glee Club's oral tradition, as do other Reuss remarks, for example: "their long standing custom of entertaining themselves with nondescript songs drawn from a floating stock of their own making will continue."[17] Only "their" in this case does not refer to a particular organization—it refers to the American undergraduate in general.

Reuss was speaking in his 1965 master's thesis, "An Annotated Field Collection of Songs from the American College Student Oral Tradition." Whether or not average students still carry on this oral tradition as they once did via musical groups, fraternities, sororities, military units, sports teams (and we can assume that to a large extent they do not), one can conclude that the Glee Club's ongoing oral tradition streams from a much broader source. That is the striking revelation of Reuss's catalog of songs, for included in his collection are two songs of interest here: "In the Halls" and "Don't Send My Boy to . . ."

Thus we see that the Glee Club's "Off the Record" collection is not entirely indigenous to Cornell. Nor is it immutable from one incarnation to the next. Reuss's study points out that "In the Halls," also sung as "On the Farm" or "In the Corps," has innumerable verse variants and a variety of refrains, for example: "My teeth are dull. I cannot chew; / It comes from opening cans of brew; / It comes from opening cans of brew," or one that is more handy for Glee Club parties which begins: "Drink beer, drink beer . . ."

He also cites the exact refrain sung at Cornell and further writes of "In the Halls" that it "undoubtedly would have to be selected as one of the two or three songs most likely to be known by nearly all college students."[18] As for "Don't Send My Boy to . . ." he records a verse that turns the tables on the usual version:

> "Don't send my girl to Skidmore,"
> The dying mother said.
> "Don't send my girl to Syracuse,
> I'd rather see her dead.
> Don't send my girl to Vassar,
> Or even worse, Cornell.
> And as for Cortland Normal School,
> I'd see her first in hell."
>
> To hell, to hell with Cortland Normal . . .

Reuss adds, "the school to be avoided is more consistently designated as Harvard than any other" and further notes the song is "joined with other college songs about as often as not," true in the case of the "Itsy, Bitsy Spider" version.[19] While the musical sources of the verses are in some dispute, the melody of the refrain is attributed to "The Battle Hymn of the Republic." (One might also suggest "I've Been Workin' on the Railroad," noting the similarity between the folk song and the "Battle Hymn.") Regarding "In the Halls" Reuss suggests the music conceivably descended from "The Quartermaster's Store," an old British army marching song.[20]

Alternate versions are not limited to the Glee Club's "Off the Record" collection. In fact there exists an alternate version of the official CUGC constitution, a parody clearly stating that in the event the president is unable to fulfill his duties, the vice president shall get doughnuts. Then too, the Glee Club's programmed repertoire has been subjected to theme and variations treatment, alternate versions being devised by members to suit the particular occasion. Returning one year from a West Coast tour only to find their luggage much delayed, the Glee Club entertained other disgruntled travelers in the airport with a revised version of Gustav Schreck's "Advent Motet," replacing the phrase "Lord Hosannah" with "Where's our luggage?" Other rewritten masterpieces include Milhaud's "Psaume 121," where the emphatic "Jerusalem" becomes "No more Milhaud" followed by the descending chromatic line in the baritones which can sound like someone falling off a building. Or the beautiful spiritual "My Lord, What a Morning . . . when the stars begin to shine," which begins ever so softly, "My Lord, what a Glee Club . . . when the booze begins to flow."

This brings us to the subject of tour burns, one of the primary sowing fields for Glee Club humor. Dating back at least to the days of the Glee, Banjo, and Mandolin Clubs, when members put a cork in the clarinet player's instrument or train crews switched cars on the men, the tour burn has become an annual event, generally intended to poke affectionate fun at the director and assistant directors. The unofficial rules suggest that a burn involve some alteration of the usual performance, but one recognizable only to the director and singers, not the audience. Frequently a slight change in words, a switch in soloists or in the song order, or a few choice photographs in the director's score suffice. But occasionally, the Club has gone beyond the call of duty, resulting in memorable moments such as the "Annie Lisle"/Genghis Kahn spoof, the ill-fated rendition of "Annie Lisle" with guitars, and the evening when instead of shouting out the final word of Brian Israel's "M'bevrashua" (in a movement with the text "Don't lose your head . . . your brains are in it!"), ten men in back each lifted a placard to spell "BURMASHAVE" across the back row.

Even the world's finest musicians are not exempt from Glee Club burns. In 1962 Eugene Ormandy had admonished the singers all week long, "Watch the beat." The evening of the concert, as the *Philadelphia Evening Bulletin* later reported, he walked into his dressing room to find a curious object ensconced in a chair—a large red beet, with slight fuzz glued to either side looking conspicuously like his balding head. The sign affixed to the vegetable read, "Watch the beet."

And so the Glee Club continues on, repeatedly proving true a statement the *Cornell Era* made back in 1870: "[We] do not believe that there is a class of people in our country who have so much fun as students."[21] Perhaps that is part of the magic of the Club—that the experience belongs to a peculiar time and place known as youth, which as a place is always within us, yet which as a time only allows us one gambol through before we feel we are somehow intruders upon the land. So too, one's days as a member of the Glee Club and a student at Cornell are numbered, and there are only so many years a member can sit back in the eleventh row of the tour bus among peers, no more or less responsible than the rest, and feel fully at home.

Perhaps, as Homer suggests, the poignancy arises precisely because the days are numbered. And so several years later, that singer who stood up and was welcomed in unexpected fashion at his first Glee Club rehearsal reaches his final Dudley dinner. He stands and recounts his most memorable moments in the Club, and then, before requesting the song which the Club will sing for him, he simply says something like: I'm beginning to realize that I'll miss this group a lot. I always felt Glee Club had a respect for our talent, always put us to the test. There's just something about it—a spirit of belonging that I don't want to lose. I've never been in a group like this . . . It has meant a lot to me, and I just wanted to say thank you.

For generations, young people have left their families and their homes and set out in search of an education. Some have arrived on a hill in central New York, where in the bleakness of winter, or the solitary nights of study, they may

48. The Cornell University Arts Quadrangle, c. 1990 (Sage Chapel at left).

have felt very much alone. Kurt Vonnegut 1944 was once in that situation, trudging between the life he loved down at the *Cornell Daily Sun* and his classes up on the Hill. When he returned to Cornell in the spring of 1993, the novelist had some advice for the students: "Get yourself a gang." For some it's the baseball team or a fraternity, for others, the people working in the same lab—regardless, most students seek out some smaller family within the larger Cornell community. With this smaller group will come many of the higher moments of life and the chance to belong to something larger than oneself. For several thousand, that smaller family has been the singular, at times idiosyncratic, and altogether extraordinary family known as the Cornell University Glee Club.

The Club would not exist were it not for the pursuit of musical excellence in rehearsal and performance—without this purpose there would be no center, no fire around which people could or should want to congregate. For the musical endeavor is precisely what allows the opportunity for everything else—to experience the heights of artistic achievement, the "golden moments" of performance, to succeed both as individuals and as part of an ensemble, to feel part of a large family, to meet friends and spouses, to touch some living and universal ethos. C. S. Lewis once wrote that in stories the real theme—usually "something that has no sequence in it, something . . . much more like a state or quality"—cannot be approached directly, but gained only through the series of events we know as the plot.[22] Just as when you are blinded by a sunspot, you cannot look directly at something and hope to see it; you can see it only by focusing on something else. And so too with the Cornell University Glee Club, which in making music over the past century and a quarter has opened the door for other miracles—leading to the formation of the Club, one of the great Cornell families in the history of the university.

This is, as always, y.a.f.e.o.t.s.s.w.g.c.a.f.c.u.t.m . . . Amen.

Epilogue

On November 5, 1993, current and alumni members of the Glee Club met in Ithaca to celebrate the 125th anniversary of the CUGC. The assembled family, gathered from across the country, represented nearly fifty years of Glee Club history. At the banquet in the Statler Hotel that evening, the group watched a video of the 1954 Perry Como appearance, and in his second speech of the day (the first being a welcome to First Lady Hillary Clinton) Cornell president Frank Rhodes noted the Glee Club had reached the "'My, you look marvelous' stage of life," later affirming that "the Glee Club is a very important part of Cornell life." Several other speakers likewise spoke about the meaning of the Club, good food and friendship were enjoyed in abundance, and the singing continued well into the night. The next morning, Saturday November 6, dawned cold, but the memorably warm celebration continued with the fall Homecoming Concert in Sage Chapel that evening. Opening with an Ave Maria chant, the Glee Club concluded the first half of the program with the world premiere of David Conte's *Carmina Juventutis.*

Conte had been commissioned to write a work for the occasion some time before, but it wasn't until he made a trip to Ithaca in fall 1992 that he found his inspiration. During that visit he joined the Glee Club at the Chariot after rehearsal one evening and, moved by the Club's spirited singing and camaraderie, he soon chose three medieval Latin texts to set—a student song (Omittamus Studia), a love song (Levis Exsurgit Zephirus), and a drinking song (Vinum Bonum). The text of the third movement concludes (in translation): "We pray thee: abound here, and may the whole company be loquacious; and so let us utter our joys with merry voice. May the devout band of monks, all the clergy, and the whole world drink equal draughts, now and for ever." When this last movement came to an end with its rhythmic four-hand piano accompaniment and the Glee Club singing, clapping, and shouting a last "Yo!" the audience burst into applause and a standing ovation.

Carmina Juventutis (Songs of Youth) could well serve as the title for this book. For the Glee Club, though it has evolved and aged as an institution, has always been composed of youth—in search of knowledge and experience, in search of love, and in search of a good time. While in the Philippines in 1966, the Glee Club inspired one reviewer to write: "A male glee club connotes and evokes College and Youth and Song. Therein lies their universal appeal. Something there is in us that stirs at the sound of male voices swelling in song."[1]

Yet youth alone does not account for the meaning or success of the Glee Club. There is in the Glee Club—indeed in the singers themselves—a combination of youth and maturity, a marriage of amateur fervor with professional discipline. On that same 1966 tour another review reported, "Their singing is an upsurge of youth, beautifully shaped and disciplined and all enjoyed their performance of truly professional skill."[2] Very likely the long-term success of the organization is explained by this combination of youth with deeper roots, with the depth and direction provided by gifted leadership. And if at the center of the CUGC spirit are the binding power of the music, a time and place called Cornell, and, in the words of Willa Cather, a feeling of "happiness; to be dissolved into something complete and great," at the foundation is the Glee Club's (and Cornell's) history. The second half of the 1993 anniversary concert concluded with the sixty-five current members being joined by more than a hundred returning CUGC alumni and an audience on its feet, all singing the Alma Mater led by a man who had been director of the Club for more than thirty-five years. With its past and present drawn together the Glee Club appeared as it truly is—an institution based on a sense of tradition constantly infused with youth and new life, and guided by the continuity of strong leadership.

Surely that continuity has been a significant factor in the Glee Club's attainment of the 125-year milestone; consider the directorial tenures: Dann, 32 years; Dudley, 21 years; Sokol, 38 years. "There is much for an ensemble to build on when there is a period of continuity," Sokol says, "which does not mean that you can't become ossified. . . . But I think overall it provides a great advantage."[3]

That continuity of leadership has now passed to Scott Tucker. As coincidence would have it, Tucker presented a background similar to Sokol's in several ways. He came to Cornell by way of Boston, having served as assistant conductor of Harvard's Glee Club and the Harvard-Radcliffe Collegium Musicum, as well as choral director at Milton Academy.[4] And he too spent his youth as a trumpet player, earning a performance degree in that instrument from the New England Conservatory in 1981, along with a degree in psychology from Tufts; he also completed a master's degree in conducting at the conservatory in 1986. But these similarities aside, Tucker represents a new generation of conductors, with different ideas about style and sound, and the Glee Club has already taken a new direction under his leadership. In 1997 the Glee Club released a CD featuring the music of

Tallis, Josquin, and Ferrabosco I; they and the Chorus performed a joint program with Ugandan artist Samite which had the audience dancing in the aisles of Bailey Hall, and on May 29, 1997, the Glee Club was heard internationally on Garrison Keillor's "A Prairie Home Companion," in an NPR program broadcast live from that same hall. At the end of his first year Tucker wrote the CUGC alumni, "It is the music which inspires us, and which binds us as in the old Glee 'Glorious Apollo' by Samuel Webbe: 'Here every generous sentiment awaking, Music inspiring unity and joy.' The joy of making music connects us to each other, to those who have made music before us, and to those who will come after."[5]

Such was the feeling on a November weekend in 1993, celebrating 125 years of Glee Club history—125 years of youth and tradition, of musical achievement, and of homecoming.

Back in 1868 the *Cornell Era* wrote, "Several attempts have been made to organize a Glee Club in the University. Will someone give us the result?"

Now that we have come to the present moment, what do we envision for the Glee Club? After hearing the group in 1994, Dick Erali wrote:

> It is the tradition that does it for me. . . . From the sequential process leading to membership to the emotional separation at graduation to the whimsical process of rekindling membership at alumni gatherings. It is this process that makes you understand your obligation to make sure that there will always be a CORNELL and a CORNELL GLEE CLUB. . . . For who will tell the story? Who will teach the songs? Who will live the traditions? This is what the Glee Club does so very well. The story is told in a manner that leaves the learner in an epidemic of "goose-bumps. . . ." The freshman is prompted, "tell me more." The learned alumnus responds with a request: "Tell me one more time."[6]

"Tradition is part of it," Sokol says, "as is vision. Each institution must be forward-looking. To perpetuate the past without change isn't sufficient to retain an organization's vitality. The Glee Club has tried to anticipate changes in artistic, educational, and social aspects of the university and to adjust its activities accordingly."

Asked as he neared retirement in 1995 what he imagined for the Cornell University Glee Club, Sokol responded:

> I hope that the Glee Club will address, first of all, musical challenges—including quality of performance, repertory, and circumstances of performance. Each generation will face the challenge in its own way. The officers and managers will set the tone for the organizational life of the members, and Professor Scott Tucker will be the keystone in setting and guiding the Glee Club's artistic and educational goals. Together their intelligence, talent, ingenuity, and hard work will assure a high standard.

The choral picture in America today is much different from what it was twenty years ago, and it will be very interesting to observe its exciting course during the next twenty years. The Glee Club, I am certain, will make a significant contribution to the choral art in America. I have ardent confidence in the Glee Club family and in their institution, Cornell.

We now look to the horizon, toward the promise of challenges and miracles unseen, and the possibility that for centuries to come people will find atop the Hill a home in song.

Timeline

1868
Orpheus Glee Club founded soon after Cornell University opens.

1869
January 21: First performance of the Orpheus Glee Club, at Library Hall.
Collegensia Quintette founded.

1870
Archibald Weeks and Wilmot Smith first adapt words to H. S. Thompson's "Annie Lisle," creating Cornell's Alma Mater.

1874
Formation of the Cornell University Musical Association.

1875
First appearance, in name, of the "University Glee Club."

1876
May 5: First out-of-town performance given by the Glee Club, in Cortland.
Cornell Glee Club first appears in the *Cornellian.*

1877
Henry Tyrell pens words to "O Tannenbaum," creating "Evening Song."

1880
May 24–29: Concerts given in Trumansburg, Auburn, and Syracuse, N.Y.

1888
First Junior Week concert given.
Cornell Banjo Club successfully organized.

1889
Hollis Dann named director.

1891
Groups become collectively known as the Glee, Banjo, and Mandolin Clubs.

1892
Glee Club first appears in Chicago.

1893
Glee Club first appears in New York City.

1895
June, July: Tour to England—first European tour by an American collegiate ensemble.
Musical Clubs Council formed and first constitution drafted.

1899
First Thanksgiving concert with the University of Pennsylvania clubs.

1901
George Coleman appointed director of Banjo and Mandolin Clubs.

1903
Dann appointed as Cornell's first instructor in music.

1904
April 1: First Cornell Music Festival opens with Mendelssohn's *Elijah;* Glee Club takes part.

1914
February: Glee Club first performs in Bailey Hall, during Junior Week.
December: Glee Club tour reaches Denver, Colorado.

1915
Archibald Davison publishes "A New Standard for Glee Clubs."

1917–1918
Glee Club silent during the war.

1921:
Dann steps down; Eric Dudley named director.

1922
Glee Club first heard on national radio.

1924–1925 tour
Concert in New York's Town Hall broadcast courtesy of the Radio Corporation of America.

1927–1928 tour
Tour reaches Dallas, Texas.

1933
Revolution in Glee Club programming begins, lasting rest of decade.
December: Musical Clubs stage Gilbert and Sullivan's *Mikado* with the Women's Glee Club.

1934
First collaborative spring concert with Women's Glee Club.

1937–1938 tour
First Christmas tour in seven years—"Oh, What a Night!"—takes beer on stage.

1941
Glee Club performs Richard Lee's "Coediquette."
Coleman retires; Instrumental Clubs fold.

1942
Dudley retires; John Kuypers named director, moving Glee Club control back into Cornell's music department.

1943–1945
Glee Club activity suspended due to war.

1945
Paul Weaver named director.

1946
May 19: Glee Club gives first concert in three years.
Weaver dies; Thomas Tracy named director, moving Glee Club outside of music department authority.

1947
Junior Week: Glee Club presents "'47 in A-Chord," signaling a return to Glee Club shows.

1950
Junior Week: Cayuga's Waiters make their first public appearance as Glee Club's small group.
Glee Club membership approaches one hundred; Tracy forms Orpheus Glee Club to handle overflow.

1951
Glee Club makes first television appearance on NBC's *Kate Smith TV Hour.*

1954
February 19: Glee Club appears on the *Perry Como Show.*
March, April: Glee Club tours continental U.S. and Mexico, appearing for the first time in Los Angeles and San Francisco.

1956
Waiters disassociate from Glee Club; Sherwoods formed.

1957
Tracy steps down; Thomas Sokol named director of Cornell Choral Music, and independently invited by Musical Clubs Council to become director of Glee Club.

1960
Glee Club moves into Sage Chapel.

1960–1961 tour
December, January: Glee Club tours Russia and England, becoming first American collegiate ensemble to tour Soviet Union.

1961

Glee Club formally embraced by the university; new Glee Club constitution drafted and Musical Clubs Council disbanded.

1962

October: Glee Club and Cornell University Chorus perform Beethoven's *Ninth Symphony* with Eugene Ormandy and the Philadelphia Orchestra, in Philadelphia and Ithaca.

1963

June: Glee Club tours England.

October 18: Fall concert given for first time on Homecoming weekend, in Statler.

1965

March: Glee Club, Chorus, and Cornell Symphony Orchestra under Karel Husa perform Beethoven's *Missa Solemnis* at Lincoln Center for Cornell's centennial.

1966

February–April: Glee Club takes three-month, U.S. State Department sponsored tour of the Far East, visiting Ceylon, Singapore, Malaysia, Thailand, the Philippines, Hong Kong, Taiwan, Okinawa, Korea, and Japan.

August 4: Glee Club, Chorus, Philadelphia Orchestra, and Ormandy perform Beethoven's *Ninth* for the opening of Saratoga Performing Arts Center.

1967

November 19: Glee Club celebrates its centennial with Bailey Hall concert.

December: Centennial celebration continues with coast-to-coast tour.

1968

CUGC Hangovers founded.

1970

January: Glee Club tours Germany.

1972

January: Glee Club tours Germany, Czechoslovakia, Austria, Hungary, and Yugoslavia.

1973

April: Glee Club, Chorus, and Orchestra perform in Carnegie Hall and the Kennedy Center under Husa.

November: First Homecoming performance in Sage Chapel.

1979

January: Glee Club tours England.

1982

July: Glee Club again tours England, performing with Dame Janet Baker at the King's Lynn Festival.

1989

January: Glee Club tours Asia, performing in Singapore, Beijing, Shanghai, and Hong Kong.

1992

January: Glee Club tours Spain, France, and Switzerland.

1993

November 5, 6: Glee Club celebrates 125th anniversary during Homecoming week-end.

1995

Sokol retires; Scott Tucker named director.

Notes

The following abbreviations and short forms have been used in the notes.

Bishop	Morris Bishop, *A History of Cornell*. Ithaca, 1962.
CU Archives	Cornell University Archives, Division of Rare and Manuscript Collections, Cornell University Library. Repository for *Cornell Alumni News, Cornell Daily Sun, Cornell Era*, Cornell University Glee Club records prior to 1966, *Cornellian*, Deane Waldo Malott papers, Edmund Ezra Day papers, Roger Henry Williams Scrapbooks.
CUGC Archives	Chronological records of the Cornell University Glee Club, 1966 to the present, located in the basement of Sage Chapel.
DeJarnette	Reven DeJarnette, *Hollis Dann*. Boston, 1940.
Malott interview	Interview conducted by the author with Deane W. Malott, retired president of Cornell University, winter 1993–1994.
NGD	*The New Grove Dictionary of Music and Musicians*. Ed. Stanley Sadie. 20 vols. London, 1980.
NHDM	*The New Harvard Dictionary of Music*. Ed. Don Randel. Cambridge, Mass., 1986.
Samuel	Harold Samuel, "The First Hundred Years of Music at Cornell." *The Cornell University Music Review*. Vol. 8 (1965).
TAS interviews	Interviews and conversations between the author and Professor Thomas A. Sokol during the 1994–1995 academic year.
Tracy interview	Interview conducted by the author with Mary Lou Tracy, widow of Thomas Tracy, fall 1994.

Preface

1. Leonard Bernstein, *The Joy of Music* (New York, 1959), 11.
2. Rainer Maria Rilke, *Stories of God,* trans. M. D. Herter Norton (New York, 1963), 49.
3. Vladimir Nabokov, *Strong Opinions* (New York, 1973), 45.
4. Isaiah Berlin, *The Hedgehog and the Fox* (London, 1953), 25, 26.

1. The Origins

1. *Cornell Era,* 1.2.3. Numbers cited for this publication, in the CU Archives, refer to volume, issue number, and page (or pages).
2. The spelling of the yearbook was changed from *Cornelian* to *Cornellian* in 1882–1883.
3. Morris Bishop's description of Ithaca at the time of the university's founding is colorful. See Bishop, 1–4; quote at 4.
4. Ezra Cornell to his wife, February 13, 1857, quoted by Bishop, 20.
5. Andrew D. White, *Autobiography* (New York, 1905), quoted by Bishop, 32.
6. Ezra Cornell to Francis Miles Finch, January 27, 1865, quoted in Bishop, 64.
7. Bishop, 90, 91.
8. Ezra Cornell to home, January 5, 1854, quoted in Bishop, 24.
9. *NGD* 7:430–31; *NHDM,* 341–42.
10. *NGD,* 7:431.
11. *NGD,* 11:188, 193–94; 7:431; *NHDM,* 142–43.
12. While several historians wrongly state that the Orpheus Glee Club never performed actual concerts, another claim that the ensemble performed at the library's third anniversary celebration appears to have confused the January 21, 1869, performance with a later date.
13. *Cornell Era,* 1.7.5.
14. The *Era* later claimed, "It is indeed fortunate that the introduction of coeducation preceded the revival of music in the University, for now the linked sweetness long drawn out, of these knights of song, need not be wasted on the desert air."
15. In an *Era* article entitled "The First Cornell Glee Club," H. W. van Wagenen 1873, a founding member of the Collegensia Quintette, claims that this group was the first glee club, an assertion contradicted by the early 1869 concert appearance of the Orpheus. The quintette did have a direct line to the first "Cornell Glee Club" however—its director, Chas. W. Raymond, initially of the Class of 1873, was still around in 1875–1876 to join.
16. *Cornell Era,* 2.13.100. According to Edith Hamilton's *Mythology* (New York, 1969), Cythera was the land near which Venus was born. Ixion was a prisoner in Hades, condemned for insulting a goddess by being bound to a wheel that revolved forever. Orpheus was the mortal musician who sought his beloved Eurydice in the underworld; his music was so beautiful, Ixion's wheel stopped still for a moment.
17. *Cornell Era,* 3.5.37, 4.17.264, 6.18.140.
18. *Cornell Era,* 7.11.82–83.
19. *Cornell Era,* 7.12.91.
20. *Cornell Era,* 7.27.211.
21. *Cornell Era,* 8.28.220.
22. *Cornell Era,* 9.30.236–37.
23. The relationship between science and music was close elsewhere. Romeyn Berry notes in *Behind the Ivy* (Ithaca, 1950, 21–22) a memorable 1880 contest between Theobald Smith 1881 and Herman Biggs 1882 for the position of university organist. Years later, Smith's studies of Texas fever in cattle "pointed the way to the control of yellow fever, malaria, and typhus," while Biggs's work contributed significantly toward the eradication of tuberculosis.
24. *Cornell Era,* 9.23.180.
25. *Cornell Era,* 10.28.3, 2.
26. *Cornell Era,* 11.19.217.

27. *Cornell Era,* 7.32.253.
28. Samuel, 7.
29. *Cornell Era,* 12.29.342, 340.
30. *Cornell Era,* 12.31.361.
31. The name later became Cascadilla Hall.
32. *Cornell Era,* 13.10.115, 13.11.128.
33. *Cornell Era,* 13.15.174.
34. *Cornell Era,* 13.29.340.
35. Bishop, 139. He also incorrectly mentions a Cornell glee club being founded in the spring of 1869, presumably referring to the Collegensia Quintette.
36. Quoted in Bishop, 48.
37. *Cornell Era,* 18.23.278.
38. Quoted in Bishop, 122.
39. *Cornell Era,* 16.4.37, 16.10.91, 16.12.112.
40. *Cornell Era,* 17.26.314.
41. *Cornell Era,* 18.23.278.
42. *Cornell Era,* 19.24.277.
43. *Cornell Era,* 16.23.241.
44. *Cornell Era,* 21.17.188.
45. *Cornell Era,* 21.2.246. His must have been quite a talent to behold—after the Commencement concert, where he apparently outdid himself, the *Era* celebrated his clear range of tone and his talent for trilling and triple-tonguing.
46. *Cornell Era,* 21.31.324.

2. Hollis Dann

1. DeJarnette, 3–4.
2. DeJarnette, 4–5.
3. *Cornell Daily Sun,* January 30, 1890.
4. *Cornell Era,* 22.17.186.
5. *Cornell Era,* 22.30.297.
6. *Cornell Era,* 24.15.179. The same phenomenon is apparent around 1920, when the Glee Club claims nearly every year that the most recent season was "one of the most successful years in history."
7. *Cornell Era,* 25.15.178.
8. *Cornell Era,* 23.21.229.
9. *Cornell Era,* 24.21.247, 251.
10. That support was not unique to Cornell—alumni of many leading institutions showed similar dedicated support of their touring minstrels. In this emerging age of alma materism the musical club concert probably came to represent both good entertainment and memories of youth.
11. *Cornell Era,* 42.6.235.
12. For the record, the Musical Clubs did perform for other causes, as in 1894–1895 when they sang at a hospital ward benefit; athletics most often were the prime beneficiaries, however.
13. *Cornell Era,* 26.15.176.
14. *Cornell Era,* 27.24.285.
15. *Cornell Era,* 27.31.3.
16. *St. James's Gazette,* July 6, 1895; *London Standard,* July 6, 1895.
17. *Cornell Era,* 25.16.187.
18. *Cornell Era,* 28.4.40.
19. Robert Kane, *Good Sports: A History of Cornell Athletics* (Ithaca, 1992), 369.
20. *Cornell Era,* 28.4.41.
21. *Cornell Era,* 30.9.115.

22. *Cornell Era,* 32.2.26.

23. DeJarnette claims the Glee Club grew into three clubs—a concert club, and two prepara-tory clubs—but I've encountered no evidence to support this claim.

24. In following years the Cornell Masque took to "trying out" its dramatic shows at the insti-tution before their Junior Week performance. The New York *Evening Sun* noted, "If no serious results are observed, they conclude that the play can be safely produced before the faculty and un-dergraduates at Ithaca" (*Cornell Era,* 33.3.119).

25. Such ventures were, of course, not without hazard. There was the time Estévan Fuertes was sent as Cornell's representative to the University of Bologna's 900th anniversary. The one-time Glee Club director and professor of civil engineering apparently was humiliated when, amid the robed delegates bearing beautiful parchment inscribed in Latin, he appeared in a Benny Rich suit with a half-sheet of note paper written in English and printed at a local Ithacan press (Romeyn Berry, *Behind the Ivy* [Ithaca, 1950], 81).

26. *Cornell Era,* 29.23.288, 29.25.310.

27. *Cornell Era,* 31.26.306.

28. *Cornell Era,* 22.29.289.

29. *Cornell Era,* 27.20.232.

30. Samuel, 9, 10.

31. An 1899 conservatory ad listed Egbert as director and an executive committee including Hollis Dann, with Treman as chairman.

32. *Cornell Era,* 28.11.130.

33. *Cornell Era,* 31.7.77.

34. *Ithaca Daily Journal,* June 5, 1901.

35. A spring 1887 *Cornell Era* mentions, however, that the Glee Club and Banjo Club had a sat-isfactory trip to Owego.

36. The instrumental clubs eventually became defunct in the early 1940s, but the joint name remained as a technical vestige until the fall of 1972.

37. Letter, Walter V. Price to Bruce N. Smith, December 19, 1989. (Unless stated otherwise, all letters, quoted or paraphrased, are in the CUGC Archives.) The *Era* also reported that during the 1915–1916 tour Dann accompanied the groups in Cincinnati, Detroit, and Cleveland, while Cole-man was with them in Baltimore, New York, and Pittsburgh, which still left four cities unattended.

38. One man wrote the Glee Club as recently as 1980 to say, "As I must have said to you before, with the director leading the Glee Club, it becomes a Choral Society, not a Glee Club."

39. Thomas Tapper, "A Wandering Capellmeister—His Chronicle," *Musical America,* October 1901.

40. DeJarnette, 13, 14.

41. *Ithaca Daily Journal,* October 16, 1903.

42. DeJarnette, 109.

43. *Ithaca Daily Journal,* April 18, 1904.

44. Ibid.

45. Quoted in DeJarnette, 31.

46. *Cornell Alumni News,* May 3, 1905, 500.

47. *Cornell Alumni News,* May 2, 1906, 356.

48. Both reviews come from unidentified newspapers, the second dated May 5, 1911. They can be found in the Music Festival scrapbooks, kept by the Department of Music, Cornell Uni-versity.

49. *Cornell Era,* 40.7.311.

50. *Musical America,* October 16, 1915, 9.

51. The letter of March 10, 1931 is quoted in DeJarnette, 33.

52. Berry, 280.

53. *Musical America,* October 16, 1915, 9.

54. DeJarnette, 124.

55. Allan Treman told of one soloist hired from the Metropolitan Opera Company to sing in a few festival cantatas. "In one cantata he had only one line and when that arrived he was looking

elsewhere or licking a cough drop and missed his cue completely" (Allan Treman, *As I Remember* [Ithaca, 1979], 42).

56. *Cornell Era*, 38.9.301.

57. *Cornell Era*, 39.5.237–38.

58. *Cornell Era*, 40.4.168–69.

59. DeJarnette, 34.

60. Bryant obviously admired her predecessor, calling him a "master conductor" in a 1934 letter, and saying, "There never has been, is not, and never will be another like you."

61. Perpetually on the lookout for new repertoire, his program from one German *Männerchor* concert has detailed notes; next to one Schubert piece alone, he notated nine different dynamic markings beside lines of the text, and wrote in the margin "(C.G.C. ?)."

62. *Cornell Era*, 46.1.55.

63. *Cornell Era*, 25.16.187.

64. *Cornell Era*, 28.16.184.

65. Headlines from *Scranton Republican*, December 25, 1894; quote from unidentified newspaper (also likely December 25, 1894), found in Roger Henry Williams Scrapbooks, CU Archives.

66. *Cornell Era*, 46.5.298–99.

67. *Cornell Era*, 48.7.440.

68. *Cornellian* (1918), 50:528.

69. Bishop, 427.

70. *Cornellian* (1918), 50:523.

71. Bishop, 434.

72. DeJarnette, 49.

73. *Cornellian* (1921), 53:430, (1917), 49:376. According to Walter Price, on one occasion the soft shoe dancer (performing in dimmed lighting) accidentally danced off the stage into the pit. Fortunately he landed on the piano and was immediately able to step back onto the stage.

74. DeJarnette, 115–16.

75. *Cornellian* (1921), 53:430.

76. *Cornellian* (1921), 53:430.

77. *Cornell Era*, 53.12.11.

78. *Cornell Era*, 53.4.12.

79. DeJarnette, 113, 121, 118.

80. *Cornell Era*, 53.4.26.

81. DeJarnette, 89.

82. DeJarnette, 115, 78, 128.

83. DeJarnette, 120–21.

84. DeJarnette, 128.

3. The Dudley Years

1. *Ithaca Daily Journal*, May 1, 1905.

2. *Ithaca Daily News*, April 18, 1904.

3. John Harcourt, *The Ithaca College Story* (Ithaca, 1983), 19. Though Harcourt says Dudley replaced Gogorza in 1906, the reviews he quotes are from 1907.

4. Ibid, 14.

5. Ibid, 17.

6. *Cornell Era*, 54.1.23.

7. Local organizers occasionally tried to put on festival concerts (as in the case of a 1925 performance of Haydn's *Seasons*). Cornell professor Paul Weaver revived *Elijah* at a 1934 Barton Hall concert with 439 singers from local church choirs, the Sage Chapel Choir, and the Ithaca College Chorus, joined by the New York Philharmonic; the concert lost money. Dann's achievement was never recaptured.

8. *Cornellian* (1922), 54:456.

9. WEAF was the country's first station to carry a commercially sponsored broadcast.

10. *Ithaca Journal,* April 27, 1925.

11. The Poulenc "Chanson à boire" resulted from the group's 1921 European tour and was dedicated to the Harvard Glee Club by the composer. (The *New York Times* claimed the piece's title was calculated to arouse melancholy thoughts in Prohibition days.) That same tour garnered another composition written specifically for the group—Darius Milhaud's "Psaume 121," which remains a fixture in the male-voice repertoire.

12. Elliot Forbes, *A History of Music at Harvard to 1972* (Cambridge, Mass., 1988), 49.

13. Archibald T. Davison, "A New Standard for Glee Clubs," reprinted in Forbes, 49–50.

14. *Cornellian* (1924), 56:438.

15. *Cornellian* (1927), 59:394.

16. *Cornellian* (1932), 64:342.

17. Roger Lewis Dann was one of twins, both second tenors. The other, Robert Harding Dann, was student leader of the group that same year.

18. *Cornellian* (1925), 57:434.

19. Letter, Romeyn Berry to George Coleman, April 15, 1931.

20. Letter, Coleman to Musical Clubs Council, April 10, 1931.

21. Letter, Berry to Treman, September 12, 1931. C. E. Treman's post as graduate treasurer was rather ambiguously passed on to Allan, who more than once in the succeeding years inquired as to who actually was graduate treasurer. In the end, given his ties to the Ithaca Trust Company (joined with the Tompkins County Trust Company in 1935), Allan inevitably oversaw most of the group's finances through the next few decades.

22. During this time a second constitution was adopted, and new rules and regulations were drawn up.

23. Letter, B. A. Hubbard to Conductor of the Glee, October 5, 1931; letter, Berry to Hubbard, October 7, 1931; letter, Berry to Treman, February 10, 1932.

24. Letter, Berry to H. C. Ballou, January 19, 1931.

25. Quoted in DeJarnette, 92–93.

26. The world of popular music, and of musical theater (which in some cases qualifies as "serious music"), of course have done much to promote the poignancy of song, if not always the art of singing.

27. Yet other instrumental organizations at the university were booming. The Cornell University Band, "thoroughly drilled in marching and in playing," took the field a hundred strong at the 1931 Princeton game. In addition to the Varsity Band an independent Cadet Band had about sixty freshmen members. And thanks to a 1919 gift from Gerard Hinkley 1915, the University Orchestra grew strong on a $20,000 endowment, offering eleven annual scholarships to upperclass players on the basis of talent and dedication.

28. Letter, Berry to Dudley, May 15, 1931.

29. Letter, Berry to Benjamin Frick, August 26, 1930.

30. A few weeks after the opening of term in fall 1895, a notice appeared in the *Cornell Daily Sun:* "Brother Savages: Jay's, Friday at 8:30" (or "Savages—8 o'clock Saturday—Oriental" depending on whose account you read). Those who remained from the England trip gathered to reminisce about their evenings at the London Savage Club and soon after, they received permission from the London organization to start an American chapter. (For a more detailed account of the group's formation, see the *Cornell Era,* 40.4.180–82.) The Savage Club of Ithaca recruited its members from Cornell's two upper classes, the faculty, and townspeople, making it a local rather than a strictly university organization. Restricted to males who could pass the "severe tests," the group met in its rathskeller off East Green Street and, for a time beginning in the 1950s, in the Toboggan Lodge on Beebe Lake. Meetings termed Social Sessions were held "every once in awhile" (*Cornell Era,* 45.4.240), particularly when there was opportunity to entertain notable visitors to Ithaca. The group remained popular with Glee Clubbers well into the twentieth century, some men such as Allan Treman joining as undergraduates and remaining lifelong members. Treman, William Corcoran 1923, Truman Powers 1930, and C. Wesley Thomas formed the Savage Club Quartet (also known as the Cornell Alumni Quartet), a group which performed with the Glee

Club at home and on tours in addition to its appearances in Savage Club shows. The Junior Savage Club Quartet consisted of undergrad members of the Glee Club, and likewise performed on Glee Club programs. The Savage Club has presented its own performances at Bailey Hall for many years and still gives an annual concert at Reunion time. For more on the Savage Club, see Chapter 4.

31. Letter, Berry to Walter Wing, January 9, 1931.

32. Letter, Berry to Hubbard, October 7, 1931.

33. The logic is a little thorny. Berry claimed youthful fervor lay with the serious music, yet the more serious members of the Glee Club became, the less often outside students attended the concerts.

34. *New York Evening Post,* January 6, 1931.

35. *Ithaca Journal-News,* December 18, 1933.

36. Letter, John McGovern to C. B. Hutchins Jr., April 30, 1934.

37. *Cornellian* (1935), 67:302.

38. *Cornellian* (1936), 68:316.

39. Musical Clubs press release, February 26, 1936 (CUGC Archives).

40. Letter, J. S. Kittle to E. W. Averill, November 9, 1937.

41. At that time Reunion and Commencement weekends were combined.

42. *Cornell Daily Sun,* March 19, 1937.

43. *Cornell Daily Sun,* December 19, 1940.

44. Thereafter differences in schedule made it difficult to coordinate—the Musical Clubs were back to Christmas tours and could no longer make the necessary time commitment. Still, for a few years the Gilbert and Sullivan productions brought students back to student performances, and prosperity back to the books.

45. The Women's Mandolin Club also started up with the Women's Glee Club, and a Women's String Ensemble was organized in 1932. By then the University Orchestra had been open to both men and women for some time.

46. In later years the Spring Concert with the women coincided with the Navy Ball, one of the original features of Spring Day.

47. Other notable pupils included Dorothy Cothran 1943, who sang on national radio while still an undergraduate.

48. *Ithaca Journal-News,* December 17, 1934.

49. Reprinted in Managerial Forms and Correspondence, 1935 (CUGC Archives).

50. Detwiler was quite humorous, writing letters off to high society friends in New York encouraging them to support the Glee Club on its 1934 spring tour. Assistant manager as well as accompanist, he came down with appendicitis just before the tour; it took two men to replace him.

51. Letters, David Ten Broeck to Berry, April 1, 1937; J. S. Kittle to Alumni (Mr. Returning Alumnus), May 21, 1937.

52. For years, the men's tour itinerary books carried a blank page in the back, marked Junior Week Dates.

53. Letter, Coffin to Thomas Ludlam, May 4, 1940.

54. Letter, H. J. Noel to John Modrall, April 10, 1941. The bit about formal attire wasn't entirely true; the men still wore costumes on occasion, and certainly the "coed" in "Coediquette" did not appear in a tux.

55. *Cornell Era,* 56.6.18.

56. Other invitations extended to the CUGC included a 1941 offer to perform with the same Rochester Orchestra and other glee clubs in an abridged version of Bach's *St. Matthew Passion.*

57. *Cornell Era,* 40.7.311.

58. Concert program from 1939–1940; publicity release contained in Managerial Correspondence for 1937 (CUGC Archives).

59. Letter, W. W. Sproul to H. Jerome Noel, January 1941.

60. Letter, Barnum to Noel, August 11, 1941.

61. Letter, Barnum to Bud Erb, February 19, 1942.

62. Letter, Barnum to Erb, March 10, 1942. Barnum emphasized this would be the case, even if the man were married.

63. Letter, Weaver to Dean R. M. Ogden, June 10, 1942 (Edmund Ezra Day papers, CU Archives).

64. Letter, Barnum to Day, March 1, 1942 (Edmund Ezra Day papers); letter, Day to Barnum, March 6, 1942 (Edmund Ezra Day papers).

65. Letter, Paul Weaver to Eric Dudley, June 11, 1941. No member of the musical staff was promoted to tenure during Weaver's fifteen-year chairmanship of the music department.

66. Letter, Barnum to Erb, March 10, 1942.

67. Musical Club Resolutions, April 20, 1942 (CUGC Archives).

68. Gerould returned to tell the story at his 50th class reunion. Some contend a mispronunciation of "Cayuga" is the way to unmask an intruder in a crowd of Cornellians.

69. Treman, 42.

70. Audition announcements, September 30, 1930; September 28, 1932 (CUGC Archives).

71. Samuel, 28.

72. *Ithaca Journal,* May 22, 1947.

4. The War Years and Thomas Tracy

1. From "The Next War"; the first two lines of the epigraph are from "Bugles Sang," while the third line comes from "Strange Meeting," *The Collected Poems of Wilfred Owen,* ed. C. Day Lewis (London, 1961). These lines are among those selected by Benjamin Britten for his *War Requiem* (1961).

2. Bishop, 539.

3. *Cornell Daily Sun,* March 18, 19, 1943.

4. Letters, April 22, 1943, and April 30, 1943 (Edmund Ezra Day papers, CU Archives).

5. Apparently a Navy glee club was formed on campus during the war years.

6. The impetus may well have been Kuypers's concern that the department *had* to send all its voice students to Dudley, whose rate for lessons was considered too high and who was further questioned on the ground that he made "special arrangements" for those students who sang in the Presbyterian choir. Kuypers requested an assistant choral director/voice teacher be hired.

7. Letter, Sabine to Day, July 3, 1944 (Edmund Ezra Day papers). In late 1945 Dean C. W. de Kiewiet wrote Kuypers to inquire about the ambiguity and questionable efficiency of Dudley's position in the music department. After Dudley spoke with de Kiewiet in early 1946, it was agreed Dudley would continue on in his present post for another year.

8. Letter, Weaver to Day, May 19, 1943 (Edmund Ezra Day papers).

9. Letter, Day to Treman, July 6, 1944 (Edmund Ezra Day papers).

10. Letter, Treman to Day, July 14, 1944 (Edmund Ezra Day papers).

11. Samuel, 30.

12. Lillian Dudley had been forced to resign in 1942, an unpleasant incident that resulted in her taking the sum total of the Women's Glee Club treasury with her.

13. *Ithaca Journal,* May 20, 1946.

14. *Cornell Alumni News,* December 1946, 235.

15. Letter, April 5, 1947.

16. Letter, Irving Blatt to Henry MacCormack, March 6, 1948.

17. *Ithaca Journal,* February 7, 1948.

18. Letter, Day to Glee Club, December 10, 1948 (Edmund Ezra Day papers).

19. Tracy interview.

20. Mary Lou Tracy also said of the Tommy Bartlett appearance: "They really carried on like comedians that day, because they had this big show the night before and they had partied practically all night. So, they were not too sharp, I guess, although they thought they were real funny."

21. *Cornellian* (1951), 83:98.

22. *Cornell Daily Sun,* March 12, 1947.

23. *Cornell Alumni News,* December 1946.

24. *Cornellian* (1951), 83:99.

25. Letter, Sociedade de Cultura Artistica to Brewer, December 1, 1950.

26. Quotes taken from a videotape of the February 19, 1954, broadcast.

27. Letter, Peter Schurman 1952 to John Hillsley, November 27, 1951.

28. Letter, Brewer to John Syme, October 22, 1953; letter, Brewer to Harold Riegelman, July 22, 1953. The performance was ultimately given at the New York Hospital–Cornell Medical Center, newly reorganized and officially titled as such that same year.

29. Letter, June 13, 1952 (Deane Waldo Malott papers, CU Archives).

30. Requoted in a letter, Brewer to Tracy, June 23, 1953.

31. Letter, Ann Hopkins (Wells 1954) to "Manager of the Glee club," October 1, 1953; letter, Rodney S. Rougelot to Ann Hopkins, October 15, 1953.

32. *San Francisco News,* March 31, 1954.

33. *San Francisco Chronicle,* March 31, 1954.

34. Letter, C. Stewart Fiske 1921 to Fulton Rindge 1951, May 2, 1951.

35. *Batavia Daily News,* March 28, 1955.

36. The distinction "specifically college glee clubs" is important, seeing as other ensembles—high school glee clubs or show choirs, for example—involve a different set of considerations, and thus would demand their own discussion. (In more recent years college glee clubs such as University of Pennsylvania's group continued to present programs different in style from the Davison model.)

As a separate note, the term "serious repertoire" is meant to include Western music from the early periods to the present day. Moreover, the indigenous music of other cultures and countries has become an important part of choral programming, and is generally considered suitably ambitious repertoire. (Here too, Cornell's Glee Club was for a long time relatively silent; most pieces were sung in English through the better part of the 1950s, something that changed significantly in the 1960s.) Admittedly, words such as "serious," "highbrow," and "lowbrow" are problematic, not least because they hinge on an acquired set of cultural assumptions—as Lawrence Levine points out in *Highbrow Lowbrow* (1988)—and they are used here only for lack of better terminology.

37. Bishop, 606–12.

38. Samuel, 32.

39. 1955–1956 Cayuga's Waiters publicity release (CUGC Archives).

40. Musical Clubs Council minutes, May 2, 1955.

41. ILMAC minutes, December 5, 1956 (CUGC Archives).

42. Letter, Grout to Treman, September 17, 1947.

43. TAS interviews.

44. The Dudley Award was established in 1947 to honor the former Glee Club director. Originally it was given to the graduating senior who "during his four years has made the most outstanding contribution to the musical and organizational life of the Glee Club"; now it is awarded to any graduate who has been a member in good standing with the Club for six semesters and two tours.

45. Tracy interview.

46. Tracy interview, Malott interview.

47. Letter, Lucius Donkle to Michael Slon, December 22, 1994.

5. The Sokol Era

1. TAS interviews. Unless otherwise indicated, all the Sokol quotes are drawn from these interviews.

2. As it happens with legends, the Sokol interception story is often retold as being the longest interception return in the history of the Rose Bowl.

3. At the high school he roped a couple of the school's star football players into joining the choir and was soon deluged with young men interested in singing in the ensemble.

4. Sokol's first appearance with the Glee Club was actually at a Cornell Council meeting at which Coach Sanford and the Cornell crew were honored.

5. Letter, A. S. Landues to Charles Yoh, undated; letter, Chauncy Grant to Yoh, May 26, 1958; letter, Albert Neimeth to Yoh, May 27, 1958; letter, Don Hershey to Yoh, May 26, 1958.

6. TAS interviews.

7. Elliot Forbes, *A History of Music at Harvard to 1972* (Cambridge, Mass., 1988), 51.

8. Malott interview.

9. CUGC Constitution (CUGC Archives).

10. Letter, William Lathrop Jr. to Malott, May 18, 1961; letter, Malott to Lathrop, May 20, 1961.

11. TASS (Moscow, USSR), December 21, 1960; *Sovietskaya Musika,* March 1961; *London Times,* January 3, 1961; undated article on the CUGC's January 4, 1961, concert.

12. *Cornell Alumni News,* February 1961, 349.

13. *Philadelphia Inquirer,* October 13, 1962; *Philadelphia Evening Bulletin,* October 13, 1962.

14. *New York Times,* August 6, 1966; *Philadelphia Evening Bulletin,* August 5, 1966.

15. Letter, Albrecht to Sokol, April 26, 1964.

16. Malott interview; letter, Falkner to Malott, January 9, 1961.

17. *Royal College Magazine,* Christmas Issue 1963.

18. *Cornell Alumni News,* November 1966, 13.

19. *Sunday Gazette* (Penang), February 20, 1966.

20. *Cornell Daily Sun,* March 24, 1970.

21. *Cornell Daily Sun,* November 7, 1969.

22. *Ithaca Journal,* May 12, 1971.

23. Presidential Report, 1971–1972 (CUGC Archives).

24. Presidential Report, 1970–1971 (CUGC Archives). The report includes an account of the arguments for and against the proposed amendment.

25. For the full version of this adventure see the account of assistant director Stan Malinowski in the spring 1972 CUGC newsletter. In the retelling, Sokol's actual words have evolved and often been reported as "Gentleman, we have the cigars, we have the slivovitz, there's nothing to worry about," or "If we have the cigars and the slivovitz, we should go on," or even, "We have the cigars and the slivovitz, we can ride on in style."

26. Editor of *The New Harvard Dictionary of Music,* Randel became dean of the College of Arts and Sciences in 1991 and provost of the university in 1995. He is a strong supporter of the Glee Club.

27. Letters, Don Randel to Provost Robert Plane, May 15, 1972, June 5, 1972.

28. Managerial Papers 1972–1973, Book 1, Part 1 (CUGC Archives).

29. CUGC Annual Report, 1977–1978 (CUGC Archives).

30. At that time known as the Intercollegiate Musical Council, the name has since been changed to Intercollegiate Male Choruses.

31. During a 1971 tour through Pennsylvania "Uncle Tom" was actually given a public performance, apparently complete with kazoo accompaniment.

32. Executive Manager's Report, 1983–1984 (CUGC Archives); program for a performance of Husa's *American Te Deum,* given in Bailey Hall on May 1, 1979.

33. About that time the group also performed in New York at the 150th anniversary of Lord and Taylor.

34. Led by Byron Adams, the group did however appear with Dolly Parton dressed in blue jeans and red bandanas in spring 1985.

35. The organization of the Glee Club's accounts and the group's good financial standing with the university owes much to John Ostrom 1951, former university controller and a member of the Glee Club Advisory Council.

36. The Glee Club eventually won the lawsuit, getting back the several thousand dollars the agency had tried to pocket.

37. At Homecoming time the following year Sokol, not feeling well, asked his associate director Slon (your author) to conduct the 1994 concert.

38. Letter, Sokol to Faculty and Students—Department of Music, May 15, 1970.

39. Letter, Murray Sidlin (then director of the New Haven Symphony Orchestra) to Cornell Chorus c/o Thomas Sokol, March 21, 1985. Many more will benefit from the Sokol legacy, thanks in part to a gift from the late Robert Engel 1953, a university trustee and presidential councillor, as well as a member of the CUGC Advisory Council. In July 1993 Engel gave $100,000 to set up

the Thomas A. Sokol Endowment for Choral Music; with contributions from others, the endowment should continue to aid all Cornell's choral groups well into the next millennium.

6. The Songs

1. This and the following quote from Weeks, as well as the early Alma Mater version cited, come from Thomas A. Sokol, "The Story of Cornell's Alma Mater" (Ithaca, 1970), published as an insert with a Glee Club recording of the Alma Mater.

2. Ibid.

3. Romeyn Berry, *Behind the Ivy* (Ithaca, 1950), 306–8.

4. *Songs of Cornell*, comp. and ed. Thomas A. Sokol (Ithaca, 1988), 25.

5. Sokol, "The Story of Cornell's Alma Mater."

6. *Songs of Cornell*, 19.

7. A 1912–1913 rendition of "Alumni Song" is worth noting, if one ribald account of that year's tour is to be believed. "Macnoe tried to make the Savannah alumni believe that he had rewritten the Alumni song by singing the last verse first. Larry Lawrence got a whiff of his breath and amid a riot the song was ended" (unidentified tour account, CUGC Archives).

8. Given the current popularity of basketball in the NCAA, one could demonstrate the decline in college song writing by citing the dirth of college basketball songs.

9. *Songs of Cornell*, 19.

10. *Cornell Songbook* (Ithaca, 1900), 69.

11. For both the first and traditional versions, see *Songs of Cornell*, 72–73.

12. *Cornell Era*, 2.3.21.

13. *Cornell Era*, 3.19.145.

14. *Cornell Era*, 5.31.246.

15. *Cornell Era*, 16.12.112.

16. *Cornell Era*, 15.19.206.

17. *Cornell Era*, 23.14.163; 20.16.188.

18. *Cornell Era*, 20.17.198.

19. *Cornell Era*, 20.16.188.

20. Letter, Robert A. Doyle to Bruce N. Smith, December 20, 1989; letter, Walter V. Price to Bruce Smith, December 19, 1989.

21. Letter, unspecified Glee Club manager to J. Brown McKee, December 10, 1929.

22. Letter, David L. Ten Broeck to "Director of Entertainment Committee, Keuka College," January 22, 1937; letter, J. S. Kittle to Otto N. Frenzel, October 7, 1937.

23. *Springfield Daily*, December 27, 1940.

24. That same year Carl Fischer Inc. of New York City published a Cornell song book.

25. Letter, R. Seldon Brewer to George W. Whitesides, August 1, 1947.

26. Letter, William Harder to Lucius Donkle Jr., January 30, 1948.

27. Letter, Justin Camarata to R. Seldon Brewer, June 27, 1958.

28. Translation: Ratibor, and the river Mississippi and the city Honolulu, and the lake Titicaca. Popocatepetl is not in Canada, but is in Mexico, Canada, Malaga, Rimini, Brindisi . . .

29. Recollection from private account of John Nicolls. The dent is still in the university mace to this day.

30. *Cornell Era*, 36.1.10–11.

7. The Odysseys

1. Constantine Cavafy, "Ithaca," in *The Complete Poems of Cavafy*, trans. Rae Dalven (New York, 1961), 36. The entire poem merits reading, especially in the context of this chapter.

2. *Cornell Era*, 25.16.186.

3. *Cornell Era*, 20.16.190.

4. In addition to Troy and Syracuse several other names from antiquity grace upstate New York towns, including Seneca, Homer, Ovid, and Virgil.

5. Quoted in the *Cornell Era,* 24.23.271–72.

6. Quoted in the *Cornell Era,* 27.13.152.

7. *Cornell Era,* 25.16.187.

8. Unidentified Ithaca newspaper, clipping in the Roger Henry Williams Scrapbooks (CU Archives).

9. *London Standard,* July 6, 1895; *Times,* July 6, 1895; *Morning Advertiser,* July 6, 1895.

10. Unidentified Ithaca newspapers, Roger Henry Williams Scrapbooks.

11. By varying accounts the accrued tour debt ranged anywhere from $2,000 to $8,000, either way an extraordinary sum for the time.

12. *Cornell Era,* 40.4.169.

13. In those days tours typically started earlier, often before Christmas, and ran through the holidays.

14. *Cornellian* (1912), 43:370.

15. *Cornell Era,* 47.4.228.

16. *Cornell Era,* 41.4.192.

17. *Cornell Era,* 31.12.136.

18. *Cornellian* (1921), 53:430.

19. *Cornell Era,* 46.5.298.

20. *Cornell Era,* 41.4.191–2.

21. *Cornell Era,* 24.14.168.

22. General tryout letter, September 30, 1930.

23. Such problems are part of any tour, and solutions don't seem imminent. In 1991 a blizzard made certain the Glee Club singers were about the only ones who made it to their concert that night, and a year later a broken bus left the group momentarily stranded somewhere in the mountains of Spain.

24. *Cornellian* (1925), 57:434–35.

25. *Cornellian* (1928), 60:247.

26. Glee Club publicity, 1930 (CUGC Archives).

27. Letters, Thomas Ludlam to C. B. Hutchins Jr., October 20, 1932; April 9, 1934.

28. Letter drafted by Glee Club management, Managerial Records 1935 (CUGC Archives).

29. H. Jerome Noel, Musical Clubs press release (CUGC Archives).

30. Tracy interview.

31. *Cornell Alumni News,* May 1, 1954, 452.

32. That moment has been repeated in various ways over the years. On the 1993 Great Lakes tour, at the open invitation to singing alumni to join the group on stage for Cornell songs, the Club's bus driver came up to sing the Alma Mater, having learned it by heart sitting through ten days of concerts. In the years in between, numerous other people—pilots, bus drivers, secretaries, sponsors, hotel managers—previously unconnected either with Cornell or singing have, through tours and through the music, become part of the Club. This ability of tours to draw people together remains one of their finest virtues.

33. "Cornell Men's Glee Club 'In Retrospect'" (internal history account, CUGC Archives).

34. Glee Club record of 1960–1961 tour communications (CUGC Archives).

35. Letter, John Fleischauer to "Members of the CUGC and their parents," September 2, 1960.

36. A copy of Sokol's 1960–1961 tour chronicle may be found in the CUGC Archives.

37. George Ecker, "Evensong, Anthems, Catches," *Cornell Alumni News,* September 1963, 19, 20.

38. Presidential Reports, Papers, Advisory Council 1962–1963 to 1966–1967; memo, Don Weadon to Executive Committee, August 12, 1965 (CUGC Archives).

39. Quoted from Newman's private recollections of the Far East tour (CUGC Archives), which provided numerous facts and anecdotes.

40. *Cornell Alumni News,* November 1966, 15.

41. Ibid., 21.

42. Ibid., 17.

43. Ibid., 17, 20.

44. Ibid., 21.

45. Letters quoted in H. Michael Newman's Presidential Report 1965–1966, found in Presidential Reports, Papers, Advisory Council, 1962–1963 to 1966–1967 (CUGC Archives).

46. Quoted in the *Milwaukee Journal*, December 13, 1967.

47. Presidential Report, 1969–1970 (CUGC Archives).

48. *Ithaca Journal*, February 2, 1970.

49. Private journal of Michael Klein 1972; James Bulman 1969 in CUGC Newsletter, spring 1970, 5.

50. Undated letter, Weigle to "Club Members."

51. Diary reprinted anonymously in *Cornell Alumni News*, May 1972, 30. "George" was tour photographer George Gull 1972.

52. *Lidova Demokracie*, January 12, 1972.

53. *Maribor Daily*, January 22, 1972.

54. CUGC Newsletter, spring 1972, 4. Articles by Sanford Shaw, Stan Malinowski, and Peter Muth 1974 have all proved helpful in reconstructing the events of this tour.

55. CUGC Newsletter, spring 1972, 5.

56. *Cornell Era*, 3.30.237.

57. CUGC Newsletter, spring 1979.

58. Letter, Jean Marchant to Peter Sherwood, July 31, 1982.

59. Manager's Report, CUGC Annual Report 1982–1983 (CUGC Archives).

60. Over time, some have replaced the "which" with "*we* Glee Clubbers . . ."

61. Much of the credit for this achievement goes to Ron Schiller and the late Mark Cardin 1987.

62. A few months later Chinese students began their prodemocracy demonstrations, brutally crushed in and around Tiananmen Square.

63. Statement made at party following the January 6 Beijing concert.

64. *Cornell Alumni News*, May 1972, 30.

65. Bishop, 136.

8. Haec Est Domus

1. *Cornell Era*, 2.13.100.

2. Kermit Carlyle Parsons, *The Cornell Campus* (Ithaca, 1968), 4, 5.

3. Bishop, 249, 210.

4. Parsons, 185.

5. Daniel R. Snodderly, *Ithaca and Its Past* (rev. ed., Ithaca, 1984), 42.

6. Bishop, 342.

7. Merrill Hesch and Richard Pieper, *Ithaca Then and Now* (Ithaca, 1983), 26.

8. Parsons, 89. The first Music Festival could have begun quoting Haydn, "Die Himmel erzählen die Ehre Gottes," although Burt Wilder, professor of comparative anatomy and natural history, was heard to raise his voice after 1903 about "the impossible musculature of angels with both wings and arms" (Bishop, 111).

9. Bishop, 291.

10. *Cornellian* (1915), 46:428.

11. Allan Treman, *As I Remember* (Ithaca, 1979), 64. The Cornell Library was torn down in 1960 as part of Ithaca's urban renewal project. The Blood building, which housed the Glee Club's former headquarters, came down next door at the same time.

12. Letter, Coffin to R. S. Rougelot, May 17, 1954.

13. Bishop, 459.

14. Treman, 127.

15. *Cornellian* (1957), 89:84.

16. Letter, Sokol to James Herson, September 13, 1961.

17. Romeyn Berry, *Behind the Ivy* (Ithaca, 1950), 168–69.

18. TAS interviews.

19. Berry, 164–65.

20. *Cornell Era,* 58.2.5. (The format of the *Era* had by this time changed radically from its earliest days, and several years were skipped. This volume came out in the late 1940s even though volume 54 dates from the early 1920s.)

21. Berry, 38. Additional information about Zinck's was provided by this book's editor, Jane Dieckmann.

9. The Small Groups

1. Letter, Robert Doyle to Bruce Smith, December 20, 1989.

2. *Cornellian* (1958), 90:106; (1959), 91:120.

3. Press release, Managerial Records 1951 (CUGC Archives).

4. *Cornellian* (1954), 86:79.

5. Musical Clubs Council minutes, May 6, 1956.

6. *Cornellian* (1957), 89:88.

7. Musical Clubs Council minutes, May 6, 1956.

8. TAS interviews. A few singers did return, and manage to balance their commitments to both groups.

9. Quoted from Jon Wardner 1979, "History of the Hangovers" (typescript, CUGC Archives).

10. *Cornellian* (1971), 103:90.

11. Until 1982, when Rob Mack 1985 assumed the post, every director of the group had been a legitimate hangover.

12. Steve Strasser, Executive Manager's Report 1983–1984 (CUGC Archives).

13. Oversize bottles of champagne are given specific names—for example "Jeroboam" or "Nebuchadnezzar." The credit for identifying this particular bottle as "Methusalem" (and enlightening me about the existence of these names) goes to Glee Clubber Eric Saidel 1997.

14. *Cornellian* (1982), 114:162.

15. *Cornellian* (1983), 115:154; (1985) 117:158; (1987) 119:114.

16. *Cornell Alumni News,* October 1981, 2.

17. *Cornellian* (1971), 103:80.

18. *Cornellian* (1988), 120:110.

19. *Cornellian* (1990), 122:65.

20. Audio tape of 1975 concert in Macon, Georgia.

10. The Club

1. Fred Hoeflinger 1969, Managerial Records 1966–1967, Book II (CUGC Archives).

2. Southern States Tour Book, January 1975 (CUGC Archives).

3. CUGC Newsletter, spring 1978.

4. Ibid.

5. Presidential Reports, Papers, Advisory Council, 1967–1968 to 1968–1969 (CUGC Archives).

6. Letter, Dick Erali to Michael Slon, February 9, 1994.

7. *Cornell Alumni News,* November 1966, 11.

8. Such collaborations naturally promote intercollegiate relations and serve to tighten up the Glee Club ranks. One year at Smith, though the women's group "was better prepared when we arrived . . . the men, sensing the quality of the 'competition,' were quickly on top of things" (Annual Report, 1977–1978, CUGC Archives).

9. CUGC Newsletter, fall 1980; tale from oral tradition.

10. CUGC Newsletter, fall 1969.

11. *Cornell Era,* 24.19.229.

12. Managerial Records, 1983–1984 (CUGC Archives).

13. *Cornellian* (1977), 109:84.

14. *Cornell Era,* 42.2.85.

15. Letter, Deane Malott to William Lathrop, March 22, 1960.

16. Richard Reuss, "An Annotated Field Collection of Songs from the American College Student Oral Tradition (M.A. thesis, Indiana University, 1965), 4–5.

17. Reuss, 21.

18. Reuss, 180.

19. Reuss, 139.

20. Reuss, 180.

21. *Cornell Era,* 3.17.132.

22. C. S. Lewis, *Of Other Worlds* (London, 1966), 18.

Epilogue

1. *Manila Times,* March 3, 1966.

2. *Sunday Times* (Singapore), February 13, 1966.

3. TAS interviews.

4. Ironically (and prophetically), Deane Malott had jokingly commented in 1993 that whenever Sokol decided to retire, one way to replace him would be to "go over to Harvard and take their director."

5. CUGC Newsletter, spring 1996.

6. Letter, Dick Erali to Michael Slon, February 9, 1994.

Index

Page numbers in boldface type refer to illustrations.

297